RT. REV. WILLIAM MEADE

[illegible], N.Y. from a Photograph.

WILLIAM MEADE

(WHEN HE GRADUATED)

Eng.d by J. A. O'Neill, N.Y. from a Portrait by Sully.

A MEMOIR OF THE LIFE

OF THE

RIGHT REV. WILLIAM MEADE, D.D.

BISHOP OF THE PROTESTANT EPISCOPAL CHURCH

IN THE

DIOCESE OF VIRGINIA.

BY THE

RIGHT REV. J. JOHNS, D. D.

WITH

A MEMORIAL SERMON

BY THE REV. WILLIAM SPARROW, D. D.

BALTIMORE:
INNES & COMPANY, PUBLISHERS, ADAMS EXPRESS BUILDING.
1867.

CONTENTS.

DEDICATION.

To the Clergy and Laity of the Protestant Episcopal Church in Virginia.

To you, brethren, this Memoir is cordially dedicated by one who appreciates your love and support during the past four and twenty years of his Episcopate — gratefully remembers the affectionate expression of your sympathy in the bereavement which this Memoir records, and earnestly prays that the brief remnant of his ministry may be so passed that the blessed bonds of peace and love which unite us in Christ Jesus, may be strengthened by our continued co-operation in promoting the interests of His Church on earth, and perpetuated in purity and bliss in Heaven.

Malvern. J. JOHNS.

PREFACE.

At the earnest solicitation of the sons of Bishop Meade, I consented, though not without serious misgiving, to prepare a memoir of their honored father. To the responsibility thus assumed, and the difficulty and delicacy of the performance, I was not insensible. As none of the many attempts to represent his personal appearance had been very satisfactory, it was not to be expected that the more difficult portraiture of his remarkable character, could be so executed as to prove generally acceptable. Any delineation which would accord with the impressions of those who knew him intimately, would be regarded as too favorable by general acquaintances, and others would perhaps pronounce against it as unreal. I have therefore abstained from any formal effort to present a full exhibition of the subject of this Memoir, and have adopted, as far as practicable, the less pretentious, but safer expedient of letting his deeds reflect his likeness, and his own clear utterances illustrate his spirit.

If his actions had always been isolated, and his communications so impersonal, that in reporting them, they might be entirely detached from the course of others, then, whatever skill the proper selection might require, it could be accomplished without the appearance or suspicion of partiality.

This, however, is not possible in Bishop Meade's case. Many of the transactions in which he was engaged, and which were most decidedly characteristic of the man, were of an official nature, open before the Church, and affecting the reputation of others, as well as his own. Some of these I would gladly pretermit. But these are the very cases in connection with which he has been most egregiously misrepresented, and most violently attacked. Under these circumstances, silence might be construed as acquiescence in the statements of his assailants — and, to leave to some later period the collection and use of the ample materials for his vindication now available, would be to risk their loss, and would justly expose me to the charge of unfaithfulness to my trust, or at least, of culpable inconsideration. In recording those cases, I have relied on his own manuscripts, together with other authentic records and cotemporary publications, venturing upon little comment beyond what their perspicuous and decided presentment required. If, in one instance, this policy has been departed from, it is because I would blush to have recorded it without a feeling of honest indignation which refused to be repressed, and which on careful revision, I see no cause to regret.

A refugee life, amidst the disturbances of a protracted civil war — with the pressure of increased, various, and sometimes very painful official services — without a study and without books, was not favorable for the preparation of the Memoir. Accomplished under such disadvantages, the considerate reader will not be exacting, and if, on perusing this volume, he experiences a moiety of the gratification and profit which its composition has afforded me, by renewing in spirit my intimate intercourse with its loved and venerated subject, then I shall be amply remunerated for the time and labor which it required.

J. Johns.

MEMOIR.

NEARLY three-fourths of a century have passed since the birth of the subject of his biography, and with this lapse of time, the companions of his childhood have disappeared, leaving but two of their number to testify of his early days. These two retain very distinct impressions of his appearance, deportment and spirit as a boy, but can recall but few incidents sufficiently characteristic for formal use in connexion with this record.

A letter from the only surviving member of his family, a sister who was five years younger than himself, contains a line which is conclusive as to the date of his birth. "In our old family Bible is written 'WILLIAM MEADE, born Nov. 11th, 1789.'"

The eldest brother, Richard Kidder, who was much addicted to genealogy, left among his papers a brief history of the Meade family. He traces to Thomas Cromwell, a blacksmith of Putney in Ireland, who was father of Thomas Cromwell, servant of Wolsey, and his successor in the favor of Henry the Eighth, but who, forfeiting that, was beheaded by his order. Oliver Cromwell was his nephew. One branch of this family was the Everards of Essex, from whom Richard Kidder, Bishop of Bath and Wells, was derived.

The paternal ancestor of the family in this country was Andrew Meade, born in the county of Kerry and kingdom of Ireland, about the latter part of the seventeenth century. Tradition says that on leaving his native country, he went first to London, and from thence came to New York, where he married Mary Latham of Flushing. Some five years afterward he removed to Virginia, and settled in Nansemond county. One son and a daughter were all the children he left. The son David married Susannah, daughter of Gov. Everard, of North Carolina. Their children were Anne, who married Richard Randolph of Curls — David, who inherited the estate in Nansemond — Richard Kidder, Everard, Andrew and John. The three elder boys were sent to England for their education, and placed under the care of Dr. Thackery, the Principal of Harrow School and Archdeacon of Surrey.

Richard Kidder, at the age of nineteen, married Jane Randolph of Curls — an aunt of John Randolph of Roanoke, who always called him "Uncle Kidder." She lived but a few years, had several children, all of whom died before the mother.

At the commencement of the conflict between the Colonies and Great Britain, R. K. Meade lived at Coggins' Point in Prince George, now the residence of Edmund Ruffin. In that eventful struggle he felt the deepest interest, and promptly participated in it in person. His name is second on the list of a party of gentlemen who, on the 24th of June, 1775, shortly after the hegira of Lord Dunmore, removed certain arms from the Governor's palace at Williamsburg, and lodged them in the magazine, of which Dr. Bland had the charge. His signature is the first appended to the following "receipt of arms:" "The subscribers acknowledge the receipt of a stand of arms, each, from the public magazine; which we do oblige ourselves to return to Dr. Theoderick Bland or order, when demanded." — Dated June 26th, 1775. ("Memoir" prefixed to the Bland papers, pp. xxiii–iv.) These active measures were soon followed by bloody collisions. In "the battle of the Great Bridge," he took an effective part, serving as Captain under General Woodford. In his letter to Col. Bland, describing that fight, the cool determined spirit of the writer is unmistakably expressed. The letter is dated "Norfolk Town, Camp, Dec. 18, 1775. The scene when "the dead and wounded were brought off, was too much. "I then saw the horrors of war in perfection, worse than "can be imagined. Good God! What a sight! What "will satisfy the Governor? You know my feelings and "my determination. I'll see this present matter at an end "or die."—(Bland papers, page 39.)

This was no momentary excitement, but the deliberate resolve of a patriot spirit, animated by a clear conviction of right and ready to stand by and sustain it at any sacrifice. He at once sold his estate on James river, distributing the greater portion of the proceeds among his relations—reserving only $3,000 for himself, which he placed in the hands of a friend to be invested for him as he might think best. Having disencumbered himself, he offered his services to his country. It is not known what position he at first occupied or through what grades he passed; but from several brief letters on army matters, addressed to Col. Bland, in May, 1777, it appears that he was then aid-de-camp to the Commander-in-Chief and one of his military family.

"As a soldier he was distinguished for his activity in reconnoitering, being a good rider, and having a fine animal—the black mare—so well known to British as well as American armies. He used to say that Hamilton did all the head work for the General, and he the riding, reconnoitering and carrying orders on the field. He was with Washington in all the great battles of the Revolution. To him was committed the superintendence of the execution of Major André, of which he always spoke with much feeling, saying that he could not forbear tears at seeing the execution of so uncommon and interesting a man, though he entirely approved the order. When Washington was taking leave of some of his aids, a circumstance occurred which showed his estimate of their different characters. To Hamilton he said, "You must go to the bar, which you can reach in six months." To Laurens, something as appropriate. To Col. Meade, whom he then called by his familiar name, "Friend Dick, you must go to a plantation in Virginia; you will make a good farmer and an honest foreman of the grand jury of the county where you live." The prediction was literally verified.

"At the close of the war, Col. Meade married the widow of Mr. Randolph, of Chatsworth, near Richmond. She is mentioned in Campbell's history as among the female contributors to the expenses of the war. Perhaps this circumstance may have first attracted the Colonel's attention to her." (O. ch. vol. 1, p. 295.) Col. Richard Kidder and Mary Meade had six children, of whom William was the fifth.*

The friend with whom Col. Meade had left the portion of the proceeds of the sale of his estate which he had reserved for his own use, purchased with it one thousand acres of land in that part of the Valley of Virginia, known as Frederick County, and since its subdivision, as Clarke. It was then a wild region, a kind of backwoods to the first settlements on tide water, and as the price indicates, not in much demand; but as it became cleared and was brought under cultivation, its superior agricultural properties were soon developed and it rose very much in value. The in-

---

*Richard Kidder Meade, born July 14th, 1746 Married Dec. 10th, 1780. Died Feb. 9th, 1805.

Mary Meade, his wife, born Nov. 9, 1753. Died June 16, 1813.

CHILDREN.

Ann Randolph Meade, born Dec. 3, 1781. Married March 23d, 1799. Died March 29, 1838.

Richard Kidder Meade, born Feb. 18, 1784. Married Dec. 19, 1815. Died Feb. 26th, 1833.

William Fitzhugh Meade, born March 16, 1786. Died September following.

Susannah Meade, born March 9th, 1788. Died Oct. 2, 1823.

William Meade, born Nov. 11th, 1789. Married Jan. 31, 1810. Married Dec. 2, 1820.

David Meade, born March 11, 1793. Married Nov. 17, 1814. Died Dec. 19, 1837.

Mary Meade, born Christmas day, 1794.

Lucy Fitzhugh Meade, born Oct. 26, 1796. Died October 2d, 1823.

[Copied from the old Family Bible.]

vestment was regarded as eminently advantageous, which is quaintly expressed by the name given to the tract, "Lucky Hit."

After the war Col. Meade went to reside on this estate, and labored diligently as a pioneer in its improvement. With his own hands he assisted in tilling the ground and in the erection of the buildings necessary for the accommodation of a family and for the purposes of the farm.

The principal building was a log house, consisting of but two rooms. This modest mansion was the birth-place of WILLIAM MEADE.

The energy of Col. Meade was not confined to the general management of his property, but extended to those operations, which involved severe bodily exertion. His daughter describes him as "hewing trees — working in iron and in leather — and, with his box of tools, keeping in repair the furniture of the log house. In those days, and in that region, mechanics were scarce. Col. Meade shrank from no labor which the proper culture of the soil or the real comfort of the dwelling demanded.

"Nevertheless he did not entirely discard books and politics, but sometimes wrote an article for the press on some subject which deeply involved the interests of his country. Nor did Washington disdain to consult him as to the choice of officers when, in the near prospect of war with France, he was called once more to head the army. The year before the death of Washington, Col. Meade paid him a visit at Mount Vernon. They had not met since the close of the war. The General was on the farm. They met in one of the fields near a pair of draw bars. Each recognizing the other, they dismounted and shook hands over them, the General insisting that he would pull down his own bars, and the Colonel that he would still be his aid!" — (Old Churches, vol. 1, p. 296.)

As he advanced in life, the effects of the exposure and hardships of his military career, became apparent in premature infirmity and painful disease, and then "he was seen moving about in his Bath coating dressing-gown with swollen hands and feet," suffering and disabled by frequent attacks of the gout. From an obituary, by the pen of an intelligent acquaintance, it appears that his death was caused by an unexpected attack of his constitutional disease, which occurred at the residence of an old friend in the vicinity, with whom he was accustomed to pass much of his time. The obituary furnishes so just an estimate of his character, that the brief extract which follows may be fitly introduced in this connexion:

"It is a melancholy reflection that the heroes of the American Revolution—the patriots of '76—are rapidly declining.

"On Saturday, the 9th inst., (Feb. 9, 1805,) at the seat of Matthew Page, Esq., in Frederick county, died Col. RICHARD KIDDER MEADE, formerly aid-de-camp to General Washington.

"While the memory of Col. MEADE is cherished with fond enthusiasm by his surviving friends, his loss will be long and bitterly regretted. His virtues, though of that dignified kind which enforce respect, were yet so tempered by gentleness and condescension that they never failed to conciliate affection. In public life his conduct was such as to secure the esteem and friendship of those accurate discerners of merit—Washington and Hamilton.

"If any virtue had a pre-eminence over the rest in his character, it was an invincible fortitude. Neither the pressure of external calamity nor the most acute bodily pain were ever known to discompose the serenity of his temper. He possessed likewise a sensibility which seemed scarcely compatible with such firmness as he exhibited.

"The death of his friend, General Hamilton, made an impression of melancholy on his mind which, it is believed, was not obliterated till the hour of his death. He had, for a considerable time, been sensible that his death was approaching, and when he spoke of that event, always mentioned it with the utmost tranquility of a philosopher and a Christian. The gout, which had long been wandering in his system, settled suddenly in his stomach, and in a few hours put a period to his existence."

A concise notice of the father is found on the first page of a few lines of manuscript by the son, commenced as a memoir of himself, but soon abandoned. "My father was emphatically an upright man. I remember to have hear him say that his teacher, the master of a grammar school in England, used to tell him, that though he would not be a learned scholar, he would be what was far better, '*vir probus.*' My father evidently took great pleasure in the thought that he was universally esteemed, what he really was, a man of great integrity — and without setting it in opposition to religion, took great pains to bring up his children in a high admiration of the '*vir probus.*'"

In the History of the Old Churches, ministers and families "of Virginia" by the son, it is recorded of the father that "he rejoiced as a citizen in those blessings which his military services had helped to obtain, and often said that there was no debt he so gladly discharged as the taxes levied for the maintenance of our (then) free and happy government. He never allowed a tax-gatherer to come to his house in search of what was due, but always anticipated this by paying it beforehand at some appointed place. The same was true of all his debts."

Another allusion to his father is in a private paper, enumerating causes for gratitude, where he specifies having been blessed with "Christian parents."

This sketch will afford the means of recognizing in the son a happy reproduction of some of the peculiar features of the parent.

The inestimable blessing of the household was the mother, Mrs. Mary Meade. Her praise has been transmitted by her privileged associates, as well as by the lips and the lives of her loving children. To their welfare she gave herself with uncommon energy and judgment as her business and pleasure, and was amply compensated by their affection and dutifulness. Her maternal tenderness was a hallowed power for the comfort and improvement of her children, and not an amiable infirmity too blind to behold and too bland to correct or even chide their faults. She had no ambition to be wiser than inspiration, and when required, she spared not the rod, yet administering discipline so gently that the chastisement was as expressive of affection as the most agreeable indulgences.

In a person of Mrs. Meade's intelligence and piety, it might be expected that religion would sustain and pervade her system of domestic education. In the autobiographical fragment,* by the son, it is stated, "On my mother devolved the religious education of the children, and faithfully did she perform that duty. A favorite topic with her was the continual presence of God, a consciousness of which she wished to have ever on our minds." With the effect of this training, especially on this son, she had no cause to be dissatisfied. The sister testifies that he was "very devoted to his mother," and adds, "I have heard her say he was very docile." He was her scholar and companion till his tenth year, at which age she believed "that other government and teachers should be found for her sons."

The high toned morality which prevailed at "Lucky Hit," forbade all habits of extravagance, and perhaps was not tolerant of certain indulgences which could not now be prohibited in the same class of society without the appearance of austerity. All daintiness of diet and expensiveness of dress was decidedly eschewed as unfavorable to manliness of both of mind and body—and something like Spartan frugality and hardness were esteemed conducive to health, honesty and happiness. If, during the boyhood of William Meade, "his clothes, both for summer and winter, were all of home manufacture," and he little heeded hat or shoe—it was not from penuriousness, but from principle, to avoid effeminacy and to secure becoming vigor and independence.

At Carter Hall, the residence of Mr. Burwell, which was about five miles from Col. Meade's, there was a select

* This fragment which will be referred to as occasion offers, is endorsed thus: "Something like an autobiography commenced. Intended to prevent anything like an heightened eulogy by some partial friend, from which my soul revolts."

school, consisting of Mr. Burwell's own boys and a few others received for this purpose, as boarders in his family. Their instructor was the Rev. Mr. Wiley, who, under the conviction that in entering upon the ministry he had mistaken his calling, abstained from the exercises of its sacred functions and devoted himself to secular teaching. For this he was well qualified, and pursued it with great enthusiasm and singular success. His reputation as a classical teacher, was not confined to Carter Hall. In the course of a few years he was elected principal of a flourishing academy in Fredericktown, Maryland, and afterwards professor of languages in St. John's College, Annapolis, where he remained till his death. Whatever his infirmities may have been, he was an able instructor, and his pupils compare favorably with those of other teachers of that period. To this school at "Carter Hall," WILLIAM MEADE was sent in his tenth year. His literary taste, and more especially his fondness for the ancient classics, were skilfully cultivated by the intelligence and zeal of Mr. Wiley. The happy effect of this training was soon apparent in the successful collegiate course of the pupil; but its most surprising result was reserved for the closing years of his life, and survives in the last volume of his numerous writings—"The Bible and the Classics"—the excellent fruit of his old age.

The desire to know something of the spirit and bearing of the boy and of the incidents connected with his school days, is perfectly natural. But where are the witnesses? Of all his companions at "Carter Hall," but one survives; he, his junior by two years, and never associated with him in the same classes. This sole witness, whose own worth fitted him eminently for perceiving and appreciating the character of WILLIAM MEADE, furnishes, in a recent reply to a letter, the following concise statement:

"I went to school with him for about two years, (I think between the years 1801 and 1804,) to a Mr. Wiley who then taught in the family of

Col. Burwell, of Carter Hall, being at the time about ten years old, and WILLIAM two years my senior. He was, at that time, as I recollect him, a boy of uncommonly amiable character, insomuch that I was at once attracted to him, and at that early period formed for him a friendship which was increased by all my subsequent intercourse with him to the end of his life. This I think was the general estimation of him in the school. He was more than usually liked among the boys. As he was in more advanced classes than myself, I have not a very distinct recollection of his standing as a scholar, though my impression is that it was excellent. He was full of vivacity, and showed much of that ardor and energy in the sports of boyhood, which has since greatly distinguished him in matters of a graver kind. In following his impulses of this sort, he would occasionally be betrayed into improprieties which brought on him the rebuke of his teacher. I have a very distinct recollection, in particular, of one incident illustrating this point. In one of his rambles on the banks of a stream which ran through the "Carter Hall" estate, he got in pursuit of an eel, which, by dint of great effort and strategy, he at length succeeded (in the technical language of the youthful anglers) *in hanging* — that is to say, in drawing up from the water, but not finally capturing it. The call to books interrupted the sport for the time. Upon going into school, his head was so full of his late exploit that he could think of nothing else. Books for the time were quite out of the question, and he could do nothing but go round among his companions, detailing his adventure, particularly dwelling on the fact that, though he had not wholly secured the slippery prize, he certainly had 'hung an eel.' At last the disturbance made by the loud and animated whispering, attracted the attention of Mr. Wiley, who, to punish his disorderly conduct and make any further communication about the eel superfluous, fastened on his back a piece of paper, on which was written, in large letters, 'WILLIAM MEADE hung an eel.'"

"After leaving Mr. Wiley's school, I do not remember to have met with WILLIAM until after he became a minister. I forbear going into any details of his subsequent life. I will, however, say, that having known him intimately during the whole time, I have never seen anything to justify the idea some have entertained, that there was anything harsh or repulsive about him, either in his character or manners. On the contrary, he always appeared to me in the light of a warm-hearted and affectionate, as well as a firm and faithful friend." — [Letter of Major Thomas M. Ambler, of Morven, Fauquier Co.]

Another significant school-boy adventure has been transmitted by uncontradicted tradition. The garden at Carter Hall was surrounded by a high enclosure, which formed an adequate protection against ordinary intruders, but did not hide the inviting fruit from the vision of those outside. The temptation thus constantly presented, was too much for boy nature—but who so active as to scale the barrier, or so bold as to risk detection? WILLIAM MEADE was the one to volunteer for the enterprise. Apart from the fine fruit, for which, through life, his appetite was extraordinary; the peril involved appealed to his intrepidity, and fondness for adventure. Aided by the boys, he was soon over the fence, and in the midst of the spoils. But the pillage had scarcely begun, when Col. Burwell, himself, surprised and arrested him in the very act. On hearing how he had effected an entrance, the Col. seems to have lost sight of the offence, in admiration of the daring it evinced. Instead of punishing the transgressor, he said, "help yourself to as many as you can eat, but take none away with you. Those who would not share the danger, shall not partake of its fruits."

In athletic exercises and juvenile sports, WILLIAM MEADE engaged with great ardor and success. The popular amusement of dancing and its associations, seemed to have had peculiar charms for him at this period. In a letter to his sister a few months after he had left home for college, he adverts to those fascinating scenes—"What would I not give to spend a few such evenings with our Virginia belles as I did last Summer, during the time of the dancing school: that was a golden age, indeed, to me."

When, at a subsequent period, he regarded that recreation as frivolous in itself, and pernicious in its influences on Christian experience and character, the decided change in his opinion must be imputed to some other cause than native austerity, or insufficient information. He could truly affirm—I speak that I do know, and testify that I have seen, and in which I once delighted.

When he had attained his seventeenth year, he was thought to be sufficiently advanced in his studies to enter advantageously on his collegiate course. The Rev. Samuel

Stanhope Smith was at this time the President of Princeton College, New Jersey, and by his distinguished literary attainments, and elegant manners, had rendered the Institution highly attractive to Southern students.

In the Fall of 1806, WILLIAM MEADE and two of his companions — William Page, of Frederick county, and William Fitzhugh, of Fairfax, matriculated as members of the Junior Class.

His first letter from Princeton will form his appropriate personal introduction, and extracts from the few others which remain, will afford sufficient information as to his life in College :

NASSAU HALL, Nov. 19, 1806.

I received my dear sister's letter, accompanied by one from brother Kidder, dated the 10th, yesterday morning; both of them gave me inexpressible delight by informing me of the health of all my friends. I thank my sister for her great anxiety concerning the manner of my admission into the Junior Class, and am glad to inform you that neither William Page or myself were deficient in anything except Kenneth's Antiquities, which we had never read. Wm. Fitzhugh being well versed in that book, was deficient in nothing.

As to our lodging in the same room, we found that impossible; but are all fixed greatly to our satisfaction. My own room-mates are very clever, sensible young men, and I hope we shall all agree well. You request a particular account of my journey, but want of time must excuse me. At some future period I will satisfy your curiosity. I cannot be so ungrateful as to omit our reception in Philadelphia. Besides the particular attention of Aunt Hair, and all my other aunts and uncles, Mr. Abercromby and his whole family, treated me in the most friendly hospitable manner. He carried us over the whole town, and often invited us to his house, to which we went very willingly, for his daughters are the finest women I ever beheld. It was with reluctance we proceeded on to Princeton, where we are safely landed, and have to suffer penance for our long vacation. Upon examination I found my purse so light as to be obliged to write for more — but for fear of disappointment, ask Mr. Bowen to endeavor to get the balance due from Pain, and send it to me by the first post. This short letter must suffice for the present. I thank you for your good advice, and will try to follow it as far as lies in my power. Remember me to all my friends, particularly to Uncle, in the most affectionate terms, and believe me,

Your affectionate brother,

WILLIAM MEADE.

P. S.—Excuse me for not returning the compliment of writing post-paid, for believe me, I have but 18 cents in the world.

NASSAU HALL, Feb., 1807.

My Dear Mother :—

Many, many thanks for your long, long expected letter, which came last Tuesday evening, not, however, before it had taken a trip to Brunswick. Here is an additional argument which ought to make you punctual, for who knows whether the next neglect may not send it on to Nova Scotia, and there be salted up among their herrings. Notwithstanding this misfortune, your letter, my dear mamma, was truly grateful to my heart, and so will all of them be while I have an affectionate heart, and I hope to die before it shall be otherwise than truly so. Your anxious solicitude, your hopes and fears for your children's future conduct will, I hope, only make me more dutiful. The thought of a fond mother's tender care, of the transport she will receive, at realized hopes, or the unhappiness she must feel at seeing her expectations blasted in undutiful and bad children, will, I most fervently pray, ever be an inmate in our breasts and warn us of our duty. Your letter was doubly satisfactory, because it assured me you were well and all round you going on happily. It merits a longer reply than I am able to give at present by reason of the urgency of college duties. You will excuse me though, I am sure, as I do not often put you off with a laconic epistle. There is nothing new worth relating, which you have not heard, and I am no politician to expatiate on the Embargo. Farmer Meade seems to have been inspired by it, for he gave me some verses full of patriotic warmth. It must have acted both as muse and subject to him, for I never knew he was a poet before. Here, then, is one advantage arising from the horrid Embargo that it has given America a poet. Let Mr. Jefferson alone. He knew that we should want Bards to sing our battles, and proposed this method to bring them out from their farm yards. Embargo born poets! beautiful name! America disdains being shackled by custom, and will have no poets dependent on the *Nine*. However, brother Kidder may call me envious, I will therefore desist. I must conclude by sending my love to all in the neighborhood, old and young — the pretty girls whom I long to see, and the boys who, I hope, are going on well with their studies. Tell Mr. Wylie I confess my neglect and will try to write soon. Remember me to all the servants, Daddy Brutus, and Aggy in particular. Thank Susan for her letter, and answer this hurried one from me.

I am your affectionate son,

W. MEADE.

P. S.—Wm. Fitzhugh is well and thanks you for your letter.

NASSAU HALL, Nov.—

My Dear Mother :—

Your affectionate letter dictated in a warm bed, and after a good night's rest, has safely arrived. I rejoice that all my friends are well, but was disappointed in not receiving a particular account of brother Kidder's leg, concerning which I cannot but feel a little uneasiness, until I am assured of its perfect restoration to strength. I beg, therefore, to be informed minutely in the next letter from Frederick.

To proceed to your next information concerning the regularity you are about to introduce in the several occupations of my sisters, I must say that I rejoice to hear of it, and hope you will succeed to the extent of your wishes.

Perhaps I may be called a trumpeter of my own fame, when I say that my mother would be highly gratified in seeing the order I observe in every one of my occupations, whether it be study, conversation with a few particular friends, or my exercise for the preservation of health. Had I time at present, you should have a particular account of them all. Perhaps you may think this but a poor specimen of the advantage I receive from my regularity, not to be able to write a long letter to my mother once in two weeks. You shall have an explanation of it. Our class is shortly obliged to appear on the Church stage, and each made to deliver an oration of his own composition. In preparing this I am now engaged, otherwise I would write you a long circumstantial, affectionate epistle. In my next I will be more explicit. You tell me Mary has been reading to you my favorite author, Watts. I know you must be pleased with his sentiments, though not more than I am myself. Would you believe me when I tell you that I had spent the whole of the evening on which I got your letter, in reading his rules for the improvement of the mind. I have an elegant English edition of that book, which I shall ever value above all others, as it was a present from a much loved friend of mine. He is a student, but unlike the greater part of them. We have been intimate since our first entrance into College, which intimacy has ripened into a friendship, I hope not of that flimsy texture which often marks youthful connexions. His name is Howell; you may, perhaps, have heard me speak of him before. I at first refused his offer, fearing lest he should be unable to procure another hereafter, but he pressed me much to take it, and preserve it as a token of his affection. Knowing how anxious you were for me to procure it, I accepted it, and hope to have the essence of it in my mind when I return to my friends.

And now, my dear mother, I must bid you adieu, with a fervent prayer that God will grant you health and happiness, and the love of your children. I am your dutiful son,

WILLIAM MEADE.

P. S.—My love to brothers, sisters, friends and neighbors. If I have a few moments to spare before the post goes out, I must scribble a few lines to Lucy.

My Dear Sister:—

I have found time to write you a few lines, but wish from my heart that I could assign some other cause for it than the following: Dr. Smith has just heard of the death of his favourite daughter, and is unable to attend on our class this evening. If I judge correctly of my sister Lucy's heart, she will sympathise with me in lamenting this unfortunate circumstance. You should feel for all, my sister, and remember what you would feel yourself on such an occasion. To leave this melancholy subject, I thank you for your letter. I think it pretty good, although it had several errors. My dear sister, improve the present opportunity of learning useful things; I assure you will never find another, so capable, and so desirous of teaching you as mamma. Love her with all your heart — be dutiful and make her happy—then you will be loved more sincerely by

Your affectionate brother,

W. Meade.

P. S.—Give my love to David. Tell him to write me how he is coming on with his studies, and I will answer his letter. Tell Mr. Wyley as he would not write to me, I am determined to write to him, and rouse him from his lethargy.

Nassau Hall, Dec. 7, 1806.

On Monday evening I received my dear brother's letter, enclosing a note of $50. It was very acceptable to me on two accounts — the one because it assured me of the health of my dear mother, and all my friends—the other because it enabled me to pay what I had borrowed, and likewise to purchase some articles that are absolutely necessary. I have in the end of the letter stated in what manner a part of the money was disposed of, the remainder, I think, will be fully sufficient for this session. Be assured, I will run into no expense which can be avoided. You desire to know how much will suffice for one year. I cannot decide accurately, but I think, exclusive of traveling expenses and clothes, $300 will be fully sufficient; if it is possible, I will make less serve me. I really think my dear brother might have devoted a few moments more to his letter, and have given me some little information concerning the farm, as he must know how very anxious I am to hear of every movement about it. Pray take time in your next, which, I hope, will be very soon, and tell me particularly how the wheat looks, how much corn you make, whether you have sold any wheat or pork, and at what price, which of the boys you hire for the ensuing year, and how you and Mr. Green come on? An answer to all these questions will afford me much satisfaction, and will not be very troublesome to you, who are so expert with your pen.

Tell mamma, my mind does not run so much on home as to cause the least neglect of my studies. At the mention of my studies, I recollect my promise in a former letter of informing you what they were. We are at present at Euclid and Algebra, in the former of which we recite five problems per day. In a few weeks we will recite Sunday lectures to Dr. Hunter. The remaining studies of this year are Navigation, Surveying, Trigonometry, Heilsham's and Blair's Lectures. As the studies of the Junior Class are easy in comparison with those of the Senior, I shall avail myself of the opportunity, and read History while I have it in my power. At present I am engaged with the American Revolution, written by a company of gentlemen in England. If my eyes will permit, I intend to be a very hard student during my residence at College. My brother must excuse my abrupt conclusion, as it is Church time, and I wish to address a few lines to my mother on the next page, when I return. Please to give my best love to all our friends, to my sisters, and to David. The only manner in which you can now evince your affection for me, is by endeavoring to make our dear mother happy by your tenderness and care of her. Adieu, and believe me Your affectionate brother,

WILLIAM MEADE.

ACCOUNT.

To Black Gown	$6.25
" Table and Chair	4.75
" Money borrowed	2.50
" Skates	1.00
" Neckcloths	88
" Shoes	1.00
" Sundry Articles	1.50
	$18.88

In my letter to sister, I promised to address my next letter to my dear mother, but without thinking, have used almost the whole of the paper in writing to brother Kidder. My mother will excuse me, no doubt, upon my promise of never neglecting her so again. I hoped long ago to have received a letter from you in your own handwriting, nor can I conceive the reason why I have not. If you do not favour me with one soon, I shall be certain you are too unwell to write, and will put no confidence in the assertions of any letters but your own, concerning your own health. Pray, my dear mother, be careful of yourself this winter. Sister has persuaded you to remove to Annfield at Christmas. I will not pretend to offer my advice, since I am certain you are the best judge. I hope you will not follow the example of sister Nancy in your letters to me; not even the Spartans could have been more laconic in writing than she was. From being so tenacious of her advice, she must have feared that it would have been slighted by me. I have no means of proving to the contrary than by assuring her that nothing would delight me more than to receive advice from her. Want of time and of paper forces me to bid my dear beloved mamma adieu. W. MEADE.

His college course, however, did not pass without serious disturbance. The year 1807 is memorable at Nassau Hall, as the year of the great rebellion, in which he was so far implicated, that with many others he was dismissed from the Institution. His own account of the unhappy occurrences is recorded in his brief autobiography:

"At the end of four or five months an unfortunate difference between the Faculty and some of the students arose, which produced a general petition from the latter to the former. Myself and many others, through want of experience, were imposed on, and signed, without consideration, an offensive document, which led to the suspension of one hundred and fifty out of two hundred students, because they did not on the spot withdraw their names, when suddenly and in a very unhappy manner required to do so. Out of the one hundred and fifty, only fifty returned. I was one of that number. My mother, whose authority was well established over her children, had only to express her desire that I should return and make any acknowledgment that might be required. It was done without a murmur. How often have I blessed God for giving me such a mother, and for this act of maternal authority especially."

After his re-admission to college, he addressed to his mother the letter which follows:

NASSAU HALL, May 21, 1807.

It gives me real pleasure to tell my dear mother that I am now re-instated in College, according to her desire and opinion of propriety; and what renders my situation more agreeable is, that in obeying the wishes of my mother and submitting to her superior judgment, I have in no manner acted in opposition to my own feelings or inclinations. An implicit obedience to your will, mamma, I hope ever to consider not as a duty only, but a pleasure. How pleasing, then, is the thought that in this act your will and my inclination do perfectly coincide. You will, perhaps, be surprised to hear of this alteration in my sentiments with regard to entering college — it is one which will contribute much to my future welfare, and perhaps, will not derogate from my honour at present. Upon mature consideration, I think the promise we made of supporting the committee, a rash step, and the means of performing it not in our power. We have assisted them as far as lay in our power, and from conversations which I have held with several of them, they appear to think that if consciousness of error, or the wish of parents incline any to enter, they would act with great propriety in so doing. It will certainly afford them greater satisfaction to see young men obtaining their education and profiting by the opportunities offered here than absenting themselves on account of that promise. Before I came, the tumult which had so long prevailed, had subsided and was succeeded by the utmost order. Many have returned, to the number of one hundred and twenty, though, I must confess, the finest young men have refused to return. Some there are whose minds were wavering at one time, but who determined to persist at last because the trustees, not content with suspending or expelling the non-retractors from college, wished to force the societies to do the same also, threatening to dissolve them in case of a refusal. They, however, did refuse in a very resolute manner — and College, societies and all were at the point of dissolution several different times. Prudence, however, at last got the better of passion and the trustees receded. William Fitzhugh, after much doubt and deliberation, had very prudently entered a few days before my arrival. His Papa's uneasiness, before I left Alexandria, was so extreme that I believe had William objected, it might have been attended with fatal consequences. You have, I suppose, before this received a letter from William Page, dated at Baltimore, assigning reasons for his determination. I must confess it surprised me a little. I will not pretend, however, to censure him, as I am liable to err so often myself, and as it was left for his judgment to determine, an adherence to the dictates of that was very proper. I think if he had remained at home one week longer, and waited till all those students who came determined to persevere, had withdrawn themselves, his opinion would have been materially altered. Perhaps, however, it will be all for the best, since he is so advantageously fixed.

All disturbances are [illegible] at an end, and I hope will never again be revived. Since I have ru[illegible] narrow a chance of not completing my education here, I will take great care never to run a similar risk, and the only piece of advice I ever intend giving to a young man on entering college will be, never to sign a *petition* on any account.

And now my dear mamma, let us take a final adieu of this subject which has afforded matter of conversation throughout the whole United States, and on which you have heard so many debates, pro and con. I will follow your advice, and avoid all conversation relating to it, with the students; indeed it seems to require little exertion so to do, as we are all wearied with it.

To change the subject then, I hope you are by this time perfectly restored to health, and have been skipping about at the dancing school with the girls. Dancing is an exercise, the moderate use of which I think, salutary both to young and old, and were you to have one quarter with Mr. Robardette, I should expect to find you quite renovated on my return. If I be not mistaken, you intended going to Lucky Hit the week succeeding that of my departure. I hope when you get there, that your health will permit you to attend to domestic affairs, since a little exercise is so beneficial to you. Brother Kidder is, I suppose, as usual, busily engaged on his farm, and in constructing the barn. It will give me much pleasure to receive a few bulletins similar to those of the last Winter, from headquarters, and grateful thanks will always be returned for them.

It is time to bid my dear mamma adieu. God grant that she may enjoy health and happiness, is the constant and fervent prayer of her truly affectionate son, WILLIAM MEADE.

P. S.—Mamma, this letter is not written as correctly as it should be. I depend upon the good news compensating for all its errors."

If he blessed God for giving him such a mother, well might she bless God for giving her such a son.

It was during his last year in college that his religious views and experience assumed a decided character. In reference to this very important and interesting subject, it is not necessary to have recourse to conjecture or inference, or the testimony of others. His own clear statement commencing with his earliest impressions, and extending to the period of his life now under consideration, furnish the very information which is desirable.

Alluding to his mother's "faithfulness in the religious education of her children," and to the favorite topic, the continual presence of God, a consciousness of which she wished to have ever in our minds"—he proceeds: "I felt the effects of this at a very early period. Indeed I cannot go back so far as to recollect a time when I was without some sense of God's presence, and, as I believe, some operation of the Spirit on my mind. At the age of, I should think, about eight years, I recollect that my mind was the subject of some contending thoughts. I was conscious of the desire to do right in the sight of God, and would resolve to do it, and at the same time I was beset with some most wicked thoughts, even to curse God. I can well remember how I would sometimes set out and run with the utmost violence, trying thus to get away from such a wicked act of the mind.

At the age of ten, when first sent to school, I wrote the day before leaving home, some thoughts as to my duty, which were very gratifying to my parents. Although much like other boys, while there, in my general conduct, yet even now can I recollect the reasonings of my mind in favor of religion, as something which, even if proving untrue, must be a happy delusion to the believer and useful to mankind. Even more than this I remember, when fourteen years of age, being most deeply distressed for one very dear to me, who seemed almost hopelessly given up to an evil habit, and being led as a last resort to pray most earnestly for him to God as the Being who alone could rescue. One night, after being in great distress weeping and agonizing in prayer, I was most sensibly relieved by the strong impression that God would hear my prayer. I have ever believed that even my poor prayers were heard among many others, far more fervent and effectual, which were sent up from righteous hearts, for the evil was averted.

I remember, also, during my sixteenth year, I would often read some chapters in the *Spectator* and *Vicesimus Knox's Essays* of a serious character, and being much affected by them, although they by no means conveyed clear and strong views of Christianity. My mind was in search of truth—my heart was in some degree longing for God as my portion. It was an age of darkness, when even the best Christians did not enter so fully into the glorious system of redemption as they should have done. It was a long time before I rejoiced in God as a Saviour. The law of the Spirit of life in Christ Jesus had not made me free from the law of sin which still had dominion over me."

"In this state of mind — my father being dead — my mother sent me to college. God made use of this separation from my friends in strengthening my religious feelings. My heart was tenderly attached to them. I had never been more than a few miles from them, and for a few days at a time before, and I was very sad. I read the few books I took with me with deep feeling — particularly

'Young's Night Thoughts,' a great favorite of my mother and elder sister. I remember that my religion partook very much of a communing with the spirit of my deceased father, and of my absent mother, whom I was ever regarding as being present with me, and whose approbation I was earnestly seeking. But God was still drawing me to himself."

After a brief narrative of the College rebellion, his relation to it, his being sent home, and his return to his mother's direction, he proceeds: "It probably gave direction to all my subsequent life. I was destined to the law, and had I been permitted to follow the example of many others who were sent home at the same time — that is, in proud rebellion refuse to return — I should at once have entered on the study of a secular profession, and what might have been the effect of the same on my moral and religious character, God knows. As it was, on returning to an almost desolate College, and humbled at the thought of the injury our own folly had done to it, my religious feelings were greatly strengthened, and this was so apparent in my letters homeward, that I soon received a letter from my elder sister, Mrs. Page, conveying to me the suggestion of our beloved mother, that I should seriously consider whether the ministry was not the path of duty. Although such a thought had never entered my mind, and everything in the state of our Church was most discouraging, yet do I well remember that I felt my determination fixed in a moment, and at once rejoiced at the thought of a life of such honor and usefulness."

When this determination was communicated to his family and friends in Virginia, it gave great satisfaction. The letters which he received from home abounded in expressions of grateful joy. His eldest sister, Mrs. Ann R. Page, to whom he was largely indebted for much excellent instruction and advice, and who, at his mother's request, had presented the subject of the Christian ministry for his serious consideration, now responded for that delighted mother and herself:

"My brother, your sentiments have in every point given the most complete joy. You have pictured out our every wish, and your Heavenly Father will enable you to perform them — will carry your mind from strength to strength. I have the supreme satisfaction of expressing this in our dear mother's name. Brother Kidder will, I expect, certainly write to you how congenial your letter was to his heart. The overflowing eye evidenced his feeling."

There was another relative and friend whose heart was deeply interested in this determination—Mrs. Mary Custis, of Arlington, D. C. — the sister of his friend, William Fitzhugh. She was a Christian lady of superior intelligence, and of a most gentle and affectionate spirit, and with evangelical views and religious experience, in advance of her day and associations.

The correspondence of these devoted cousins commenced early — was frequent and familiar, sometimes playful, but generally very serious, and very salutary in its influence upon the young student. Her discernment and sensitiveness in connection with his character and usefulness, and the judgment and fidelity with which she communicated with him, and expressed her solicitude in reference to his professional qualifications and efficiency, appear in the following extract from a letter written at a later period, but recurring to the important purpose now formed:

April 20, 1819.

Ultimately, with tears and anxious desires for yourself, your ministry, and your mission, my soul was poured out in prayer. Unpossessed, however, with that assurance of faith which many possess, both for themselves and others, those tranquil emotions which succeed the unburdening of the heart to God, gave way once more to a trembling anxiety, which I have ever been subjected to on your account. I looked back to the circumstances connected with your entrance into the ministry — your letters written to me whilst you were in College were re-perused, and though fraught with many of those amiable feelings which resulted from the pious care of your excellent mother — the very possession of those feelings seemed to beguile you into self-righteousness. You know who has said, "God often leads his servants blindfold into the sanctuary,' and thus it certainly was with you, for no deep feeling of unworthiness seemed to appal your entrance. I desire to thank God that you have been gradually led to perceive the depravity of an unrenewed heart. In your enlarged intercourse with the world, I sometimes fear, evils may be elicited which you dream not of. Should it be so, I humbly trust you will be preserved from such a manifestation of them as shall give the enemies of religion cause to triumph. May every high imagination be checked in its first rising — every feeling inimical to a "single eye" to God's glory, be bathed in the tears of an early repentence. May the arms of our divine Saviour uphold you continually — the Spirit of Grace dwell in you richly, and a constant dependence on the Father and Creator of all things, annihilate self in your bosom! Such would be my daily prayer for you, if I *could* daily be fervent in prayer, but warm words from cold lips, reach not the throne of grace."

If the Princeton letters alluded to were available, they would, no doubt, fully sustain the statement relative to the dimness and defectiveness of his personal piety at this period, and the inadequacy of his perception of the nature and responsibilities of the office to which he, sincerely, yet in much remaining darkness aspired. But of this we have decisive proof under another form. After recording his prompt determination to devote himself to the ministry, he furnishes a frank disclosure of the state of his own mind:

"While there was a sincere and lively desire to do good to my fellow-beings by promoting what I believed to be necessary to happiness in both worlds, there was still a very indistinct and imperfect view of the Christian system and the gospel ministry, and I was entering the latter blindfold in a considerable degree. I was, however, working out my salvation with perfect sincerity, and honestly preparing to teach others to do the same."

He proceeds: "I had only one or two religious associates, and but few helps to advancement in divine life. I took pleasure, however, in reading a few pious books and was engaged in a warfare with my body. In order to get away from the temptation of eating too much at dinner, I would sometimes take a good book and stroll so far from the College, that at the sound of the horn for dinner, I could not reach it in time. Many were the resolutions then made, and many the resolutions then broken. By this process, God was preparing me for a fuller understanding and more humble reception of the doctrines of grace.

"As one evidence of the imperfect views I had of religion and the ministry, and of the low state of piety in our Church, let me state that in passing through Baltimore, on my way home, I went to the theatre, where I saw an old schoolmate of my earlier years, who having been living there for some time, had learned that the theatre was no place for me, and expressed his surprise at finding me there. I never remember before that, to have heard it condemned." (Autobiography.)

His College course was drawing to its close. The following letters written during the last session of his senior year, show his sentiments and action in the transition period, from youth to manhood.

NASSAU HALL, June 13, 1808.

* * * * * I feel anxious for the arrival of the time when I shall embrace my beloved mother and all my dear relatives, not because I am discontented at present, but because it is the nature of man to long for coming happiness. I expect to bring with me my young friend from Jersey, who is the warmest friend I ever had. Some of his qualities I will state more particularly when we meet, and some you will immediately perceive on the first acquaintance. If he should come, you must treat him just as you would myself, for he lives in a neighborhood much like our own for hospitality and rural simplicity of manners. I wish I could bring him, heart and all, and give him to some of our fine girls, but the poor fellow has, I fear, parted with the first portion of himself, so that they must seek husbands for themselves.

I am now devoting all of my spare time to French, to enable me to read those eloquent preachers who endeavored to disseminate true religion through the unhappy land of France. In three months I cannot learn much, only elementary principles, and how to jabber a little *Francais*. I shall learn at least to beg for mercy, when our land is overrun by Bonaparte, which is a circumstance the warm *Fed's* are very apprehensive of, though I can never agree to it. Do not think I ever meddle with politics because a word slips out now and then, that way inclined. I have read nothing but Pickering's letters and Gardner's speeches. The former I revere as a firm, honest patriot; the latter I admire as a bold, independent orator, but must condemn him as a very punctilious man of modern honor. All good men I will openly applaud; proved villians I may condemn, but of doubtful characters I will be silent. The characters of a politician and divine are not easily blended, or at least form an unnatural and unprofitable combination.

Adieu, my fond mother. May Heaven guard you from distress either of mind or body; may the gratitude of your children cheer you through the remainder of life; may you live to see them flourishing in happiness and virtue, and may the expectations formed of your son be verified."

WILLIAM MEADE.

NASSAU HALL, July 1st, 1808.

My Dear Brother:

It is now five o'clock in the morning, and I am just returned from a salutary bath at a run of water, a mile hence. This little circumstance is related, to prove that the strengthening of my body is not overlooked in the cultivation of my mind. In your affectionate letter of the 22d ult., you reminded me that my own hands were to supply me with the comforts of life, and advised a careful attention to my health. I have ever expected this, and look forward with pleasure to the time when alternate study and labor shall keep me in constant employment. As to any carelessness of health, I am too sensible of its value, to sport with it heedlessly. Three or four hours of each day are devoted to exercise. The hottest sun that has ever shone on the classic land of Princeton, never confined me within the College, at the appointed time for exercise. The happy consequences of this regularity, are an uninterrupted health, and a greater fondness and capacity for study. To books, I never give less than ten hours per day; more should be given were my eyes sufficiently strong to bear more, but they require indulgence, and I cannot read at night without pain.

Sometimes, when I reflect on our poverty and on the necessity of my speedy liberation of you from further expense, I wish they were so strong as to let me study twelve or fourteen hours in the day. I would lop off one year at least from my professional study. But, again, I look on their weakness as a kind dispensation of Heaven—as one of those which we term evils; but which in truth are only manifestations of the Divine goodness in offering us stimulants to virtue. Were my eyes perfectly strong, love of reading, and perhaps ambition would keep me perpetually at books, my health would have perhaps been already sacrificed, and little time would have been spent in devotion, in meditation, and reflection. I might now be picturing to my worldly mind the beauties of fame, of office, of popular eloquence, and all the gewgaws which offer charms to the vain heart of man. I might have been engaged in such contemplation, quite estranged from my God, and certainly not half so happy as at present, while looking forward through the humble, obscure, though, I hope, useful and respectable life I am about to lead. Never, unless necessity (arising from the weakness of my sight which made me lay aside my book very frequently) had led me to retire in my own mind, would I have made any virtuous resolutions, which only paved the way for my ready entrance into mamma's choice of a profession.

Thus have I reason to bless my God for this apparent evil. It has forced me to be temperate, and to refrain entirely from liquors. The clear water of the brook will quench my thirst better than the richest wines — the simplest nutriment will appease my hunger better than the choicest dishes of the epicure.

Having satisfied you with regard to my health both of body and mind, I will reply to your question concerning the studies of this session. They consist of Chemistry, Astronomy, Logic, Political Philosophy and Theology. Our class has in some manner gotten a little behind hand, and we are now forced to make it up by assiduous study. In answer to your request that I would not be unmindful of College distinctions, I must say that it has come rather late, for two months will terminate our course. There are forty-four in our class, and about twenty-five or thirty distinctions are usually distributed. I will only promise that your brother's name shall not be found among the last on the list. Whether it will lie in the neighborhood of the top, remains a secret locked up in the minds of our Professors. As soon as the determination is made, you shall be informed; but let me ask you not to raise your expectations high, as the fall may be grievous.

Your cautions on the score of economy shall be observed. I will not spend one farthing unavoidably, but many must be spent necessarily. Certainly I can never spend more than half as much hereafter, wherever I shall live. At this place, the expense will be inconsiderable. Whatever shall be the result of your joint deliberations in respect to the place of my residence during the next year, shall meet with my cheerful compliance. Cousin Molly Custis is very anxious for me to live with Mr. Addison, and wishes me to grant her permission to ask his consent, supposing that it would meet with mamma's approbation. Perhaps it would be more agreeable to you all, if I should live with Mr. Belmaine, or return here immediately. We can agree on this point in the fall, and therefore I will dismiss it from consideration till then.

It gave me not a little uneasiness to hear that my expenses here are equal to the value of the crop at the present price, but let us all derive good from evil, by economy, industry, and every domestic virtue. I really am of the opinion that the embargo will be serviceable to our neighborhood, for it must lessen that pride, which, we have ever thought, threatened destruction to its prosperity. If this affliction should not suffice, you, my dear brothers, and myself, mutually strengthening each other, will, in spite of the odium fixed on singularity, dare to set example of true agricultural simplicity, so necessary for the permanency of that happy union, which now connects so many virtuous, yet extravagant families in Frederick. I am happy to hear that mamma is making Virginia cloth, and with the greatest pleasure will receive the present she is preparing of a coat. If my sisters are knitting any stockings for me, ask them to make them larger than the rest. I strongly suspect the little jades are about to surprise me with their industry, to present me with some valuable marks of their love.

I cannot go on writing in this hurried, careless manner any longer, without apologizing. You know it is necessary for a preacher to write a plain, large, and easy hand. I cannot do this, and therefore intend, as soon as I return home, to alter mine entirely. Being, at present, much in want of time, I do not think it criminal to write as fast as possible, since my friends will not ascribe it to a carelessness of affection. You do me wrong, in supposing that I ever harbored narrow opinions of your fraternal liberality. I always thought that our general happiness was uppermost in your heart, and looked up to you in that respect as a just father. I trust that my whole conduct, through life, will prove the truth of this assertion. Although I have often united with mamma and sister, in censuring some of your resolutions, yet be assured, I have admired, in secret, those steady principles of honor, justice, and piety, taken from the example of our dear departed father, and which directed all your actions, in contradiction to the trivial ridicule manifested by others, who make custom their guide, without ever retiring into their own minds to consult its propriety. When we have settled together, we shall be able to defy the assaults of ridicule, whether they be directed against supposed penuriousness, against a weak humanity for servants, or any other principles which mark our actions. We will cultivate friendship with our virtuous neighbors, but let the strictest friendship subsist between ourselves. Let it be the aim of our lives to set examples of piety, contentment, love, charity, and every Christian virtue. That I should be exemplary is indispensably necessary. A minister of religion is a light, set on an high hill, to light others to glory. This light must not be dim or deceitful to travellers. That I may be able to make my light shine clear to the sight of men, is the constant prayer of my heart to Almighty God.

Against the temptations of the world, I will fortify my mind by principles of religion. That I shall ever fail in any great affair, I am not much

much fearful; in the small concerns which are also weighed in the balance of God, I fear I shall often be found wanting. I know this much, that I place my confidence in God I am anxious for the promotion of His glory, by the diffusion of His religion through the hearts of men. I would rather be a worthy minister of the humble and lowly Jesus, than the first magistrate of our country, decked with all the glories of his office.

I never will disgrace the profession, by undertaking it, unless qualified by learning, zeal, and uprightness. As for the gaudy flowers of oratory, they never shall disfigure the pulpit where I stand. If important truths, wholesome warnings, and advice delivered in the simple style of nature, which is warm and impressive, have no power over the hearts of my hearers, they must seek for some others to please their fancy.

Give my love to all the neighbors. I hope they are well and happy. Tell mamma I long to see her long winning letter, which must be very long to compensate for my long unfulfilled expectation. The embargo has certainly stopped sister's pen, and Susan's and David's, and in fine all of you have felt its influence. My love to them all. I remain

Your most affectionate brother,

W. MEADE.

In the College of New Jersey, it was customary for the Faculty to signifiy their estimate of the comparative scholarship of the prominent members of each graduating class, by the award of "honors," or complimentary recognitions, which were announced to the audience at Commencement, and given to the press for publication. The prizes thus proposed were most potent appeals to youthful emulation. The competition for the highest honors was always very spirited, and the ardor of the candidates was often intensified by the rivalry of the two literary societies of the College — each eager for the success of its own members, and constantly stimulating them to efforts to secure its triumph.

As the preceding letter discloses, there was at the rural home beyond the Blue Ridge and in the hearts of the unostentatious inmates there, an assurance that William could excel, and a true desire that his superiority should be apparent. The elder brother communicated to him these aspirations of the domestic circle, and in the name of their honored and beloved mother, expresses the hope that he would not he indifferent to College distinctions. This, of itself, would be sufficient to rouse his energies, if they had been slumbering, in the pending race for Academic honor. He received the communication without disturbance—alluded in reply to certain duties and discouragements, and cautions against any high expectations, lest the disappointment should be the harder to bear—but he had, and could not but be conscious of, those endowments which guarantee success. In a few months the contest was decided. Out of a large class, he and two others were proclaimed to be of equal merit, and entitled to the "First Honor."

The policy of such distinctions has been seriously questioned. He has recorded his own testimony, founded on experience:

"I was doubtless somewhat hindered in my religious progress, by the fact that I was one of the candidates in a class of forty, for the highest honor, which was divided between myself and two others." (Autobiography.)

The Cliosophic Society of which he was a member, exulted in his success, and addressed to him a letter of cordial thanks and congratulations.

CLIOSOPHIC HALL, September 5, 1808.

Sir and Brother:

The members of the Cliosophic Society, feeling grateful for the honor conferred upon the Institution by your exertions, have unanimously voted you their thanks, and determined to present you with a diploma as a testimony of their brotherly affection. It is also expected that you will, as soon as convenient, act in conformity to that law of the Society which specifies the highest reward and the greatest insignia of honor, Cliosophians can oestow upon conspicuous merit. I shall not attempt to describe the pleasant and joyous sensations, which our late triumph excited, and which have already been so fully expressed by your brothers.

We hope that you have too much strength of mind to regard the invidious, unfounded assertions of malicious rivals, whose disappointment at the decision of the Faculty, has been expressed in scurrilous observations upon the most worthy members of that honorable body, and in ungentlemanly detractions from your merit. Your honor becomes apparent in proportion to their abuse. Trusting that your subsequent conduct will be such as to gratify the expectations of all, and that rigid virtue will be the companion of your future life. I remain

Your affectionate brother Cliosophian,
JAMES MOORE WAYNE.
(In behalf of the Cliosophic Society.)

MR. WM. MEADE.

Of the orations usually appointed for Commencement day, the Valedictory, which carries with it a recognition both of superior scholarship and excellence as a speaker, was assigned to him, and formed a graceful close to his Collegate course.

The following letter, addressed to his mother from Dr. Smith, President of the College, preceded his return home by a few days:

Madam:

I have the pleasure to inform you that your son has just finished his course of College studies with great credit to himself. His talents, his application, his principles, and morals are such as may justly afford a virtuous and affectionate parent the sincerest, purest consolation. It will not be long I trust, till you embrace a son worthy of you.

With the greatest respect and the best wishes for your happiness,

I am, Madam,
Your obedient humble servant,
SAMUEL SMITH.

At this period, the Church had no Theological Seminary. Divinity students either returned to College, as resident graduates, to avail themselves of the advantage of extensive libraries and general literary association, or else placed themselves under the guidance of some minister eminent for his ability, to receive such instructions as he might have leisure to impart, and to learn from his example.

During WILLIAM MEADE's last session at Princeton, the arrangement for pursuing his professional studies was often the subject of correspondence between his family and himself. In a letter to his mother, written June, 1807, this passage is found: "Cousin M. Custis takes a warm interest in my welfare and writes me very affectionate letters. She is anxious that I should spend the next year with Mr. Addison, and from many considerations, I enter warmly into the plan. A good and constant example, mamma, is of more real utility to a young man, than any collection of precepts. I am averse to returning here immediately, because I should find only young men like myself. The first entrance of ecclesiastical study is the most important, since *then*, the opinions of the many subjects which have unfortunately divided Christians, are formed. I wish to form them from mature reflection, aided by the advice of a virtuous and well-informed minister. Such a man is Mr. Addison supposed to be. Cousin Mary promises to ask him whether he will receive a young student of divinity into his house, and guide him by his counsel. If it meets with the approbation of my mother, I would prefer it to any other plan. Yet be assured, I will follow implicitly your advice, however different it may prove from my opinions or wishes."

The conclusion was in favor of an application to the Rev. Walter Addison to receive him as a student, and the negotiation which was conducted by Mrs. Custis resulted successfully.

After his graduation, Mr. MEADE returned to Virginia, and remained there for a short time, enjoying the society of his honored mother and other beloved relations and friends. This interval of study was rendered memorable by his engagement to Mary Nelson, daughter of Philip and Sarah Nelson — an event which gave great pleasure to both families.

When a "month or two" had been passed "at home" amidst the most pleasing associations, affording a salutary recreation both to mind and body, well deserved by his academic diligence and success, he again left his native valley and repaired to the residence of the Rev. Mr. Addison, to live in his family, and study divinity under his direction.

Mr. Addison was remarkable for extreme mildness and simplicity, combined with extraordinary decision, where principle and duty were concerned. In the ordinary intercourse of life so gentle and compliant, that one might imagine a child could lead him, and yet, when occasion demanded, not only immoveably firm, but heroically aggressive. His admiring pupil states: "In him I became acquainted with one of the best men, and saw one of the purest specimens of the ministerial character. He was faithful and bold in reproving vice from the pulpit and elsewhere, though one of the meekest of men. He was of English parentage and born to large landed possessions on the Maryland side of the Potomac, opposite Alexandria." This fine estate, extending several miles along the east bank of the river, was gradually wasted away by mismanagement, and at last, its once wealthy proprietor was reduced to penury. To penury was added the great affliction of increasing dimness of sight, terminating in blindness. Both of these evils, he bore with most exemplary resignation, and both were, as far as possible, alleviated by every attention and comfort which affection could bestow. "He lived to a good old age," as his pupil further states, "loving all men, and beloved by all who knew him—to the last the happiest and most grateful of all the happy and grateful ones, I have ever seen or known. In my visits to the District afterwards, I ever felt it to be my sacred duty, and it was my high happiness, to enter his humble dwelling. But this was never done without bursts of feeling and of tears on both sides. Such was the man of God with whom it was my privilege to spend some happy, and I trust not unprofitable months—the period of my stay being abridged by a weakness in the eyes, which altogether prevented study."

"Parson Addison," as he was then commonly called, was

more noted for the attractive excellence of his personal character, than distinguished for theological learning. The great advantage which his student enjoyed, was afforded, not so much by oral instruction, as by the meekness, humility and holiness of his Christian life.

Mr. MEADE's indistinct and imperfect view of the Christian system, at the time of his determination to devote himself to the ministry, has been represented in his own language. Happily he has also left us his own account of the time, place and instrumentality connected with the entrance of clearer light, and the experience of its decided power. "It was while reading under his (Rev. Mr. Addison's) direction, that the first clear and satisfactory and delightful view of the necessity and reasonableness of a propitiation for sin by our blessed Lord, was presented to my mind. I shall never forget the time, or the instrument, or the happy effect, and how I rose up again and again from my bed, to give thanks to God for it. The book which was instrumental to it was 'Soame Jennings on the Internal Evidences of Christianity.' Mr. Wilberforce's work (Practical View) about the same time was put into my hands and gave the cast and coloring to my religious views."

The weakness of his eyes — an infirmity from which he often suffered during his whole life — now rendered it necessary that he should intermit his studies. A few months at home and his eyes were sufficiently improved to permit him to resume his regular professional reading. He was evidently very partial to Princeton. Though there was no Divinity School there, yet a few young men who were preparing for the ministry resorted to the place as affording superior advantages to theological students. To avail himself of those advantages Mr. MEADE returned to Princeton, in the summer of 1809, but his expectations were soon and sadly disappointed. A few days after his arrival, he was seized with a violent fever, which brought him to the verge of the grave. During this severe illness and tedious recovery, his thoughts very naturally turned with more than usual tenderness, to his family and friends at his distant home, and yet he was by no means insensible to the sympathy and friendly services which he received from the people of the place. In his reply to a letter from one of his sisters, he writes: "How rejoiced am I to hear that you are happy and well, neighbors, visitors, and all. The sincere and fervent ejaculation of my heart is, that you may long continue so. Never I believe was there more happiness condensed into any one society, equal in dimensions with that of which we are members. At least, no band of relatives and friends ever possessed better or more abundant material for true Christian felicity, than the members of our neighborhood. The more I see of the vain world, the more attached do I become to the society in which I was born, nurtured and educated. Little do you know, you young generation, whose eyes have never peeped over the mountains, that you inhabit the Paradise of our State, and, my great attachment adds, of all the States, for I verily believe the valley of Frederick contains more real friendship, piety, and happiness than any other spot in the land. My partiality for a native spot, however, does not encroach on my judgment and blind it to the merit of others. On the contrary, my friendship and good opinion of the State and place in which I now am, have been greatly augmented since my last visit. My indisposition, which drew some of the kindest souls to see me, and led to a most extensive acquaintance in the State, showing me, that hospitality and Jersey were by no means unharmonious names, has made this addition to my esteem. Were I not bound by the ties of religion and friendship to my own State, and were the valley covered with the lake, which Mr. Jefferson imagined, overspread where you reside, I should prefer this to any other State I have yet visited. But Virginia shall ever be the scene of my labors. Oh that I could see her already what my hopes and fancy portray!"

The following letter, without date, appears to have been written to his sister, Mrs. Page, before his departure from Princeton:

My Dearest Sister :

For three years have I now been a stranger to my home, and for three years have held communion, ah! sweet communion with the best of sisters.

By the guidance of Providence, a letter from herself, and my dearest mother, first directed my heart to the noblest of sciences, and the best of professions.

To epistolary communion with my Christian friends, how much delight and profit do I owe. It is now drawing to a close. I come among you perhaps never to part more, unless my Master, Father, and Redeemer shall order. To His will, may I ever be willingly obedient.

I come among you, my dear friends, with sentiments of the tenderest love, and the most ardent wishes to make the glory of our blessed Redeemer shine brightly throughout the hearts of all.

My beloved sister, you whose heart beams with so much ecstacy and comfort on the cause I am about to undertake, and whose prayers so often ascend to Heaven in behalf of your brother, rejoice alway, that his heart is every day more and more set on his glorious mission. Each day some new and precious light, coming down from the Father of lights, seems to dawn upon his soul, teaching him the blessedness of religion. Prayer, and every religious exercise are no longer duties, but the most glorious privileges given to poor condemned mortals, by which they may regain that purity of nature, and perfection of bliss, for which the Almighty first intended us, but which our first parents lost by their disobedience, and the restoration of which, is the merciful end of the Christian mediation.

There is surely no happiness on earth but to serve the Lord. To serve with a willing, zealous, and glad heart is felicity little lower than that of the angels above. They enjoy His presence, and so does the Christian, only removed at a greater distance. Oh! my dear sister, what a choice have we made. How glorious are our prospects. Happy here, and divinely, transcendantly happy for ever hereafter! Should we ever forget to pray most fervently for our dear mother, that good instrument in the hands of Almighty God for converting souls to His kingdom? How can we ever love her enough, for that watchful Christian care with which she reared our tender souls to piety and virtue.

May it be our sedulous endeavor hereafter, to smooth the path of her declining life — to comfort her anxious heart by showing in our lives, and by every filial office, that her labors have been blest. Let the tenderness of our love soften the least anguish that may disturb her bosom, and, as her life and labors have been devoted to our good, so may ours be now employed in making the best of mothers, the happiest of mothers also.

Your affectionate brother,

WILLIAM MEADE.

Though restored to health, it was thought better for him not to resume immediately his regular course of study. Accordingly he left Princeton, indulged himself in a short visit to Parson Addison, and hastened to his earthly Paradise in the happy valley. In a few months, when he had just entered upon his twentieth year, he consummated his engagement with Miss Nelson. From a congratulatory letter addressed to him on the occasion by Mrs. Custis, and dated "Arlington, Jan. 30, 1810," it appears that the marriage occurred the next day:

"I learn with joy, my dear William, that you will to-morrow be the happy husband of Mary Nelson. May every blessing attend you both!— congenial minds — souls attuned to heavenly pleasures — friends approving — these are delightful auspices. How few such unions seem to bless mankind. How often is a life of suffering the penalty of a connection formed on the ignominious principle of aggrandizement. Monday night Kidder's arrival surprised us. He only staid to see you a Benedict, and brought to us the welcome news, and your letter and your Mary's. As you are *one* now, she will not think I have slighted her, if I do not address her on a separate paper."

If WILLIAM MEADE did not serve seven years *in advance* for his Mary, their marriage certainly subjected him to quite that term of service, very laborious in its nature, and very diligently and perseveringly performed — though no doubt he could have testified, as did the Patriarch, that "it seemed to him but a few days for the love he had to her," and which he, at a later period, so affectingly recorded in his "Recollections," "printed for private circulation."

His circumstances at this time and his independent, manly course, are best learned from his own frank relation: "This step, (marriage) compelled me at once, and for many years, to labor with my own hands for a support. My mother gave me a small farm, out of order, much injured by the tenant, and without a house on it. My wife had nothing. I began at once to build a small house. Myself and one or two hands burnt the lime-kiln, which was used in building. I was in attendance, almost without intermission, night and day, from Monday morning to Saturday night. I assisted to tend the workmen who built the house. On the farm I helped to plough the first field that was cultivated, and, as I did for many years, scattered the seed with my own hands. I did all this because I was resolved never to incur debt—a rule to which I have strictly adhered ever since, and which, in the good Providence of God, has been the means of greatly increasing my property and enabling me to divide a sufficient portion to my sons. Had I, at an early period, been too proud or too indolent to work, or had I not been a rigid economist, and even subjected myself to ridicule for what seemed a needless singularity to some, I should have been forced to sell, at a very low price, my portion of my father's military land, which has since so increased in value, as to enable me to give to each of my sons, as much to begin life with, as I desire they should have."

Such proceeding, however, was not compatible with much study, or favorable to those intellectual habits which are so important to professional proficiency. "The step," to one in his circumstances, may have created the necessity of which he speaks; but, was it necessary that a step so seriously interfering with his preparatory course of reading, should *then* be taken? Ought not a youth in his twentieth year, and who had scarcely commenced his theological training, to have resolutely avoided any, and every entanglement with the affairs of this life, which would retard and impair his education for the sacred service to which he was dedicated?

At a later period of his life, no one could give to this question a more prompt and decided affirmation than he did. Consciousness of the disadvantage under which, notwithstanding his fine intellect and subsequent application, he labored, in consequence of not having had early and thorough systematic drill in the elementary branches of theological learning, gave peculiar emphasis in his testimony. And the sad effect of premature engagement and marriage in other cases, where there was not the redeeming power which his talents and temperament afforded, made him avail himself of every proper occasion to caution students against a hasty "step" which might cripple them during their whole professional course.

The following hints on this subject are extracted from the 18th Lecture of the "Pastoral Office:"

"1st. Be not in too great haste to marry, or make engagements. Take time for consideration and consultation. Let judgment and conscience, and religious principle, and prayer have their full share in deciding your choice. Do not trust to the first appearance and exhibitions of character. You will not understand me as condemning all reference to the feeling of love, or as denying that there is a sympathy and congeniality of character most important to conjugal happiness, and which must be consulted. I only warn you against drawing your standard from novels, poets and sentimental writers, as weak young men and women do, to the ruin of their peace and comfort through life.

Do not rush into matrimony on your first entrance upon the ministerial life. Wait until you can form a proper estimate of your own abilities, and ascertain what station you will be able to get and retain. Some, by neglecting this, have chosen companions who were inferior to those with whom they were afterwards to associate, and have become ashamed of them; while others have succeeded in securing those who were doomed to the mortification of seeing their husbands sink instead of rise — of being obliged to sink with them, to the great unhappiness of both, and to the disappointment of friends.

Wait, therefore, until you have found your proper level, and then choose one to suit yourself, and those with whom you are both to associate."

Candidates for orders would, with very rare exceptions, be seriously injured in their devotional character, if not entirely alienated from the proper spirit of the ministry by the manner of life led by Mr. MEADE at this time.

His personal piety was, from its first formation, remarkably direct and practical. He had a happy facility in associating his religion which he loved, with his secular pursuits in which he was diligent; blending them so naturally and continuously in his daily walk as to exemplify the Apostolic precept, "Whatsoever ye do in word and deed, do all in the name of the Lord Jesus, giving thanks to God and the Father by Him." His laboring with his own hands was performed, not to accumulate wealth, to gratify "the lusts of the flesh and the lust of the eyes, and the pride of life"; but for conscience sake, to maintain his household in godly simplicity, and himself, pending his preparation for the ministry, and afterwards in the discharge of its duties for many years, without pecuniary fee or reward. Manual labor so conducted, he regarded as much a part of his moral obligation, as his daily devotion. It did not hinder but help his growth in grace, and enable him to walk with God as truly in the operations of the farm, as in the services of the sanctuary. This period of much bodily exercise, but of moderate mental activity, witnessed no loss of interest in reference to the sacred office to which he had devoted himself, though there could have been little progress in those studies which are prescribed as suitable preparation for its responsible services.

Of all this, he was fully aware—"the weakness of my eyes—my sickness at Princeton—my early marriage and the necessity of resorting to much manual labor, of course, all prevented even a moderate share of theological preparation for holy orders. Very little indeed in those days was required."

"The Course of Ecclesiastical Studies established by the House of Bishops in the Convention of 1804, in pursuance of a resolution of the preceding General Convention," together with the then existing canons relative to "the learning of those to be ordained," and the several "examinations" they were required to pass, relieved the Church from the censure implied by the preceding remark and devolves it where, when called for, it properly belongs—upon the persons whose duty it is "to take heed that those whom they present, be apt and meet for their learning and godly conversation to exercise their ministry duly to the honor of God and the edifying of His Church." The qualification for admission to Holy Orders, so far as literary and theological attainments are concerned, was higher then, than now. The culpable remissness of those entrusted with the examination of candidates, still too often neutralizes the canonical provision, and would, not unfrequently justify the report, that "very little preparation indeed, in these days, is required." A serious evil, not to be remedied by mere legislation, but by greater fidelity on the part of the examiners, on whom must still rest the great responsibility of keeping the learning of the ministry up to the standard which the Church has wisely established.

As the period of Mr. Meade's ordination approached, he was much disturbed in reference to certain ecclesiastical regulations which, as a minister of the Church, he would be bound to observe, but which, as some represented them, he was neither prepared to approve or practice. As an honest man, he freely communicated his difficulties to the

Bishop of the Diocese. The following statement of his scruples and the letter of Bishop Madison on the subject, together with the account of the examination and ordination, are transferred from the pages of "Old Churches in Virginia" to this volume, as here specially pertinent:

"But before speaking of some circumstances attendant on my ordination, it may be well to allude to a correspondence between Bishop Madison and myself some months before that event. It is the more proper to do so, as it will serve to correct some misunderstandings which have gone abroad with respect to us both, and which have had a bearing on the Virginia Churchmanship of that day. Passing through Philadelphia a year or more before my ordination, and staying at the house of an Episcopal clergyman, I heard some severe strictures on one or more of the ministers of our Church in some other diocese, or dioceses, for violating the rubric of the Prayer Book by abridging the service. It was designated by no slighter term than perjury in the violation of solemn ordination vows. I learned afterwards that such charges were made elsewhere. In examining the canons of the Church, I also found one which seemed positively to forbid, under any circumstances, the admission into an Episcopal pulpit of any minister, not Episcopally ordained. I was aware that it was impossible to use the whole of the service in very many of the places where I might be called to officiate, and well knew that ministers of other denominations preached in many of our old Episcopal Churches, and indeed that it was questioned whether under the law, our ministers had the exclusive right to them. I also saw that there was a canon forbidding servile labor to the clergy, while from necessity—for the support of a young family—I was then taking part in the labors of the field, which in Virginia was emphatically *servile labor*. Wishing to enter the ministry with a good conscience, and correct understanding of my ordination vows, I wrote a letter of inquiry to Bishop Madison on these several points. To this I received a very sensible reply, nearly all of which, I think, the House of Bishops, and the Church generally, would now endorse, though there would have been some demurring in former times.

BISHOP MADISON'S LETTER.

Dear Sir:

I received your letter by Mr. Bracken and approve of your conscientious inquiries respecting certain obligations imposed by the canons. You know that every society must have general rules as the guides of conduct for its members, but I believe the Episcopal Church is as lenient as any other religious society whatever. The subscription required by the candidate is, that he will conform to the discipline and worship of the Protestant Episcopal Church in the United States. At the time of ordination he promises to conform to the canons. With respect to the Book of Common Prayer, an adherence is required, wherever the situation of the Church will permit; it happens, however, too often, that the minister must be left to his own discretion, particularly on occasions when it may be necessary to abridge the service, or where there may be no clerk, &c. No oath is administered or required, and that adherence to the Book only is expected, which may tend to further religion and good order in a religious society; for there can be no doubt of the superiority of forms of prayer for public worship. Before sermon, many ministers, I believe, prefer a prayer of their own, and if it be well conceived, I suppose no objection would be made. His private prayer may certainly be determined by himself. With respect to the use of our Churches by other societies, the general rule is often dispensed with, especially if the party wishing the use will assist in the preservation of the building, or the preacher be of known respectable character. Too often indeed our Churches are now used entirely by other sects. The canon could never intend that a minister should be entirely prevented from following any occupation which was creditable. Hence the practice of physic, &c., is not deemed inconsistent with the ministerial profession, nor I conceive any other business which is free from a kind of public odium. It would be unfit for a minister to keep a tavern or grog shop, &c., but certainly not to follow any occupation, where good may result both to the community and to the individual. The honest discharge of clerical duties, with a life preaching by example, are, in reality, the principal requisites; when these are manifested, and the piety and good behaviour of the minister cannot be questioned, he need not apprehend the rigor of canons, or any other spiritual authority. I am, Sir,

Yours very respectfully,

J. MADISON.

October 10, 1810.

"Remarks: — Some years after my entrance on the ministry, I was conversing on the subject of dispensing with the regular service in preaching to the servants in their quarters, with one of our most eminent ministers, when he maintained, I doubt not, most conscientiously, that I had no right to open my lips in preaching to them, without first using the service according to the rubric. A very great change has recently come over the minds of some of our clergy on this subject — judging from some things seen in our religious papers, in which more latitudinarian views are taken than I ever remember to have heard of formerly."

In reference to the rigid and uncompromising construction of extravagant rubricians, the venerable Bishop Griswold was wont to say in his sententious way, "The service of the Protestant Episcopal Church is a *reasonable* service." The members of the Council which adopted the canons of the Church in the Confederate States were of the same mind. Regarding the rubrics as sufficiently directive and obligatory as to the use of the Book of Common Prayer, the canon on this subject was omitted in the new code, and a prolific cause of dispute was thus judiciously retired.

The friendly author of a brief biographical sketch published in a Philadelphia paper, alluding to Mr. MEADE's conscientious scruples occasioned by the canon forbidding servile labor, represents it as a canon of Virginia, and then, with the morbid aptness to regard all that is supposed to be wrong at the South, as heading in slavery, ascribes the prohibition to the prejudice which slavery produces against all such occupation. The amiable author is scarcely excusable for a statement so totally erroneous. *He* ought to have been better informed. The canon was adopted by the General Convention in conformity with the LXXV Canon of the Church of England entitled, "Sober conversation required in ministers," which ordains that "ecclesiastical" persons, "shall not give themselves to any base or servile labor." The spirit of the prohibition is found in those canons of the early Church, which forbid all secular service on the part of the clergy, "Let not a Bishop, Presbyter, or Deacon, undertake worldly business; otherwise let him be deposed." (Apost. Canon, VI.) The Diocese of Virginia has never legislated on the subject.

As to the Canon concerning the officiating in Episcopal congregations, by persons not Episcopally ordained, the declaratory resolution passed by the General Convention recognizes, all that charity for others should ask, and as much as a due care for the sound teaching of Episcopal congregations allows.

In reference to the particulars enumerated, the letter of Bishop Madison satisfied Mr. MEADE that he might with a good conscience, promise canonical obedience, and he now made his arrangements for early ordination.

Williamsburg, where the Bishop resided, was about two hundred miles from Frederick County. Mr. MEADE performed the journey on horseback, and, with the requisite testimonials, presented himself to the Bishop for ordination. Once before, when quite a youth, the hands of the Bishop had been laid upon his head. His account of the service is brief and unsatisfactory: "My confirmation took place at a very early period, during the first and only visit of Bishop Madison to this part of Virginia. I have but an indistinct recollection of his having heard some of us the Catechism at Church, and as I suppose, laying his hands on us in Confirmation afterwards, perceiving that we said our Catechism well. But as to both of them, especially the latter, I have relied more on the testimony of other persons, than on my own certain remembrance." (O. C., p. 22.)

Now, by this second imposition of hands with prayer, he was, on Sunday, Feb. 24th, 1811, solemnly authorized to "execute the office of Deacon in the Church of God."

His examination took place at the Bishop's, before breakfast; he and Dr. Bracken conducting it. "As we went down to the Church," he relates, "companies of students with guns on their shoulders, and dogs at their sides, met us on their way to the country, attracted by the frosty morning which was favorable to the chase; and at the same time one of the citizens was filling his ice-house. On arriving at the Church, we found it in a wretched condition, with broken windows, and a gloomy comfortless aspect. The congregation which assembled, consisted of two ladies and about fifteen gentlemen, nearly all of whom were relatives and acquaintances. The morning service being over, the ordination and communion were administered, and then I was put into the pulpit to preach—there being no ordination sermon." (O. C. p. 29.)

A venerable Christian lady, extensively known, and much loved in the Church in Virginia, and now in her eighty-first year, has kindly furnished a few "personal recollections of the early life of Mr. MEADE":

"The first time I ever saw WILLIAM MEADE, (as we used to call him,) was in the year 1811, when he came down to receive Deacons' orders from Bishop Madison. I was then living in York with my sainted mother, the grandmother of his two wives.

Before he came, the reputation of his having devoted himself, soul and body and spirit, to the service of God, had gone before him, and we looked forward to his visit with mingled feelings of respect and curiosity; for such things were rare in those days. I was then a seeker of righteousness. Oh! so anxious for my soul's salvation, thinking I should get good to my poor soul from being with him. His dress was a plain suit of home-spun. At that time he was a husband and a father, and spoke of his Mary in a way to gratify her numerous relatives. He only spent one night with us. In those days, though there were pious people in the house, we did not have family prayers. It was very cold weather; the whole face of the earth being covered with snow. I did not see him again, but we heard of his saying, when he went into the old Church at Williamsburg, and saw the few assembled there, that 'he wondered if it was emblematical of his ministry?'"

Before, and at several periods subsequent to his ordination, a rumor was circulated which he thought that, justice to another as well as to himself, required him to contradict, and later in life to commit his statement to writing. A copy of the manuscript found among his papers is here inserted:

PROSPECT HILL, near Millwood,
Clarke Co., Dec. 15, '51.

Having been asked twice, within the last year or two, whether it is a fact that I was anxious to enter the ministry of the Presbyterian Church, but was dissuaded from it by Dr. Hill, of Winchester, and having an accurate recollection of the circumstances which attended a report of such design on my part many years since, while a candidate for orders, I think it well to commit the same to paper.

Shortly after my return from College, Dr. Hill visited me at my mother's house, and expressed great pleasure at hearing of my design to enter the ministry, and particularly the ministry of the Episcopal Church, as he believed I could do more good in that than in any other. I became quite intimate with him and fond of him, and was often at his house in Winchester. During all the time of my candidateship he ever held the same language of pleasure at my purpose of entering the ministry of the Episcopal Church. During the summer before I was ordained, I was one day surprised by a visit at my mother's from Mr. Balmaine, the Episcopal minister at Winchester. While sitting in my mother's chamber, Mr. B. suddenly, in his peculiar manner, and to the surprise of all, said to me, "You must not let Mr. Hill persuade you to join the Presbyterian Church." I expressed my astonishment at what he said, and that such an idea had ever entered into any one's mind, for I never had had a thought of such a thing. Mr. B. said that there was such a report in Winchester, and he had come down to see about it. He returned, much relieved by my assurance that there was not the least foundation for it. Shortly after this, on going to Winchester, I saw Mr. Hill and mentioned what had occurred, when he told me that he had been exceedingly annoyed by the report, which he said contained something else, viz: That he had employed the Rev. Mr.

Shannon, a Presbyterian minister who occasionally preached near my mother's, as his agent in the work of proselyting me. I often mentioned these things at that time and for years afterwards, when the report was mentioned, not only to correct the impression of my wish to relinquish the design of entering the Episcopal ministry, and adopt another, but to do justice to Mr. Hill."

WILLIAM MEADE.

Mr. MEADE conjectured that this oft-repeated and annoying report might have originated in a misapprehension of the nature and design of the correspondence known to have passed between Bishop Madison and himself. Less than this, however, would have afforded occasion for the story and given it plausibility, in the then deeply depressed condition of the Episcopal Church. His own testimony on this subject, though exceedingly painful, is so important in its relation to his ministerial life and labors, that its omission here would be inexcusable.

"Infidelity was then (at the time of his ordination) rife in the State, and the College of William and Mary was regarded as the hot-bed of French politics and religion. I can truly say that then, and for some years after, in every educated young man of Virginia whom I met, I expected to find a skeptic, if not an avowed unbeliever. I left Williamsburg, as may well be imagined, with sad feelings of discouragement. My next Sabbath was spent in Richmond, where the condition of things was little better. Although there was a Church in the older part of the town, it was never used, but on communion days. The place of worship was an apartment in the Capitol, which held a few hundred persons at most, and as the Presbyterians had no Church at all in Richmond at that time, the use of the room was divided between them and the Episcopalians, each having service every other Sabbath morning, and no oftener. Even two years after this, being in Richmond on a communion Sunday, I assisted the Rector, the Rev. Dr. Buchanan, in the old Church, when only two gentlemen and a few ladies communed. One of the gentlemen was a resident in the upper country. One of the old clergy who was present, did approach the chancel with a view of partaking, but his habits were so bad and so notorious that he was motioned by the Rector not to come. Indeed it was believed that he was not in a sober state at the time."

"So low and hopeless was the state of the Church at this time, but a few of the clergy even attempting to carry on the work, and only one person having for a long time been ordained by Bishop Madison, and he from a distance — and a most unworthy one — it created surprise, and was a matter of much conversation when it was understood that a young Virginian had entered the ministry of the Episcopal Church. Even some years after this, when I applied to Judge Marshall for a subscription to our Theological Seminary, though he gave with his accustomed liberality, he could not refrain from saying that it was a hopeless undertaking, and that it was almost unkind to induce young Virginians to enter the Episcopal ministry, the Church being too far gone to be revived. Such was the general impression among friends and foes."

His account of his reception as a minister is of great interest.* "I had, however, through the State, many most respectable and influential relatives. Some still rich, other of fallen fortunes, both on my father's and mother's side, who were still attached to the Church. These things caused my ordination to excite a greater interest, and created a partiality in favor of my ministry. But still, there were many who thought it so strange a proceeding, that they were ready to accept, as a probable mode of accounting for it, an opinion expressed by one or more, and soon put in circulation, that there was something unsound

* With his characteristic modesty, he prefaces this reference to his family and self with the apologetic remark that it is done "at the risk of being charged with even more of egotism than has already been displayed", the statement "being necessary to the right understanding of the whole subject I have taken in hand."

in mind, or eccentric in character, at any rate, a want of good common sense, or I would not make such a mistake as to attach myself to the fallen and desperate fortunes of the old Church. Some strange speeches of this kind were made. Nor were they or their effects confined to Virginia or to that time. I am not sure that their influence has ceased to the present day. One good, however, resulted from them, viz: that certain views of religion, and certain modes of life adopted by me, and supposed to be contrary to what were supposed to be the doctrines of the Episcopal Church—certainly contrary to the sentiments and practice of the people—were ascribed to this natural defect, and were kindly dealt with, instead of awakening hostility, which under other circumstances might have been excited. Certain it is, that my ministry, from the first, was received with a favor, which neither my imperfect theological education, nor my most unfinished sermons, nor anything else about me, were entitled to." (O. C., pp. 30, 31.)

Those who listened to his discourses would say that to represent his ministry simply as "being received with favor," would convey a very inadequate idea of its acceptableness. Wherever he preached, a crowd gathered to admire, if nothing more, his manner of reading prayers and the eloquence of his sermons—not the eloquence formed by the arts of oratory—but flowing from a heart pervaded by intense interest in his message and for his hearers, and which the peasant and the philosopher could alike appreciate and enjoy. And when he wrote that there was nothing in his "unfinished sermons," or "about himself," to entitle his ministry or himself to be "received with favor," he no doubt expressed his own honest convictions, and yet as certainly affirmed, what all who heard him in the pulpit, or knew him personally, would positively deny. As a minister of the gospel, he was highly gifted. His youthful appearance at the first—the manly presence into which this matured—his sound and vigorous and well-balanced intellect—his naturally brave and feeling heart were very important contributions for efficiency in his sacred office. And when to these are added a voice singularly sonorous and sweet, and a manner very earnest and persuasive, it is unnecessary to say that he was capable of the highest order of eloquence.

But the elements in the preaching of Mr. MEADE, to which its peculiar interest and impressiveness are to be ascribed, was the evangelical truth which it presented, with great clearness and emphasis. The Church sermons of that day were, with few exceptions, meagre and impotent discourses on ethics, with some infusion of natural theology, and rare and remote references to distinctive Christian doctrine. Alluding to this, Mr. MEADE states: "In the Church in Virginia, with the exception of Mr. Jarrett and perhaps a few others, I fear the preaching had, for a long time, been almost entirely of the moral kind." "Blair's sermons, on account of their elegant style, and great moderation in all things were most popular." "The sickly sensibility of Sterne's sermons (and especially of his Sentimental Journey) was the favorite style, and standard of too many of our clergy. After entering the ministry, I heard several of such most faulty exhibitions of Christian morality. It is no wonder that the Churches were deserted, and the meeting-houses filled. But the time had come, both in the English and American Church, for a blessed change. (O. C., Vol. I, p. 25.) In Virginia, the works of Bishop Porteus, Wilberforce and Hannah More, were largely instrumental in the happy result. They were republished in this country, and introduced more evangelical views into some of the most influential families in Virginia. A desire for the pure word of life began to spread among the laity, and when this desire was not regarded by their own clergy, other teachers were resorted to, and their own neglected. Under these circumstances, when a beardless youth, in his home-spun dress and with his boy-like collar and black neck ribband, stood up in the pulpit, zealously preaching "Jesus Christ and Him crucified," as the Saviour of perishing sinners, it is not surprising that wherever he officiated, the Church was filled with attentive hearers, and some began to entertain the hope that better things were in reversion for the old Church in Virginia.

The Rev. Mr. Balmaine, who had been a chaplain in the United States Army during the war of the Revolution, and who had married a relative of President Madison, was the minister of the parish in Frederick county. He resided in Winchester, and preached alternately there and in the Stone Chapel near Millwood. His character is briefly sketched by Mr. MEADE, who, in the spring of 1811, became his associate: "My connexion with Mr. Balmaine was most pleasant and harmonious. He was one of the most simple and single-hearted of men. He was also very generous and disinterested, but, like too many of the ministers of that day, he thought there was no harm in the dance, the game of cards, and, sometimes, the free use of the cup. For the last ten years of his life, however, he was a changed man. Some of the most eloquent extempore effusions I ever heard, were from his lips while standing in the chancel on Sacramental occasions, when he referred with tears to past errors, and sought to make amends by thus testifying to evangelical doctrine and holy living."

In the Old Stone Chapel, in the erection of which Mr. MEADE's father had taken an active part, and in which for many years, his honored parents had been accustomed to worship, surrounded by their children; to which he had often been carried an infant in his mother's arms, and when a boy, on horseback behind his father—where in after life he was destined to bend again and again as a mourner, and where he hoped at last himself to find a grave near the remains of the many loved ones, there sleeping in Jesus — there he now commenced those stated services, which continued for five and twenty years of his ministerial life, "Living and laboring on a small farm, and having no design or wish to go elsewhere."

In the "recollections," by Mrs. J. Nelson, referring to his visit at the time of his ordination, it is stated that "at that time he was a father." The event had occurred but a few weeks before, and of course had been announced to absent friends, especially to the family at Arlington. That letter is lost, or very probably it would furnish a specimen of wild joy, and extravagant description such as few would credit of WILLIAM MEADE. There is however, something to sustain such a conjecture, in letters which remain. Mrs. Custis, in a congratulatory communication to Mrs. Meade, alluded to Mr. MEADE's glowing account of the boy's excellencies, both corporeal and mental, and made playful overtures to pre-engage Philip for her own daughter Mary, (now Mrs. Gen. Robert Lee,) but with the proviso that he must prove "very good and very wise." Mrs. Meade in a letter post-marked Feb. 11, 1811, and addressed to Miss Susan Meade, then on a visit to Arlington, alluding in modest terms to her infant, sleeping near her says, "But do not credit WILLIAM's exaggerated accounts of his personal perfections. He is not a beauty even in my eyes," and, "as to his intellectual perfections, I can give you little information on that score, as they have not yet developed themselves." Referring to the condition annexed to the betrothment proposed by Mrs. Custis, she remarks, "Tell Cousin Molly the condition on which she offers her precious Mary, are no easy ones, 'To be very good and very wise,' falls to the lot of few of the sons of Eve. But tempting is the prize, it must be confessed; sufficiently so, to induce a strenuous effort to obtain it. However, I expect Mary will not consent to wait for Philip. Her bright eyes will lead captive many a poor youth, I suppose, e'er he will have escaped the light branches of hic, hæc, hoc, &c., and amongst her train the happy selection will, I suspect, be made before that period."

To this letter Mr. MEADE appends a few lines intended for Mrs. Custis:

> "Hip! Gee! Woo! Wha! and the plough,
> Hic! Hæc! Hoc! and the Latin Grammar.

No! No! Mr. Philip! You shall learn to say the words in the upper line before spring, and then with all solemnity I intend to consecrate you to the hands of the plough. Teach Mary to wash and spin and cook, and we will make a match of it, Cousin Molly. Mary, my wife, she does think him handsome, and so he is. He laughs killingly; he cries sweetly; he opens his mouth, above all, in imitation of mine! Good-bye."

With a heart alive to the delightful charities of domestic life, and a circle of relatives and acquaintances suited to exercise every feeling of affection and friendship, it is not strange that he should have "no design or wish," to leave the beautiful "little farm on which he lived" so happily, and labored diligently with his own hands to support his family, whilst, in public and private, he freely and faithfully preached to the people the unsearcheable riches of Christ. But this happy arrangement was soon to be, for a time and partially interrupted. Christ Chnrch, Alexandria, had just become vacant. The last Rector was from the West Indies, where his wife whom he had abandoned, still lived. After coming to this country he married again. The wife whom he had forsaken, pursued him to Alexandria, when he quickly disappeared, and was heard of no more. This was not the first instance in which the parish had suffered from the unworthiness of its ministers, and now, desirous to avoid a repetition of the evil, the vestry determined to secure the services of some one of known worth and ability. With Mr. MEADE they were acquainted, and to him they made an unanimous and earnest appeal to come to their relief. The very peculiar circumstances of the congregation, of which he was well informed, enforced the appeal and determined his acceptance of the invitation, with the understanding that he was to spend "a considerable part of the year in Frederick, visiting Alexandria during that time, once in four weeks." It could not have been expected that this arrangement would be durable. It continued but two years. Finding it impossible to do justice to both congregations, he withdrew from his connection with Christ Church, Alexandria, and gave himself again wholly to his first love in Frederick.

His temporary residence in Alexandria was by no means a profitless experiment. It was productive of a reform in certain practices, which were irregular and injurious, in the cultivation of a taste, on the part of the people, for decidedly evangelical preaching, in the adoption for the first time, of an instrumentality for good, which, in after life, he often employed with happy effect, and in the formation of acquaintances and associations, which, in the good providence of God, led to measures most influential in the gradual revival of pure and undefiled religion in many parishes.

The irregularities, to the correction of which he addressed himself, were connected with "the place of baptism and the qualification of sponsors." "At an early period," he writes, "I resolved to oppose myself to the practice of private baptism, without due cause, on account of its shameful dishonoring of the ordinance. When I went to Alexandria the Fall after my ordination as Deacon, I found that up to that time, the old custom had prevailed of private baptism, with more or less merriment. I determined to make a change. I communicated my purpose to one or two of the best of the laity, but found they feared the result. 'Let us try it,' I said, and accordingly addressed the congregation on the subject from the pulpit, setting forth the law of the Church, and the great prostitution of the ordinance by reason of its violation, and begging them to bring unbaptized children to the Church, on a certain Sabbath and at a certain time appointed. God blessed the effort. There was but one refusal, and that only for a few months. The same thing occurred at a later period of my ministry, both in Norfolk and Petersburg. The most interesting of all my services at those places were the public baptisms. They were separate occasions, the hymns as well as the prayers, were suited to the occasion. Exhortation both before and after the Baptism, were altogether on that subject. The afternoon of certain Sundays was devoted to such services and many were the attendants."

With regard to sponsors, the error lay in making the request a mere compliment, and in placing in that relation those utterly destitute of personal piety, and, not unfrequently, youth who had themselves scarcely come to years of discretion. The impropriety of this practice was too palpable to stand exposure, and it easily yielded to his affectionate and judicious remonstrances.

Mr. MEADE aimed to reform the pulpit as well as the font. The prevailing style of preaching has been noted. From the character of several of the Rectors of Christ Church, it is a fair inference, that in their teaching there was little to inform the mind, rouse the conscience, or lead the enquiring to the "Lamb of God, who taketh away the sins of the world." "The Gospel, it is to be feared," writes Mr. MEADE, "had not been clearly preached in times past. It was now attempted, and though most imperfectly done, as to style and manner, God's blessing was granted. The services were well attended. Many were added to the Church of such as gave good proof afterwards, that they would be of those who should be saved." (O. C., p. 32.)

The change which he so humbly records was not a freak

of religious excitement, occasioned by the powers of a popular preacher, and on his removal sure to be followed by a relapse. It was a holy and wholesome resolution in the spiritual taste and appetite, and has been so perpetuated, that, from that period, none but an evangelical ministry, has found favor in Christ Church.

Mr. MEADE was, early and always, partial to that mode of ministerial usefulness, which consisted in the circulation of judicious tracts and larger treatises on those religious subjects, which the state of the Church seemed to need. Many of these he wrote himself and was zealous in inviting others to the work. When he found anything in print which promised, in whole or in part, to advance the good cause, he was diligent w:th his pen in preparing it for use, and liberal with his means in publishing it for distribution. He thus relates his first experiment: "It was during my stay in Alexandria, that I procured from the library of Mr. Custis at Arlington, the folio edition of Bishop Wilson's works, which had been presented to Gen. Washington by the son of Bishop Wilson, and which works had been recommended to me by Bishop Madison. By the help of Mr. Edward McGuire, who was then preparing for the ministry with me, I selected from the various parts of that large book, a small volume of private and family prayers, which have gone through three editions, and which, being freely circulated among the families of Virginia, contributed greatly to introduce what was indeed a novelty in that day — the practice of family worship." (O. C., p. 34.)

A distinguished politician who has long been in public life, was a few years since, on a visit to one of his constituents. Before the family separated for the night, the stand, with the Bible and the Book of Prayer was set out, and the head of the family read a chapter and said prayers. When the service was over, the visitor observed, "Well! what a change in old Virginia! When I first canvassed this district, family worship was almost unknown; but now in nearly every house I visit, the members assemble as you have done, to read the Scriptures and unite in prayer before retiring to rest." This salutary change in the religious usage of the families of Virginia, may, without liability to the charge of credulousness, be annexed to the record of the work of the young parish minister and his student in Alexandria.

In his autobiographical sketch, he mentions in connexion with this date, the commencement of an acquaintance, which soon ripened into a devoted friendship, and continued without intermission till terminated by death. "It was during my stay in Alexandria that I formed a strong attachment to my most estimable friend, Mr. Francis S. Key, of Georgetown." The rare genius of this distinguished gentleman — his great natural refinement and grace — and his extraordinary conversational powers, combined with his intelligent, ardent, and active piety, rendered him a charming companion, and an invaluable friend. He was highly gifted us a poet, and though the pieces which he has left us, are few and brief — evidently produced without effort or elaboration — they speak to the patriotism and the piety of the people, and have embalmed his memory in the History of the Country, and in the devotions of the Church which he loved. No one could more highly appreciate his personal excellencies and enjoy his lovely Christian spirit, than Mr. Meade. In evangelical sentiment, and in reference to the benevolent and religious enterprises of the day, they were of one mind and one heart, and hand in hand, rejoiced to labor for their advancement.

The vicinity of Alexandria to Washington, enabled some members of Congress who were attracted by the character and preaching of Mr. Meade, to attend the services in Christ Church. John Randolph, of Roanoke, and James Milnor, who was then a Representative from Philadelphia, were among his occasional hearers. Mr. Randolph, who was distantly connected with him, and always called his father "Uncle Kidder," regarded him with singular favor, both as a man, and as a preacher. When, at a subsequent period, his conscience was roused, and he became alive to the importance of religion, he communicated freely with Mr. MEADE, and with their mutual friend, Mr. Key. Some of his letters addressed to them under these interesting circumstances, and preserved in "Garland's Life of Randolph," and in the "The History of the Old Churches, and Families of Virginia," are well worthy of perusal, as exhibiting the exercises of a great but eccentric intellect, under the awakening power of divine truth.

Mr. Milnor's connection with Mr. MEADE, commenced at a period when his religious character, and new purposes of life, were receiving their form and direction. At such a crisis, it was a gracious providence which brought him, though only occasionally, under such spiritual teaching as was rare in those days; and into association with a minister whose intelligent zeal, and godly life, were well calculated to guide and and animate him, in the pursuit of truth and duty. How largely he was indebted to his salutary association for those clear views, which determined him to relinquish a profession which had secured to him honor and wealth, and to devote the rest of his life to the ministry of the Gospel, is one of those disclosures reserved for the last day

Another brief notice will complete the history of the new and eventful acquaintances which Mr. MEADE records as formed at this time. "It was during my short stay in Alexandria, that the Rev. Wm. H. Wilmer, assumed the charge of St. Paul's congregation; and at the close of my ministry there, that the Rev. Oliver Norris, took charge of Christ Church. These beloved brothers, coming from Maryland with those views of the Gospel which the evangelical clergy and laity of England, were then so zealously and successfully propagating there, contributed most effectually to the promotion of the same in Virginia, as is well known to all of their day." (O C., p. 34.)

These devoted men, with their brother who has thus borne his affectionate testimony to their faith and efficiency, formed the clerical trio, honored of God as His instruments in resuscitating a Church, which many regarded as hopelessly dead. Mr. Norris was the first of the three to "finish his course with joy," having made full proof of his ministry in the parish which he served, and in aiding to diffuse through the Diocese those views of evangelical truth and order, which have been so signally successful in its revival. Early in its increasing light, he was called to rest from his labors, but its dawn had rejoiced his heart, and he closed his eyes in blessed hope.

The Rev. Wm. H. Wilmer survived Mr. Norris but two years. By his happy influence from the pulpit and through the press, and in the councils of the Church, he contributed to its growth and symmetry The Journals of the Diocese and of the General Convention testify to the honor with which he was regarded whilst living, and the sense of bereavement caused by his lamented death.

This recital of the measures successfully adopted and of the friendships formed by Mr. Meade, whilst Rector of Christ Church, shows that his short sojourn in Alexandria was not a mistaken and fruitless experiment, but an important episode in his life, distinctly marked by activities and alliances, profitable and pleasant at the time, and suited to promote his usefulness in the future. It must not be unnoticed, that here also originated the movements which led to the resuscitation of the Church in Virginia.

For seven years, from 1805 to 1812, there had been no Convention in Virginia. The few zealous ministers labored faithfully in and around their respective cures, but they labored apart, without the benefit of conference and co-operation. The Bishop was, perhaps unavoidably, devoted, to a great extent, to the interest of the College over which he presided with distinguished ability, and from which he derived his support. Here and there an isolated congregation, favored with a faithful pastor, gave signs of life; but the Diocese at large had sunk into a lamentable lethargy. In the spring of 1812, Bishop Madison died, and the parishes were thus deprived of even the imperfect supervision and infrequent services which his connection with "William and Mary" permitted him to render.

The first voice that was raised to rouse and rally the supine and dissociate members of the Church, and animate to such action as was demanded for its preservation from total extinction, was heard from the lips of the young deacon who ministered in Christ Church, Alexandria. The Rev. W. H. Wilmer concurring with him as to the course proper to be pursued, they addressed a letter to the Rev. Dr. Buchanon, who was Secretary of the Convention of 1805, "requesting him to call a special Convention in May. In compliance with this notice, the meeting was held at the time designated (May 13), and in the city of Richmond. From the Journal of that year (1812), it appears that fourteen of the clergy and twelve of the laity were present. The election of a Bishop was the important business of the meeting, and after discussing it and fully determining it to be expedient, the Rev. Dr. Bracken, a Professor in William and Mary College, was nominated. The election appears to have been by joint ballot. Twenty-three of the twenty-four votes cast, were found to be for Dr. Bracken, who was accordingly declared to be duly elected Bishop of the Protestant Episcopal Church. When the testimonial, recommending him for consecration, was being subscribed by the members of the Convention, Mr. MEADE, who had endeavored to effect the postponement of the election, declined signing the document. Edward McGuire, the lay delegate from Christ Church, Alexandria, also declined, as did the Rev. W. H. Wilmer, and his lay delegate from St. Paul's, Alexandria, who "having been detained on their journey, and coming in during the act of signing the testimonial; placing their refusal on the ground of not having been present at the election, and perhaps of not being acquainted with the individual." (Autobiography.) Mr. MEADE's refusal was not because of anything incidental to the proceedings, or from mere preference for some other person, but from the honest conviction of the "unworthiness" of the Bishop elect.

His conscience was not satisfied by simply withholding his sanction, and leaving the responsibility entirely upon those whose votes determined the election. He did not deem his duty discharged without using every lawful means to prevent the consummation of a proceeding which he believed would prejudice the cause of religion, and seriously interfere with the prosperity of the Episcopal Church. With that moral courage for which he was distinguished through life, "he declared his intention to make further opposition" before others whose consent would be necessary to the proposed consecration. This painful duty, however, he was spared. For reasons not recorded, those appointed to arrange for the consecration did nothing. The Journal for 1813 contains the entry: "The Rev. Dr. Bracken, who was elected Bishop of this State by the last Convention, gave in his resignation, which was accepted." Here the matter ended. The discernment and resolution of a young deacon arrested and nullified the almost unanimous action of the Convention, and saved the Diocese an infliction, greater perhaps than it could have well borne. The occurrence is of no further importance here, than as it furnished occasion for the manifestation of that nobleness of spirit which regards right, rather than popularity, and of that intrepidity which prefers standing alone by duty, to companionship with the multitude in doing evil; and which is not unfrequently honored with a triumph unattainable by faint-hearted and compromising policy.

Of the Convention of 1813, and of its impression on himself, Mr. MEADE has left us an affecting description: "It was attended by a mere handful." "Our deliberations were conducted in one of the Committee rooms of the Capitol, sitting around a table. There was nothing to encourage us to meet again. When I left it, it was under the impression that it would be our last." "I well remember that, having just read Scott's 'Lay of the Last Minstrel,' as I took my solitary way homeward, I found myself continually saying in relation to the Church in Virginia, in the words of the elfish page, '*lost! lost! lost!*' and never expected to cross the mountains again on such an errand."

In the gracious purpose of Divine Providence, which had better things in reserve for the Church in Virginia than recent events would indicate, the very failure which had so dispiriting an influence, only left the way open for a movement which was already in preparation. The hour was indeed of great darkness, but the dawn was nigh. What to man's vision was hopeless extremity, proved to be God's opportunity. Before another Convention met, the auspicious measure was in progress. The Rev. Mr. Dashiel, of St. Peter's Church, Baltimore, had, at a recent General Convention, become acquainted with the Rev. Dr. Moore, then Rector of St. Stephen's Church, New York. He had heard him preach the gospel with zeal and power, in several large Churches, and also eloquently advocate the introduction of more hymns into the Prayer Book. Mr. Dashiel was so favorably impressed by the ability and spirit of these performances, that he wrote of him to the Rev. Messrs. W. H. Wilmer and Oliver Norris, as the man to raise up the Church in Virginia. These gentlemen immediately communicated with Mr. MEADE on the subject, and he and Mr. Wilmer entered into a correspondence with Dr. Moore, which led to his election at the next Convention. The whole proceeding, when once commenced, was perfected with singular dispatch. From the Journal of 1814, it appears that on the 5th of May, "the Rev. Richard Channing Moore was declared to be duly elected to the Episcopate of the Diocese of Virginia." The General Convention met the same year and month in the city of Philadelphia, and on the 18th of May, not a fortnight after his election, Dr. Moore was consecrated in St. James' Church, Bishop White presiding.

Mr. MEADE, who had been so active in securing the services of Dr. Moore, expresses himself as in some respects disappointed at the commencement of his administration. "I was not so well pleased with him at first as I expected. He brought with him more of New York, than was to my taste, or the taste of many others. But his good sense, his amiable disposition, and sincere piety, gradually accomodated him to the clergy and people of Virginia; and we all loved him more and more to his life's end, and he became more and more one of us every year." With his entrance upon the duties of his Episcopate, "a favorable change commenced. Hope sprang up in the bosoms of many hitherto desponding. Bishop Moore had some fine qualifications for the work of revival. His venerable form, his melodious voice, his popular preaching, his evangelical doctrine, his amiable disposition, his fund of anecdote in private, and his love for the Church, all contributed to make him popular and successful, so far as he was able to visit and put forth effort."

The Monumental Church in the City of Richmond, having been completed, and the congregation organized, a memorial from the vestry, was presented to the Convention of 1814, "praying the right of representation." It was granted. Among the proceedings of the second day, the following entry is found:

"*Resolved*, That the Rev. WILLIAM MEADE, be requested to deliver a discourse in the Monumental Church, in this City, at the hour of eleven, A. M., on the next Sabbath day, appropriate to the occasion of admitting *that* Church into the General Church of this Diocese."

It is surprising that the only reporter of the services on that solemn occasion, was neither of the Convention, nor a resident of the city. Mr. Randolph happened to be a sojourner in Richmond, and extracts from two of his familiar letters to his friend Key, written at the time, are more satisfactory than many formal notices.

RICHMOND, May --, 1814.

"MEADE is expected here daily. There is a general wish that he should preach the first sermon in the Monumental Church. What an occasion for a man who would not sink under it! He might do a great deal of good, were he to yield to the desire of the congregation, and establish himself among them; but where is the field in which he would not do good?"

RICHMOND, May, 7, 1814.

My Dear Friend:

Mr. MEADE tells me that he expects to see you in a few days, and I cannot let him depart without some token of remembrance. He goes away early on Monday morning, so that to guard against failure, I write to-day. He has made an engagement to preach in Hanover, thirty-five miles off, on Monday evening. No man can respect or admire his zeal, more than I do; but I fear he will wear himself out, and that the sum of his usefulness, will, on the whole, be diminished, unless he will consent to spare himself. I must refer you to him for what occurs here, except the eagerness of all classes and ranks of people to hear him. No man can be more generally revered than he is.

Mr. MEADE will preach to-morrow in the new Church. He is anxious on account of a silly piece which was stuck into his paper. He has had no time for preparation on so useful a subject, and is uneasy that public expectation has been led to it. Indeed, who could treat it as it deserves? Certainly no man whom I have ever heard.

I left the letter open that I might say a word about my friend's discourse. He explained, in a few satisfactory and appropriate words, why he should not touch upon a subject, which many of his hearers had been led to expect he would treat, (the burning of the theatre, on whose site the new Church was erected), and then gave us a most excellent sermon, on the pleasure of a true Christian life. A prayer which he introduced into his discourse, that the heart, *even if it were but one*, of the unconverted, might be touched, was most affecting. He preaches this afternoon at the Capitol, on the subject of the Bible Societies.

Sunday, 2 o'clock, P. M.

When Mr. MEADE resigned the Church in Alexandria and returned to his charge in Frederick county, he was still only in Deacons' orders. The precise time of his ordination to the Priesthood is not known. It occurred, however, before, and but a short time before, the consecration of Dr. Moore. The Episcopate of Virginia being yet vacant, Bishop Claggett, of Maryland, was invited to officiate, and admitted him to Priests' orders in Alexandria, "about two years after" his resignation of Christ Church. The sermon was preached by the Rev. Simon Wilmer, a presbyter of the Diocese of Maryland—"a faithful brother" —warm-hearted, and active in his ministry, who, in the parishes with which he was connected, and in "journeyings often," carried the light of the gospel to many who sat in darkness. It would be no mistake to number him with those whose labors helped to improve the tone of preaching, and the state of religion in his day. Of Bishop Claggett, and the examination, Mr. MEADE writes: "So far as I know and believe, he entertained sound views of the gospel, and was a truly pious man. There was much of the Englishman about him, I presume, from his wearing the mitre, and his mode of examining me—that conforming so much to the character of the English University examinations. Besides a number of hard questions in the metaphysics of Divinity, which I was by no means well prepared to answer, but which he kindly answered for me, he requested that I would, in compliance with an old English canon, which had been I think somewhere incorporated into our requisitions, give him an account of my faith in the Latin tongue. Although I was pretty well versed in the Latin language, yet, being unused to speak it, I begged him to excuse me. He then said I could take pen and paper and write it down in his presence; but he was kind enough to excuse me from that also, and determined to ordain me with all my deficiencies, very much as some other Bishops do in this day."

Mr. MEADE's relinquishment of Christ Church, Alexandria, and his return to his "earthly paradise" in the Valley of Virginia, have been noticed. He is now to be viewed as the minister of a country parish, occupying his own house, which his own hands had helped to build, cultivating the small but fertile farm, from which the support of his family was derived, and ministering with diligence and success to a people whom he delighted to serve in the gospel, and by whom he was revered and loved.

The building occupied by himself and family, was of very moderate dimensions, and in conformity with the principles of its proprietor, perfectly plain in its finish and furniture — more so, than at a later period, and with more ample means, would have been required by his conscience, or agreeable to his taste. It was situated in a rich and beautiful country, and afforded an extensive prospect of the Blue Ridge, which, no doubt suggested its name, "Mountain View." Here he sought and found his chief earthly happiness; not in aimless intercourse and profitless indulgence, but in pleasing and salutary social occupation, endeavoring "from time to time to sanctify his own life, and those of his family, and to fashion them after the Rule and Doctrine of Christ — that they might be wholesome and godly examples and patterns for the people to follow."

Mr. MEADE would be considered a strict disciplinarian, but with so much good sense, and affection, that his control commended itself to those whom it influenced, and gained both their judgment and love. Alluding to his "domestic habits," he writes, "I was devoted to my most excellent wife and three children." The touching memorial of the former which he prepared, discloses a heart alive to the most tender affection which that relationship involves, and experienced in the happiness which its purest exercise imparts. His fondness for children was remarkable; one was rarely in his company without being dandled on his knee, if not mounted on his shoulder and borne sportively round the room. In his short rides on horseback over his farm, he was often seen with one behind him, or if too young to be trusted there, placed on the pummel and supported by his arm. It was not unusual when he was writing, for the youngest to be sleeping on the floor at his feet, another seated on his knee, and a third close by, freely amusing himself with his playthings. His house had not apartments enough to afford, what would seem to be the indispensable accommodation of a separate study. "For the first twenty years of my ministry," he writes, "I had no study, most of my sermons were written in the chamber or dining room, and in the midst of children and servants," and no doubt he might truly have added, whilst engaged in the nursery service, which the judicious Hooker dignified by his example.

He was now indeed less favorably circumstanced for regular reading or composition, than during the period of his candidateship. To reconcile the many and diversified demands of the parish, with the time and labor indispensable to the management of the farm, was no easy undertaking. There were times, when his conscience was disturbed by the apprehension, that he might not be giving himself sufficiently to those studies, which were requisite to the efficiency of his ministry. But when moved by this suspicion, he endeavored to apply himself, more assiduously to his books, he was soon compelled to relax his efforts, by the painful consciousness of a physical infirmity to which he was subject through life, and which at times, seriously interfered with his professional pursuits, and produced the conviction, that it was useless for him to aim at extensive and profound professional learning. "I often ask myself," he writes, "when much occupied by my farm and giving little time to study, am I not guilty of violating my ordination vows? I would then, for a time devote myself to more study, but soon my eyes began to fail, and my head was affected with vertigo, and I became satisfied it was not the will of God that I should study to be a great divine or eloquent preacher. Had I not been a farmer, my health must soon have failed. A minister to a town congregation, for any length of time, I could not have been, during the first twenty-five years of my ministry, or indeed at any subsequent period, though I have been enabled to study and write more for the last ten years."

His conclusion that it was not intended that he should become an eloquent preacher, was no doubt very honest, but certainly very erroneous. Unless his cotemporaries were incompetent judges, or false witnesses, he rarely preached without producing a decided impression. His written sermons were simple in structure and style, and scriptural in their substance and spirit, and were delivered with a solemn earnestness, which rendered them both interesting and effective. His extemporaneous discourses and addresses were often highly felicitous and of great power and pathos. After one of his happiest efforts, a clerical brother observed to him, "you preach so much more eloquently without your manuscript, why do you not always extemporize? He replied, "I cannot rely on it, for I can never tell whether I shall succeed or fail. With me, such eloquence is too *accidental*." Perhaps not so accidental as he allowed himself to think. Without proper preparation the product of the pen is as uncertain, or immature and insipid, as the fruit of the lips; and other things being equal, the latter will, in the glow occasioned by the light and warmth of an intellectual and congenial assembly, ripen as surely, and with more beautiful tint and more agreeable fragrance and flavor, than the uniform temperature of a study can produce.

Whether Mr. MEADE became "a great divine," it would be premature to attempt to determine at this period It will be more opportune when the record of his professional acquirements and labors, afford adequate means for forming an intelligent decision. In the manner of his life and his habits of study, as noted by himself, there is nothing to render improbable the humble conclusion, which he so frankly expressed.

An incident, illustrative of his habits, occurred about this time. His friend Mr. Key, accompanied by Rev. Mr. Horrell, of Maryland, paid a visit to Mountain View. Mr. H. had never seen Mr. Meade. He was not in the house when the visitors arrived, and they seated themselves at the door, awaiting his return. It was not long before a person approached, dressed in home-spun, with a powder-horn and shot bag around him, a gun on his shoulder, and the tail of a fox stuck in the front of his hat. Mr. Key introduced the stranger as the Rev. Mr. Meade, and was not a little amused by the astonishment of Mr. Horrell, at the appearance and accoutrements of his friend, who soon explained the marvel. It was his habit, he said, to study a little, and farm a little, by turns. When his weak eyes warned him to desist from reading and writing, he was accustomed to walk about his farm to inspect and assist in its operations. Within the last few days, the premises had been visited by a fox, which had committed serious depredations on the flock and poultry. Hoping to encounter the marauder in his walk, he had taken his gun with him. He was not mistaken in his expectation, or his aim. A single shot sufficed to prostrate the spoiler, and he had brought the *brush* home, to amuse the children.

It would be great injustice to Mr. Meade, to suppose that with him, his agricultural interests had the ascendency. His parochial work, so far from being slighted as of secondary consideration, was regarded as paramount, and was performed with a punctuality, devotion and energy, worthy of imitation by those who are freed from his cares. In addition to the stated services at the Stone Chapel, and in Winchester, he frequently officiated elsewhere, both in Frederick, and in the adjacent counties. By such missionary labors the Church was established at several important points in that section of the Diocese. Alluding to these ministrations and their fruits, he writes, "When I first began to preach at the Chapel in Frederick, there was not a Church except that in Winchester, within twenty miles around. From a distance of twelve miles around, I would often see worshippers there. There are now no less than ten excellent Churches, where there were only two indifferent ones."

There was a class in the community, whose claims to ministerial attention Mr. MEADE felt very deeply, and from the first, endeavored to perform faithfully, those duties which his relation to them involved. Although there were not as many slaves in the Valley, as in the Tide-water counties, yet even there, they were sufficiently numerous to require special religious services. For these he made the best provision which the nature of the case allowed — officiating for them himself, both in season and out of season — engaging others to do the same, and also to assist by preparing short sermons, catechisms, and tracts, suited to their capacity, to be used in families in the way of oral instruction. In reference to some of these labors he writes, "When preaching at the Chapel, I used often to minister to the servants there in the afternoon, and sometimes in the morning at some of the quarters, on my way to Church, in the summer season. One day in the week was devoted to them on the plantations, being at one farm about breakfast time, and another at dinner time. There were about fifteen plantations thus visited, so that the intervals were long, especially when visits to the neighboring counties, took me from home, as was often the case, there being such a demand for my services in the vacant parishes. The overseers too, would often defraud me of many of my hearers, by having some particular business for some of the hands."

After the erection of a new Church at Millwood, the Stone Chapel was appropriated to the servants. The example of furnishing a separate place of worship for them, was followed in different parts of the Diocese. Along the course of James River, several of the owners of large plantations, provided suitable Chapels for the accommodation of their servants, where at the convenience of the minister of the parish, they could be assembled.

Although from motives of expediency, Mr. MEADE did liberate some of his servants to emigrate to another State, yet at no time had he any scruples as to the lawfulness of slavery. At a later period of his life, his experience and observation led to a change in his views as to, even, the expediency of emancipation. When he was consulted on the subject by a clerical brother who thought of following his example, he advised, as the most humane course, that if he could not retain his servants himself, he should provide them with good masters.

For the abundant and useful services rendered by Mr. MEADE, he, for at least the first five years of his ministry, received no pecuniary compensation, but depended on the yield of his farm, for the support of his family. When at last, his congregation did contribute, the amount was not appropriated to his own use, but by an arrangement suggested by himself, distributed to aid several of the approved measures of Christian benevolence. His disinterested course in this respect, seems to have been misrepresented, and unfavorably construed by some, or there could have been no occasion for the following certificate preserved among his parochial papers.

"Before Mr. MEADE was regularly settled as a minister in this parish, he thought it right to refuse any compensation for his services; but after he was so fixed, and officiated regularly, he consented to receive a subscription, declaring at the same time, that no part of the money resulting therefrom should be appropriated to his own private purposes, but to those of public utility."

Winchester, 7 July, 1816. "ALEXANDER BALMAINE."
(Senior Minister of Frederick Parish.)

This arrangement was strictly adhered to, for at least five of the five and twenty years of his ministry in Frederick county, and if he subsequently received any salary, its amount was too inconsiderable for record—not a moiety of what he expended annually for benevolent purposes.

It is evident that Mr. MEADE had no misgivings as to the propriety of the usual mode of clerical support. He knew it to be an ordinance of God, that "they who preach the gospel, should live of the gospel." And though from considerations peculiar to his own position, and others arising from the circumstances of the Church in Virginia, he long expressly declined any remuneration for his own labors, yet in due time he did not shrink from the delicate task of expounding to his people, the Scriptural right of the ministry, to adequate compensation for their services, and the corresponding obligation of the laity, to make suitable provision for their maintenance. His explanation of his own course is brought out in connection with his views of the effect of the sale of the glebes. Had they been continued beyond "the lives of the incumbents, I am well persuaded the effect would have been to perpetuate, in a great degree, the same kind of ministers, and seriously to interfere with the real prosperity of the Church in Virginia. It has been well for the Church in Virginia that the old order of ministers should pass away altogether, and that a new set of young men, of other views and character, imbued with the love of souls, and not seeking for sordid lucre, should engage in the work of resuscitation. Nothing could have been more unfavorable to success than the least plausibility to the charge of seeking the priest's office for a piece of bread. Such dishonor had been brought on our Church, by this disposition of her old orders of ministers, that I felt it a solemn duty to avoid even the least appearance of it, and therefore preferred to give myself, in a great measure, to manual labor, and to the strictest economy, rather than press for a support. During the twenty-five years of my ministry in my little congregation in Frederick parish, my salary did not average more than $250 or $300. I have been blamed for permitting this, and thereby encouraging a criminal neglect; but, in justice to myself, I must record that while I did not press my own claims—my farm yielding a support to my family—I ever distinctly told my little congregation, that I should expect them to do more for other objects. And they have always done so. According to my calculation, from about twenty-five or thirty families, composing the congregation, there has been annually, for the twenty-five years, at the end of which I gave up the charge, not less, on an average, than one thousand dollars sent out of the parish. Not only this, but since the congregation was called on to support a minister who needed a larger salary, it has contributed in money, and otherwise, not less than one thousand dollars per annum, a larger amount than any country parish in the Diocese."

That "one thousand dollars sent out of the parish," is made to perform a double part. In its first intention, it is the salary of the minister, which he distinctly declined applying to his own use, and then, at his suggestion, it is sent abroad as the contribution of the parish to benevolent purposes—though in reality the contribution of their minister. It operated in a way to produce a pleasant mental illusion in the people, as if they were both complying with their obligation to provide a salary for their minister, and also giving liberally to extra parochial charities. Mr. Meade expresses himself satisfied with the result of this arrangement. Some of his successors in the Rectorship have not been so well pleased with its fruits.

In a discourse which he delivered in the Stone Chapel, on the duty of contributing to the support of religion and its ministers, he expressed himself very decidedly, maintaining that the "high and interesting relation" between pastor and people, "was instituted by Christ himself," and that the laborer is entitled to his wages, by a divine ordinance, which every Christian should esteem it a privilege and a pleasure to obey. He referred to the origin of the prejudice against this arrangement, which had been so extensively prevalent in Virginia, and to the injury to religion which must ensue, unless the error was corrected.

"There was formerly an establishment here. When, at the Revolution, this was broken up, there arose various sects—in each of these, there were some, with more zeal than prudence, and more bigotry than either zeal or prudence, with whom it became the fashion to revile everything belonging to the old establishment. The clergy were called *paid preachers*, *hirelings*, &c. Then others wanted nothing but the honor and pleasure of being laborers in God's vineyard; till at length the people have generally been persuaded that it is wrong to pay the ministers of religion, and the consequence is, and ever will be, that religion has suffered, and will suffer, except this be altered. Its ministers are forced to resort to every shift and craft and trade to support themselves, and are then abused as being greedy of filthy lucre. This is generally felt and acknowledged among all sects. Except there be a decent support for the clergy, the ministry will inevitably fall into the hands of very illiterate persons, and others, who will be obliged to connect it with every kind of trade, with the exception of some disinterested persons, who will step forward with a proper zeal to uphold the cause."

"I have spoken thus to contribute my part toward the diffusion of proper sentiments about this duty."

He proceeds to assign other reasons for addressing his congregation upon this subject. "I owe it to the religious character of this society to state to them their duty. I have been often asked whether I did not receive anything, and how much, for my labors in this neighborhood. Heretofore, I have been unable to answer in any other manner than in the negative, but at the same time, have stated the reason why it had been thus, with a belief that it would not be so in future. It is evident that the character of this society would suffer injury, from such neglect, especially now, that a more liberal spirit is showing itself in many of the old congregations."

"But I must yet, before I conclude, make known my will and determination with regard to any contributions that may be made. As to the propriety of this I have had my doubts, and notwithstanding I shall do it,—expect more censure than praise, both here and abroad, where it may be mentioned." "As it ever was my intention from the first dedication of myself to the ministry, to require and accept compensation for my services, so it never was my intention to apply such to private uses, while my paternal estate was sufficient for those. I have never yet seen cause to repent and change such a resolution, and do not think I adhere to it through obstinacy, or vain glory—at least I have prayed, and endeavored to think right on the subject. After the most mature deliberation, I have determined to make known this on the present occasion. I will state one or two reasons for this":

"In the first place, by declining any private appropriation, and devoting it to religious or charitable uses, I cannot be chargeable with more ostentation, or be suspected of more vain glory, than I have been guilty of for the last five years, during which time I have received nothing and have had the credit from some, and the censure from others, of laboring gratuitously."

"My duty to you, religion, and mankind makes me receive it, and my wish is thus to spend it."

"In the next place, what would be the construction put upon it without such avowal? Why, that heretofore, from some motive or other, I have not wished it, but that now, from the difficulty of the times, I was constrained to fall on this mode of subsistence. Were I in real want, I should then feel it to be my bounden duty to myself and family to receive it for such purposes. This being not the case, I have no wish, so to receive and use it."

"When I compare my situation with that of my brethren in the ministry generally, with those who labor much more, and have a bare subsistence—out of fraternal sympathy with them, I am strengthened in my resolution to grow no richer, and live no better by means of the ministry."

The benovolent purposes, to which he proposed to appropriate the contributions placed at his disposal, were, "the education of poor and pious young men for the ministry"—"the publication and dissemination of good books to help the labors of the preachers"—"the distribution of the Bible among the destitute"—"and to carry the knowledge of the Lord to the heathen world." For these objects, with the exception of "the distribution of the Bible," there were no societies then existing in the Protestant Episcopal Church, in America. He was in these respects in advance of his times, and destined to lead, in forming and conducting the associations subsequently organized for the important purposes, which he commended to the patronage of his people.

Mr. MEADE did not expect to escape censure for this address, or to secure unanimity in the action which he advocated.

"I well know that this, and all such things, will be condemned by a nice sensibility, and critical refinement, but I well know that this same sensibility and refinement and fearfulness of censure, prevent many things from being done that ought to be done. If a man expects to be useful in this world, he must expect to be suspected and misrepresented. If he set his light on a hill, the winds will blow it—most prefer to hide it under a bushel. There are times which call for extraordinary exertion and sacrifice. Examples must be set, before they can be followed. We must neither seek the praise, nor fear the censure of men. We must not do our good works to be seen of men, nor omit to do them in the most effectual manner, through fear of being seen. But what am I saying? good works! Alas, all our works are mixed up with sin. We have need to beg pardon for them all."

These extracts from his discourse, defined his position, and explained his motives in a manner perfectly in keeping with that manly independence, and self-denying generosity, which the fitting occasion never failed to manifest.

Persuaded as Mr. MEADE was, that the Doctrine, Sacraments and Discipline of Christ, as held by the Protestant Episcopal Church were according to the commandments of God, and having solemnly engaged to give faithful diligence to administer the same; he made it his study to teach the people committed to his care, so to receive and keep them.

With regard to doctrine, being well assured that all that is necessary to eternal salvation, is contained in the Holy Scriptures, it was his prayerful purpose, and effort, to derive from that sacred source, the truths on which he relied for ministerial usefulness; and whilst he was faithful to declare the whole counsel of God, he was careful to teach nothing as necessary to salvation, but that which might be concluded and proved by the same infallible authority. His sermons were decidedly evangelical in their character and free from the sharpness and rigidity which result from strict adherence to theological system. With the analogy of faith and the law of proportion as his map and metre, he was secure against serious deviation from the way of life, and in no danger of misleading those whom he was ordained to guide. In presenting doctrines and duties which were unpopular, and unpalatable, he was not dictatorial or denunciatory, but parental and persuasive — in meekness instructing those who opposed themselves—and "by manifestation of the truth, commending himself to every man's conscience in the sight of God."

The irregularity in the administration of baptism, and the carelessness as to the character of persons received as sponsors, which then generally obtained, were noticed in connection with his Rectorship of Christ Church, Alexandria. The same evils prevailed in the parish of Frederick county. Here also, and with like success, he addressed himself to their correction.

But there were other practices very popular among professing Christians, and sustained by a kind of prescription, which increased the difficulty of their abatement. Such were the fashionable amusements of horse racing, card playing, theatrical performances, and balls. It is not surprising that communicants should partake of these demoralizing amusements, when it is recollected that under the Colonial establishment, many of the clergy, not only "did such things, but had pleasure in those who did them." In these practices the Church and the world were generally so identified, that with rare exceptions, it was only by the parish register, or at the communion table, that professors of religion could be discerned. The ways of Zion mourned, not only because so few comparatively came to the solemn feasts, but because, of the few who came, so large a proportion "worshipped the Lord, but served their own gods."

The change which had taken place in the character of the clergy, and in the teachings of the pulpit, were preparatory to an improvement in the deportment and spirit of their parishioners. The "new order of ministers" who came preaching the Kingdom of God with plainness and power, were the precursors of a salutary reform in the sentiments and practice of those who professed and called themselves Christians. In furthering this movement, Mr. MEADE was behind no one of his brethren. Of the manner and result of his efforts, he has left a brief notice:

"At an early period of my ministry, I took my stand, and never departed from it, and found it the easiest and best. Some of my young communicants were going from place to place, from ball to ball, even as the veriest devotees of pleasure. I affectionately warned them of their fault, but without effect. After due time and deliberation, I wrote to them again, stating the only terms on which I could receive them to the table of the Lord. It seemed strange to them, their parents, and friends, that I, so young—that I, who had been with them at the dancing-school—their companion from childhood—their relation—should take such a step. But I stood firm and would not retrace it. At length, one after another yielded, and I had no more trouble of this kind during my ministry. The same thing occurred in relation to a wedding, soon after I entered the ministry. At a place where I expected, and had a right to expect, more respect, the fiddle and dances were introduced into the room where I was sitting, without any warning, and my retreat for a time intercepted. As soon as I could, I escaped, and ordering my horse, (the night was dark and I intended to have remained) went several miles to a neighbor's house. My conduct was well understood, as I wished it to be, and I have never since been thus treated. A little decision will save a minister much trouble!" "I see no cause to change my opinion and practice on such subjects."

The course thus indicated, was not the action of a morbid temperament, or of that adventitious austerity which is often produced by the life of a recluse, whose habits disaffect towards all social pleasures, and dispose him to suspect evils where none exist—or the effect of the prejudice of an earnest mind occasioned by insufficient knowledge. Mr. Meade was naturally of a genial spirit—very companionable—in youth fond of its active sports, and specially devoted to the dance, as is evident from his college letters, and with so little suspicion of any impropriety in the amusement, that, in one of those letters, he playfully proposes that his venerable mother should take a few lessons, to benefit her health. Now, how changed in his views and practice! To what is this complete revolution to be ascribed? He had become a new creature in Christ Jesus. Old things had passed away—all things had become new.

The letter which he addressed to his young communicants, has been preserved, and it furnishes an expression of his renovated taste and judgment, which leaves nothing more to be desired:

My Young Friends and Parishioners:

I trust that the good Spirit of God, has moved me to address you in the following friendly admonitions: I pray it may guide me throughout, both in manner and matter, and also incline your hearts to receive the same and profit thereby. I should be utterly unworthy indeed of the high trust reposed in me by Almighty God, I should be criminally wanting in that duty I owe to the Church of Christ, and to you and your parents, as professed members of the same, if I were to see and know that any of you were about to take a step, or were living in a manner injurious to your own souls, and dishonorable to the character of religion, and I, not to endeavor in the most affectionate manner, to warn you of the evil and persuade you to avoid it. Silence in such a case, would not only be a neglect of duty but actual criminality. I cannot suffer such a sin to rest upon my soul.

If I am rightly informed, some of you who are regular members of that Church in which I minister, are about to enter on a scene of gaiety and revelry, utterly inconsistent with those solemn vows you are in the habit of making around the table of your crucified Lord. By that act and those vows, you do most solemnly separate yourselves from the world, renounce its pomps and vanities, devote yourselves to Christ, to lead a new life in His service, and outwardly incorporate yourselves with His Church, which He declares is not of this world. By thus joining the Church, you impose much upon yourselves, and God and man require of you, more than of others. What might be wrong in others, becomes doubly so in you, who, by this act make much higher professions, calling yourselves Christians. As a minister of the Church, I also am more particularly bound in duty to you, and should leave no means untried to persuade you to do all that is right. Hence this letter.

The painful feelings with which I enter on the task of reproof, are only mitigated by the hope of success, and the consciousness of duty. If those to whom it is addressed will only read it with the same desire of being improved, as I feel, that it may render service, I shall not despair. To some of those who intend being of this party of worldly pleasure, it was my full purpose to have addressed a letter, the same in substance as the present, immediately after their visit to Winchester. I have much lamented, and now more than ever, that unavoidable circumstances prevented the execution of my design — since it would have been more likely to have produced effect, than at the present. I felt much mortified and distressed at that event, which all serious and reflecting persons must condemn, which brought dishonor on the Church of which they were members, filled their parents' hearts with sorrow, and exposed themselves to much censure and even ridicule. I had hoped and believed that their own mortified feelings and painful reflections in consequence of that strange and unjustifiable step, would have been a sufficient punishment and corrective of their error, but their present disposition to renew a course of conduct so unbecoming the character of serious *Christians* and *communicants*, forbids such a hope or belief.

I cannot therefore suffer another occasion to pass by without the performance of my duty, and begging them to take into serious consideration the propriety of their conduct. I do not ask you to take my opinion, or that of any human being, but to carry this matter before your God and Saviour; and with a sincerity and earnestness becoming poor weak creatures, who ought to "fear always," and "tremble at any temptation;" ask Him if you can go on in the course of life you are leading, and yet be safe. Consult the spirit of our holy religion, and see whether it allows such a mixture with the world, and such an enjoyment of its vain and giddy pleasures.

It were impossible, in the short compass of a letter, and written in the very limited period allotted to the writing of it to answer the many pleas which the world offers in behalf of such enjoyments, and to enforce the many powerful reasons which should make Christians renounce all these *false ways of happiness*, and avoid all such alluring temptations of Satan. In humble dependence upon the Divine blessing, without which, the most convincing arguments and powerful representations would fail of their effect, I shall, with great brevity and true affection, mention a few reasons why you do wrong to profess and call yourselves Christians, and yet join yourself to the world in its unhallowed, expensive and dangerous dissipations.

In the first place, let me beg you ever to keep in mind and solemnly to feel, that you are professors of religion, and of a religion which requires much of its disciples. The author of it, the blessed Saviour, whose obedient servants we ought to be, declares that he came to save us from this present evil world, and purify to Himself a peculiar people. He declares that His disciples "are not of this world"— they are not "conformed to the world," but are "renewed in the spirit of their minds," and "not as the world give I unto you," said this same Saviour; but we ask if the gay assemblies of the children of fashion, the dressing, feasting, idle conversaion and bodily gestures performed for the pleasure and admiration of men, is of this world or of God? Are they suitable to the character of serious Christians? Do they agree with those feelings of penitence, that confession of guilt, those renunciations of the pomps and vanities of the world, those self-dedications of themselves, their souls and bodies, which they make on every reception of the Holy Sacrament? Is religion a mere name or profession? or is it a reality, a new life? Is it allowable to make such vows and professions with our lips and contradict them openly in our lives? Should we not fear lest God should apply and address to us the words of the Psalmist, "What hast thou to do with me, that thou shouldest take my covenant within thy mouth?" Be assured, my young friends, religion is a serious business; it should not be trifled with. We may have the form of godliness, and be destitute of the power thereof; we may have a name to live, and yet be dead in trespasses and sins; may think we are rich and well off, and yet be blind and naked and poor and miserable in the sight of God. Such I cannot but fear is your case, when I perceive you so anxiously set upon the vain pleasures of the world, unmindful of the high vocation wherewith you are called, and neglectful of those superior pleasures, which God is ready to bestow on all who sincerely seek after His favor. The inconsistency of such things with your character and profession as Christians, ought of itself to prevent the step you are about to take. This is one of those places and affairs in which it is better to err on one side than the other. All must acknowledge that in every age there have been vast numbers of the best of Christians who have thought such places and amusements improper and dangerous, and therefore to be avoided; but none have ever considered it a duty to go to them or a crime to stay away; they have never recommended them as a good school for virtue and true piety; the furthest they have ventured to go, has been to allow them to young people as being not sinful; saying and hoping, that as they grew up and became more serious, they would leave them of themselves, out of a preference for the more solid and noble enjoyments of religion.

Now it should be the rule with all Christians to avoid doubtful places and things. The salvation of our immortal souls and the favor of our God are things of such unspeakable importance, that we ought not to expose them to the slightest hazard. We should rather throw away all such pleasures, which none will contend are absolutely necessary to our existence or comfort, than run the least risk about our souls. Indeed, we are such weak creatures, so easily overcome by temptation, and allured by pleasure into excess, that we should fear to trust ourselves in doubtful places. "Lord, lead us not into temptation," is our daily prayer. How can we use it, and then rush into the snare? We should recollect that the Scripture says, "He that doubteth is damned," that is, he who doubteth whether anything is sinful or not, and yet does the same, is condemned and does wrong We should recollect that the Apostle, both by example and preaching, enjoins Christians to attend, not only to what is lawful, but what is expedient.

Moreover, my young friends, what a poor opinion must such conduct in professors give to the world, of the joys and excellencies of religion, when they perceive any of us come begging for some of their vain pleasures. Well may they say, "What! is your religion so poor and barren that it will not support you? Must you come over to us to partake of our short-lived pleasures?" They will either undervalue the pleasures and excellencies of religion, or doubt the sincerity of those who profess it, and yet seek their happiness elsewhere than in its lawful and pleasant enclosures. The latter conclusion will be more frequently adopted by those with whom you would associate on such occasions. Yes, be assured, young ladies, you not only lose the favor of God, incur the censure of the more pious, and destroy the peace of your souls, by driving the Spirit of God far away from you, but you actually sink in the esteem of the world, when you profess to be Christians, and yet live like worldlings. Whatever you may think of the guilt or innocency of these things, the men of the world who are wise in their generation and good judges of consistency of conduct, see a manifest contradiction between religion and worldliness, and they often express their astonishment at those who thus act; the more evil disposed triumph when they can get a professor of religion among them, because they know that thereby, religion, the object of their hatred, is disgraced; they tauntingly exclaim, "Where is the superiority of religious people over us? they are as fond of worldly pleasures as we are, nay, some of them go beyond us in their excessive fondness of pleasure." "Oh! shame, where is thy blush?"

My friends, the world marks our conduct. It sees you when weeping around the table of the Saviour, and hears you in your solemn vows and renunciations of the world, and sees you again in the vain dress and fashion of the world, and in the undignified dance; it hears you speak in the light and vain language of mammon, it notes down the same, and repeats it, till it becames the common talk, and all this is set down as the defect of religion — religion is indeed wounded, cruelly wounded in the house of her friends. It is not an enemy that hath injured her, but her own familiar friend in whom she trusted. While on this subject, I cannot forbear mentioning to some of those to whom this letter is addressed, how they have been the frequent theme of such censure and laughter — their fondness for pleasure and dress and fashion, and its inconsistency with their religious profession is the common talk of the country, far and near. "These are they, it is said, who come from the bosom of a society reputed to be the most religious and domestic in the State; these are they, who are educated by the most religious of parents, and here they are traversing the county in quest of worldly pleasure." My young friends, these things ought not so to be. Very few indeed are there, even in our own Church, who think of frequenting such places, and the Holy Sacrament at the same time.

I feel, I acknowledge that I am personally much mortified at this. With what unfeigned pleasure have I instanced the young ladies of this neighborhood as proof that such pleasures are not necessary to happiness. For a long time they seemed to have lost all relish for them, and I had hoped that they had formed a strong and durable relish for the pleasures of piety. How disappointed am I now to see so many of them, turning out again in defiance of every argument to the contrary, and seeking their pleasure in the vain resorts of dissipation! But I will not despair of being yet able to offer them as examples to others, and of seeing them amomg that company of amiable and respectable young women who have voluntarily given up the world, and chosen that good part which shall never be taken away from them, and those noble pleasures which will ever increase in brightness and glory.

There are two arguments usually adduced by such as wish these things to be innocent, to which I would make a brief answer. It is said many good and pious people have indulged in these things and thought them innocent. With more propriety it might be said, *some* than *many*. It is conceded that there have been some of zeal and piety who have occasionally lent themselves to these places and amusements, and not considered them sinful. But is this conclusive proof that they are right? A greater number of pious people have thought otherwise, and would it not be safe to take the opinion and follow the example of the majority? Besides, are there not some peculiar seasons and circumstances which may account for the opinion of the few pious people who have gone before us? May we not make allowance for a dark and corrupt age in which they lived? for a lukewarm and worldly clergy, who were themselves to be often found at the ball-room, the theatre, the horse-race and card-table? Was it to be wondered at, that the private members occasionally visited such places with such sanction? I make no doubt that many of those who are now quoted in favor of these things, would, if alive, unite with Christians in condemning them; and when upon earth, and in the occasional practice of such things, they were not devoted to them, their hearts were not given to them — they rather complied with such things as the custom of the day, than sought after them as their happiness. If truly pious, their hearts were fixed where alone true joys are to be found. Now suffer me to ask you plainly, and you should answer the question candidly to yourselves, "Is this your case? Are these pleasures only secondary and indifferent to you? Is religion your chief concern and highest happiness? Are your hearts set upon righteousness? Is peace and joy shed abroad in your souls by the Holy Ghost?" Oh! my young friends, I fear you cannot answer these questions satisfactorily to yourself or to God!

But there is another argument by which the young encourage themselves in such indulgences, and which from peculiar circumstances of delicacy, it is more painful to answer. It is the permission and sometimes the wish of parents. Far be it from me to lessen that reverential feeling due from the child to the parent. But I cannot think that I dishonor my revered parents, because I may think God and the Scriptures think and speak differently on one particular subject from themselves. Our parents are liable to err as are others, and perhaps under different circumstances they also might have thought otherwise. We should examine the sacred Scriptures and endeavor to find out the will of God from them on all subjects. But what is the present case? Will any of you say that your parents urge you against your will, judgment and conscience to go? Do they not merely permit, fearing lest a refusal might be more injurious than that permission? Were any of you to say, 'My parents, I fear to go — it is a place of pleasure and temptation — my happiness is elsewhere — it is contrary to my profession as a Christian." What parent would urge it one moment longer? Lay aside these false excuses, I beseech you for God will not accept them, and your own hearts must condemn them. View the naked truth that you are "lovers of pleasure, more than lovers of God." I tremble for your situation. You are going on in a course of life which I fear will end in everlasting ruin. You are loving that world which is at enmity with God, and I wish to persuade you to turn to true religion for happiness. It is the want of its true enjoyment, which makes you seek after the pleasures of the world. "Were all men happy, revellings would cease." "These are the sad opiates for inquietude within." Oh! then, seek to be truly happy — begin at once to enjoy yourselves — devote the youth and prime and vigor of your days to the God and Saviour who love you — leave the world and its poor fugitive enjoyments. "Lean not on earth; it is a broken reed at best, and oft a spear; and on its sharp point peace bleeds and hope expires." Lay not up material for repentance; be not among those wretched disappointed creatures who cry out upon the world when it is too late, "Oh! had I weighed it in my fond embrace, what darts of agony had missed my heart." How would I rejoice to see you turning from the world to your Saviour, and with your whole heart seeking the peace of religion. Then would you say that you never knew happiness before — then will you rejoice with a godly mirth, and the world and its pleasures will lose all their beauty.

"As by the light of opening day
The stars are all concealed,
So earthly pleasures fade away,
When Jesus is revealed."

Let me remind you, young ladies, that you are only pilgrims and sojourners upon earth — you must soon die, and appear before God and Christ to account for the manner in which you have spent your time and talents upon earth. And what will all these pleasures avail you in that day? Oh! how will one hour spent in the service of God outweigh thousands of such unsubstantial pleasures! You may be very soon called away from these things; how soon, God only knows — some one of you perhaps before the period of this revelry shall arrive. Are you ready to die? Live then in such a manner now as you will wish you had done when you come to die. Thinking as I do, how could I have said less to you than I have said, or less plainly? I know I shall have your approbation at one time or other. I wish it may be soon, lest it should be too late.

Before I conclude, I must once more refer to a point already touched upon. You are communicants. To take the sacrament of the Lord's Supper is a serious thing, ought to be done seriously and only by serious people — to such only can it be consoling and serviceable. So far from doing good, it must do injury to any not rightly disposed in their hearts, and correct in their lives—to those who eat it unworthily it is condemnation. The manner of life you live, the amusements in which you delight, I must ever think entirely incompatible with a worthy receiving of the sacrament. While you continue to partake of it in your present state of heart, you only encourage yourself in a false belief of your safety, and suppose that by uniting with Christians on such occasions you will be saved. You also set an injurious example to others, and bring reproach upon the character of the Church of which you are members. Let me therefore, as your friend, relation and minister, advise you to relinquish the one or the other. "Ye cannot serve God and mammon." And though I may not feel myself justified in refusing the sacrament to such of you as frequent such places, and love such things, but are in other respects observers of the forms of piety, yet I must say that I shall never administer it to you without the most painful feelings, without the deepest regret, and the most perfect conviction that you are eating and drinking unworthily and unprofitably to yourselves and most injuriously to the church.

I wish you to take this matter into serious consideration, and before God, and by the help of the Scriptures, examine whether your hearts are right, and whether you ought to receive the Holy Communion under such circumstances.

Let me observe to you that there are now very few indeed even in our church, who ever think of connecting these things together, and the young ladies, before they come to the communion, bid adieu to all such scenes of gaiety and dissipation.

And now, I commit this labor of love and trial of my ministry to the blessing of my God, and pray Him to impress it on your hearts and make it to bring forth in you the fruit of good living. Say not, my young friends, that it is now too late to recede. It is never too late to do what is right. Take courage, call on God to help you, and dare to do what religion and conscience directs. Let not the fear of man bring you into a snare: break off boldly now, and the task is done. You will no more be solicited. Separate yourself from the world — walk worthy of the high vocation wherewith you are called — live as dignified immortal beings ought to live — be not satisfied with the lower gratifications of sense, when you may enjoy the noble pleasures of the soul.

I have thus plainly stated to you my advice and opinion. I hope you will receive it with proper feelings. Let me beg you to relinquish your present plan; let me urge you to substitute some other pursuit in its room. Instead of preparing for this ball, let me persuade you to undertake the serious work of self-examination. Let me persuade you to try the pleasures of religion, and when the day and hour of the entertainment arrives, spend that time in contemplating the pleasures of piety on earth and its glorious rewards hereafter. I think you will never repent it, but on the contrary, ever rejoice at it.

And now, whatever may be the course you shall take, my affection and anxiety for your souls shall be the same, and if I shall suffer the mortification of seeing you persist, I shall lament your conduct, shall pray for your forgiveness and conversion, and live in the hope of seeing you yet penitent. Should you relinquish it, then will I go before my God with a glad heart and offer my thanksgivings, and pray that this act of self-denial may be the first step to your thorough establishment in true religion.

I remain, your sincere and affectionate friend,

William Meade.

P. S.—I cannot but express my desire that each of you would take a copy of this letter, not because of any peculiar merit of style or sentiment, but as a memorial of my friendship to your souls, and desire for their welfare. Though it might fail of its complete object now, the time may come when you may read it with other eyes and other hearts; or should God think proper to call me hence before you, it would remain as a remembrance of my good desires toward you.

Some few seem to have been unmoved by this tender appeal, but it so commended itself to the consciences of his parishioners, that the changed tone of sentiment, together with his own judicious firmness, soon relieved his cure from the reproach of such inconsistency.

A few loose leaves of manuscript found among his papers, endorsed "Card Playing," contain his testimony against this pernicious practice. Although the record is fragmentary and incomplete, as if merely made to aid his memory, when he deemed it proper to express his sentiments in public, it needs no interpreter, and is the more valuable because the last paragraph was penned near the close of a long life, and is the deliberate annexation of his testimony and seal to the uniform teaching of his extended ministry:

NOTES ON CARD PLAYING.

"When we enter any society we are bound by honor, not only to obey its rules according to promise, but to promote its welfare, and have reference to the wishes and opinions of its members.

Every man entering a society, civil or religious, gives up a portion of his individual liberty for the public welfare. Without this, all is confusion and anarchy. The worst days of Israel were, when 'every man did that which was right in his own eyes.'

Besides the special regulation of the different branches of the Church of Christ, there are some great principles and laws of God for the whole Church.

Whatever we do, we must do all to the glory of God. We must in love and gratitude do all the good in our power—love our neighbour as ourselves, and not tempt him by evil example. We must deny ourselves—be not of the world, though in the world—denying all ungodliness and worldly lusts, living soberly, righteously and godly, avoiding things inexpedient. Some things may be lawful which are not expedient. 'If my brother be offended, I will eat no flesh while the world standeth," said the Apostle. Avoid the appearance of evil, and let not your good be evil spoken of.

We should join with the minister in winning souls to Christ. With David we should say, if the Lord forgive, 'then will I teach transgressors Thy way, and sinners shall be converted unto Thee.' What an honor! What a privilege!

But to be more particular: What is it to renounce the devil and all his works? that evil being who rebelled against God, and instigates to all evil? the world, with all its pomp and vanities? the flesh, with all its sinful lusts? What are these pomps and vanities? Legion is their name

— vain dressing — theatrical exhibitions and games of chance — wasting time and money — giddy dances, unbecoming the seriousness and penitence of an humble sinner.

Our baptismal vows are not intelligible, except thus construed.

I would especially emphasise that of wasting time in games of chance, a most fascinating employment to the idle.

Games of chance in every age have been condemned as a perversion of God's institution — the lot — a sacred ordinance for the decision of certain questions by the Lord Himself. 'The lot is cast into the lap, but the whole disposal thereof is of the Lord."

If the history of its perversion could be written, if only of one year's operation throughout the world, or in our land, what a volume of sin and misery would it be? What waste of time and property and talents? beggary and wretchedness of wives and children? Is it fit for the sons and daughters of the Lord — the redeemed — the sanctified thus to associate with them? The testimony of more than one ruined gambler has been published in his autobiography of late years — that his first card was cast in the company of professing Christians, who taught him its use in a game for amusement. What a thought, that the first lesson was learned from a member of the Christian Church — perhaps a parent, a sister, a wife. Oh! how many have bitterly bewailed the consequences of their own example! Much injury is thus done even by the pious — the greatest injury by them. 'It was not an open enemy that has done me this wrong, but mine own familiar friend, in whom I trusted.' 'Wounded in the house of my friends'!

It is said, 'we play only for amusement, no stake, or only a barley corn.' Alas! how mistaken! How different the actual result! It may be a stake infinitely more than the thousands of the desperate gamester — reputation as a Christian professor. Certainly nothing can be gained —

how surely something lost, even in the estimation of the worldly and pleasure-loving. And may not something more be lost in injury to others? 'We must have something to kill time.' To *kill!* to *murder* time, the great gift of God, in which to gain an eternity of glory. 'Oh! time, time!' said a dying man, when the clock struck one; 'it is fit thou shouldst strike thy murderer to the heart!'

Is there nothing which can give life to time, to fill it with blessedness? Where is the Bible, with its interesting varieties of style, and narrative and doctrine? Where are the good books, of which the world is full? Where are the works of charity, which the hand of a Dorcas was wont to do? Where are those domestic duties which the virtuous woman of Solomon delighted in, and by which she excelled above all favor and beauty?

Misery, poverty, shame, and ruin, have first entered some happy family, in the shape of a pack of cards. Little did father and mother know, that they were dealing out death to their children—training them up in the way of death, instead of life. Oh! the bitter tears which have been shed by some wretched wife, some broken-hearted mother, some father, whose gray hairs have gone down in sorrow to the grave; some promising young Christian, who, at his confirmation, spread joy through the bosoms of minister, bishop and friends—perhaps, shall I say it? angels rejoiced over him for a time—but as angels have fallen, so have such.

The case of some one recently mentioned in our public papers—twenty-seven years an ornament to the Church, a blessing to society, his house the abode of bishop, clergy and other friends—but the fatal bottle and the cards—the first, doubtless, tasted only in small quantities—the last, only for amusement, perhaps in the company of Christians, were his ruin—reputation, property, lost! He was seen on the street, all mangled and dead, having been cast out of some gamblers' den—hell, let it be called.

'He that despiseth little things.' Time is a very little thing compared with eternity, and yet this little thing mis-spent, is an eternity of misery. One small spark, one small leak in a vessel, is a very little thing, but, oh! the conflagration! Oh! the shipwreck!

Is it any sin for children to play with fire? Ought parents to do it, and thus lead their children to destruction?

There is something fascinating and overcoming in it, (card playing) as in taking stimulating drinks. Danger is, it (private play) stimulates and prepares for public use and this, for something else. Ought *wives* to do it, seeing so many have been made wretched by their husbands? Ought members of the Church, seeing what evil report, what disgrace in times past, it has brought upon religion by its ministers and members? How many gamblers declare that their first game was played in a private house, with some professor of religion, and for mere amusement. A notorious one, in his memoirs, says this of himself. Is it not probable that many such, have done the same? The first game has been for mere amusement. It very easily glides into gaming for some slight stake, to make it interesting. Then it increases as the love of ardent spirits, until we are unhappy without the excitement. The first cast of the dice, may be the first step to the gambler's grave. Touch not — handle not the dangerous instrument. Beware of edged tools — trifle not with fire. A Christian professor, who engages in this, will soon find himself in evil company.

All professors should be longing to do good to others — to win over the irreligious to Christ, and *not to see how much worldliness they may indulge, without forfeiting their place at the table of the Lord. Hinderers* of religion are a very injurious class in the world — lovers of pleasure — the lukewarm — the servants of mammon. "Little children, keep yourselves from idols" — most true of all engrossing pleasures. BORDERERS — how often, dangerous, unworthy characters — unhappy — unsafe — always liable to be entrapped and drawn over the line.

In ladies, especially young ladies, how evil in its effects. If they go thus far, use them in their chambers, will not the young men use them in taverns, and gambling-houses, those dens of iniquity? If they play for amusement, will not their brothers play for a stake?"

Septuagenarius, the author of this, was travelling through a certain part of Virginia, once the seat of gaiety, refinement, and dissipation, where the card table was the daily and nightly amusement of most families. He passed by house after house, farm after farm, and enquiring for the families, found that those who had formerly inhabited, were only remembered, as those who had been. The older ones had gone away or died — the young men had gambled away the property and died the death of drunkards, and the whole society was changed. The card table, surrounded by some at first for amusement, had become a snare. In forty years the whole society was changed.

A few resolute Christians can make a great change."

The following letter, written at a later period, to a parishioner on the subject of horse racing, completes his testimony against the fashionable amusements of that day. Though the practice reprehended is now comparatively rare among those who profess and call themselves Christians, yet the letter affords so admirable an example of pastoral fidelity and affectionate interest and judicious address, that its insertion is important as a manifestation of ministerial character:

My Dear Sir: Trusting that the following communication will be received in that spirit of affection which dictates it, I take up my pen to address you a short letter, on the subject which for a few moments engaged our attention, just as we parted, on the morning that I was last at your house I was not a little surprised, and yet more distressed, to find that you advocated the practice of racing under any circumstances or to any extent, for I had supposed the contrary. Since that time I have suffered what I will not attempt to describe, from learning that you are largely embarked in furnishing the instruments for this (as I must deem it) most demoralizing occupation, and that it is even said, that the regular training is not dispensed with on God's holy Sabbath. In regard to this latter circumstance, I cannot but hope and believe that it is founded in mistake. I have accordingly so expressed myself. The subject has not been out of my mind for many minutes together, since our conversation, and I am sure you will excuse a minister of religion, and one who sincerely desires your welfare, and that of your family, for unburthening himself, and spreading his grief before you.

I should be unworthy of the high trust reposed in me, were I not to seek, by all proper means, to avert evil from those over whom I have the slightest spiritual superintendence. Let me then address to you a few words of remonstrance, as one holding an office in the Church of God — as a father of many children — and as an immortal being, who must soon bid adieu to this earthly scene, and appear before the tribunal of Omnipotence.

And first let me say, that among the circumstances which encouraged me when undertaking the erection of that building, which I hoped would prove a great blessing to ——— and the country around, the pleasure you expressed and the interest you took in it, held a conspicuous place. I, in common with many others rejoiced in the hope that a better day was at hand — that order, sobriety, morality and religion, were about to receive an effectual help from our efforts. The officers of the Church were multiplied, and spread over a large surface, in order the better to watch over its interests, and promote the cause of religion. Yourself was requested to accept the place of vestryman, and consented to the same. Now I pray you, my dear sir, to consider what influence the countenance you give to this practice, is calculated to have on the cause of re igion, and on the interests of that Church which you are specially bound to promote. The Episcopal Church has for a long time laboured under many and great disadvantages, and its ministers especially, have felt the heavy pressure of them. Those who are unfriendly to it, are ever ready to hold up to public view anything in the conduct of its members or officers, which is calculated to bring reproach upon it. The vestrymen of the Church will be regarded as the representatives of its principles and character, and by their conduct, will be judged. On this account, as well as many others, I confess, I feel deeply concerned, in common with many others, the best friends of religion and the Church, in this parish. And what considerations are there of profit or pleasure, which can for a moment compare with an injury inflicted on religion? Let me entreat you to examine this whole subject, and see how far your example may prove pernicious to the whole neighborhood around, injurious to the best of causes, and detrimental to your own reputation. I confess my hopes of reformation in the vicinity of the three churches, which Providence has planted in this part of His vineyard, are sadly fallen by the prospect of the regular establishment of this species of demoralizing amusement, which is so universally condemned by the sober and serious part of the community.

But I must address you in another and most affecting relation of life. You are a father of many dear children. In your presence, and with your consent and approbation at the altar of God, their mother, in their name, renounced all the pomps and vanities of this wicked world — all the sinful lusts of the flesh, and all the works of the devil. With much pleasure, and in the spirit of prayer, did I perform this act. Let me beseech you as a father to consider whether you are acting in conformity with that solemn dedication — whether you are consulting the best temporal as well as eternal interests of your children. On the contrary, are you not lending the influence of your example, to that which has proved the ruin of thousands of the youth of our land. One need only travel over the State of Virginia, and enquire for the descendants of those families which were once devoted to this practice, to be convinced that the judgments of God are visited upon it, to many generations.

My dear sir, I feel a lively interest in your family. I desire the eternal welfare of your children. I know you love them and wish their happiness. You would have them to be industrious, sober, moral, and I hope, religious. You would wish them to associate with the best society, with the most excellent of the earth — but let me ask if familiarity with the practice in question and fondness for horse racing is likely to benefit your children, and make them all that you would have them to be? Oh! how many parents have been brought down in sorrow to the grave, by the misconduct of children, who have been led into the society of the wicked, by an early attachment to this, and other species of gaming! With a view therefore to the immortal beings, whom God has given into your charge, let me pray you to give this subject a serious consideration.

And for your own sake, my dear sir, for the sake of that never-dying soul which is within you, I entreat you to enquire, whether this is not a mode of increasing an estate, which a bountiful God has already made abundant, calculated to injure your everlasting peace. "What shall it profit a man to gain the whole world and lose his own soul?" I have thus, my dear sir, very hastily, in the midst of much duty, presented to you some of the thoughts, which have lately agitated and distressed my mind As a minister and friend, I could not be at peace, without at least the effort at remonstrance. I hope and believe you will justly appreciate my motive, and regard this as an evidence of fidelity to the high trust reposed in me. Such remonstrances have sometimes been happily successful, and great good has resulted from them. My prayer to God is, that the present effort may not be in vain.

You have it in your power, by your example, to do much good or evil, in your family and in the neighbourhood around, and, holding an office in the Church of Christ, to promote, or injure the reputation of religion. Think upon the evil which may, and must result from the continuance of this practice, and then think on the good which might follow the trivial sacrifice, of that which the good and pious of every age have condemned. Of this thing I am sure, that by the encouragement of racing, you can do no good to your family and society, and may do much harm. Whereas by the contrary course, you will secure the approbation of the best members of society, and will remove any occasion of censure from the Church, which is already the subject of conversation, and must be more and more so, as it becomes generally known.

Let me request that you will preserve this as a memorial of the interest I feel in your welfare. With whatever feelings it may now be received, perhaps the hour may come, when more solemn views of eternity present themselves, and when the heart is made tender by affliction, and then, if not now, you will feel, that this letter was the best evidence of my pastoral solicitude, and that its entreaty ought not to be disregarded. At any rate, I am sure we are all hasting to a time, and place, where there will be no difference of sentiment on the subject. There, you and I, and your children, and servants and neighbours, will meet before the great Head of the Church. God grant it may be a happy meeting. May none of your children, servants, and neighbours, have cause to lament, that they have been injured by the practice, to which you now lend your countenance.

I will only say in conclusion, that my prayer shall be offered unto God, that he will convince you of the evil which must result from that in which you are engaged, and that you may rejoice many hearts by the decided and utter condemnation of what now grieves and distresses them.

I remain your sincere friend and affectionate pastor,

May 2, 1831. William Meade.

In reference to the fashionable amusements of that day, the views of Mr. Meade, and his clerical friends, the Rev. Dr. Wilmer and the Rev. Mr. Norris, of Alexandria, entirely accorded, and no doubt had a decided influence upon the sentiment and legislation of the Diocese on Lay Discipline. This will be noticed in its proper place.

(*Associations.*)—It has been stated that, at the commencement of Mr. Meade's labors in the Valley of Virginia, that section of the Diocese was almost destitute of the services of the Protestant Episcopal Church. His endeavors, by occasional itinerations as a voluntary missionary, to supply in some measure this lamentable deficiency, resulted in the restoration of some parishes, and in the formation of new ones. As these succeeded in procuring their own ministers, he found himself sustained by a band of zealous brethren, ready to co-operate with him in the good work, in which he had been the solitary but successful pioneer. Still, the number was very inadequate to the extent of territory, and its dispersed population. To provide for this lack of regular service, the clergy of that district agreed to meet from time to time in their several parishes, and at points of missionary interest, to engage in a series of religious services, and thus, an expedient commended by a Convention during the Episcopate of Bishop Madison, was, for the first time, attempted in practice.

One of Mr. MEADE's co-workers in this expedient was the Rev. Benjamin Allen, afterwards rector of St. Paul's, Philadelphia. He was singularly suited for the services which this measure involved. His intellectual powers and attainments were not extraordinary, but his zeal was irrepressible and his activity untiring. He preached often, and wrote much, though his preparation for the ministry had been hurried, and his way of studying was always desultory. He was wont to say of himself, that he could not endure confinement — a few hours, and he was "like a wilted cabbage-leaf." On his horse, however, he was at home. The saddle was his study, and he was much in it. He read, and meditated, and made notes, and composed sermons, as he rode, and was ready for preaching whenever he reached any of the many places where he was accustomed to officiate; and there were few neighborhoods in the counties of Berkeley and Jefferson which he did not thus frequent. To him, the recurrence of the period for the meeting of the brethren was a festival, and by his bright spirit and animated services, he contributed his full proportion to the profit and pleasure which they afforded.

The Rev. John Thompson Brooke is mentioned by Mr. MEADE as, at a later period, another and a junior member of their clerical association. He was born in Maryland, of Romish parents. He was educated in their Church, and, when a boy, had sometimes acted as attaché of a priest in the pantomimic evolutions of their ceremonial. When he had attained the proper age, he was entered as a student (of law) in the office of the late Chief-Justice of the Supreme Court of the United States, who at that time resided in Fredericktown, Md., and was at the head of the profession, which he adorned by his personal excellencies, not less than by his eminent forensic ability.

When young Brooke was admitted to the Bar, he became a candidate for practice in his native county, and was so successful that he soon found the income from his business sufficient for his support. Though of a languid bodily temperament, he was of a very jovial spirit. With a keen perception of the ludicrous, and uncommon powers of humorous imitation and song, his company was solicited wherever conviviality was proposed. Both his professional success and his soul's salvation were imperilled by that dangerous faculty of administering to the mirth of others, which often proves suicidal to the light-hearted contributor. But in his case, God, who is "rich in mercy" and often leads by a way which we know not, was pleased to order it otherwise. In His gracious providence young Brooke was prompted by mere feelings of companionship to attend service in a Protestant church. There, unknown by any of the congregation, the Word preached was sent with awakening power to his heart. The next morning, he was alone with the pastor in his study, earnestly enquiring, "What must I do to be saved?" A mind thus wrought upon by the Holy Ghost is not usually slow to perceive the suitableness and sufficiency of the provision set forth in the Gospel, or to appropriate it when known; and one of the earliest desires connected with this experience is to bring others to Christ. This desire soon and powerfully possessed the soul of the new convert to the faith of the Gospel. His opportunity as a layman did not satisfy his longing spirit. Believing that he could be more efficient in the ministry, he relinquished the Law and became a student of Theology, in the Alexandria Seminary, where he completed the prescribed course, and was admitted to Holy Orders.

From the hour of Mr. Brooke's conversion, the reality was strikingly indicated by the outward and visible change in his manner of life. Never afterwards did he, even in private intercourse with his familiar friends, indulge those powers which had previously rendered him so attractive in worldly society. The transition, however, was not from gaiety to gloom, but to an habitual sobriety, perfectly compatible with cheerfulness, and with the exercise and enjoyment of all the pure charities of the social relations. Thus chastened and refined by grace, he consecrated his gifts and acquirements to the ministry of reconciliation, and became an able and faithful preacher of the Gospel, sound in his teaching and of exemplary walk and conversation. His mode of preparing his sermons was peculiar. His custom was to think them out carefully, even to the very language, and memorize them accurately as thus composed, and then he was able, without having committed them to writing, to deliver them with as much precision as if he read from a manuscript, and with all the freedom and impressiveness of extempore address. His first parish included the churches at Martinsburg and Hedgesville. Both there and in other more extended spheres, to which he was subsequently called, his labors were blessed with much usefulness, till he fulfilled his ministry and entered upon his reward. This sketch is due to the memory of one who is named by Mr. MEADE as a member of their Association, and who rendered valuable aid in the revival and extension of the Church in the Valley.

Mr. MEADE has left on record his brief but decided testimony in favor of Associations. "We assembled generally in each other's parishes—having meetings among ourselves, and at private houses, for special prayer—taking up collections for missionaries in the Western part of Virginia. The first two who went to Virginia beyond the Alleghanies—the Rev. Charles Page and the Rev. William Lee, were sent out by our Society. These Associations were attended by much good, and no evil, so far as I know, and believe. I have ever encouraged them since entering the Episcopate. Bishop Moore did the same, before and after that time, as being important auxiliaries to Bishops, especially in large dioceses. I regard it as an evil omen when ministers favorably situated, are averse to such means of their own, and their people's improvement, though I do not mean to say, that there are not some good and pious men, who regard them in a different light." (Old C., M. and F., vol. I, p. 42.)

A country clergyman with two or three, and sometimes four churches under his care, and officiating in them in rotation on Sunday only, necessarily labors to great disadvantage. If the weather or any other cause, interferes with his appointment, then an interval of four, six, or eight weeks, passes without service in that congregation. When ministrations are so rare, the instructions from the pulpit must be very limited. If on any occasion, its stirring appeals to the heart and conscience, prove awakening, the impression is apt to disappear, before another opportunity, or, in the absence of the teacher preferred, the anxious inquirer seeks counsel of others, and is liable to be led off, and lost to the Church in which he was roused to consideration. The quarterly association secured to each parish, in addition to its stated services, a series of ministrations, conducted daily and for several days in succession, and thus provided in some measure, precisely what was needed. The interest manifested by the clergy extended to the people. Large congregations assembled. Persons not often seen in religious meetings, were attracted to these, and so brought under the influence of the Gospel, both during the public administrations and during the intervals of service, in personal intercourse with ministers and other Christians. Their minds were thus, under very favorable circumstances, and for an unusual length of time, kept in contact with divine truth, and any religious concern produced, instead of being dissipated at the close of the single service, was often, by the succession of services, cherished and matured into abiding piety. Wherever these meetings were held, salutary results were witnessed. The "association," which is still conducted under the more Church-like name of "Convocation," became the popular usage of the Diocese, and not a few of the members of the Church in Virginia trace their first decided religious impressions to these meetings, and testify to their instrumentality in forming and advancing their Christian character. Nor were the people the only gainers. The clergy in attendance derived profit and pleasure from these associations. Confined to their regular parishes, and isolated from their brethren except during the few days of their annual Convention, there is danger of losing that expansion of spirit and activity, which the Great Commission enjoins, and of becoming contracted into parochial, if not personal selfishness. The generous *esprit du corps* degenerates into religious *egoism*. Shut out from that professional companionship which promotes individual improvement by the opportunity it affords to take knowledge of those whose example shows a more excellent way by animating to increased endeavor for higher attainments in the divine life, and more devoted and efficient zeal in the Master's service, the parish minister is liable to acquiesce with satisfaction in his own measure, and plod on in the routine of his official services, in unsuspecting, though deteriorating self-complacency. "The association" by affording the clerical brethren frequent opportunities for benefitting by each other's services in the desk and the pulpit

—for comparing experience in reference to the difficulties, and the helps in their parochial duties—for consultation as to the means of increasing their usefulness, and for the extension of the Gospel—for prayer with, and for each other, and for their people—provided a happy counteractive to the evils described, and an excellent expedient for promoting personal piety, and professional efficacy—for strengthening the blessed bond of clerical brotherhood, and kindling to greater zeal the spirit of evangelization. Such has been the uniform testimony of those who have availed themselves of its advantages. It is to be hoped that a usage, which has almost become an institution of the Church in Virginia, will be perpetuated, and under the Divine favor, perpetuate and extend the rich blessings of which it has been productive.

(*Death of his Mother.*)— The mother of Mr. MEADE was still living, when he resumed his connection with his parish in Frederick county. She was spared to see, in his piety, influence, and growing usefulness, a most satisfactory answer to her unceasing prayers, and to receive a rich reward for the excellent example, judicious counsel, and firm but loving discipline, by which, under God's blessing, he had become a son worthy of such a mother. His filial affection and reverence were unsurpassed, and the event of her death, which occurred on the 16th of June, 1813, in her sixtieth year, pierced his manly breast with such sorrow, as he had never felt before. There was indeed everything, of which the nature of the bereavement admits, to sustain and solace him in his affliction. But it was deep and abiding. The loss of a beloved mother sunders a ligament of such exquisite delicacy and tenderness, that though the wound may cease to bleed, its sensibility remains through life, and the suffering is often renewed under the pressure of memories, which, though they re-produce the sorrow, are too sacred and salutary to be resisted.

A manuscript was found among Mrs. Meade's papers,

containing two prayers which she composed and used privately for years, also a letter of advice to her children, designed for their benefit after her decease. These papers are given as intimately connected with the biography of her son, and as a pattern for pious mothers, who desire to be found faithful in the performance of parental duty:

1. (*Prayer for Herself.*)—"Thou art my Creator, Oh, my God! and Protector. Thou are the ultimate end of my being and supreme perfection of my nature. Under the shadow of Thy wings is perpetual repose, and from the light of Thy countenance flow eternal joy and felicity. Grant me, Oh! blessed Judge of angels and men, this felicity, and not only me, but the whole of the human race. I beseech Thee to look upon my infirmities and pity my weakness, and give me those things, which Thy wisdom sees proper for me. Give me such a portion of Thy grace as may influence my heart to an humble imitation of my divine Redeemer and Advocate. Let the perfections of my mind be my first and great concern, but after I have exerted my best, though feeble endeavors, let me rely only on Thy mercy. Let this divine attribute, so necessary for man, be ever present with me, and make me as ready to forgive, as to ask forgiveness. Grant me to make every duty my delight, and to be afflicted only with my crimes. Make me to fulfil the duties of wife, mother, friend and mistress, most faithfully. Let Thy wisdom direct my intentions, and Thy blessing be upon all my actions. Be my God forever and ever, my guide even unto death. I ask it through the merits of my crucified Redeemer, in whose incomparable words I pray to be further heard. Our Father," &c.

2. (*A Prayer for Grace to perform her Duty to her Children.*)—"Give me wisdom, Oh! great Creator, to discharge my duty as a parent most faithfully. Teach me to form the minds of my children to virtue—to train them up in the love of infinite wisdom and mercy. Grant them docility of

temper which may make the instructions of a fond parent their delight. Teach me to arrange instruction and amusement in such due order, as may produce a succession, both pleasing and beneficial. May they have engraven on their hearts, every virtue — truth, justice, mercy, humility and charity, in thought, word and deed. Make them wise as serpents, and harmless as doves. If Thy wisdom sees proper, bless the endeavours of their affectionate parents, to make such provision for them, as, with their own care and attention, may enable them to pass through life with comfort to themselves and the happiness of assisting passengers less fortunate. If Thou seest contrary, Oh! great Creator, Thy will be done. I will with the assistance of Thy divine power, endeavour to make it mine."

Amen. Amen. MARY MEADE.

3. (*Advice to her Children.*)—"From your earliest infancy, my dear children, I have endeavored to train you up in the paths of virtue, to make you sensible of your dependence on your Creator, Protector, and continual Benefactor, under the shadow of whose wings, is perpetual repose, and from the light of whose countenance flows eternal joy and felicity. May truth, justice, mercy, humility and charity, in thought, word, and deed, to the whole race of mankind, be practiced by you with delight. Think not either, or all of these desirable virtues difficult to attain. Apply but to the fountain of all wisdom and goodness, with a sincere and determined resolution to exert your utmost endeavors to obtain them, and all will be easy. Your tender affection and love for each other, I have often remarked with tears of delight. Continue this happy union, my beloved children, and let the loss of an affectionate parent, bind you more firmly to each other. You are young and frail, and consequently an uninterrupted state of harmony is not expected to subsist between you, but endeavour to come as near it as possible. Strive, each succeeding day, to make progress in conquering a propensity to dispute with each other. The eldest,

I hope, will set the example. Never glory in getting the victory in a dispute. It is false glory, for disputes generally arise from the most trivial causes. Glory rather in getting the command of your passion. This, is productive of every good — it ensures the approbation of infinite wisdom, of your own mind, and of the virtuous part of mankind. Think for a moment, before your passions get to an unjustifiable height, and impose on yourself the task of silence. This done, reflection will follow, and I hope there are none of you, but are blessed with such dispositions, as will feel more joy in forgiving an injury than in triumphing over an adversary. This victory obtained, I must caution you against an error which may be the consequence of it. The result of a virtuous action must be self-approbation, but let not this degenerate into vanity— an error common to mortals, and which ought therefore carefully to be guarded against, for it is not only contrary to the precept and example of our blessed Saviour, but disgusting to man — the brightest virtues are tarnished by it, and lose considerably their lustre. "Pride was not made for man"—therefore, my children, if you are happy enough to place your whole aim and ambition in virtue, and are conscious that you possess it, in some points, superior to your fellow mortals, let it not cause you to look on others with contempt. God, who only knows the heart of man, may see in them virtues which your penetration cannot discover, and though they may be wanting in what you excel in, they may possess qualities of a higher dignity, particu'arly if adorned with humility. Should it be your fate to be separated, let it not diminish your affection for each other. Let a constant correspondence subsist between you, in which you must communicate in the tenderest terms, the defects you may hear ascribed to each other. This is a nice and delicate point, but certainly one of the first proofs of friendship. To them alone, let the subject be mentioned, nor ever deceive yourselves or others by supposing you participate in the injustice done a friend or fellow mortal, by calumny or detraction, while you with ease or indifference, make it the subject of common conversation. Ere I say adieu, let me once more entreat you to be kind and affectionate to your fond father, and other kind benefactors, and be united in the strictest bonds of harmony as brothers and sisters. Let those to whom Heaven has been most bountiful, bear with the weakness of the younger or inferior. How delightful the reflection to have reformed perhaps a froward brother or sister, by lenity, prayer and rectitude of conduct. A few more lines, and then farewell. They relate to your behaviour to domestics. From your earliest infancy, my dear children, I have taught you to treat them with complacency, kindness and humanity. This I must forever justify, but positively forbid familiarity with them. Never will you be respected by them, if you make companions of them. Adieu, my children, and let the following lines be a rule for your conduct. Never think a thought, speak a word, or do a deed, but what you may be safe in setting about, with these words: 'Oh! God, my Maker and Judge, I do not forget that Thou art witness to what I am doing." Heaven preserve and direct you to His divine presence, most fervently prays your affectionate mother,

MARY MEADE."

Such were the prayers during life, and such the posthumous address of the sainted mother, to whose hallowed influence on her son, the Church is indebted for blessings, the extent of which will be fully known, only in another world.

The removal of both parents devolved on Mr. MEADE a responsibility which he truly recognized, and he promptly addressed himself to the conscientious discharge of the offices which it involved. The generosity which he evinced in connection with the voluntary arrangement he had made, in changing the distribution of the paternal estate, for the accommodation of a brother, marked all his transactions with the other members of his family, and indeed was only one, in a series of deeds of liberality, which, as occasion offered, adorned his life, and benefitted and bound to him, in gratitude and admiration, those who were capable of appreciating his unselfish and beneficent course.

His sisters now especially needed a friendly counsellor, both in reference to their temporal interests and their religious obligations. His prompt and judicious fraternal guardianship appears in the following letter, which, immediately after their mother's death, he addressed to them jointly. It was evidently designed for their perusal only, and was composed without any studied reference to its style. Yet it so well illustrates the spirit, principles and practice of the writer, and is so admirably calculated to be of use to others in similar circumstances, that it would be culpable not to give it permanent publicity:

"To My Three Younger Sisters."

My Dearest Sisters:—

Will you listen to the kindly admonitions of a brother who loves you dearly, and would see you happy eternally, and would persuade you so to live on earth that when you die, you may be exalted to Heaven? The removal of our dear mother from the scene of sickness and sorrow to one of bliss and perfection, has made a great alteration in our family. The course and order of things which has subsisted for the last thirty years, must now be changed. "Old things must pass away, and all things become new." Our mother, our guide, our counsellor, our example, our head, our centre around whom we moved, and who kept us in our orbits, is now taken from among us, and we no longer hear the sweet accent of her voice, no longer behold the angelic smile of her countenance, and are no longer guided by her rule and immediate counsel. She has left us separately to follow by ourselves those good principles, which, under Heaven, she taught us and practiced before us, while living. "By them, she, though dead, yet speaketh."

We are all affected, much affected by this change, but none so much so as my three single sisters. They are thrown into a new course of life—they are thrown out of their old employments—the tender nursing and watching over the best, the kindest of mothers. Hitherto they have been dutifully and continually engaged in all those filial attentions which her weakness called for, and in relieving her from those family cares which she could not sustain. These are no longer required. Praised be God! our mother has now no troubles, no pains, no sickness. She is a ministering angel, brightly hovering about the mercy-seat of God, chanting His praises, and going on errands of love—perhaps (exstatic thought) often despatched with good thoughts, kind monitions and sweet consolation to the hearts of her children. Yes, yes, "there is no pain among the blessed," sorrow and sighing flee away from them, God with His own hand wipes away all tears from their eyes. And our mother is among them—certainly, most certainly.

But my sisters are almost without employ—they feel a vacuum within—something is wanting and something must be found as a subsitute, or they may fall into a state of idleness and listlessness, than which nothing is more to be feared, since it exposes us to every temptation and leads the way to a vain, worldly, and irreligious life. It is also the state of all others, in which Satan, our great enemy, delights to find us, for then is his time to get us into his employ.

I fear, I tremble for my sisters, my two younger sisters Mary and Lucy, especially. My sister Susan is, I trust and believe, too firmly fixed in right principles, and too long habituated to good actions, ever to depart from them (the grace of God preventing her.) I say I fear, I tremble for you, my dear Mary and Lucy, for although at present you show good dispositions, and have ever been kind and dutiful and submissive to mamma, and from her have received the knowledge of what is right; and though in our elder sister you have more than many mothers are to their children, yet still I fear your age is so critical, the world so seductive, pleasure so enchanting, the tempter so wily, and by nature we so prone to supineness, so ready to follow the common custom of others, so averse to taking up the cross, and leading a holy, useful, heavenly life, careless of ridicule, unmindful of opposition, and mainly intent upon doing that which is right.

These things make me to fear for you. I feel a godly jealousy over you. My heart's desire and prayer for you is, that you may be saved, not only from misery hereafter, but from this present evil world, in the first place, as necessary to the former. You have now no mother to watch over you, to urge you continually to that which is right, and to restrain you from that which is wrong. You have no mother on whom to expend your love and thoughts, on whom to bestow your affections. You must then find out something, my sisters, about which to engage yourselves, if you would be either happy or religious, if you would please God or that sainted mother, who now looks down from Heaven upon her children.

I have determined to write down some thoughts for my sisters on the right way of appropriating their time and property, so as to derive that benefit from them which God intends, so as to make them blessings instead of curses. I would affectionately warn them against some things which I may think will injure them. I have (I trust) devoted myself to the service of mankind. My duty is publicly and privately to administer advice wherever it is needful or proper. My first duty is to my own family. Oh! that we may all unite in the blessed work of doing good and living righteously. May we be a band of brothers and sisters firmly united. Oh! may we be just such as our dear mother, and Heavenly Father, would have us to be. May we live together "blessing and being blessed," and, though separated time after time by death, as now from our dear mother, may we be reunited in Heaven, and form a happy family above!

There are two things on which I would ground the following advices: The first is that my sisters have much time at their disposal, the right use of which will be required of them by God who gave it. The second is that by the providence of God they are possessed of a property, the annual interest of which will be far more than they should wish to expend in their present state. I would beseech you, my dear sisters, so to expend these gifts and talents of God, that they may bring you in an eternal interest and treasure. I hope that you will spend your time and property like Christians. They are given you to use, not abuse, to use for the benefit of others, as well as yourself; this is not only your duty but your happiness. Those who receive time and property both from Heaven, have much to answer for, and have much wherewith to make themselves and others happy. The property affords employment for the time, and the time enables them to spend their property usefully and joyfully.

"A capacity to do good, not only gives the title to it, but makes the doing of it a duty," said a great man, to which we may add the neglect of it a crime. I would beseech my sisters, out of love to their souls, to begin at once to live on this principle — to redeem their time, to spend as much as possible of it in a useful way, to themselves and others. We have but a little while to live in this world, and in that little to prepare for an endless eternity. It becomes us then to spend it in the best manner.

Perhaps there are no persons more exposed to the temptation of spending their time in idleness, in dress, in visiting, and in trivial, worldly conversation, than females at the age of my sisters, without a mother to employ or restrain them, and without families of their own to engage their thoughts and attention. Sorry, sorry should I be, to see my sisters fall into the manners and habits too common to the young women of our day — grieved to the soul should I be to see them delight in the vanity of dress, in visiting, in trivial reading and conversation. They will say perhaps that I do them wrong — that I fear badly of them — they cannot possibly fall into these habits — they cannot so injure the spirit, so disobey the precepts of their beloved mother. I hope not, I pray not, but alas! the frailty of poor mortals, how apt to turn aside! how prone to forget the best precepts and examples, when the mother who gave them is no more! How gently, how gradually do we fall into the ways of the vain and idle world. My dear sisters, prayer, holy reading and employment, are the only things which can keep you from going astray, from depending on the vanities of the world for your happiness. Hitherto you have been close to the side of the best of mothers; she has been your sweet and interesting companion. You will now form others, but beware, lest you form such as will lead you into an intimacy with the world, whenever you go out into company (which should be as seldom as possible.) Be on your guard against anything you see or hear, lest you be gradually accustomed to what may be wrong. You should pity, but beware of those votaries of fashion who rove from one pleasure to another, who delight in revellings, whose continual conversation is about dress, and visiting and balls, and novels. These persons are ill employed, they are unhappy within—they know not the joys of true religion—instead of going to God, they go to the world for happiness, and this sooner or later must turn to anguish.

If you will begin now at once to live religiously and usefully, it will become easier every day. You will become more and more pleased with your choice, as you grow up. You will become independent of the world. You will establish an intercourse between God and your soul, which will continually enlarge itself, and afford you increasing happiness, and should you hereafter become the mothers and mistresses of families, you will be prepared for performing a Christian part in these relations. Oh! my sisters, you little know how much depends on your present choice, on your first entrance into life. On it perhaps the whole character of your future life depends. "Now is the accepted time, now is the day of salvation." If you now turn into the wrong course, how hardly will you get back into the right one. It is ten times easier to set out right and go forward, than, having set out wrong, to turn back and get into the right way. Our dear mother has been heretofore leading you in the right way. She has let go your hands; she has gone up to Heaven, but she still beckons you onward. You will not return. You will not turn aside into the paths of folly and vanity. You will not love idle company, and trifling books and dress and pleasure, when she taught you to love good books as your companions, to think of your souls rather than your bodies, to do good rather than to seek pleasure in idleness and frivolity. I trust not—Oh! God, I pray not. Oh! God, take my sisters under Thy care. Be Thou more than a mother to them. Teach them the true happiness and the best way of spending their time. Do Thou "guide them by Thy counsel" while on earth, and "afterwards receive them into glory."

I would now say something to my sisters about the duty of rightly spending incomes. I say it is more than sufficient to support them in a decent Christian manner. I hope they do not wish to live in any other way. I hope they will never make their happiness to consist in dress. Now this is all the expense they will be at about themselves. They will always, while single, live with one of their brothers, or with our dear sister or cousin. My sisters cannot certainly wish to expend all of their income on themselves. I hope, and will not believe, that they would desire to lay by and amass more than they have. Here then, my sisters, is a fund given you by Heaven, and that parent who is in Heaven, to do good with, to relieve the poor and distressed, to enlighten the ignorant, to comfort those who mourn. Resolve then, now at once, that you will spend only so much on yourselves as Christians should do. (I do not wish you to dress meanly, or too singularly, but plainly and modestly,) and give the rest to pious and charitable uses. That is the true way of enjoying your estate — that is the way whereby you will please Him from whom you hold your property and all other things in this world, and that which is to come.

I would not have my sisters to be ostentatious of their charity — far from it; the very reverse — scarcely to let their right hand know what their left hand doeth. I would have them be as secret as possible. I will associate myself with them and throw in all that I can give from my family. I will look out the proper objects of charity, and the best modes of usefulness. Many will present themselves. God will direct us how to dispose our charities. He will second our disposition by guiding it into the most useful action. There are a thousand ways of doing good which will present themselves to such as seek them. One only would I mention — assisting to publish good books and disseminating them. I wish to be engaged in this. I wish annually to publish a selection from the writings of some eminent Christian. My sisters might here assist me in two ways; first in copying out the selection, and then in the publication, with their money, if necessary. If only one soul be improved and comforted by such a book, what a feast to a Christian heart! We might employ some pious man to travel about through our State, and sell at a cheap rate, some good books which we might get published, and when it was necessary, give them away. How many poor families are deprived of much pleasure and instruction, by want of good books to read. While we are feasting our own minds with such a variety of good books, we should feel for others. We might greatly assist to mend the morals of our State by disseminating small tracts to the poor as well as sick — hymns and catechisms for children, &c. We might begin on a small scale and enlarge — others would join in the work, and we might give away and sell at a cheap rate, many hundreds annually. This is one way, nor does this require much money to put it in execution.

Many others will present themselves to you. There are many poor families in different places, who would be much relieved by a little assistance; some poor children might be educated, some poor orphan be supported.

Ah! how much better will it be, thus to spend whatever is not absolutely necessary for comfort and decency, than in dress or vanity or pleasure, or in increasing a principal already fully sufficient. We ought to look upon it as an honor of the highest grade, to be allowed to do good—it is the highest pleasure—it is a holy luxury to a humane heart. We should seize on any opportunity to do good, with rapture and delight. Doing good is the reward, the pleasure of Christians while on earth. There is no greater happiness on this side of Heaven. It was a high compliment once paid to a great man, "that as to the wealth of this world, he knew no good in it, but the doing good with it." We are nothing the better for anything we possess, merely for the propriety's sake—it is the application only which gives it its real value. Let me say to my sisters as a certain person once did to his friend on his accession to an estate: "Much good may it do you,—that is, much good may you do with it." But again, I would caution my sisters against ostentation, or thinking highly of themselves for anything they may do, or propose to do.

One of the holy fathers has well said, that, "it is truly excellent to do great things, and yet esteem ourselves as nothing." Nothing makes us so agreeable in the sight of Heaven, as to rise high by our good actions, and yet sink low by our humility. I hope and pray that this may be the case with my dearest sisters. By thus acting they will enjoy the truest happiness in this life—they will escape the vanity of the world—they will live above the world—others may see their good example and take pattern after it—they will thus enjoy a Heaven below, as far as permitted to mortals, and they will prepare themselves for Heaven hereafter—and they will be received into it with these rejoicing words of our Saviour, "Come ye blessed children of my Father, inherit the kingdom prepared for you from the foundation of the world."

(*Colonization Society.*)—In the year 1817, the American Colonization Society was organized in the City of Washington. Its object was to procure by purchase, sufficient territory in some suitable locality on the Western Coast of Africa, and to provide for the removal to such place, of those free persons of color who were willing to emigrate to the land of their forefathers. It was neither sectional or sectarian in its origin. Some of the most eminent men from each of the great divisions of the country, aided in its establishment and were numbered among its patrons. Its list of members exhibited the names of persons belonging to different religious denominations, and its funds were furnished mainly by contributions from the several Churches of the land. Disconnected from the Government, which cautiously abstained from any official association with the enterprize, it afforded no encouragement to party spirit, and no occasion for party interference. It was truly and simply a great scheme of Christian and patriotic benevolence to benefit the country and ameliorate the condition of the class of persons to be colonized, and through their instrumentality, gradually introduce the blessings of civilization and religion among the savage and imbruted hordes of Africa. It was sanctioned by the deliberate opinion of the most distinguished statesmen. Mr. Jefferson, in a letter, dated January 11, 1811, writes: "You have asked my opinion of the proposition, to take measures for the procuring on the Coast of Africa, an establishment to which the people of color of these United States, might, from time to time, be *colonized*, under the auspices of different Governments. Having long ago made up my mind on this subject, I have no hesitation in saying that it is *the most desirable measure which could be adopted* for gradually drawing off this part of our population." And again: "It may perhaps be doubted whether many of this people would voluntarily consent to such an exchange of situation, and but few of those advanced to a certain age in habits of slavery, would be capable of governing themselves; *this should not, however, discourage the experiment, nor the early trial of it*, and propositions should be made with all the prudent *caution* and *attention*, required to reconcile it to the interest, the *safety and prejudice of all parties.*"

Mr. Clay's opinion was thus expressed: "I would not, I could not believe that man, in the pursuit of the vilest cupidity, in the prosecution of purposes of the most cruel injustice, which had constantly marked the African slave-trade, could accomplish more than might be attained in a cause, which was recommended by so many high, honorable, and manly considerations. *Such is the cause in which this Society is engaged.*"

In December, 1816, the following resolution was passed by the Legislature of Virginia:

Resolved, That the Executive be requested to correspond with the President of the United States, for the purpose of obtaining a territory on the Coast of Africa, or at some other place, not within the States or territorial governments of the United States, to serve as an asylum for such persons of color as are now free, and may desire the same, and for those who may hereafter be emancipated.

Resolutions to the same effect were passed by the Legislatures of Maryland and Tennessee. The Convention of the Diocese of Virginia, habitually careful to avoid all extra ecclesiastical legislation, adopted the following resolutions on this subject: "On motion of Mr. Needham L Washington, *Resolved unanimously*, That this Convention express their approbation of the object of the Colonization Society, and offer up their hearty prayers for its success." "On motion of Rev. William H. Wilmer, *Resolved*, That a committee be appointed to address the Board of Managers of the Colonization Society, and to express the approbation and good wishes of this House."

In conformity with these resolutions, a strongly commendatory address, prepared by Dr. Wilmer, as chairman of the Committee, was approved by the Convention and entered on the Journal. (Journal of 1819.)

It was not to be expected that a measure of this kind could progress without being suspected and opposed. The Quakers and other abolitionists regarded it as an artful device of Southern planters to get rid of free persons of color, that they might hold the slaves in greater subjection and security; whilst certain extremists in the South, mistrusted it as an incipient move in the line of emancipation.

It was openly resisted by both parties until those in the South, surprised at the strange alliance in which they found themselves, were led to a more careful consideration of the subject, and with few exceptions exhibited their characteristic magnanimity, by becoming its friends. This was a subject upon which Mr. MEADE, like Mr. Jefferson, "had long ago made up his mind." He had not to wait, and watch the direction of public opinion — he was ready and able to lead it. Both his judgment and his heart were in favor of the noble enterprize, and from the first he stood forth as its advocate and supporter. Not only with his funds which he liberally appropriated, but, as far as compatible with his parochial engagements, by his personal services, and frequent correspondence, he zealously contributed to the formation of the Society. It is to be regretted that none of his letters are available. A few from others show the importance attached to his influences and services, and his earnest activity in the cause.

At a meeting of the Board of Managers, held in Washington, D. C., April 7th, 1819, at which the Hon. William H. Crawford, one of the Vice-Presidents, presided, resolutions were adopted which led to the appointment of Mr. MEADE as the Society's Commissioner to negotiate with the Governor of Georgia for the purchase of a number of captured African slaves, who, having been brought there contrary to the laws of the State and of the United States, became the property of the State, and were advertised to be sold publicly on the 4th of May, in the town of Milledgeville. Mr. MEADE accepted the appointment, and with this commission connected an agency to explain and advocate the objects of the Society, as opportunity might occur. In a few days he left his home on this embassy, and was absent for several weeks, during which he visited some of the principal Southern cities, diligently engaged in public and in private, both by speaking and the circulation of appropriate publications, in setting forth and commending the colonization cause. His instructions contained in the letter addressed to him, by the Secretary of the Society, will more fully explain his special mission:

"*To the Rev.* WILLIAM MEADE, *Agent of the American Society for Colonizing the free People of Color of the United Sates:*

The Board of Managers of the American Colonization Society request that you will proceed to Milledgeville, in Georgia, to request His Excellency, the Governor of Georgia, to deliver to you the Africans mentioned in the accompanying advertisement and resolution of the Board, agreeably to the law of Georgia, passed the 19th of Dec., 1819. You are authorized to make such arrangements with the Governor, in behalf of the Society, as may be deemed necessary to comply with the stipulation of said law.

Upon receiving said Africans, you will please have them sent to Smith's Island, at the mouth of the Chesapeake Bay, where they will be provided for at the expense of the United States, till the proper season arrives for their being sent to Africa, unless you find that they can be more advantageously taken care of for the present, in Georgia.

The manner of executing this duty will be left to your discretion, with such advice as you may think proper to take in Georgia.

You are authorized to draw on David English, Cashier of the Union Bank of Georgetown, Treasurer of the Society, for the necessary funds for the objects of your mission. We anticipate, however, from the benevolent and liberal spirit of the people of Georgia, that you will receive sufficient supplies for that purpose in Georgia. From the character we have heard of his Excellency, the Governor, we have no doubt you will receive from him, all the aid in his power in promoting the benevolent object of your mission. As the Managers have been obliged, from the circumstances of this case, to act without having particular information as to the amount of expenses, and many other circumstances, it is not intended to preclude you from exercising your discretion after your arrival in Georgia, as to the extent you may consider it advisable to act, under the Resolution of the Board. Your knowledge of the views and resources of the Society, will enable you to act according to these views, so far as they come within the resources of the Society, after you have acquired the necessary information in Georgia.

If it would facilitate your operations to have your drafts on the Treasurer payable in Philadelphia or New York, arrangements can be made to pay them there, upon giving time. It will be advisable for that purpose, to make your drafts payable thirty days after sight.

By order of the Board, E. B. CALDWELL, Secretary.

WASHINGTON, April 15, 1819.

True copy from the Minutes, JOHN UNDERWOOD, Rec'dg Sec'ty.

On his return, he wrote from Charleston, S. C., to his friend, Dr. John Brockenbrough, of Richmond. The object of his letter, as is apparent from the reply, was to inquire if it would be advisable for him, on his route home, to make an effort in behalf of the Society in the city of Richmond.

RICHMOND, 8th June, 1819.

My Dear Sir:

I have postponed replying to your letter from Charleston as long as possible, with the hope of giving you some information on the subject you have so much at heart, that could be consolatory, but you will find this letter barren, or worse than barren. Mr. Rice has been absent almost ever since you left us, and Mr. Mercer only reached the place a few days ago. Those were the only persons from whom I expected any intelligence. Mr. Mercer, after making an address to the people of Fredericksburg, formed a Society there very respectable in its number and character. Here he has had no encouragement, and I believe will attempt nothing. His address at Fredericksburg has caused a good deal of excitement on the part of those unfavorable to the scheme, and we are all so excessively harassed here about our debts, and pecuniary concerns, that I am confident it would not only be unavailing, but injurious, to make any efforts to form a Society, either publicly or by individual applications.

You can form no idea of our worldly sufferings. Our citizens are gloomy, dispirited and irritable. All their golden visions are vanished, and they are left languid and restless. In truth, almost every man seems astonished at his own folly and infatuation, and I, amongst the number.

Mr. Mercer, I presume, wrote to you, and would more fully explain his motives and plans. I have nothing more to add than assurances of *our* affectionate regards.

Yours, most truly,
JOHN BROCKENBROUGH.

The Committee of Arrangement appointed by the Society, were earnestly engaged in endeavoring to secure the favorable action of President Monroe, in facilitating, by all proper means, the negotiation for the contemplated African territory, and for the transportation of the captured slaves purchased from the State of Georgia. The difficulties and the delays experienced were disheartening, and but for the zeal and determination of those to whom the business was intrusted, it must have utterly failed.

Whilst this application was being ably and perseveringly pressed at Washington, Mr. MEADE was induced to visit the Northern States, and present the claims of the Society to the people of that section of the country. That his mission was well received, may be gathered from a kind and encouraging letter to Mr. MEADE, by the Hon. Timothy Pickering:

SALEM, Sept. 12th, 1819.

Dear Sir:

My son informs me that you expect to remain at Newburyport till to-morrow morning. I therefore address you to say that, after consulting with Mr. Pickman (whom you saw) and my son, (and I have not time to advise with others) it has seemed to us expedient that you should pursue your original plan of visiting Portland as well as Portsmouth, and not hasten your return for the sake of attending a meeting of gentlemen in Salem; which we think had better *follow* a meeting in Boston, our metropolis, where there is much wealth, much humane and Christian feeling, and great liberality.

Such men are not exempt, however, from the feelings of human nature, and will probably think that the occasion should be offered to them of *taking the lead* in Massachusetts in this important business. A noble display of liberality there, cannot fail to have a salutary influence on other commercial towns; and it is from the fruits of commerce alone, (by personal acquisition or inheritance), that contributions can be raised in New England. We have no rich farmers.

Portsmouth is the commercial capital of New Hampshire, as Portland is of Maine, which may now be considered as an independent State, and where therefore the objection applied to Salem may be viewed as superseded.

The subject also is a new one, and has barely been *heard of* by a small number of our citizens. It may be expedient to introduce it into our newspapers, to excite public attention, and prepare the minds of the intelligent and humane to enter upon it with adequate zeal.

I visit Salem at least weekly, often coming hither on Saturday afternoon, and returning home the next Monday forenoon. Should you be here a week hence, you may hear of me at my son's.

With affection and esteem, I am, dear Sir,

Your friend and servant,

TIMOTHY PICKERING.

The Rev. WILLIAM MEADE.

On Mr. MEADE's return from the North, he received, in Philadelphia, a letter from his friend, Mr. Key, informing him that President Monroe still held the application of the Committee under advisement; expressing some anxiety as to the result, and urging Mr. MEADE to come on to Washington:

GEORGETOWN, 8, 1819.

My Dear Friend:

Mr. Crawford's fears are realized. The President has forgotten his promises, and what simple courtiers were we, to suppose it would be otherwise.

We have it all to go over again. But never fear. We shall bring him back to the point we had gained. He is gone, and we must write to him, and get him to give his orders at once, in black and white.

Mr. Crawford had a talk with him and the Attorney General, and I have seen them both. All the difficulties that we had before removed about the vagueness of the law, and the difficulty of its execution, re-appeared. Mr. Crawford tried to remove them; *econtra* the Attorney General. The President thought that he could not purchase land, therefore could make no settlement, nor any provision for receiving the captured negroes in Africa. He desired the Atterney General to take the law and examine it, and give him his opinion. The Attorney General said, that without further examining it, he would at once advise him to do nothing, that Congress would soon meet, and pass another law, in which they might say plainly what they wanted done. Mr. Crawford said the law was just what it ought to be, and presented neither doubt nor difficulty.

Thus they broke up. Nothing was done. Caldwell has seen Mr. Crawford and the Attorney General also, and we have not met to compare notes since. I went to see him, but he was gone to Alexandria. I spent several hours with Mr. Wirt. He acknowledged that he was uninformed about the business; thought our plan impracticable, but concurred in all our wishes. I found him reading our report, and he says he will read everything about it and consider it. I think he will be a friend, at any rate, not an enemy. He seems to fear the danger of some excitement among the slaves, in consequence of our proceedings, and made some observations on the subject that deserve to be considered. He said the President would certainly appoint Bacon the agent, and that we ought to write to him and remind him of what had passed between us; as to which, he had no doubt, he would do what he had promised, and intimated that he would not oppose us. He added that he would write to the President to-day upon the subject.

We must, therefore, immediately prepare to carry on a correspondence with the President, and I will prepare a letter for our Committee to sign and forward, as soon as Gen. Mason (who is one of us, and the only one who has any weight) returns, which I hear, will be to-morrow.

We shall all, that is Caldwell and myself, be, in consequence of this state of things, a good deal wanted here. Nevertheless, if you think it more important that we should meet you in Philadelphia, we will do so, at least I will, if possible. My idea is that the President will appoint an agent, two, if we can find another, (which, by the bye, we must do, and I wish you to look about for another), that he will send a ship of war to the coast, and probably a transport with the colored men from this country, as laborers, and some agricultural implements, and that he will authorize him to settle in our territory and make preparations for receiving the captured negroes, and I think this will do.

I wish you to bring on a dozen of the sermons you sent me, the 'Plea for Africa.' I have promised one to Mr. Wirt. The one I had, I lent, and cannot get again. I think it calculated to help us greatly.

If we have no meeting in Philadelphia, I think you had better bring on Bacon with you, and the sooner you are both here, the better, unless you are doing something material, of which you will be the best judge.

May God bless you.

Ever your friend,

F. S. Key.

Caldwell, I presume, has written, and given you an account of our diplomatic adventures.

When the Society obtained position and facilities for action, enabling it to pursue successfully the benevolent purposes for which it was formed, the officers at Washington were fully able to conduct its ordinary work. The presence and services of others were neither solicited or needed, except in connection with the annual meetings, which increased in attraction as the operations of the Society extended. In these Mr. Meade was ever much interested, but as his personal agency was no longer needed, and other objects more intimately pertaining to the ministry claimed his consideration and influence,—to these his time and powers were now almost exclusively devoted.

(*Education Society.*)—Education was a subject which early and earnestly and through life, engaged the thoughts and energy of Mr. Meade. At the close of his college course, it was the theme which he chose for his valedictory address. His private resources were liberally used to aid deserving youth in pursuing those studies which would fit them for usefulness in the various departments of life. To his sisters, on coming into possession of the property which they inherited, he specified this as an important mode of doing good with the means at their disposal. When, in 1818, certain ministers and laymen assembled in the District of Columbia, at the laying of the corner-stone of a church, proposed the formation of a Society to assist pious, but indigent students in preparing for the ministry, he was with them in their consultations, to animate and further the scheme, by his zeal, wisdom and liberality. It was well conceived and has been efficiently executed. To relieve the delicacy of the beneficiary, the aid rendered, was to be regarded as a conditional loan, to be returned only, if, at any time, the recipient should be in circumstances to do so without any embarrassment. In many instances this has been done, and thus, the same sum has been available for the support of several students in succession. At first they were not required to connect themselves with any one academy or college, but were authorized to pursue their studies in any respectable institution most convenient for themselves. The disadvantage of this soon became apparent, and in connection with other weighty considerations, suggested the expediency of the less expensive and happier arrangement subsequently adopted.

This society, which was occasioned by the interest felt for one who was known to be pressed by pecuniary difficulties in supporting himself, whilst engaged in his preparatory course, and, in its incipient action, was quite limited, expanded as the necessity for such patronage was disclosed, and soon proved a most important auxiliary in the cause of theological education, not only by directly aiding beneficiaries themselves, but by contributing to the support of professors engaged in their instruction. In his "History of the Protestant Episcopal Church in Virginia,"

Dr. Hawks states, "It has steadily pursued its course of usefulness, and commended itself to the affectionate interests and cordial support of its friends, both in Virginia and elsewhere. In proof of this, it is only necessary to relate what it has done. Nearly one-tenth of the clergy of the Protestant Episcopal Church in the United States, have, in whole or in part, been assisted by this Society. One-sixth of the present clergy of Ohio, one-eighth of those of Pennsylvania, one-fifth of those of Maryland, and a large proportion of those of Virginia, have derived aid from its funds, while it is now affording assistance to about one-seventh of all the students in the several Theological schools of the Church in the United States." (Vol. I., p. 211.) Mr. MEADE's interest in the prosperity of this Society never declined. He availed himself frequently of the press and the pulpit, to testify to its great usefulness and commend it to the constant and generous support of the Church.

(*Theological Seminary.*)—With the revival of the Church in Virginia, there was a great demand for ministers to officiate in the resuscitated parishes, to take charge of new congregations, and to visit missionary districts. In one of his addresses to the Convention, Bishop Moore states: "In every section of the State which I have visited (and these visits have been very general), I have observed the most sincere and ardent attachment to the Church. From the temper of the people, I draw the most pleasing conclusions, and my mind is perfectly convinced, that, were it possible to procure a greater number of faithful ministers, those ministers would be received with joy by the vacant parishes, and provision made for their support." As a provisional arrangement, lay readers were appointed, and often with good effect. Still the cry continued, and extended, for educated men, apt and meet for the entire service of the ministry, and who could give themselves wholly to the work. It is not surprising that both clergy and laity felt the importance of prompt measures for meeting this encouraging requirement, and of the necessity of providing for the competent instruction of such as were moved of God to devote themselves to the ministry. But the great expense which any suitable arrangement would involve, and the apparent impossibility of procuring capable instructors, without depriving some influential congregations of their esteemed rectors, were formidable difficulties in the way of any plan which promised success The providence of God was preparing a way.

"Bishop Moore laid before the Convention of 1815, a letter from Dr. John Augustine Smith, President of William and Mary College, proposing that the Episcopal Church should establish a Theological Professorship in that Institution. The overture was referred to a committee. They reported favorably, and recommended "that the Bishop and Standing Committee be authorized to adopt measures for the promotion of an object of so great magnitude, and which may under the blessing of God be productive of the most beneficial consequences." This was adopted. The subject was resumed in the Conventions of 1820 and 1821, when resolutions were passed recommending the establishment of a Theological School in Williamsburg. A Board of Trustees was appointed, with instructions to adopt the most efficient measures for accomplishing it, by raising funds, selecting professors, &c., and to correspond with the Standing Committees of Maryland and North Carolina, to ascertain whether the members of the Church in those States were disposed to co-operate in the important measure. Maryland was heard from through her Bishop, the Right Rev. James Kemp, D. D., who declined the proposal for reasons not complimentary to the Christianity of Williamsburg, or the Churchmanship of Virginia. North Carolina was silent. The Trustees, however, proceeded to establish the School. The Rev. Reuel Keith, D. D., whom they chose as the professor, became also the minister to the congregation in Williamsburg, and was prepared to instruct any candidates who might be sent there. During two years, only one presented himself. The experiment was a failure, but that this was in no respect to be imputed to Dr. Keith, is evident from the signal success and distinguished reputation which he soon attained in a different location. On various accounts Williamsburg was found to be an unsuitable place. The attempt was abandoned, and Dr. Keith resigned the parish, and withdrew.

The circumstances which led to a renewal of the experiment elsewhere, are not furnished by any official record, but may be gathered from a letter preserved among the papers of Mr. MEADE. It is from the pen of Mrs. S. H. Smith, daughter of Dr. Thomas Henderson, of Georgetown, D. C., and wife of Gen. F. H. Smith, Principal of the Virginia Military Institute. It bears the date of March 10, 1860. *Extract.*—"About the time that Dr. Keith left Williamsburg, it was my father's desire to establish such a school in Georgetown as would be the foundation of a Protestant College, to be located in the District. In prosecution of this purpose, he followed him as far as Philadelphia, in hope of meeting him at the General Convention, then in session. Not finding him there, he returned home, and wrote to him to come and take charge of this academy, which in a very short time, brought Dr. Keith again to Georgetown. Mr. Frank Key met the Rev. Messrs. Hawley, Wilmer and yourself at my father's house. At his house, after repeated interviews, these meetings resulted in a determination to open a school for the prophets in Alexandria. My father was directed to prepare the address. At my request he gave me these facts in writing, many years ago." From this statement it would seem, as if all the action of the Convention was regarded as terminated in the failure at Williamsburg, though the Board of Trustees still existed, and upwards of $10,000 had been secured for the object. The probability is, that the result of the consultations at Georgetown were communicated to the members of the Board, who, influenced by the considerations in favor of Alexandria, especially by the prospect of obtaining the services of Dr. Wilmer and the Rev. Mr. Norris, in connection with the course of instruction, adopted the plan to which the subsequent sanction of the Convention was accorded. Those contributors, who had subscribed with the understanding that the location of the school was to be in Williamsburg, consented to the change of the place. So the important enterprise, which seemed in danger of being abandoned, was renewed under promising auspices in Alexandria.

Deeply interested as Mr. MEADE was in the effort to provide for the education of students ef Theology, and co-operating, as he did, in the measures adopted by the Convention, it is doubtful whether the Williamsburg arrangement had the approval of his judgment. The change presented the important undertaking under a more promising aspect, and he devoted himself to its accomplishment with full purpose of heart. In the Conventions of 1824–'5–'6, he was the medium of communication between the Board of Trustees and the Convention, and in the reports which he laid before that body, his views and expectations with regard to an Institution, which, under God, was mainly indebted to his judicious and persevering exertion for its establishment and growth, are embodied.

"At the last meeting of the Trustees, the Rev. Reuel Keith was engaged as Professor in the Institution, and requested to hold himself in readiness whenever it should go into operation. He accordingly settled in Alexandria, in October last, and has had under his charge, since that time, from twelve to fourteen students, thirteen of whom are candidates for orders. There are at present under his care, eleven young men, pursuing their studies with fair prospect of their future respectability and usefulness, and it is expected that not less than twenty will wish to enter at the ensuing session." "The more advanced class has recited to the Rev. W. H. Wilmer, who has had charge of the Department of Systematic Theology."

"The Trustees take great pleasure in contemplating the present state and encouraging prospects of the School, and in bearing testimony, as far as they know and believe, to the zeal, fidelity and ability, with which the professors have discharged the duties of their professorships. The whole course of studies has been entirely conformed to the canons of the Church."

"Williamsburg is too remote and inaccessible to justify the hope that students can be obtained for a Theological Institution at that place. The experiment was tried there for one year without success, and no hope of success seemed to present itself in time to come. No sooner was the trial made in Alexandria, than the number of students and the means of supporting the indigent among them, increased beyond the most sanguine anticipations."

"All that is wanting to complete success under the blessing of God, is the liberal co-operation of the friends of the Church." "We cannot hope for a full and permanent supply of ministers from any other source than the Institution we commend to the liberal patronage of our members." "The number of pious young men desirous to devote their lives to this sacred cause, is continually increasing, and the disposition to aid the more needy of them to procure a suitable education, is increasing in an equal degree; and to us do both the pious youth and their benevolent patrons look for an Institution which shall furnish them with that instruction, by means of suitable instructors." (Journal of 1825).

Mr. MEADE's expectations with regard to the effect of the change of place, were soon realized, and the Convention confirmed the action of the Trustees by a resolution, "that the Theological School of Virginia be located for the present, in the town of Alexandria."

(*Journal of* 1826.)—"From the present prospects of the School, the Board entertain the hope that it will be prepared to take a respectable rank among the similar institutions established by the Church. The General Seminary of New York has been for some time in successful progress: a Diocesan School in Ohio, is about to commence its operations also, with encouraging prospects of success. Experience has proved that there is ample room and demand for the Theological School of Virginia. By its local convenience, and by its accommodation to the habits and manners of our Southern country, it attracts, without conflicting with the interests of the General Seminary, a patronage and support, which otherwise, would be lost to the cause of the Church. Many of the students now attached to it, would have attended no Seminary, and probably would have been alienated from the Church."

"Although the Diocese of Virginia was the first to move in this enterprise, and after action had been commenced by the General Convention, was very explicit in disavowing opposition to the General Seminary established in New York, yet there was a party in the Church, who insisted that, that 'Seminary was 'not only *General*, but *exclusive of all others*, and who denounced the Virginia School as *schismatic*.' Most threatening letters came to Bishop Moore, calling upon him as a Bishop of the general Church, bound to guard its unity, to interpose and prevent the establishment of the Seminary at Alexandria. Every assurance within the limits of self-respect was given to quiet this morbid sensitiveness, and allay this uncharitable suspicion, but the churchmen of Virginia were too much accustomed to such aspersions to be swerved from their purpose. The fulminations were impotent to arrest the good work on which they had entered. In a little while, the controversy occasioned by the removal of the General Seminary to Connecticut and in connection with the Kohn legacy, led to a more thorough investigation of

Diocesan rights, and settled the question by a formal recognition of the lawfulness of Diocesan Seminaries, and other Dioceses have followed the example of Virginia without let or hindrance.

When the subject was first agitated, Bishop Moore, whose mind had not been particularly directed to it, was not clear as to the judiciousness of the proceeding in Virginia, and his gentle spirit was troubled for a time by the audacious attempts to intimidate him. In one of his addresses to his Convention, he thus alludes to his difficulty: 'When the attempt was first made in the Diocese, my mind was impressed with considerable doubt, as to the utility of the measure, from an apprehension that it might interfere with the General Seminary at the North, but after the most serious reflection, the doubts I have entertained have been removed, and my *mind is now satisfied with a full conviction of the necessity of the undertaking*. The Church in Virginia is now favored with the labors of several of her native sons, who have been educated in her own school, and others are presenting themselves under similar circumstances, who, I trust, will prove equally successful.' In his affecting address at the close of the Convention, to the clergy and laity assembled at the Chancel, he said: 'Seven young men, six of whom are alumni of that Institution—from which we have received so much benefit and advantage,' and 'from which we have reason to expect still greater results'—have this day been admitted to holy orders. Men, from whose labors parishes which have been destitute for many years will be supplied, and the Word of Life communicated to those who have looked to us for spiritual help. Yes! the walls of some of our Churches, in which the voice of the Gospel has not been heard for twenty years, will again resound with the good tidings of salvation, and wake the prayers and praises of our people.' 'My heart vibrates with joy at the glowing prospect presented to our view, and my soul rejoices in the prosperity of our Zion.' " (Journal, 1818.)

In noticing and commending the purpose of the Trustees "to apply to that Convention for their continuance and support in the further prosecution of their design," Bishop Moore observed, "*The individual through whose instrumentality the School was first set in motion*, has consented, should the Convention countenance the undertaking, to engage with all his energies in the work, and to go in person through this State, to raise a fund for the permanent establishment of a Theological School in the Diocese of Virginia."

Mr. MEADE was truly the father of this Seminary. Its prosperity became his business, his study, and his delight. He visited it, often watched and prayed over it with parental supervision — labored for it "in season and out of season," by his pen — in the pulpit, and through the press — absenting himself for months from his loved home, in itinerating through the Diocese, and occasionally elsewhere, to solicit funds for its permanent endowment — always ready with that sound sense and practical wisdom for which he was distinguished, to aid in its management, and finally consenting to add to his other weighty responsibilities, the service of Professor of Pastoral Theology, preparing and publishing at his own expense, a volume of lectures, which became the text book in that department. That he was often harassed and burdened by the difficulties inseparable from such an Institution, no one need be informed; but he was abundantly compensated by its signal success and great and growing usefulness. If his monument should bear no other inscription than "The father of the Theological Seminary of Virginia," it would identify the resting-place of the mortal remains of one, to whose instrumentality in founding and cherishing that Institution the Church at large, and especially the Church in Virginia, owe a debt of gratitude which no epitaph can adequately express.

It might be supposed that those extra parochial services would seriously interfere with the claims of his own special cure, and that his congregation would unavoidably suffer, by his devotion to Institutions of Diocesan, and even more general character. But this was far from being the case. Very satisfactory information on this subject may be derived from the parochial reports made annually to the Convention and entered on the Journal. From this source it appears that the number of communicants in Frederick parish, at the commencement of his ministry, was fifty. In a few years, Winchester, and Wickliffe became independent congregations, and Mr. MEADE's charge was confined to the Stone Chapel. From the last report, just before he was placed in a new relation to the Diocese, it appears, that the communicants at the Chapel alone, exceeded the original number in the whole of what was then Frederick parish:

"FREDERICK PARISH, Frederick County."

"During the past year, the minister has occasionally extended his labors to a distant part of the county, and feels grateful to the great Head of the Church, that those labors have not been altogether in vain. Nine new communicants have been added to the Church during the past year. Fifteen children have been baptized, four of whom were colored. A Sunday School has lately been re-organized in the parish, with some prospects of usefulness. The attendance of the congregation on public worship is punctual, and the observance of the forms of the Church regular and devout: and what is still more gratifying to the minister, there is the encouraging hope, that a goodly number belong to the invisible Church of Christ, and will be found among the Redeemed, in the great day."

WILLIAM MEADE.

In an earlier report he mentions, and for reasons which he states, some of the measures which he had found useful in the Churches to which he then ministered, and which show his thoughtful diligence, in laboring for their improvement. "The state of the congregation is considered good. The attendance on divine worship, with a few exceptions, is very regular. The number of communicants has been increased by the addition of eight, during the past year. The number of baptisms is twelve, one of which is an adult. The Societies of females, formed in the two congregations for the purpose of promoting domestic and foreign missions, and the education of pious young men, promises very effectual and permanent support to these important objects. In the Chapel congregation, very handsome collections have been made for these purposes, for some years past; in the congregation at Winchester, the efforts have but just commenced, though with very flattering prospects of success." "The minister of the parish, encouraged by the success with which it has pleased Heaven to crown his endeavors in this cause, begs leave to state to the Church, the method which, by experience, he has found most effectual, in the hope of inducing his brethren to make trial of the same. Believing that the great duty and need of raising up, and properly educating pious young men for the ministry, and of supplying the destitute parts of our own land, as well as the nations of the heathen world with the ministrations of the Gospel, only requires to be fully and frequently placed before the hearts of Christians, as we do the other duties and doctrines of religion, in order to induce them to take a lively and active interest in the same—he has for some years past, been pursuing the following plan: He has supplied himself with a number of the best religious magazines of the day, which give a full view of all the spiritual wants, as well as religious exertions and charities of the whole Christian world; from these, he has always been able to collect a great variety of most interesting and edifying pieces on all those subjects, which are most dear to every Christian heart, and which, from time to time, he reads to the congregation. In the country congregation, he has for some years been in the habit of having meetings for this purpose at private houses, on some day of the week, where a number of the families most convenient, assemble together. A few hours are spent in prayer, singing suitable hymns, and reading the above mentioned selections. Sometimes the ladies are engaged in some work, which is disposed of for the benefit of the cause; and the younger members of the family are brought in also, and encouraged to take an interest in what is passing. The minister can truly testify for himself, and those of his charge, that these meetings are unusually interesting, and have the effect of drawing the hearts of those present towards the important objects laid before them."

As evidence of which, he states that for some years past, he has, by means of these meetings in the Chapel congregation, "collected about one hundred dollars annually, which for the last two years, had been sent to the General Missionary Society of the Church. At the same time, the communicants of this congregation have been contributing between fifty and an hundred dollars annually to the Education Society of the District of Columbia, besides liberal subscriptions to the Theological Seminary of Virginia. In the Church at Winchester, a female Society for promoting the education of pious young men, and for missionary purposes, has been formed within a few months, and promises to do well. In order to give proper information to the minds of the members, and also to impress proper feelings on their hearts, in regard to these subjects, the minister has occasionally substituted, on Sunday afternoon, the above mentioned extracts in place of the sermon, and has reason to believe that this plan is not only pleasing, but will be improving and profitable." "The minister of the parish has been thus particular, because he thinks the time has arrived, when it behooves every minister to make full trial of his minisrry in this respect, and because, he believes, that there is not a congregation in the Church, from which something may not be obtained from willing hearts, if the subject be properly and frequently presented to them. He is firmly persuaded, that no other plan will produce half the effect, or will long continue in operation; and therefore urges his brethren, to adopt that, which his own experience for many years, has proved to be successful." (Journal 1824.)

Neither now, nor at a later period, when his responsibilities were still more extended and laborious, had he any cause to say, "They made me the keeper of the vineyards, but mine own vineyard have I not kept." It was indeed diligently and judiciously cultivated, and, blessed of the Lord, it brought forth its pleasant fruit in due season.

In 1826, the venerable Bishop White made known to the Convention of the Diocese of Pennsylvania, his desire for an assistant in the Episcopate. For this purpose, a special Convention was called to meet in Philadelphia, the 25th of October.

Both the clergy and the laity were divided in their preference, one part of each order being in favor of the Rev. Byrd Wilson, D.D., who had retired from his distinguished position in the judiciary of the State, to give himself to the work of the Christian ministry, and whose purity of character, and intellectual cultivation, had reflected honor on the profession from which he withdrew, and fitted him for the sacred services of the holy calling to which he was now devoted. Another part of each order had united on the Rev. WILLIAM MEADE, as their choice. This fact was communicated to him in a letter from the Rev. Gregory T. Bedell, D.D., of St. Andrew's Church, Philadelphia:

PHILADELPHIA, Sept. 7th, 1826.

Reverend and Dear Brother:

You have no doubt heard, before this, of the sudden and great change in the mind of our Bishop, in respect to an assistant, and the call of a special Convention, for the purpose of electing such an officer, if it be deemed expedient. It must have gladdened your heart to have noticed for some time past, that the cause of evangelical religion is making rapid progress in this Diocese, and this cause would gain every thing by the delay of this appointment. Of this fact, those of our Brethren, who do not view the subject in the same light in which we do, seem to be perfectly aware, and this will account, in a great measure, for the present unexpected effort to hurry us in the election. By many of the Brethren, Clergy as well as Laity, friendly to the cause of evangelical religion, it was deemed advisable to have a meeting as soon as practicable among themselves, and to consult about the business. This meeting has taken place, and all who could conveniently be assembled, were present, when, after solemn prayer to God for His especial direction, the following resolutions were unanimously adopted. Let it be borne in mind, that the meeting was composed of a majority of those, in our view, favorable to vital piety, and also of those Laymen, whom we believe truly converted unto God. It was resolved,

First, That we will feel ourselves called upon in conscience, to give our votes for that Brother, of whose soundness in the faith we are all persuaded, and who shall have the largest number of votes, at a meeting to be held by our friends on the day previous to the assembling of the Convention.

Second, It is expedient that one of the Brethren now present, visit those of our Brethren in the country who could not be present at this meeting, and confer with them, and that brother Boyd be requested to perform this duty.

Third, That this meeting cordially unite in favor of our Rev. Brother William Meade, of Virginia, and are fully persuaded that he is the person most likely to command the largest number of suffrages for the important office to be filled.

Fourth, That Brothers Allen and Bedell be requested to visit Brother Meade and to confer with him on the business now before this meeting.

Fifth, That the friends of religion generally in the Church, be earnestly requested to pray for this portion of the Lord's vineyard, at the present critical juncture, and that at 6 o'clock on the morning of every Lord's day, private prayer be offered for Divine direction and assistance, and social prayer at such times as shall be most convenient."

It will startle you, no doubt, to hear that upon you has the choice of the Brethren here been fixed; our unhesitating unanimity convinced us that the hand of the Lord was in this thing, and we were constrained to fall down before Him in devout thanksgiving for vouchsafing to us, one heart in this business. We were strengthened and took courage. Our hopes now, Brother, under God, rest upon you — on no other can we, or shall we be so perfectly united. Can you add to the weight upon our hearts, the heavy burden of a refusal to be named? We ask you not for an approval. We ask you only to be willing to leave the matter in the hands of the Master you have served. We ask you only not to forbid us to give you the warm support of more than twenty who are now praying for the prosperity of Zion. We wish you but to be still, and see what the will of the Lord is. We have reason to apprehend that some who think not with us, will seek to gain a refusal from you, and then use it to the injury of our cause. We wish you not to arm our opposers with a weapon against us. Further, we ask nothing. We wait upon God for His direction. My indisposition has prevented the contemplated visit, but in the name of the Committee and of the Brethren generally, who see eye to eye with us,

I sign myself,

Your friend and brother in the Lord,

G. T. BEDELL.

What reply, if any, was returned to this communication, is not known.

A letter of a different character, in relation to the same subject, was received from the Rev. James Montgomery, D. D.:

PHILADELPHIA, Oct. 12, 1826.

Rev. and Dear Sir:

It has been my intention for some time past to write to you, but have postponed the execution of it until I could feel fully persuaded that it was my duty to express to you candidly and explicitly my views in relation to the important subject which is to occupy the approaching Special Convention of this Diocese, and the motives which influence me in opposing the strenuous efforts in your behalf. Ever since it was understood that you were to be the candidate of one side, I have thought it but right to communicate to you the grounds of the stand which I feel myself bound to make against you. To this I feel prompted by candour, and by the deep interest I have long felt and expressed in your character. Be assured, there is no one for whom I cherish a higher regard, and for whose Christian sincerity and singleness of heart, I feel a more profound respect. I speak to you the genuine feelings of my heart, feelings which I have not withheld whenever your character has been the subject of discussion. But, in reference to the *Episcopate*, I must say that I consider your partial and inadequate views of the nature and obligations of the episcopal constitution of the ministry a disqualification. You will remember that we had some conversation on the subject at my house, when you frankly acknowledged that you had not paid much attention to it, and had not read some of the standard writers upon it. I could not but consider you then as very inadequately informed upon points, which in my *conscience*, I hold to be indispensably important —so much so, that I will never give my vote to any one, in whose sentiments on those points, I have not the most implicit confidence. It is upon such grounds that I shall feel it my solemn duty to oppose your nomination, and I want you to be assured that I shall do it without any diminution of the high sense I entertain of your excellence, or of the affectionate regards which I have felt towards you, and with which you will ever be remembered by

Your friend and brother,

JAMES MONTGOMERY.

To this letter Mr. MEADE replied:

Rev. and Dear Brother:

I have just received yours of the 12th inst., and have only one complaint against it, and that is, its too flattering style, which, acting upon the vanity of poor human nature, may do harm. The friendly spirit I truly appreciate, and in the same spirit I now reply. Your communication was by no means unexpected. Such an one, either verbal or epistolary, I calculated upon, in consequence of what had passed between us. When the first intimation reached me that it was proposed to support me for the contemplated appointment, the first thought that rose in my mind was, that yourself was the author of the scheme, and this opinion was expressed to those friends with whom I conversed on the subject, and at the same time my reasons for the supposition were stated. It is because of such an opinion expressed, and reasons given, that I feel it a duty to make this communication, lest some misunderstanding arise.

When we were last together, and in the unreserved interchange of friendly thoughts and feelings, our conversation more than once turned on my views of ecclesiastical polity and church matters generally, when you emphatically declared your conviction, that with my general sentiments on religion, and my mode of reasoning on its doctrines (particularly referring to a sermon I preached for you), I would certainly be brought to what you considered orthodox views of the Church. You further stated that you had a design upon me, and from the manner in which you spoke, the thought was raised within me that you looked forward to the event now in agitation, for you expressed a conviction that such an appointment would infallibly set me right on all points. Such remarks were well calculated to make impression on such a frail being as myself, and that impression was occasionally conveyed to others, though not in a serious way.

You perceive, then, the reason of this letter — lest perchance these things should be remembered and brought against you in the way of reproach for inconsistency, and lest you might suppose they came from myself, in the way of complaint. They were stated by me before I knew of your opposition (for indeed I did not certainly hear of it till your letter came,) and I hope they have not been thought of, or, if thought of, will never be spoken of by any to whom I may have spoken.

But, my good friend, even if you had said the above in the utmost seriousness, and intended them to be understood in the manner they were, I can now give you an honorable acquittal, by stating that though since we were together, I have read more extensively on the aforesaid subject, and though I am, upon every examination into the history of our Church, and of its character, more attracted to it, more convinced of its accordance with Scripture, and its tendency to promote true religion, and banish error from the Christian world, still I cannot *ex animo*, subscribe to some inferences which you and others draw from the doctrines and constitution of the Church, and in which indeed I cannot but think you go both beyond Scripture and the Church. Although, therefore, I think you place an undue emphasis on certain points, yet you act consistently and conscientiously in withholding your vote from one thinking differently, especially when another is proposed whom you think more correct, in your estimate. I will only add that I sincerely pray that all who are engaged in this transaction may be endued with the wisdom which is from above, pure and peaceable, that a spirit of moderation may pervade the whole proceeding, and that God himself may preside in the midst, directing their deliberations to His glory and the welfare of His people. The adversary will be also there, I am sure, to set on fire the tongues and hearts of disputants, from hell, and his agents upon earth will then be ready to exclaim, "*Tantæne animos cœlestibus iræ.*" And even if soft words should be the order of the day, let all beware lest an enemy should say,

"*Mel in ore, verba lactis,*
Fel in corde, fraus in factis."

I have only to add that my wife sends her love to you, and sincerely thanks you for your honest zeal in her cause. My own will be reserved until we meet, and will then be proportioned to your merits and my feelings.

Yours sincerely and affectionately,

WILLIAM MEADE.

Those on each side were active in their endeavors to secure the election of their favorite. The press, correspondence, and personal influence, were plied to the limit of Christian propriety. The excitement pervaded the Diocese. The Church generally participated in the interest, and awaited the result with great solicitude.

When the Convention had assembled, and the clerical vote was taken, it appeared that of the ballots cast, there was a majority of one, in favor of the Rev. Mr. MEADE.—But as there was one of the clergy (the Rev. Byrd Wilson) who, though in attendance at the Convention, neither voted nor was present when the ballots were deposited, it was contended that though the Rev. Mr. MEADE had received a majority of the clerical votes *cast*, yet not having received the votes of a majority of the clergy *in attendance*, no nomination had been made. Such was the decision of the Chair, and divided as the Convention was, that decision could not be reversed. For the same reason it was useless to make another attempt to nominate. From the demonstration made, it might have been safely concluded that the vote was stereotyped, or if not, so slight a change on either side would be decisive, that both deemed it prudent to avoid the experiment, each hoping to gain strength by delay. So the Convention adjourned, without having accomplished the object for which it had assembled.

Whether the decision of the Chair was parliamentary or not—whether the candidate whose course gave occasion for the decision comtemplated such a possibility, and whether, when the hindrance which he caused, became apparent, he ought not to have obviated it by decisive action of his own—are questions not necessary for discussion here. Mr. MEADE would no doubt have proved a blessing to that or any other Diocese over which he might be placed. But for himself—who can estimate the trials to which he must have been subjected if the efforts of his friends had succeeded in effecting his election, and securing his acceptance? God, in His good providence reserved him for more congenial associations, and for a sphere of usefulness for which he was pre-eminently adapted.

With Bishop White himself, and many of those who favored the election of the Rev. Dr. Wilson, Mr. MEADE had always been in most friendly intercourse, and he now felt it to be his duty to attempt to heal the dissensions with which he had been innocently connected, or at least to separate himself entirely from the strife. With this view he visited Philadelphia in November, and after an interview with Bishop White, in which he communicated to him his design, and received his approval, a meeting was arranged, in which each of the opposite sides was to be represented by three of its prominent supporters, to whom the proposal of Mr. MEADE was to be submitted. This meeting was held in Bishop White's study, both he and Mr. MEADE being present. The arrangement proposed by Mr. MEADE was unanimously accepted. The action to which it led, and the result of the effort will appear from the following documents and correspondence:

(CIRCULAR.)

PHILADELPHIA, Nov. 24, 1826.

Sir:

At an interview which took place on the 18th inst., (in the presence of the Rt. Rev. Bishop White, and the Rev. Mr. MEADE, of Virginia) the Rev. Messrs. Kemper, Boyd, Bedell and DeLancey, and Messrs. Binney and Samuel J. Robbins concurred in the expediency of putting the annexed question to the clergy and principal laymen of the Churches, and of meeting on Monday the 18th of December, 1826, at the house of the Bishop, at 7 o'clock, P. M., to communicate their opinions.

The undersigned are prepared to answer the question in the affirmative; and it is understood that those who so answer it, pledge themselves to act in conformity.

You are respectfully requested to transmit your opinion, written under the question, to the Rev. Jackson Kemper, so that it may be received by him on or before the 15th day of December next.

We are, Sir, very respectfully,

Your obedient servants,

JACKSON KEMPER,
GEORGE WELLER,
JOHN C. LOWBER,
CHARLES WHEELER,
JAMES MONTGOMERY,
J. R. INGERSOLL.

HOR. BINNEY.

QUESTION.

Is it expedient not to propose the choice of an assistant Bishop at the next State Convention, nor at any future time, during the life of the present Bishop, without at least six months' previous notice to the clergy and Churches, by the Bishop?

(CIRCULAR.)

Rev. and Dear Sir:

Since the adjournment of the late Special Convention, the subject which then interested us so much, and in relation to which we were so happily united, has assumed a new aspect, under which it becomes our duty to view it, and to decide upon the course hereafter to be pursued. Hitherto, we trust, we have acted according to the will of our Lord Jesus Christ, and with a pure intention to seek and promote His glory. Let us still keep our eye single, continue instant in prayer, and watch the leadings of His providence, nothing doubting that He will favorably regard our sincere endeavors. The change which has taken place ought not to diminish our hopes, or prevent us from using all suitable means for the accomplishment of our ardent wishes. The Church is under the care of its ever-living Head. Its interests are never lost sight of, and its purity will eventually be secured. For a time it may mourn in captivity; the world may lay waste her fair palaces, and trample under foot her sacred enclosures; but the time to favor Zion, yea, the set time will come, when the servants of the Lord will take pleasure in in her stones, and favor the dust thereof.

The Rev. Mr. MEADE, while attending the late General Convention, after the most serious consideration, and having referred the matter to the Lord, made known to some of his friends that he had come to the conclusion, not to accept the office of an Assistant Bishop in this Diocese, under existing circumstances, if it should be offered to him. His reasons for this determination he did not state. It is supposed however, that the present divided state of the Church, and the opposition of the present Bishop, were among the chief.

Under these circumstances, Mr. MEADE considered it a matter of no little importance to the peace and prosperity of the Church, that the choice of a Bishop in this Diocese, should not take place during the lifetime of the present Diocesan; provided that a pledge could be obtained from those on both sides of this interesting question, that the matter should not be brought forward except by mutual consent, and after a sufficient notice.

To deliberate upon this subject, Mr. MEADE requested a few persons on both sides, to meet at the house of Bishop White, on Thursday, 16th inst., when it was agreed by all present, to propose the following inquiry, in order that the opinions of the brethren throughout the State might be ascertained.

PROPOSED INQUIRY.

Whether it is expedient not to propose the choice of an Assistant Bishop at the next State Convention, nor at any time during the lifetime of the present Bishop, without at least six months' previous notice to the clergy and churches by the Bishop?

Messrs. Kemper, Bedell, DeLancey, Binney, Robbins and Boyd concurred in the expediency of putting this question to the clergymen and principal laymen of the churches, and of meeting on Monday, the 18th of December next, at the house of the Bishop, at 7 o'clock, P. M., to communicate their opinions.

It was understood at the meeting that every person answering to the above inquiry in the affirmative, should consider himself pledged not to bring forward the subject himself—to oppose its being brought forward by any other person, and in the event of its being proposed, to refuse to act in reference thereto.

We deem it proper to state the reasons which have operated upon the undersigned to consent to the above inquiry, and to think favorably of the proposed stipulations.

First. We thereby retain the Rev. Mr. MEADE as our candidate, trusting in God that at some future time he may be elected without opposition.

Secondly. We thereby consult the peace of the Church, which could not fail to be interrupted by pressing the matter at the approaching Convention.

Thirdly. An example of forbearance is thereby furnished, which cannot fail to recommend the cause we serve.

Fourthly. An opportunity is afforded to all persons concerned, to become better acquainted with the character of Mr. MEADE, who must be beloved wherever he is known.

Lastly. The election of an Assistant Bishop will thereby be put off, until it may be had, without inferfering witn the wishes of the present Diocesan.

GEORGE BOYD,
G. T. BEDELL,
SAMUEL J. ROBBINS.

PHILADELPHIA, Nov. 26, 1826.

PHILADELPHIA, Dec. 16, 1826.

To Rev. MR. MEADE,

Rev. and Dear Brother:

It has been stated here, and seems to be the impression of some of those who are most deeply interested in the matter, that at the meeting alluded to in the enclosed circular, you made a statement to the following effect: "If the election of an Assistant Bishop for the Diocese of Pennsylvania be agitated by those who voted for *me*, at the late Special Convention, during the life of the present Diocesan, *I will not accept the offer*, *should I be chosen*—but should the subject be brought forward by the other party, I am willing to be taken up as a candidate." Will the fact that I am a member of this Diocese be a sufficient apology for my asking you, whether or not you *did* make such a declaration? If you did not, will it be agreeable to you to state (as far as you may deem it proper), what you *did* say, on that occasion? My best respects to Mrs. M. and to Mr. Nelson's family.

Yours very respectfully,

J. W. Ridgely.

P. S. If you think proper to favor me with a reply, I should be glad to receive it as soon as practicable.

Dec. 23, 1826.

Dear Brother:

Yours of the 18th inst., has just come to hand, and I make not a moment's delay in answering it. You say, "It has been stated here, and seems to be the impression of those most deeply interested in the matter, that at the meeting alluded to in the enclosed circular (that is, a meeting at Bishop White's, on the 16th of November) you made a statement to the following effect,—"if the election of an Assistant Bishop for the Diocese of Pennsylvania, be agitated by those who voted for me at the Special Convention, during the life of the present Diocesan; I will not accept the office should I be chosen. But should the subject be brought forward by the other party, I am willing to be taken up as a candidate." You wish to know if any such statement was made by me, and if not, what was said. Certainly no such statement was made at that meeting. Those who suppose so, must have confounded what I said to several individuals at other times and places to the same effect, with what passed on the occasion alluded to. After having spent some days in Philadelphia, and earnestly endeavored to ascertain the path of duty, it seemed to me, very clear, that, under existing circumstances, the agitation of the subject of an Assistant Bishop any longer, until the state of things had greatly changed, would be very wrong indeed, and that it was incumbent upon me to exert what little influence I might have to prevent it. It seemed to me also, that the proper course to be pursued, was to say to both parties, "Let me advise and entreat you to desist from what must be injurious to religion and the Church." "To my supporters I say, if you will not follow this counsel, then you must choose some other candidate, since I absolutely refuse." To those who were opposed to my election I say, "if you persist in the agitation of the subject—things may be as they were,—I return to that perfect silence hitherto observed, and if any choose to vote for me and succeed, the subject will then be fairly before me for consideration." Such was the languge I used in speaking to brothers Boyd, Bedell, DeLancey, and Montgomery, as well as I remember, some days before the meeting at Bishop White's. I was pleased to discern a disposition in them and others, to adopt the method I recommended, and when we came together at Bishop White's, such an agreement appeared as to the pacific course to be pursued, that no such sentiment or expression as that ascribed to me, was called for. I said but little; nor was much needed—that little was in opposition generally to the office of Assistant Bishop, and especially under existing circumstances, in Pennsylvania. By the expression of the sentiment and resolution above mentioned, to the individuals also specified, and to some few others, I meant to go as far as I could, in condemning either party which should adopt so improper a course. It becomes me, however, in candor to say, that the more I reflected upon the subject, the more unwilling I felt to be at all engaged in it, and the less probability appeared of my being induced under any circumstances to accept the office. So that, if on the evening alluded to, I had been called on to renew the sentiment and declaration, I should have declined from a consciousness that it would be wrong to suffer myself to be a candidate for an office, which nothing could induce me to accept under the circumstances contemplated. It becomes me also, here to allude to a few words which passed between brother Boyd and myself at St. Paul's Church the evening before I left Philadelphia. He said they all agreed as to the propriety of postponing all further proceedings in relation to the election, until a different state of things should arrive, but still wished to look forward to myself, at some future period as the person to fill the office of Bishop. I replied to him that it was a matter for themselves to determine whom they should keep before them, as the object of their wishes and hopes, and that I could not tell what might appear to me the path of duty, at some future day, and under a change of circumstances,—but that I could not encourage that hope, when I saw no probability that I could ever be induced to remove from my present situation, where Providence seemed to have planted me. After all that passed between myself and those friends, who honored me with their suffrages for an office, to which I am too unequal, I feel surprised and sorry to perceive in the printed circular you have sent me, that terms are used, which are calculated to make the impression on those who read it, that I consent to be held up as a candidate, in the hope of more union, and by so consenting, give reason to believe, that I may and will accept the same under more favorable circumstances. I feel it my duty to say, that however pleasing the thought of promoting peace (which was the first that presented itself to my mind) and however powerful the appeal would be to my feelings, should agreement take place in behalf of myself, yet even that does not appear to me to have any thing like the weight of those considerations which oppose your wishes in this behalf and constrain me to spend and be spent in the much humbler sphere which Providence has assigned me. Such being the result of all my prayers and reflections and consultations, and being more and more confirmed every day, I feel it my duty to communicate the same through you to our common friends, with the desire that they will henceforth turn their attention to some one, more worthy of and suitable to the important and difficult station to be filled. If with sincere prayers for direction, and a single eye to the glory of God, you seek the path of duty, it will be made plain before you; and God Himself will send you the Bishop of His own heart. Let me beg you to remember me affectionately to all the brethren. My wife desires to be remembered kindly to you. May you be useful and happy in the gospel ministry, is the prayer of

Your sincere friend and brother,

W. MEADE.

PHILADELPHIA, Dec. 27, 1826.

To Rev. W. MEADE,

Rev. and Dear Brother:

It has fallen to my lot to address you again on the same subject which constituted the interest of a preceding communication. The plan proposed has resulted in no such termination as you desired, as there was an almost universal disinclination among our friends to bind themselves by a pledge, inasmuch as by so doing, they might be constrained to go counter to the evident leadings of God's good providence. We deeply regret that any such course has been pursued, as it has had no small tendency to give dissatisfaction to some of our warmest friends, and has given our opponents much cause of boasting, as if they had overcome us by some master-stroke of policy. As matters now stand, there is every probability that this most important question will be agitated at the next Convention, and we only desire to act as God may evidently appear to direct. If you withdraw from us, we may be defeated, as there is no other individual upon whom there can be so unhesitating an union, and if our counsels are divided, the prospect of having a Bishop such as we desire, will almost be totally precluded. In this case would it be right — would it be consistent with your duty to God and to His Church, to deny us the privilege of placing on you this office? I know your objections, but are they to stand, when the interests of religion are so deeply concerned? What has been gained by the conciliatory course you have so generously desired to pursue? It has been said that your course was dictated by the certainty that opposition would be made to your consecration, and that you did not choose to meet the issue of this question. Can your friends suffer you to rest under this imputation? But, my dear brother, there are still more serious matters weighing on our minds. Since the tremendous annunciation of Bishop Hobart under the signature of J. H. H., in the *Recorder*, we have been led to examine the whole matter with most painful anxiety, and we have concluded that should Bishop Griswold and Bishop Chase be removed by death, that we might now be able to succeed in the consecration of one who viewed the matters of serious religion in the same aspect with ourselves. It is incumbent on us, if possible, to add to the House of Bishops. You cannot but have noticed the hostile attitude of Bishop Hobart, and permit me to ask if you are not willing to help us, as we must fight this battle, or else be held for ages in the same bondage under which the Church has already too much groaned? Will you desert us in this extremity? We put it to your conscience in the sight of God. Would it be possible for you to contemplate the blasted prospects of the Church in this Diocese, while the conviction must ever press upon your mind, that you might have prevented it?

Bishop White would be personally opposed to you — so he would be to any one we should elect — but it must be known to you, that he would be less opposed to you than to any other individual we could name, and the very fact of your election would soon entirely dissipate all his unpleasant feelings. But as a servant of Him who counted no sacrifices dear, so that the salvation of perishing sinners was accomplished, are you not willing to encounter a short, temporary inconvenience? We, who have desired that you should be set over us in the Lord, have not stirred in this business without commending it to the Lord; and the train of providences has been so wonderful, that we cannot but see that our steps have been directed. With the same reliance on our Master, and the same sense of our great responsibility, and with the same confidence in you, our brother, we desire that we may not be disappointed in our hope. Agreeably to the wishes of a large meeting of Clergy and Laity, I have written this letter, and have expressed my feelings strongly, because I do feel most deeply how much the welfare of our Zion is connected with this application. We ask of you, my brother, that you will return one simple answer, and we point you for that answer to the 11th chapter of the Acts of the Apostles, and the 17th verse, last clause.

We think that we have acted in strict accordance with the will of God. We have no wish apart from His good pleasure. If, in a far different sense from that expressed by our present Diocesan, we are compelled to see the death of the child, we shall mourn in sackcloth, until God sees fit to remember Zion in His mercy.

I remain, my dear brother,

Yours, in the Lord,

G. T. Bedell.

A speedy answer, if you please.

Millwood, Jan. 4, 182

Rev. and Dear Brother:

Yesterday's mail brought me your letter of the 27th ult., and I seat myself to comply with your request of a speedy answer. The subject of which it treats, important as it is, having now been so long before my mind, and the occasion of so much prayer, reflection and consultation, I do not require more time for deliberation. The conviction that it is my duty positively to decline the high honor and sacred office you and your friends would put upon me, only gains strength from time and reflection. In your first communication on this subject, your only request was that I would not absolutely refuse to be put in nomination for the contemplated office, but allow my friends to proceed as Providence seemed to direct, and defer any decision on my part until all the circumstances could be placed before me, and the will of God made more evident. Unexpected, unwished for, nay, opposed to all my strongest and dearest ties upon earth as this request was, yet did it appear to myself, and those friends with whom I had an opportunity of consulting, as one which a man solemnly devoted to God could not with propriety refuse, at any rate without much and serious consideration. Under this persuasion, I silently assented to the request, not knowing what might be the will of God, and determined sincerely to seek after it. The more I reflected on the subject, the more were my feelings and judgment opposed to the proposition, yet, so short was the space of time allotted for the decision, so distant the scene of contest, and so ignorant was I of the circumstances transpiring, that I felt it my duty to persevere in the silent course I had adopted, and permit my friends to proceed in the measures they had commenced. It is a matter of great consolation to me that in so doing, I intended to do right, and if I erred, God will bring good out of evil. To show the progressive state of my mind with regard to this interesting subject, it becomes me to mention that as the period of the decision approached, (although I did not feel myself permitted to forbid my nomination after all that had occurred), I became so persuaded in my own mind, that it would not be proper for me to accept the office, if offered to me, that I declared to many of my friends, that unless stronger and more numerous arguments than I had either heard or thought of, were offered to me (and I felt sure none could), I should certainly refuse. Providence happily relieved me from the painful task of contradicting the wishes, and disappointing the zealous efforts of so many known and unknown friends. I felt happy in the belief that I had done what appeared to be duty, and that good would be the permanent result.

It seemed that my duty, however, would not be complete without an attempt to postpone, and by postponing, at least to mitigate an evil which threatened so much mischief to religion and the Church. In this, you inform me I have failed. If I have erred in judgment, as doubtless many suppose, I pray God to avert the evil likely to ensue.

If those who think differently err (as I fear they do), may God either correct their error before it is too late, or bring good out of it to His Church, which not even the gates of Hell, much less the errors of its friends shall destroy. As to the motives to which you say my conduct is ascribed (in withdrawing from this contest), I hope I have learned ere this, to take comfort in the Apostolic words, "It is a small thing for me to be judged of man's judgment. He that judgeth is the Lord." But ought we to be either troubled or surprised at such things, when we are conscious of so much corruption working within, of so many selfish motives ever operating upon us, of so much sin mixing itself with our very best deeds? Let it rather lead us to scrutinize and purify our motives, and endeavour that our actions be singly directed to the glory of God. Let it also produce another most desirable effect, in making us more charitable in our constructions upon the conduct of others. When we are conscious of being influenced by the best motives of which human nature, aided by Divine grace, is capable, and yet men ascribe our conduct to selfishness and cowardice, let us resolve that we will not follow their example, but will banish all unworthy suspicions from our bosoms, and cherish that charity which "hopeth all things," unless indeed the contrary be too evident, and the cause of sacred truth demands the exposure of hypocritical design.

I have thus, my dear brother, through you, opened my heart to those friends who have hitherto endeavored to elevate me to a station for which I think Providence never designed me. In sending this refusal to co-operate with them, I also send my most earnest prayers for Heaven's direction and blessing to them, in the very important work in which they are engaged. May God grant to your prayers, one, who from the best of motives desireth the office of a Bishop, and in the best of ways, shall perform every duty of the office. And may the God of peace be with you, prays

Your sincere friend and brother,

WILLIAM MEADE.

REV. G. T. BEDELL.

PHILADELPHIA, Jan. 5, 1827.

Rev. WILLIAM MEADE.

Rev. and Dear Sir:

The interest you took when last in this city, in promoting an understanding between the Clergy and Laymen who were on opposite sides upon the question of an Assistant Bishop, entitles you to know the result of the measures then adopted on your advice. I therefore take the liberty of enclosing you a printed circular, which, after the meeting at the house of Bishop White, was signed by the Rev. Mr. Kemper, a few other gentlemen and myself (Mr. De Lancey having been absent from the city), and addressed to the Clergy and Laymen in the Diocese, whose opinions at the late Convention had coincided with our own. On the evening of the 18th of December last Mr. Kemper, Mr. DeLancey and myself attended at the Bishop's study, agreeably to appointment. The Rev. Mr. Boyd and Mr. Robbins were also present. The Rev. Mr. Bedell was, it was said, unable to attend by reason of an engagement. It was stated by myself, I believe, that we were prepared to express the sentiments of our friends upon the proposition which had been drawn up at the previous meeting; and it was asked whether Mr. Boyd and Mr. Robbins were ready to do the same. The reply given by one of those gentlemen was, that they were not; that they had received but few answers from those to whom they had addressed a circular upon the subject, but that judging from communications made by five out of eight gentlemen from whom an answer had been received, and from conversations with the Clergy and Laymen in the city, it was not believed that the proposition would be assented to, at all events Mr. Boyd and Mr. Robbins were then unable to express any such assent.

It was asked on our part, whether a further meeting was desired, to give another opportunity for collecting the opinions of gentlemen who had omitted to answer the circular. Mr. Boyd replied that he was willing to attend such a meeting if others wished it, but that he would not say he desired it, and finally, upon both Mr. Boyd and Mr. Robbins saying that they did not believe there would be an assent to the proposition, the meeting was adjourned, with an understanding that if they should perceive any good in another meeting, before the first of the next year, they were to give us notice, and we would again ask the Bishop to receive us in his study. The time has now expired without any such notice.

This, Reverend Sir, is, I believe, an accurate but concise statement of the occurrences at the Bishop's house on the 18th of December.

The circular is sent to you, that you may know in what spirit we communicated with our friends. They promptly answered us in the same spirit; so that we were authorized to express the assent of 21 clergymen and 47 laymen of the Diocese to the proposition which had your approbation, and ultimately that of all the gentlemen convened at the house of Bishop White on the 18th November. What is to be the result of the dissent which I think may be inferred from the last conference, I cannot predict. That we are again to witness a scene, at the recollection of which the friends of the Church ought to weep, I hope is not possible; but as the interview at which the proposition in question was stated and adopted, was, I think, at your suggestion—and as certainly my own part in it was exclusively induced by your declaration, that if this course should not be acceded to by those who professed to be your friends, you would not permit them to use your name in the controversy, I have thought it my duty to make the communication to you. I beg to assure you that no part or vote which I may have taken or given in this matter, is otherwise than perfectly consistent with the sincere personal respect of

Reverend and dear sir,

Your friend and servant,

HOR: BINNEY.

HORACE BINNEY, ESQ., Jan. 11, 1827.

Dear Sir:

Yours of the 5th inst., has just come to hand, and I feel it my duty to acknowledge the same, not merely in courtesy, but to assure you of the continuance of those views and sentiments which influenced my conduct while in Philadelphia, touching the subject of your letter.

It was not without much and serious deliberation, nor without previous conversation with individuals on both sides of the question, that they might consider it well, and not be hastily led into any measure, that I obtained my own consent to be the author of the proposition submitted. Still thinking that it is the measure most likely to conduce to the peace and prosperity of the Church, I regret that it does not prove more universally acceptable. If I have erred and recommended an injudicious course, I pray God to defend His Church against the injurious effects of it. Most sincerely do I hope that all the objections which presented themselves to my mind against the first agitation or renewal of this subject, may prove groundless, and not only the actors in it be justified before God and man, in all that they have done, or shall do, but that the result may be for the glory of God and the good of His Church. The path of duty now appears plain before me. In accordance with a resoultion taken and declared while in Philadelphia, I must now absolutely and entirely withdraw from all future participation in this controversy. In so doing, I only act in compliance with what appears to be my duty from various other considerations. As one solemnly devoted to the service of Almighty God in any station he might assign me, I did not feel myself permitted in the first instance to refuse any consideration of so important, and so unexpected a proposal, lest I might be disregarding the voice of God. I therefore silently consented to be voted for, resolving honestly to seek, and steadily pursue the path of duty. All the reflections of my own mind and all the advice of my best and most judicious friends have conspired to form and fix a resolution, not to accept the office, even if offered under the most flattering circumstances.

Some days before the receipt of your letter, I had communicated this determination to those friends who had honored me with their support for the important office to be filled. In so doing, I have the pleasing consciousness of having endeavored to make my whole conduct proceed from the best motives, of which my corrupt nature is capable, and now commit the event to that Providence who maketh all things work together for good.

In conclusion, allow me to hope that the next Convention in Pennsylvania may be as different from your apprehension, as the last General Convention was from mine, and that the result of both may be most favorable to the cause of true piety throughout our Church.

Accept for yourself, my dear Sir, the assurances of my high esteem and the best wishes for your temporal and eternal welfare.

Your friend and servant,

W. Meade.

(*Ante Communion service*).—During the deep depression of the Church in Virginia, when her extinction was predicted by some, and assumed by others, the rubrical directions connected with the prescribed forms of public service, and various offices set apart in the Book of Common Prayer, were very imperfectly observed. The Church itself had almost disappeared, and it could scarcely be expected that her peculiarities would be maintained in full and symmetrical order. Public services were rare—prayer-books scarce—the liturgy when attempted, of necessity conducted in a fragmentary and feeble way. With the revival of the Church, and the increasing opportunities and facilities for religious services, there was a readiness on the part of ministers and people, to renew the suspended privileges of the Sanctuary by conforming to the order for prayers, as indicated by the rubrics. This was not, at once, equally practicable in all places, but it was generally and honestly essayed. Mr. MEADE relates, that "when in 1811, I took charge of the congregation in Alexandria, so unaccustomed were the people to join in the service, that I tried in vain to introduce the practice, until I fell on the expedient of making the children, who, in large numbers, came weekly to my house to be catechised, go over certain parts of the service and psalms with me, and after having thus trained them, on a certain Sabbath, directed them to respond heartily and loudly in the midst of the grown people. They did their part well, and complete success soon attended the plan."

"The practice of those who engaged in the resuscitation of the Church in Virginia, was, to use the morning service and litany, and to omit the Ante-Communion service except on Communion days. This was introduced among us by the brethren who came from Maryland—the Rev. Dr. Wilmer, Norris, and Lemmon, who doubtless believed that it was according to the design of those who arranged the American Book of Common Prayer. They quoted as authority the declaration and practice of the Rev. Dr. Smith, who, as may be seen in the Journals of our earliest General Conventions, took a leading part in the changes of the Prayer-Book. Dr. Smith, after leaving Philadelphia, settled in Chestertown, Maryland, where it was declared he never used the Ante-Communion service. Dr. Wilmer was one of his successors, and said that it was affirmed also, that Dr. Smith avowed himself to have been the author of one or more of the rubrics, on the meaning and design of which, rested the question of obligation to use the Ante-Communion service every Sabbath, and that he had in view the permission to leave it optional with the minister. I am aware that Bishop White expressed a different opinion, and that his practice was otherwise. Nor do I purpose to discuss the question, or to take sides, but only to state the authority on which the Virginia custom was advocated."

"From the first every minister has been allowed the free exercise of his conscience and judgment in regard to it. For a time Bishop Moore, who had been accustomed to the fuller service in the city of New York, was disposed to urge the same on the clergy of Virginia, but, after some observation and experience, became satisfied that it was best to leave it to the discretion of each minister, and though in his own parish, he always used it, never required the same in his visits to others."

This diversity of practice was by no means peculiar to the clergy of Maryland and Virginia. This was intimated to Bishop Hobart, by Mr. Meade, in a conversation which occurred during the session of the General Convention, in 1823. To the statement that some of his own clergy, chiefly in Western New York, indulged in this practice, he was unwilling to assent. But, at the opening of the General Convention of 1826, he took Mr. Meade aside, and said, that on inquiry he had found that Mr. Meade was correct, and that he "meant to propose something, which, he thought, would satisfy all parties, and produce a happy uniformity throughout the Church."

This plan was soon introduced into the House of Bishops, where it was passed unanimously, and sent to the House of Clerical and Lay Deputies. Here also, with some slight modification, it was adopted and transmitted to the several Dioceses for consideration, preparatory to final action by the next General Convention. The preamble declares, that "the House of Bishops, solicitous to preserve unimpaired the liturgy of the Church, and yet desirous to remove the reasons alleged from the supposed length of the service, for the omission of some of its parts, and particularly for the omission of that part of the Communion office which is commonly called the Ante-Communion, do unanimously propose to the House of Clerical and Lay Deputies the following resolutions":

Resolution 1, provides that the minister shall not be confined to the Psalter as divided, or the selections, but may substitute any other Psalm or Psalms, except on those days on which "proper Psalms are appointed."

Resolution 2, provides that the minister might read only a portion of the lessons, not less than fifteen verses; and on other than Sundays and holy days, when morning and evening daily prayer is used, that he might substitute other portions of the Old and New Testament for the prescribed lessons.

Resolution 3, provides an alternate for the preface to the Confirmation service—the Bishops finding the existing one, is frequently not well suited to the age and character of those who are presented for this holy ordinance.

Resolution 4. To provide against the injurious misapprehension of certain terms in the first collect in the office of Confirmation, proposed to insert the words "in baptism" between "hast vouchsafed" and to "regenerate"—thus identifying baptism and regeneration, and declaring them convertible terms. And then to guard against the error of supposing that the regeneration in baptism, is "the renewing of the Holy Ghost"—it is declared to be a titular kind of regeneration or investment promissory, actual possession to be secured with the terms of the covenant.

Resolution 5, provided for rendering the use of the Ante-Communion service obligatory on all Sundays and other holy days."

At this same Convention, a canon was introduced, designed to render the use of the Ante-Communion as proposed, *immediately obligatory.* As this, if passed, would secure the fifth resolution at once, as a law of the Church, and leave the other parts of the plan to the uncertainty of Diocesan action, and of confirmation by the next General Convention — the movement looked suspicious and awakened painful apprehension in the minds of some — lest it might be a plan under the influence of the whole in prospect, to enact a part forthwith, and then abandon in the future, those provisions of the plan which rendered this particular part passable.

Sometime after the adjournment of the General Convention, the existence of these unpleasant impressions was made known to Bishop Hobart. He promptly addressed the following letter to Francis S. Key, Esq., with a request that he would communicate its contents to Mr. MEADE, adding as a reason for not writing to him, that he did not know his post-office.

NEW YORK, Jan. 30, 1827.

FRANCIS S. KEY, *Esq.:*

Dear Sir:

My friend, Judge Emott, intimated to me some short time since, that he thought you and Mr. MEADE were unpleasantly impressed with the circumstance that the original propositions from the House of Bishops were connected with a canon enforcing the Ante-Communion office; inasmuch as the former propositions would not be definitely acted upon until three years hence, and the latter would go into immediate operation. I ought to mention to you that this canon was not brought forward by me, and though in favor of it, yet as soon as I discovered that it was not regarded as quite fair, by those who omitted it (the ante-communion service), to enjoin its use before they were allowed to abbreviate in other respects, the service, I proposed to the Bishops, that this subject should assume the shape in which it now comes forward. I do assure you, that my object was, to settle the discrepancies which prevail in the use of the liturgy, in a manner suiting all parties; and I was highly gratified by the frank and cordial support which this attempt received from yourself, Mr. MEADE, Mr. Henshaw, and others. If successful, I flattered myself that one principal cause of crimination among us, would be removed, and that the contentions thence resulting, might be settled and prevented. I have been very much surprised, that this matter has not been received in the same spirit which dictated it, and that propositions which do not leave out any one part of the liturgy, but enforcing all, merely give license to shorten two, should be represented as attacks upon the liturgy, which endanger it, when the very object is "to preserve it unimpaired." The license, too, as to lessons in the week, I consider most necessary. Having prayers on Wednesdays and Fridays and Saints' days, I have been forcibly struck then, as well as at Confirmations, with the unsuitableness of the prescribed lessons. So, in the Confirmation office, the present preface has always struck me as insufficient and rather tame, and the expressions in the prayer are liable to be misunderstood, and create serious objections, (I have found, on the part of many,) to receiving the ordinance. The object of the proposed prayer, was not to relinquish the expression of regeneration as applied to baptism, but to guard against the misconstruction that would make this, synonymous with renovation, sanctification, conversion, or any other terms, by which the renewing of the Holy Ghost might be denoted. I can account for those who are satisfied with a state of things in which they think they have sufficient plea for shortening the service as they please, being opposed to propositions which aim at producing uniformity. But I cannot account for the opposition of those who contend for this uniformity. They would prefer, as it seems rigidly enforcing the whole of the service as it now stands (as in the *Charleston Gospel Messenger*, p. 23) by the authority of the Church. But this is not so easy, nor I think so desirable a mode as that which, by a "little legal liberty" seeks peaceably to prevent "license without bounds."

You must not blame the Publishing Committee in New York, with the delay in publishing the Hymns. They were ready for publication in a few weeks after the meeting of the Convention, but the copyright committee in Philadelphia have not yet decided who shall have the copyright. Both these matters should have been entrusted to the same committee. I was much pleased with the unanimity, with which, in the committee, we got through that matter, and think we shall have a very good set of

Hymns. I have been erroneously supposed to be opposed to Hymns. On the contrary, I was in favor of the Hymns set forth in Baltimore in 1808. The only apprehension has been the exclusion of Psalms. The Hymns set forth, exhibit as I conceive, the exercises of the penitent, believing and devout soul.

May I ask you to give to Mr. MEADE the explanations on the first page of this letter, as to the Canon, &c., and to convey to him my best regards. I do not know his post-office, or I would write to him.

I am, Dear Sir,

Very sincerely Yours,

J. H. HOBART.

Mr. Key forwarded this letter to Mr. MEADE, to which he replied:

MILLWOOD, FREDERICK Co., Virginia,
Feb. 10, 1827.

Right Rev. and Dear Sir:

I received last evening a letter from my friend, Mr. Key, enclosing one from yourself, designed for myself as well as him. I should be wanting in common courtesy as well as Christian feeling, not to reply to the message sent to me therein, especially as it was connected with a remark that you would have communicated the same by letter, had you known my direction.

It is indeed true, as stated by your friend Judge Emott, that a very painful impression was made upon me by the manner in which the canon relating to the Ante-Communion service, was introduced. It was the more painful, because so unexpected from what had passed between us, and because it fell upon a heart softened by the blessed assurance, that a spirit of conciliation was to be the ruling spirit of the Convention. I was previously prepared to rejoice in the proposition from the House of Bishops, because the subject had for the last six months occupied my thoughts and engaged my prayers at a throne of grace. I earnestly desired that some method might be devised which might put a stop to dispute, which I have long considered as disgraceful to the Church, and injurious to religion. I had almost come to a conclusion to introduce the subject myself, if no one else would. At any rate, I had determined (as I mentioned to you in New York) to speak of it to Bishop White, as well knowing his sentiments on the subject, and urge him to do this last act of kindness to the Church. The transactions of the Pennsylvania Convention, and some intimations thrown out (as I understood) and indeed Bishop White's addresses would, however, have prevented my taking any steps in such a manner, for reasons sufficiently obvious. It was, however, with equal surprise and pleasure that I found from yourself and Bishop Cross, that other heads and hearts had been engaged in the same cause, and must we not believe under the influence of one Spirit?

This pleasure was indeed for a time suspended, or rather turned into chagrin and disappointment by the canon above mentioned. The readiness with which the House of Bishops consented to make the desired alterations, at once restored me to my first pleasing assurance. It gives me additional pleasure to learn from your letter, that yourself was the author of the proposition. At the very time of receiving your letter, I was engaged in looking over the Psalter and the Lessons (which I had been long intending to do), in order to come to a conclusion in my own mind as to the expediency of the proposed change. The result of my examination as to the Psalms is, a full conviction that the plan of leaving the selection of a Psalm or Psalms to the minister, as Bishop White advocated in the first Conventions of the Church, is the best, and indeed the only good one. I am surprised that I was never struck before with the imperfection of the present mode. Let any one read over the Psalter, and strike out those which are peculiar to David's state of mind under his troubles, and which contain certain passages which, in their present translation, at least are objectionable as a part of public worship; those also which are peculiar to the Jewish nation and to ancient times, and which, by comparison at least, are unsuitable to Christian worship, and he will find the number of Psalms likely to interest and edify a Christian assembly, very much reduced. According to the present plan of division, many of the best Psalms are never read at all. For instance, in perhaps four-fifths of our churches there is no afternoon or night service, and thus one-half of the Psalms are left out as to them, as they only use the morning division. Again, there are some of the divisions which contain the damnatory Psalms, which we dislike to hear, or read in public, and therefore turn to the selections, although there are some of the finest Psalms in the same division, which are of course, lost to the service. This plan also brings the selections, especially one or two of the shorter ones, into too frequent use, to the neglect of other Psalms. Again, two-fifths of the Psalms are read over two or three times each year, and it often happens that these are the most indifferent. Now, surely, any minister might do better than this for himself, and regularly present to the congregation the most interesting and edifying Psalms. Many of them are long enough to answer one at a time, and sometimes two short ones are together, which may be conveniently read. The plan proposed, I therefore think, far to be preferred.

As to the lessons for Sundays, although many of them are sufficiently short, and others could not with propriety be curtailed, yet there are many others which might, not only innocently but usefully, be abbreviated. Witness the chapters in St. John, and I would particularly refer to the 25th of St. Matthew, all of which is appointed to be read at one lesson, but which consists of three distinct parables. The first of these is only thirteen verses, the second and third are about twenty, and are most impressive lessons, whose effect, in my opinion, would be greater when read separately, than when all three are read together. The lessons then would be more like the Epistles and Gospels at present, and I believe more useful and impressive.

So far as they go, I am therefore pleased with the alterations, and can see no harm, but much good from them, but, though I would have been opposed to the general omission of the Litany, as proposed to be allowed in the first instance, yet I should be glad to see such permission granted on Communion days, when the service is so much lengthened, and other excellent prayers added. This is particularly desirable in the country, where all the congregation must stay in, during the administration, or be improperly engaged without the house, waiting for those who commune. I hope such alterations will yet be made, or at least silently be permitted. Upon the whole, I am more and more deeply impressed with the conviction that if some arrangement suitable to the state of the Church, and according with the general sentiment as to the inexpedient length of it, be not made, a heavy guilt will rest upon us. Nothing can prevent it but pride, obstinacy, prejudice and uncharitableness, and if we will bite and devour one another, we shall be consumed one of another, and become a laughing-stock to our enemies that malign us. I have seen the objections in the *Recorder* and the *Gospel Messenger*, and should like to see the defence in the *Christian Journal*. If you can procure a copy of the number which has it, you will confer a favor by sending it to me.

I have said nothing as to the proposed change in the Confirmation service, not having examined the subject as I wish, and intend to do. It seems to be good so far as it goes, but why could not another prayer on the same plan be introduced into the baptismal service, and allowed to be used in place of the one which we must now use, but which I never do without pain, because its plain literal meaning contradicts my belief? I have thus, my dear sir, freely laid open my sentiments to you in relation to the subjects now agitating the Church. I sincerely hope the measure proposed may secure the integrity and uniform observance of the service, and thus remove one fruitful source of much uncharitable feeling amongst us. Although I cannot be a High Churchman, according to your view of the subject, yet I trust my conviction of the excellency and spiritual character of the Episcopal Church, and my attachment to her doctrine, discipline and worship, will ever make me desirous to know and do what will promote her best interests.

Sincerely hoping that you may succeed in infusing a spirit of conciliation into those who usually think and act with you, but now differ from you, and that you may enjoy the satisfaction of seeing much good arise from your exertions, I remain, with the best wishes and prayers,

Yours respectfully and affectionately,

WILLIAM MEADE.

Sickness detained Bishop Moore from the General Convention which adopted the resolutions prepared by Bishop Hobart, and transmitted them to "the several State Conventions, to be acted upon at the next General Convention, according to the 8th article of the Constitution." When a copy reached him, the whole proposal met with his decided condemnation, and in his address to his Convention he fully expressed the fears which he experienced—stating that the Church had prospered in the use of the Liturgy handed down to us by our fathers—that the proposed alterations would destroy uniformity of worship—that it would render the public worship of God as various as the minds of the Clergy—that the old members of the Church would be grieved—that the guards to uniformity being removed, innovations would be multiplied—the people lose their reverence for the services, and the Church receive the most vital injury. The high estimation of the Liturgy expressed by distinguished divines of other denominations was adverted to, and the hope and prayer uttered, that "the Church in Virginia will never be induced to depart from her prescribed forms, but will defend the Liturgy in all its integrity, and prove to the Christian world that we reverence the opinions of our fathers, and are satisfied with that system of doctrine which they venerated, and which they so highly valued."

After this earnest address, the proposed alterations were referred to a select committee. In their report, made the next day, they recommended a series of resolutions, declaring each of the changes to be "uncalled for and inexpedient," and that "the delegation to the next General Convention be instructed to use their exertions to prevent their adoption." This report was then laid upon the table. At the Convention of 1829, it was called up and carefully examined, and discussed in Committee of the Whole. The result was, the recommendation of the following preamble and resolutions, which were adopted by the Convention:

"The Convention of this Diocese having had under long and serious consideration, the proposed alterations in the rubric, relative to the order of our service, and also to the proposed additions to the Confirmation service, is constrained to express its dissent from the proposed changes, believing that they are not likely to effect that most desirable end contemplated by the advocates of the same; therefore,

Resolved, That, zealously attached to the Book of Common Prayer and other offices of our Church, this Convention is desirous that no alterations should take place in the same, at this time."

On these proceedings, and the manner in which the whole plan was disposed of, Mr. MEADE observes: "But for this appeal (Bishop Moore's to the Virginia Convention of 1826), and a tender regard to the feelings of the Bishop, I believe that the Church in Virginia would, by its silence at least, have consented to the action of the General Convention, although none of us were satisfied with some things in it. I took occasion at another Convention (1829), when the delegates to the General Convention were directed to vote against the proposed change, to declare my continued conviction, that the action of the General Convention had been, on the whole, calculated to do good—though I meant not to oppose what had been determined on in the Convention of Virginia. The adoption of the changes would have effected much of what now seems to be desired. Had the change proposed, whereby the meaning of baptismal regeneration was fixed at the lowest point, been adopted, there would have been, by anticipation, a protest of the whole Church against all that flood of error, in relation to the effects of baptism of infants, which has since been brought in by the Tractarian heresy. I would not, however, be understood as endorsing Bishop Hobart's mode of explaining our baptismal service, as I believe another is more consistent with the whole tenor of our service, of which, the hypothetical theory, or the judgment of charity is the way for their true understanding. The lead which Virginia took in opposition to the measure, was followed by some other Conventions; and as it failed to give general satisfaction, Bishop Hobart proposed its withdrawment, and it was accordingly withdrawn, and the obligation to use the Ante-Communion service on every Sabbath, was left to rest on its former doubtful foundation. The Bishops had indeed expressed their opinion that it was obligatory, but, it was, of course, only an opinion, wanting the force of law, as the General Convention had never adopted it, nor did the Bishops claim more for it."

The whole measure seems to have been an ingeniously devised plan of the Bishop of New York, to effect two objects which he had much at heart—uniformity in the use of the Ante-Communion service, and of faith in the matter of baptismal regeneration. The first was to be accomplished by legislative action, rendering that unquestionably binding, which, the proposal itself, recognized as being by some, considered of doubtful obligation. The second was to be effected by an authoritative interpolation of the first Collect of the office of Confirmation, so as to confine *regeneration* to the administration of Baptism, as then, and therein, surely conferred—also defining it as solely "*titular*," and "guarding it against the misconstruction which would make this synonymous with renovation, sanctification, conversion, or any other words by which the agency of the Holy Ghost might be denoted."

The practical objection to the use of the Ante-Communion service on all Sundays and holy days, was, that except when there was communion, it unnecessarily extended the service, which, on ordinary occasions, was said to be long enough without this addition. To conciliate those who took this ground, it was proposed to give to ministers liberty to curtail the Lessons to fifteen verses each, and the

Psalter for the day to a single Psalm, to be selected at will —thus saving time by the abridgment in the Lessons and Psalms, to allow the Ante-Communion to be read, without making the whole service longer than the simple Morning Prayer, as now prescribed. The object, clearly, was not to effect greater uniformity in general, but to secure the use of the Ante-Communion on all Sundays and other holy days; and the policy was to legalize great diversity in the use of the Lessons and Psalter, in consideration of enjoining the use of the Ante-Communion, as proposed. It would not be easy to explain this *partiality*, or to justify the cost at which it was to be gratified.

The proposal to limit and settle by authoritative declaration, the theological import of the term *regeneration*, and bind it to the administration of Baptism, was liable to more serious objection, especially if there be "a more consistent explanation." The one proposed might indeed have proved "a protest, by anticipation, of the whole Church against that flood of error in relation to the effects of infant baptism, which has been since brought in by Tractarian heresy"—but this, on the supposition, would only have been the protest of legalized error against that which was not —an antagonism in which the truth has no interest, and could receive no benefit except in their mutual extermination.

The Church may be satisfied that a measure which strangely numbered among its supporters those who were generally found in opposition to each other, should have been defeated by as extraordinary a concurrence of others, who rarely harmonized in Conventional action.

The Church had not yet attained the state necessary to effect what had been honestly purposed, but happily failed in the form in which it was essayed. Perhaps the only plan which could have succeeded, would have been to leave existing formularies untouched, and as Mr. MEADE elsewhere suggests—to act according to precedent in other cases—prepare an alternate collect to be used after Baptism, consisting of such expressions only as would not be unacceptable to the advocate of either theory on the subject. Where this course has been pursued, it has had the happiest effect in abating dissension, and obviating difficulties experienced by honest minds. Beyond such provision nothing can be judiciously done, till it please God, all see eye to eye, and can conscientiously and intelligently concur in the definite expression of positive truth.

(*Assistant Bishop.*)—In his address to the Convention of 1828, Bishop Moore expressed his earnest desire for the appointment of an assistant in the performance of the duties of the Episcopate.

" Before I conclude, there is one more point to which I think it my duty to call the attention of the Convention, and as a year must necessarily elapse before a final determination of the question can take place, we shall have full time allowed us for reflection and deliberation."

" Although my labors during the past year have been equal to the labors of any preceding twelve months, still from my advanced age, it is impossible for me to calculate on a long continuance of such effort and exertion. It is my wish, provided the Convention think proper, so to alter the Constitution of the Church, as to admit of the consecration of a suffragan or an assistant Bishop in this Diocese. It was proposed several years ago, in consequence of the great extent of the Diocese, to divide it into two parts, in order that the parishes might receive episcopal visitations more frequently, than is prescribed by the canons. As this purpose can be secured by the appointment of a suffragan, or an Assistant Bishop, I would recommend to the Convention,— so to alter the Constitution as to secure the contemplated measure. It is my sincere desire that a Bishop should be appointed during my life, and as such an appointment can now be made with perfect unanimity, it is expedient that it should be done. It will give me pleasure to unite in labor with the man of your choice. It will render me happy in the hour of my departure, to know the individual to whom I am to resign the arduous duties of the Episcopate—to whose care this peaceful, quiet Diocese shall be committed. May the Almighty direct us in all our doings with His most gracious favor, and further us with His continual help."

To this earnest appeal, so reasonable in itself, and most affectionately expressed, the Convention promptly acceded. The committee on the state of the Church, responded to it, in language of filial respect and sympathy, and, to prepare the way for effecting the measure, proposed by their Right Rev. Father in God, recommended "that notice be transmitted to the several vestries of the parishes of this Diocese, that it is proposed to annul and abolish the first sentence of the sixth article of the Constitution, which declares, "there shall be but one Bishop," "to manage its concerns." This resolution was then adopted, and in the ensuing Convention, the constitutional impediment was removed—the votes standing—ayes, 45 ; noes, 17.

The way having been thus opened for further action, Mr. Hugh Nelson offered the following resolution: "that this Convention deem it expedient, considering the age and bodily infirmity of our beloved Bishop, to proceed to the election of an assistant Bishop, who is not to be considered entitled to the succession, but that it shall be the duty and right of the Convention of Virginia, on the demise of our venerable Bishop, to proceed to the election of a principal bishop as a successor to the deceased bishop." When the question was taken on this resolution, it was carried—the vote being—ayes, 50; noes, 13. As there was no division of the question, it is more than probable from the names of those in the negative, that their opposition was not to the measure, but to the restriction upon the succession, and it may be charitably presumed, that not a few of those in the affirmative, so cast their votes, to secure the measure, intending, as was afterwards done, to instruct the delegates to the next General Convention to bring the subject of the election of Assistant Bishops before that Body, to obtain such legislation as would regulate the number of bishops each Diocese may elect—prescribing the circumstances under which a suffragan, assistant, or co-adjutor, may be chosen, and also the duties of such bishops"—expecting that the wisdom of that Body would some how remedy the unaccountable error into which the Convention of Virginia had fallen. Be this as it may, the remedy was in due time provided, and the serious evils otherwise inseparable from the restriction, were thus prevented.

After the adoption of Mr. Nelson's resolution, the Convention having engaged "in secret prayer, to God," proceeded to the election of an assistant bishop. "On counting the ballots, there were found twenty-five votes in favor of the Rev. WILLIAM MEADE, D. D., and two blank ballots, so that the Rev. WILLIAM MEADE, D. D., was declared to be duly nominated and appointed by the Clergy, and then the said appointment was presented to the order of the lay delegates, and upon a ballot being taken by them, there were found in favor of the Rev. WILLIAM MEADE, D. D., thirty-six votes, being the whole number of votes given in—and thereupon the Rev. WILLIAM MEADE, D. D., was declared duly elected."

To the testimonial of the Diocesan Convention, to be transmitted to the General Convention which was soon to assemble, the names of all the members present were affixed, except two of the clergy, probably the two, who, at the election, had cast in blank votes. One of these, the Rev. Adam Empie, D. D., a most estimable and prominent Presbyter of the Diocese, and at the time President of William and Mary College, was influenced in withholding his vote and signature by conscientious doubt as to the entire fitness of Dr. MEADE for the responsible office of a bishop. As a minister, Dr. Empie was warm hearted and evangelical, but perhaps somewhat ultra in his opinions on certain points of external order and ritual observance. Under the influence of these opinions, he felt it incumbent on him to insist upon tests of meetness for the Episcopate, which the standards of the Church do not recognize,—and which, those in authority, have, in no instance avowed, in considering and deciding on the right of a bishop elect, to be consecrated. Dr. Empie had not been long in the Diocese. He knew, however, that Dr. MEADE was the only person spoken or thought of, as assistant bishop, and that when Bishop Moore had recommended the measure, and urged it because then, "such an appointment could be made with perfect unanimity,"—the illusion needed no interpretation. But Dr. Empie had heard, (he does not say from whom,) rumors relative to the Church principles and unrubrical practices of Dr. MEADE, which, if true, would bring him under the ban of the tests, which Dr. Empie had allowed himself to superadd to those prescribed by the Church. To satisfy his own mind, he addressed to Dr. MEADE the following letter of exposition and interrogation:

WILLIAMSBURG, March 23, 1829.

Rev. WILLIAM MEADE,

Rev. and Dear Sir:

My thoughts have lately been turned to the subject of our next Convention, and the election of an Assistant Bishop. The choice of a Bishop, always important, is peculiarly so in the present divided state of our Church. If, under God, anything can save her from divisions and schism, it is the House of Bishops. But that House cannot possibly effect this unless they are unanimous in their councils and their measures, and the only possible way of completely securing this, is by unanimity of sentiment upon all the important points on which Churchmen are unfortunately divided. As the members of the Church, therefore, value her unity, her peace and her prosperity, they are bound to elevate to the Episcopate those only who will harmonize with the existing Bishops in their leading sentiments and measures.

As to myself, I hold that the primary, essential and indispensable qualifications of a Bishop are deep piety, fervent zeal, a good fund of theological knowledge, much religious experience, and a deeply evangelical spirit, connected with evangelical views and principles, not in the Party, but in the Scripture sense of these terms. And in the next place, though of secondary importance, yet I hold it to be an essential prerequisite in a candidate for the mitre, that he should harmonize with our present Bishops on all those important points in which diversity of sentiment might endanger the peace, the union and the prosperity of the Church,—and this I hold to be essential, not merely as a matter of prudence, but on the ground of revealed obligation.

I am not a Party man, neither am I ultra. I believe myself to be, in the fullest sense of the term, strictly evangelical, and at the same time I call myself a High Churchman, and I hesitate not both to approve, and to condemn some things, both in the high and low church party. But I cannot, with a clear conscience, vote for or recommend to that sacred and responsible office, any man who does not cordially hold to, and who will not faithfully maintain all the distinguishing peculiarities of our Church. For this would be, to surrender the sacred deposite into the hands of one, whose principles would naturally lead him to betray it. I am not so rigid as to allow no latitude of interpretation, and no diversity of sentiment, upon difficult and disputed points — but we cannot be called Churchmen unless we agree in the following particulars: A ministry of three orders is of Divine, or at least of Apostolic appointment; none but Bishops have authority to ordain, and therefore Lay and Presbyterial ordination cannot be Scriptural or valid, though God, no doubt, will always accept the religious services of all who serve Him in the best manner they know how. Whether forms of prayer be, or be not of Divine appointment, as they are established and required by the Church, we are in duty bound to use them according to her requirements, nor can we go contrary to the express provisions of Rubrics or Canons, without incurring the guilt of breaking our ordination vows and violating laws both divine and human. Necessity, of course, will justify a departure from rubrical or canonical requirements, but mere motives of expediency afford not the slightest justification, and that conscience must be morbidly diseased, which sees no moral obligation in every part of our ordination vows. The only possible justification for rubrical and canonical irregularities is, in the case of those who, at the time of their ordination vow, did not think these irregularities excluded by that vow, and who, through the inadvertence of the ordaining Bishop, were suffered to promise conformity and obedience in their own sense. From what our laws require, there is no exemption, except through the medium of our general ecclesiastical legislature. Though we are at liberty to use our influence to alter existing laws and usages by legislative enactments, yet we are not at liberty to destroy the peace of the Church, or to carry our point by means of disunion and schism. What we cannot effect short of a dissolution of our ecclesiastical union, we must be contented not to effect at all. Besides, a Bishop ought not to stand pledged to any Party, or be ready to go any lengths that their unbridled zeal may carry him, but be determined resolutely to use all the means in his power, either to prevent or punish all irregularities or infractions of the laws. Lastly, though some Churchmen may persuade themselves that it is not necessary to use the Ante-Communion service every Lord's day, yet I think it necessary for various reasons, that every Bishop should use it, and require all whom he ordains to use it regularly, and I think further, that he should be strenuous for the integrity of the Church, and the House of Bishops, and faithfully oppose everything that might lead to schism. For any one prepared to go full lengths with the leaders of the Low Church Party, I cannot support, and I think no true friend of the Church can, or ought to support. As to other disputed points not involved in the above remarks, inasmuch as they do not necessarily compromise any of the essential principles of our Church, nor put in jeopardy the integrity of our American Zion, I leave them to the conscience of every individual.

Thus, my dear sir, I have freely stated to you my views, and told you what qualifications I require in the individual to whom I give my suffrage for the Episcopate. In these views, this decision and this communication, I am governed purely by a sense of duty to God and the Church You are held up as a candidate for the Bishopric. I wish to vote for you, if my conscience can be satisfied upon the preceding points, and I thus unceremoniously ask the expression of your present views and future intentions, because the subject is all important, and because I hear it said from various quarters, "Mr. M. is lowest of the Low Church — he observes neither rubrics nor canons — he believes Presbyterial ordination as valid and Scriptural as Episcopal — he is a Party man, and pledged directly or indirectly to the support of Party principles and measures."

May the Great Head of the Church direct, overrule and prosper us in all things, to the glory of His name and the welfare of His Church and people.

Respectfully and affectionately,
Your friend and brother,
A. Empie.

To Rev. Dr. Empie,
Reverend and Dear Sir:

Your letter of the 23rd ultimo, has been duly received, and seriously considered. High and holy indeed is the office of Bishop in the Church of Christ. Solemn and fearful should be every step taken by those who would conduct any one to that office. Modest, silent, delicate, backward, and scrupulous in the whole transaction, should be that man whom his brethren and friends would appoint to such a station. Every thing having the least appearance of promoting himself, such as courting the favor of others, boasting a great zeal for the Church, is odious, and should be carefully avoided. If the general tenor of his life, and his well known and established sentiments, are not sufficient to recommend him, no profession or promise made for the occasion, ought to avail. Neither should any one throw a temptation in the way of such person, to recommend himself by a favorable exposition of his opinions, and by fair promises of what he is to do. In this view of the subject, my dear sir, I feel a very serious objection to your letter, and a reluctance to make answer to it. The more modest and virtuous among our citizens, deeply lament the course pursued by our candidates for civil offices, who, presenting themselves before the people for public favor, subject themselves to be questioned and examined, and are tempted to commend their principles and character, by vain boasting and all the arts of acquiring popularity. I trust, however, that the sacred office of Bishop will never be thus secularized, or degraded, but that the wishes and entreaties of friends, grounded on personal acquaintance and authentic information, and not the ambitious desires of aspiring individuals, will bring them forward for this most holy office. Reflect for a moment on the mode you have adopted, and read over your letter, and then say if it be not objectionable. You say that I am held up as a candidate for this office, and that you wish to vote for me, if you can do it conscientiously, and declare that you will not, unless I hold certain principles which you lay down, and will pursue a certain course which you point out. What a temptation here is to commend myself, to make professions and promises, and thus to gain your vote, which is hung up as a lure before me. Only set down and frame an answer to your letter, which shall be satisfactory to yourself, and see if it would not look very like one soliciting your vote, one, which, at least in this suspicious and uncharitable world, would be charged with such intentions.

If there were no other method of ascertaining the sentiments and habits of the proposed candidate, if he were one of a close and reserved character, or but lately come among us, or lived at a distance, some excuse might be found in such circumstances, for drawing forth his real sentiments in the way you have adopted. But surely none of these circumstances occur in the present case. The person proposed was born, baptized, educated, confirmed, and ordained in the State of Virginia and in the Episcopal Church. This has been the scene of his ministerial labors for more than eighteen years — the State is filled with his friends, acquaintances, relations and brethren, with whom he is on terms of unreserved communication. Moreover the Bishop of the State, under whose government he has lived for fifteen or sixteen years, is well known to you. From all these sources it were surely practicable to collect evidences, to enable you to form your opinion and determination. Upon reflection, I am sure you will perceive the greater propriety of such a method, however honest and upright your intentions, while adopting the one you have chosen.

I had thought indeed of making no other reply to your letter than the above objections, and a reference to the sources mentioned, but upon further reflection, there are some points in your letter, which can be answered, without subjecting me to the temptation and imputation alluded to. You lay down certain principles or rules which must be embraced and obeyed by him who shall be deemed worthy to receive your vote and be elevated to the Episcopate. Now if there be any of those principles or rules, which I do not assent to, it becomes me in candor to declare them, so that my silence may not leave you in any doubt, as to the proper course of action. Now some of the indispensable requisites you mention, I have not.

1st. You lay it down as a principle that the only way of preserving the peace and promoting the prosperity of the Church, is by maintaining unanimity of sentiment among the Bishops on all the important points on which Churchmen are unfortunately divided. You hold it to be an essential prerequisite in a candidate for the mitre, that he harmonize with the Bishops on these points. Peace and unity are indeed most desirable things among all Christians, especially among ministers and Bishops, but, as experience proves, very difficult to be obtained, and sad have been the effects of adopting wrong methods for ensuring them. The Romish Church labored long and hard at this, endeavoring according to the doctrine of its own infallibility, to bring the minds and conduct of men to the one faith and practice. As to its success I need not tell you. The Church of England, from which we derive ours, nobly protested against the doctrine of infallibility, asserted freedom of thought and inquiry, and erected the Scripture as the standard of truth, and not the Pope, his Cardinals and councils. Our fathers, of enlightened minds and enlarged hearts, laid a broad foundation on which private Christians, Ministers and Bishops, differing on points which had divided the Church, might stand together, stand upright and fearless, nor should any attempt to force others from the stand because in certain points they differed. This is one of those features in the Church of England and America which has ever recommended it most strongly to the minds of the most judicious, moderate and humble. In this it surpasses all others. If it had required that unanimity of senti ment which you demand for the House of Bishops, I appeal to your candour, exercising itself upon the knowledge you possess of ecclesiastical history, would she, in all human probabili ty, have been the blessing to mankind she has been? Would she have conciliated so many enemies, and been such an example of unity and peace? Warmed by true charity and guided by discretion, she opened her arms to receive Calvinists and Arminians, High Churchmen and Low Churchmen, and bid them bury and forget their differences in her peaceful bosom. Accordingly we find in every period of the Church some of her most burning and shining lights, laymen, deacons, priests and bishops have ranked under these different parties or denominations. But you would alter this long-established character, and admit none to the order of Bishops at least, who were not of the same way of thinking on all these points which divide Churchmen, with the present House of Bishops. Think, I pray you, my dear brother, upon this doctrine, and see how it at once closes the door against any improvements, no matter how much needed. The House of Bishops, not being infallible, may err in some of their views and councils. If none must be admitted but those who think with them, error may thus be perpetuated. As well let them fill up their own vacancies, and choose more whenever wanted, if none be admitted who differ from them in points deemed important. This is really interfering too much with the right of all men to draw their opinions from the Word of God. A whole Diocese may differ in some points deemed important in your opinion, from the majority of the House of Bishops, and may choose a man to be their Bishop who thinks with them — and shall they be denied their choice because he does not accord in sentiment with the House of Bishops in disputed points? Our general constitution not only does not sanction this doctrine, but has provided against it, by requiring the consent of only three of the Bishops to the consecration of a Bishop.

Unquestionably, the trial of a man proposed to the office of Bishop should be his conformity in life and doctrine, first, to the Word of God, and next, to the articles and regulations of the Church, not to the opinions of the existing Bishops. So far from this being absolutely necessary to the peace of the Church, that every effort must be directed for its accomplishment, I am firmly convinced, and declared the same in the last General Convention, that the greatest danger to which the peace of the Church in these United States is liable, arises from the over-anxious desire of some to bring our ministers into one way of thinking and acting, and the attempt to do it by measures which cannot be justified by the mild and tolerant spirit of our Church. I will still lift up my warning voice to our High Church brethren, and say to them, "beware."

You next proceed in your letter to lay down certain principles, of which you say, "We cannot be called Churchmen except we agree in the following principles." The first of them is, "that the three orders are of divine, or at least apostolical appointment — none but Bishops have a right to ordain, and therefore Lay and Presbyterial ordination cannot be scriptural or valid." Now, as to this first principle, the Bishops are not all agreed. Bishop White, for instance, the Presiding Bishop, refuses to go thus far, and maintains that the Church has nowhere asserted the invalidity of other ordinations, that she "contents herself with asserting the apostolic origin of our own, without undertaking to condemn others." I believe there are one or more who will not go all lengths with you — are these disorganizers? I have, on several occasions read over the argument in favor of Episcopacy, and ever concluded with entire satisfaction in the words of the consecration service, that "to those diligently reading the Scriptures and the Holy Fathers, it evidently appears that from the Apostles' times there have been these three orders of ministers." More than this, our Church requires not even its Bishops to believe, and he who would demand more may be conscientious, may be scriptural, but he has gone beyond the Church, he has departed from the spirit of the Episcopal Church of England and America. He is adding to the demands she makes of her ministers. Look through our ordination and consecration services, and our Articles, and see if you can find such. Whether God did positively ordain this form of church government as essential to the existence of a Church—what deviations from it would render ordination invalid—are points about which the most wise, learned, pious and devoted Bishops and other ministers have certainly differed, and I think it venturing very far to say that none must any longer differ, all must consent to be High Churchmen on this point, or be no Churchmen at all. I would that all embraced what I believe to have been the Apostolic form. With none other would I be satisfied myself, but I dare not say God hath ever in this point rejected those whom He hath accepted and so highly blessed in others. This is as far as I can go, which leaves me far behind the goal you have erected. I have, however, the consolation of knowing that I herein agree with a noble company of Bishops and other ministers, whose labors in the Gospel, and whose zealous attachment to the Church, has never been questioned, and whom I could only hope to follow at a great distance behind.

Another demand you make is, that he who receives your vote should not only use the Ante-Communion service himself, but require it of all whom he ordains, to do the same. As this subject is now before the Church, and will probably be determined in some way at the next General Convention, I might very easily dispose of it by saying, that whatever the Church ordains will be binding upon me—but, as I set out with the determination to refuse my assent to any demands which you do not make in accordance with my views, I should say that were I now a Bishop, and called on to ordain, I would not feel bound to insist upon the observance of this rule, more than of some others which are neglected—as, for instance, the rubric as to public baptism—nor indeed so much, because the obligation of this is, I believe, sincerely questioned by some—that of the other, by none.

And now, my dear sir, as to all the other parts of your letter which seem to be written as concerning some lawless person who feared not God, nor regarded man, who was fit "for treasons, stratagems and spoils," who was indifferent to the peculiarities of the Church, who disregarded rubrics and canons, set at nought ordination vows, was pledged to a party, and ready to go all lengths with it, I must refer you to some other source for the confirmation or fabrication of the reports which come to you from various quarters. As to my love of peace, and my independence, and all those things which 'tis so easy to boast of, but not so easy to practice, you will excuse any professions or promises. Perhaps, however we may both be spared any trouble on the subject, as the Church has not yet decided on having an Assistant, and many circumstances may arise to save it from the calamity of a Low Church Bishop.

I beg you will believe me when I say, that however much I may have dissented from your opinions and condemned your rules, I am very far from being offended at the plainness with which they have been declared, and hope that you will receive this answer in the same spirit of brotherly kindness in which, I can assure you, it is written. With best wishes and prayers, I remain

Your friend and brother in the Lord,

April 3, 1829. W. MEADE.

WILLIAMSBURG, April.

To Rev. WILLIAM MEADE,

Rev. and Dear Sir:

Your favor postmarked 5th inst., has just come to hand, and though I wrote with a view to information, not controversy, I feel it due to myself to make a few remarks in reply, while I sincerely thank you for the candor with which you have expressed your sentiments. I was indeed desirous of knowing those sentiments, but rest assured, my letter never would have been penned if I had not thought it probable, from conversations with you last Spring, that your sentiments coincided very nearly with my own. And so strong did this probability appear to me, that I refused to credit several things said of you, and expected soon, by means of your reply to my letter, to have it in my power to refute them in your own language. This, in connection with what I said in my letter, gives you fully my *reasons* for writing to you.

Had I known, or had I possessed the means of knowing, what I now do, I should not have troubled you with my inquiries, or subjected you to the "temptation" of which you complain. Those with whom I communicated, either barely expressed their *opinions*, instead of their *convictions*, or alleged what I would not credit, or stated that they did not certainly know your present sentiments, inasmuch as they believed your opinions had undergone some change I am a stranger here, my dear sir, nor can I be presumed to know, what may be very well known to the members of the Diocese at large, nor can you expect me as a Christian, to govern my decisions or my conduct in so important an affair as that of the Episcopate, by the mere opinions or contradictory assertions of others. This was the *difficulty*, and these the *reasons*, that led me to address you, and but for these reasons, as stated in the preceding section, the *insignificancy* of my solitary vote would have bound me to silence. For my vote and influence are, in this Diocese, too insignificant to deserve your attention.

Here, however, I must remark, that I do not agree with you in your views upon this point. You object to my inquiries as involving a "*temptation*" and a "*threat*," and as calculated to ensnare the virtue of the candidate for civil and ecclesiastical offices. I hold it to be the *duty* of such candidates to make their sentiments fully known. I hold it to be not only the privilege, but the duty, of their supporters to demand an explicit avowal of those sentiments in all vital points, and I hold that no one can answer it to his conscience or his God, if he elevates to an important office, an individual of whose views and principles he is not well assured. Unless it can be proved that constituents are at liberty to act the part of traitors to their own duties, and interests and consciences, the right of instructing those whom they employ as their agents, is unquestionable.

As to my "indispensable requisites" for the Episcopate, you misunderstand me. I did not say that the candidate for the mitre *must* harmonize with the House of Bishops on *all* the important points on which Churchmen are divided, but "all those on which diversity of sentiments might endanger the peace, the union and the prosperity of the Church" (see second section of my letter). My reason, too, for making them *indispensable*, is not, as you state, because it is necessary to think as the Bishops do, but because Scripture requires it. I place it on the ground of "revealed obligation." Nor hastily do I, as your letter supposes, place among my indispensable requisites, all the points in contest between High and Low Church. I propose not to exclude from the Episcopate either Calvinists or Armenians, High or Low Churchmen. I leave to the conscience of every individual, every disputed point except those I specify; and those I insist on, because required by Scripture or by the Church, and essential to her prosperity and her integrity. These, too, I aver the Church has never compromised. These she has always made indispensable, nor can she possibly do otherwise without betraying her trust, and I therefore neither exalt the Bishops, nor abridge the right of private judgment farther than Scripture and the Church, absolutely require. All that the Church has left indifferent, open or undecided, I still leave so. This is my answer to your second argument.

You say farther, in support of your views, that our constitution requires for a consecration the consent of only three Bishops. By looking to the 6th Canon of 1820, you will find this to be a mistake, and though there is danger from rigorously exacting uniformity in minor points, there is still greater danger from compromising the essential principles of our Church.

To my position, "none but Bishops have a right to ordain—all other ordination, therefore, is invalid," you object the opinion of Bishop White—that the Church has not asserted the invalidity of other ordinations, and that she requires us only to believe that our ministry is Apostolical. I have no wish to enter into controversy, and therefore briefly observe in passing, that by the House of Bishops I mean a majority of its members, not the opinion of one or two; that, if my memory serves me, you mistake the opinion of Bishop White. He does not admit the validity of Presbyterial ordination in *general*, but only in case of emergency, where no other could be had. About this we need not dispute, for it is irrelevant to the subject, and necessity knows no law. That, if the Church does not by her words, she does by her actions, assert the invalidity of Presbyterial ordination, for she always re-ordains those who come from churches that have not Episcopal ordination ; and that, in requiring us to believe our ministry Apostolical, she makes that ministry, to the exclusion of all others, binding upon our consciences, just as much as the Christian Sabbath, Infant Baptism, and the New Testament Canon, all of which stand on Apostolic authority.

You argue further, that because some learned and pious men have held different views on the subject of Episcopacy from those which I expressed, therefore mine are untenable. Answer: I support it as the doctrine of Scripture, of primitive Christianity, of the Church, and of a large majority of her standard writers. The fact of a few having dissented from this doctrine, is no proof that it is not true, for exceptions only prove the general rule. If a few learned and pious dissentients are sufficient to disprove a doctrine, then no doctrine of our religion, however vital, is safe. As I should deny him to be a Christian who did not believe the Divinity of Christ, so, my dear brother (and you will, I trust, pardon this honest avowal of my opinion), I cannot in conscience admit him to be a Churchman who does not hold to the exclusive validity of Episcopal ordination, for "*Ecclesia in Episcopo*" is almost an article of primitive faith.

As to those parts of my letter which you say "seem to be written to some lawless person," you do me injustice in ascribing them to me as my sentiments, for I mentioned them merely as reports, and as a reason why I asked from you a statement of your views. Though I had not believed one syllable of them, I conceive they would still have justified me in the course I have taken. For no honest man is, or ought to be, afraid of avowing his sentiments.

"The calamity of a Low Church Bishop"—Low and High Church, my dear sir, are words used with much latitude. There are some Low Churchmen to whose views I have no objection, and there are both Low and High Churchmen whose elevation to the Episcopate I should regard as a "calamity."

In conclusion, permit me to remark that you will do me an act of injustice, if you ascribe this correspondence to the importance I attach to my own vote or opinions. I am conscious of no motive but a sense of duty to the Church, and its Divine Head. I knew very well before I wrote, that should I even withhold my vote, I should stand almost, or quite alone, in the opposition.

With every sentiment of respect and affection, I am, Rev. and Dear Sir,

Your friend and brother in Christ,

A. EMPIE.

April 20, 1829.

Rev. ADAM EMPIE,

Rev. and Dear Brother :

In your last, which has just come to hand, there is one sentence which, in justice to myself, I must object to. It is in these words: "You argue further that because some learned and pious men have held different views on the subject of Episcopacy from those which I have expressed, therefore mine is untenable." Surely, my dear brother, you cannot find such false reasoning as this, in my letter, wherein I object so decidedly to raising up any human tribunal, as the infallible standard and judge of truth. I would not dare to pronounce any one certainly and undoubtedly wrong in a matter of this kind, merely because the great majority of the wise and pious were against him, much less if only some, or a few as you suppose were against him. So far as it is permitted to resort to human testimony and opinion, I should acknowledge the duty of bowing to the sentiments of the greater number of the wise and pious, supposing them, and those differing from them, to be equal as to the qualifications for deciding wisely and candidly. If you will reperuse my letter, you will discover no such reasoning as that contained in the above quotation. My argument is this: that because some of the most wise and pious of the Bishops, Priests, and Deacons of the Church of England and America, holding sentiments differing from yours, have, under the liberal constitution of that Church, been freely admitted to their several offices, and because there is nothing in Articles, or Ordination, or Consecration services, which demand such sentiments of candidates, therefore you are wrong in establishing a new rule of admission, and are not justified in stigmatizing as no Churchmen, those who conscientiously believe, and zealously support, what the Church plainly requires, but are unable to go beyond this. In this opinion I am more and more confirmed. The practice of the Church has ever been according to this, and she could never have otherwise designed Her reordination of ministers coming from other churches, is, on many accounts, proper and consistent, but does not, in my opinion, require of us a positive belief that their previous ordination was certainly invalid. Such a reordination is proper, because many of our churches believe that their former ordination was unsound, because others believe that it was doubtful, others that it is at any rate safest and better to adhere to the primitive plan, and because the peculiarities of our Church require a solemn promise of conformity thereto. On these accounts it was proper to reordain, but still it does not follow that we must all necessarily believe the previous ordination to be null and void in the sight of God, in order to be sincere Episcopalians. Bishop Hoadly, as quoted by Bishop White, denies that such a construction should be put upon the act of reordination. It appears to me that our Church very wisely forbears either to assert or deny the validity of other ordinations, but contents herself with asserting that ours is Apostolic, and requires us to love and support it as such. Bishop White asserts this, and quotes Bishop Hoadly in answer to Dr. Calamy. The letter objects to the Church that in its ordinal it maintained the divine appointment of the three orders, and urged this as a reason for non-conformity. The Bishop replies that the service pronounces no such thing. "There is some difference," he says, "between these two sentences, 'Bishops, Priests and Deacons are three distinct orders in the Church by divine appointment;' and 'from the Apostolic times there have been Bishops, Priests and Deacons.'" "It appears to me our Church wisely stops here, and leaves it to her members to draw their own conclusions from the fact, thus affirmed. Accordingly, some have conscientiously inferred that God must have appointed Episcopacy, as the Jewish Priesthood, to be invariably and forever received, so that deviation from it, is separation from the true Church of Christ. Others, not finding the same positive institution or command, dare not place it on the same high ground, and exclude those who adopt a different form; at the same time from its analogy to the Jewish Priesthood, and the general resemblance between the two systems, from the example of the Apostles and the practice of the primitive Church, and the many excellencies of the mode, feel bound to adhere to it, and would have all others to adopt the same.

Such are evidently Bishop White's sentiments, and in his pamphlet he declares his belief that they were the sentiments of the great body of Episcopalians in America, in which respect, he adds "they have in their favor unquestionably, the sense of the Church of England," and as he believes, "the opinions of the most distinguished prelates for piety, virtue and abilities." But I must desist, or we shall certainly get into controversy, which I believe, neither of us have any wish to do. It was merely to correct your great error, in imputing such false reasoning as I stated in the beginning of my letter, that I took up my pen. What has followed seemed unavoidably to grow out of that conviction. In conclusion, allow me to assure you that the thought "of your writing under sense of great self-importance," never entered my mind, and let me beg you on the other hand, not to suppose that I have regarded you as being so insignificant as you represent yourself to be. I doubt not that you have acted under a sense of duty. I will only add, that should I ever be called to that high station, for which you think my principles unfit me, I shall feel thankful to any brother who would convince me of such unfitness, and, except my errors can be corrected, will most certainly decline an office, of which on many other accounts I feel myself most unworthy.

William and Mary College, May 2, 1829.

To Rev. William Meade, D. D.

My dear brother Meade, I do not write from the vain desire of having the last word, for say what you will in answer to this, I shall not reply.

I only resume my pen to communicate a few additional remarks, for which my former letter left no room; and while I am writing, I may as well say a word or two on yours of the 20th ult., just received.

I have said that two of the prerequisite qualifications of a Bishop are, that he should believe the exclusive validity of Episcopal ordination, or if you please, the invalidity of Lay and Presbyterial ordination, and that he should feel it his duty to require the use of the Ante-Communion service — you say "the Church does not require" these qualifications, and that I am establishing "a new rule of admission," to the Episcopate — and the proof you bring is, that some learned and pious men have been made Bishops though they were destitute of these qualifications. Now, my dear sir, I am disposed to call this in question. Can you prove it to be a fact? Name the men in England, or in this country, who have been made Bishops, while those who elected and consecrated them, knew them to be at that time, destitute of the above named requisites. It has, indeed, afterwards appeared, that some were destitute of one or the other of these requisites, but so also has it afterwards appeared that some were Unitarians. Can we therefore, from their sentiments, argue with certainty the sentiments of the Church? Does it follow that they were deliberately admitted, knowing them to entertain these opinions?

Bishop White's "Care of the Episcopal Churches," was written at a time of great and difficult emergency. I do not think it safe to apply his arguments and facts to ordinary cases. As to myself, I cannot admit either all his arguments or positions. He seems at that time to have imbibed much of the spirit and principles of Bishop Hoadly and Stillingfleets Ireaicum; and I take the liberty, therefore, of referring you for what I think the views of the Church on these points, to Laws' three letters to the Bishop of Bangor.

In your last letter, you seemed to me to make Episcopal ordination necessary in our Church, only because it is the established usage and required by our Church. This likewise savors of Bishop Hoadly's notions. But I hold it to be utterly subversive of Episcopacy. It partakes of the nature of Erastianism. It makes Episcopacy binding on the ground of expediency, not of duty. It refers it to the authority of usage of the Church or of the State, instead of fixing it on its only proper base, the authority of God. It must either stand on revelation, or on expediency — on the will of God or the will of man. If on the will of God, it is always and exclusively binding, if on expediency, Lay ordination among Independents and Presbyterial ordination in Scotland are as binding and sufficient, as Episcopal ordination is in England. This converts the ministry into a nose of wax.

The argument founded upon the opinions and conduct of some, in the troublous times of the English Church, I do not think fair or conclusive, any more than that founded upon Bishop White's Essay. They were forced by the emergency of the times into opinions, concessions, and measures, some of which, under different circumstances, they themselves would not justify and which, at all events we cannot approve as consistent, and scriptural.

May the Great Head of the Church direct, overrule and bless us in all we say and do, in such a manner as will best promote the glory of His name, and the welfare of His Church and people.

I am, reverend and dear sir, with sentiments of sincere esteem and affection,

Your friend and brother,

A. Empie.

Dr. Empie's scruples were not removed by this correspondence. It produced, however, not the slightest alienation, but rather a better understanding and increased mutual esteem.

The restriction as to the succession was a surprise to many members of the Convention. It was certainly so to Dr. Meade; and, though he accepted the appointment, he became more and more sensible of the embarrassing nature of the condition annexed, and was strongly tempted to recall his acceptance, and so escape the evils which he apprehended. Under these circumstances he addressed two letters to Bishop Moore, only one of which is extant:

July 1, 1829.

Right Rev. and Dear Sir:

I earnestly pray, and entreat you, and all my brethren to do the same, that neither you, they, nor the Church may have cause to lament that act, on which your letter congratulates me. Sure I am that the grace of God alone can enable me to fulfil any expectations, however humble, which may be entertained concerning me. I thank you for the pleasure you express at the event, and the prospect of its complete fulfilment. Should Providence see fit to consummate it, then will it be done — if otherwise, let us acquiesce with becoming humility. You beg that I will write to you, and if practicable, accompany you on your journey to the North. The latter is impracticable, by reason of previous engagements — the former, I have thought of doing for sometime past, as soon as I could ascertain that you had returned to Richmond. I made several efforts to see you soon after Convention arose, but failed in each, Providence preventing. I wished freely to converse with you on the subject of that condition annexed to the appointment, which was so contrary to every expectation excited by your address, and the resolution of the Petersburg Convention, and which, I supposed, was against your own wishes and principles. I was not aware that such a condition was contemplated, until the moment it was done, being absent from the house during the discussion — and a very few moments after, it was submitted to my decision, and an immediate answer requested, as the business of the Convention was closing, and the testimonials to be prepared. In this state of confusion of thought and feeling, I gave a verbal assent to a verbal communication, without ever seeing the resolution of the Convention, or knowing anything of what had passed in the House. A few moments' reflection satisfied me that I had been precipitate, and ought to have insisted on time for deliberation. It was however, too late, I thought, to recall my acceptance, and I shrank from seeming to demand more honor than the Convention had thought proper to bestow, or from doing anything which might disturb the peace and harmony of its deliberation. I endeavored indeed to reconcile those who were dissatisfied with the proceedings, and to induce them to hope that it was for the best — at the same time resolving to take the matter into full and impartial consideration, and either continue to accept, or resolve to decline, as my conscience and judgment should decide. It was to aid me in forming this decision, that I was anxious to see you, for the more I thought upon it, the more objectionable it appeared to me, and the nearer did I come to the determination to decline making any use of the testimonials furnished, and to state in a circular addressed to the members of the Convention, my reasons for so doing. Resolving however to do nothing again in haste, or without the best advice, and expecting that the subject would undergo public discussion, and learning also that you were satisfied and pleased with the measure, and being urged by some friends who were opposed to it, to continue my acceptance, I determined to give it farther consideration, and not be guilty of a "repentance which might need to be repented of." My own reflections at home, unaided by any advice from friends abroad, or by any public discussion of the merit of the question, have not changed my first impressions as to the evil tendency of the measure. Some of my brethren with whom I have conversed, have said, that they are also opposed to the principle, but consented to thus act, in order to secure the most perfect unanimity, and under the full persuasion that in this instance no evil would arise, as the succession was perfectly secure. It would indeed be presumption in me to suppose that my merits were such, as to make this sure, and thus save the Church from the evils of a contested election; but even were this perfectly certified, would it be right to consent to a principle which appears to be mischievous in its general operation? I confess it appears to me that in a Church constituted as our's, and in a country such as our's, where the election is by the people, or their representatives; and where, as experience shows, such painful circumstances attend Episcopal elections, it is dangerous to multiply those elections more than needful, and thus hold out temptation to ambition, party spirit, and all the evils attendant thereon. The man who is thus conditionally elected, or who expects the succession, should he secure the good will of the Church, is ever tempted to adopt the acts of popularity, or if he should be above this, is still ever liable to be charged with it, when he is yielding to the dictates of his own heart and conscience, and by kindness and love securing the affection of his brethren and the Church. In the performance of his duty, he may sometimes give offence, and then the offended may rouse a party against him, and threaten him with the disappointment of his expectations, and thus produce strife between him, and them, and in the whole Diocese. Should there be rival candidates for the office of assistant Bishop, as in all probability there generally will be the party defeated, instead of yielding up their opposition, and uniting for the good of the Church, will still retain their favorite candidate, and endeavor to strengthen their forces against the death of the principal Bishop, hoping to triumph over him, who had succeeded in the first election—and what heart-burning, and jealousies, and suspicions must arise during such a contest as this? Even should one person be decidedly the choice of the great body of the Church when elected assistant, in the course of a few years some other might arise who would perhaps be preferred by a portion of the Church, and then again, jealousy and suspicion would be expected, between the aspirant to office and his friends, and the assistant Bishop and his friends, and who shall say what evil may ensue? I have only heard of two arguments in favor of this restriction—the one is, that the Convention has no right to appoint a successor who is to be the Bishop of those who are to come after us, and who alone have the right to choose their own rulers. But might not this argument be used against electing any Bishop for life? Half of that generation over which you were chosen to preside, has passed away, and another half has taken their place, and had we no right to appoint you as Bishop to our children? We must introduce the doctrine of frequent elections, and make the office of Bishop to expire periodically, in order to do away this objection. The only justifiable ground for having an assistant Bishop, is, the inability to perform the duties of his office, either through his infirmity, or the great extent of his Diocese, and when this necessity arises, then is there as much right and propriety in appointing an assistant to be the Bishop of those who are to come after him, as there was in the first instance, to appoint a Bishop in the Diocese during life, and who should be the Bishop to those yet unborn. Such appears to me, to be the state of the case. The other argument in favor of the condition is, that it affords a salutary check to the assistant by putting him on trial, and making him feel that his promotion depends on his conduct during this trial. But is not this reversing the order of things? Should not a man be sufficiently tried before he is made Bishop at all, and ought not this very distrust to be a reason against appointment, and also a reason why he should not accept it, seeing that such doubts and fears are entertained of him? Might not this also be an argument in favor of electing every Bishop for a term of years on trial, in order to see whether he will appear worthy? If it is feared that he will invade the rights of the principal Bishop, and usurp undue authority, I cannot see that this condition would serve as an antidote — for if the assistant is disposed to this, and has only the majority of the Church on his side; if he should prove the more popular of the two, in his ministrations, calculating on this, supported by the Church, he may encroach upon the rights of the superior, and not fear to lose his election at the death of the superior. It appears to me that the only effectual antidote to this evil, is, the adoption of a principle expressed in a resolution of the House of Bishops at the time of Bishop Moore's election, viz., that while the assistant Bishop is competent to any of the duties of a Bishop, the extent to which that power shall be exercised, shall be regulated by the Convention, with the consent of the Bishop. Such a principle as that, I think highly important to preserve the peace of the Church. The assistant Bishop should be allowed to exercise no power, and perform no acts, except under the direction of the Convention, and with the consent of the Bishop. Should he trangress these rules, he then is liable to be tried, and degraded from his office altogether; but any other method of degradation, such as that contemplated in this conditional election, would, it seems to me, be attended by the most unhappy consequences to the Church. Another difficulty attends the present case. The resolution does not say what is to become of the assistant Bishop, should the election fall on some other person. Is he to be the assistant still, or does his office expire? Those with whom I have conversed, differ on the subject. Some say, he is the assistant to Bishop Moore, and at his death his office ends. Others say he is assistant Bishop of Virginia, and will continue as such, if not promoted. Many perhaps thought nothing about it, and the resolution does not settle the point. The Diocese might not choose to have him as an assistant, and it is not very likely that he would wish to be assistant to some other who might be put over him. But does not all this render the office of Bishop more uncertain, short lived, and less respectable, than we are accustomed to consider it, and ought to consider it? Low Churchman as I am, I feel opposed to a measure which seems to me to derogate from the dignity which God and His Church have given to the office, and which also appears likely to make it promotive of discord, rather than of peace.

I should be truly glad to hear your sentiments on the subject. You have seen, heard, read and thought much more than I have, and are qualified to correct any errors into which I have fallen. As the Convention has done it, I really wish it to be right, and should be glad to hear anything which can be said in its behalf. It would be a great relief to my mind to have its expediency made apparent. I should feel much more satisfaction in presenting myself for consecration, could I have some arguments to oppose those which weigh on my mind against the measure.

Although I see nothing unlawful or unconstitutional in the act, yet, as the principle is fraught with evil, I do not think that I can, with a clear conscience, ask for consecration, unless other views are presented to my mind.

* * * * * *

BISHOP MOORE'S REPLY.

RICHMOND, July 8, 1829.

Rev. and Dear Sir:

I perceive from your communication of May 24th, and the 2d inst., that your mind has been disturbed by the restriction connected with your election to the Episcopate. As you have desired me to express to you what may be said in favor of the measure, it will be necessary to take a view of both sides of the question, and by a comparison of the effects of one mode with the other, we shall be able to ascertain from which principle the greatest difficulty may arise.

I must observe to you, prior to my observations on the subject, that I have been informed by a prominent member of the Convention, and that member your ardent friend, that the measure was reflectingly adopted;—not that the principle should bear upon you in particular, but as a principle by which all our institutions, both civil and religious, should be regulated.

When the election of an Assistant Bishop took place in my native State, and it was determined that the person elected should, in case of survivorship, succeed Bishop B. Moore, I strongly disapproved of the measure, and for the following reasons:

First: I took it for granted that provided the succession to the charge of the Diocese should be made to depend on a future election, the then candidate would consider himself obliged to promote the cause of peace and good-will with his brethren; be more courteous in his intercourse with the clergy, and less disposed to act oppressively in the administration of the canons of the Church.

Secondly: I concluded that as the Bishop of New York had been elected by ourselves, it was but reasonable that those who might be alive at his death, should enjoy the privilege of choosing such a person as would be most agreeable to them.

Thirdly: That if we, (at the period alluded to) possessed the right to choose an assistant Bishop, and to say that such assistant Bishop should succeed to the Diocesan, we had an equal right to choose two assistants, as the Diocese was large! and with equal propriety to say that the succession should belong to them in turn; and by that means prevent future Conventions, to the third generation, from the choice of a Diocesan.

Fourthly: It was my opinion that a second election would prevent a man of tyrannical temper from exercising a disposition of cruelty; and by conforming to principles of generous moderation for a time, a habit of kindness would be produced, a habit productive of comfort to himself, and of benefit and advantage to the Church—a habit from which he would never be disposed to depart.

On the other hand, when a man of sound principles, affectionate disposition, good sense and ardent piety, presents himself as the candidate, I should think there would be no danger, in placing him beyond the reach of disappointment. But would not the qualifications above enumerated render him certain of obtaining the office of Diocesan at a future day? Would any man think of opposing an individual thus fitted for the appointment? an individual, who, by the conscientious discharge of his duty, must necessarily attach the great body of the clergy and laity to his interests?

In your case, there does not appear to me to be any difficulty. The vote in your favor was unanimous. The clergy and laity love you; you are the man of my choice, and the Church in Virginia looks up to you as a nursing father.

Should the condition of your election to the Episcopate be brought forward as an objection to your consecration, I should be obliged to receive it with great allowance. I should conclude that the objection would be more to the man, than to the condition; and that the presumption of a deficiency in High Church principles would constitute the chief impediment. I cannot believe that the Bishops, or the House of Clerical and Lay Deputies will oppose your consecration. The measure would be of a character too high-handed, and might produce effects which all moderate men would deplore.

I call myself a High Churchman, but as I have seen some acts performed by men of that denomination which have made me shudder, I think it high time to take into counsel those who are moderate in their views, and, by preserving a balance of power, preserve the present unity of the Church.

The Convention of Virginia cannot be charged with a disposition to call in question the proceedings of other portions of the Church, who have acted differently from themselves, in the choice of an assistant Bishop. They have passed resolutions, calling on their delegates, to entreat the General Convention to enact a law on the subject whereby all future misunderstandings may be obviated, and in which the *duties*, and the number, of assistant Bishops shall be clearly defined.

You ask me, provided I have any doubts as to your fitness for office, to say so. So far from having any doubts, you are the man of my choice. You have the best claim to the appointment, having taken the Church by the hand when her case was hopeless, and having largely contributed to that prosperity with which the Almighty has so signally blessed us.

With love to Mrs. Meade and all friends, believe me, most sincerely and affectionately,

Your friend and servant,

RICHARD CHANNING MOORE.

P. S.—I shall leave this as soon after the 25th of this month as possible, and will endeavor to be prepared to preach, should it be required.

As the General Convention was to meet in less than six months from the election of Dr. MEADE, the canons required that "all matters relating to the consecration," should "be deferred until the said meeting." In the month of August, the General Convention assembled in Philadelphia. Before the House of Bishops could take order for the consecration of Dr. MEADE, it was necessary that the House of Clerical and Lay Deputies should transmit to them their "approbation of his testimonials," "their assent to his consecration," and a prescribed "testimony" in his favor, "signed by a constitutional majority of their own body." When this was proposed, it met with very decided opposition. Nothing was alleged affecting his moral character, or intellectual qualifications, or soundness in the faith. These were all amply certified. Nor was any exception taken to his churchmanship. No doubt there were persons present to whom his well-known moderate views were very unacceptable, and who were disposed to avail themselves of *any* reasonable objection for withholding their consent. But in the earnest and able discussion which lasted for several days, no one was heard to maintain that Dr. MEADE's *unwillingness to deny the validity of all orders not Episcopally conferred*, was good and sufficient reason for refusing assent to the consecration. This important and delicate case, as before the General Convention, and in its determination, is thus stated by Dr. Hawks in his "History of the Church in Virginia," page 275–8:

"No speaker expressed himself in any terms but those of the utmost respect toward the bishop elect. His worth and fitness were not questioned, but a matter of principle was supposed to be involved in the restriction put upon the right of succession.

The argument against the consecration turned chiefly upon constitutional objections. It was, in substance, that the constitution did not contemplate the possibility of a Bishop without a Diocese; and that, according to the spirit of that instrument, it was at variance with the system of Episcopacy (as received by the Protestant Episcopal Church in the United States, associated under that constitution) not to guard against the possibility of such an event in the Church as that of a Bishop at large. It was said that Virginia had not the right to impose any such restriction; and on this head an argument was deduced from the state of the Church under the several colonial governments, when, notwithstanding the distinct rule exercised over the several colonies, the Church was one, and but one, united under its only Diocesan, the Bishop of London. That, consequently, after the revolution, it continued to be one, and was not made up of many independent churches then coming into union for the first time, and reserving certain rights while they surrendered others. Certain it is, that the Church in Virginia (whatever may be the proper theory on the subject) always was, in her practice, independent, and deemed herself at liberty to act accordingly, up to the period when she gave her assent to the great charter of union. In fact (as was correctly remarked in the course of the discussion), our ecclesiastical legislature was here perplexed with the same delicate and intricate question which has been so much agitated in the halls of civil legislation: State sovereignty and the powers of the general government came into collision.*

It was also contended, that to impose the restrictions under discussion, was a deviation from the general course pursued relative to coadjutors, or assistant Bishops. Instances might indeed be adduced to the contrary, and some too in very early times; but these are to be deemed exceptions to the rule.

On grounds of policy also, it was argued that a restriction upon the succession was to be deprecated. Factious and ambitious presbyters would be tempted to raise parties for themselves in opposition to those possessed of an Episcopate, the exercise of which was to cease upon the death of the Diocesan; and laymen of influence, it was said, (if such reduction was countenanced) might be led to impose it for the purpose of keeping a temporary Bishop in subjection to their control, and thereby destroying his independence.

The result of the deliberations and discussions in the House of Clerical and Lay deputies was, that the testimonials of Dr. Meade were signed by a majority of the members, and sent up to the House of Bishops. Before, however, that body proceeded to the consecration, it sent down to the lower House a declaration, as follows: "The Bishops "cannot proceed to this important measure, without de-"claring their disapprobation of the provision in the elec-"tion of Dr. Meade, which prevents immediate succession "to the Episcopacy, on the decease of the present Bishop "of the Diocese. Nevertheless, this being a new case in "questions of consecration in the Church in this country, "the Bishops, entertaining no doubt of Dr. Meade's suc-"ceeding to the Diocesan Episcopacy, in the event of his

* In the Committee, the Rev. Dr. C. E. Gadsden, deputy from South Carolina, remarked, that "if the rights of Virginia were disregarded, he believed that neither his own, nor any Southern Diocese, would be again represented in the General Convention."—J. J.

"surviving the present Bishop, have not permitted the preceding consideration to be a bar to his consecration. But "they cannot proceed to it without declaring unanimously "their determination, nor without recommending to the "future members of this House, now that the peculiarities "of this case will have ceased, not to give such further "countenance to the innovation, as might be construed to "bind it on the Church to her lasting injury." And with this *protestando*, the Bishops proceeded to the consecration, which took place in Philadelphia, on the nineteenth of August, 1829."

It is painful, but due to truth, to state, that, pending the deliberation in the House of Bishops, Bishop Ravenscroft declared his unwillingness to concur in the consecration of Dr. MEADE, unless he was satisfied as to the soundness of his church principles. In justification of his demur, he alluded to a correspondence on the subject between Dr. Empie and Dr. MEADE, in which the latter had evaded certain test questions which had been submitted to him. The difficulty was confined to the speaker. It certainly had no influence upon the action of the House of Bishops, though they may have indulged him with an opportunity for settling his own mind on a subject in reference to which it is unaccountable that he should have experienced any uncertainty. Dr. MEADE and himself were natives of Virginia, and for six years had been fellow presbyters in the same Diocese, throughout the length and breadth of which, Dr. MEADE's moderate views in Church policy, were as notorious, as his own violent ultraism. A personal conference which Bishop Ravenscroft proposed, and which Dr. MEADE promptly declined, was useless, so far as any additional information was concerned, and, under the existing circumstances, inadmissible, because indecorous. Bishop Ravenscroft ought to have known Dr. MEADE well enough to be assured that if such an inquisition, at this juncture, was a necessary preliminary to his elevation to the Episcopate, he would remain a presbyter.

Bishop Moore had informed Dr. MEADE of the representation made by Bishop Ravenscroft in the House of Bishops, as to the evasive character of his replies to Dr. Empie's interrogatories, and Dr. MEADE authorized Bishop Moore to say, that if desired, he would immediately publish the correspondence for the use of the Convention. This was stated by Bishop Moore in the House of Bishops in the presence of Bishop Ravenscroft. There was no call for the correspondence. The House took order for the consecration of the Bishop elect on Wednesday, the 19th of August.

Soon after Bishop MEADE's return to Virginia he wrote to Dr. Empie in reference to the representations made by Bishop Ravenscroft:

Sept. 1, 1829.

Rev. and Dear Sir:

Very unexpectedly, and contrary to my wishes, I am led to refer to the correspondence which took place between us during the last winter. At our late Convention, in Philadelphia, I was informed that Bishop Ravenscroft, on his way to that place, spoke of that correspondence in terms not very creditable to myself. He declared that I had returned evasive answers to every question proposed. The same statement, as Bishop Moore informed me, was made by him to the House of Bishops. Thinking it possible that some rumor of this correspondence might have gotten abroad, with the usual misrepresentations attending such things, I had put the letters in my trunk. On being informed that Bishop Ravenscroft had thus spoken, I requested Bishop Moore to inform the Bishops that the correspondence was at hand, and ready for their inspection; moreover, that if the members of the other House required them, they should be put to press without delay. Bishop Moore made this communication to the House of Bishops, in the presence of Bishop Ravenscroft. Nothing more, however, was said about the letters, and I brought them home, without having occasion to use them for any one.

I do not write, my dear sir, to complain of any use you may choose to make of our correspondence (though others censure you for it), as there was not a word which I could wish to conceal from any human being, but, in justice to yourself, I wish to know whether you represented me as being guilty of disingenuous evasions, or whether Bishop Ravenscroft was put in possession of the whole correspondence, and made that charge against me of his own accord. I have not admitted into my own mind the thought, that you could have made a statement so contrary to truth, and so inconsistent with your own acknowledgments, which give me credit for the greatest candor, and I have uniformly declared my conviction that you had never expressed such a sentiment.

Nevertheless, it would be gratifying to me to have your own authority for the denial, which I hope you will afford me ere long. I will only add that the difference which subsists between us on subjects which I am still convinced, are left by our Church to individual opinion, will, I trust, on neither part, interfere with our zealous co-operation in every measure calculated to promote the cause of our Redeemer. I pray that God may abundantly bless you in the station in which His Providence has placed you, and make you an instrument of much good to the cause of literature, as well as of religion, in our State.

May a gracious Providence watch over you, and your dear family, during the season of sickness, and preserve you in health and safety, for increasing usefulness during your future life. With best regards to all friends in Williamsburg, I remain

Your friend and brother in the Gospel of Christ,

William Meade.

William and Mary College, Sept. 11, 1829.

Rt. Rev. and Dear Sir:

The contents of your letter have been a source of surprise and regret, as I had thought our correspondence buried in oblivion, or flattered myself, that I had discharged my duty in such a way, as to give no possible cause of offence. But, without further preliminaries, I hasten to make such remarks as the matter of your communication seems to demand.

As I knew Bishop Ravenscroft was intimately acquainted with your opinions, character and ministerial practice, I wrote to him to learn what he thought on the subject of your election to the Episcopate, and I at the same time *expressly* stated that I wished everything that came from me on this subject should be regarded as *confidential*. Bishop R., with his usual frankness, was kindly pleased to give me his views, and his reasons for not thinking you a proper candidate. I told him I thought he was laboring under some mistake on the subject; that I was told you had altered both in sentiments and in practice, and that I was determined therefore frankly to address you personally for information. This led to our correspondence, after which I informed Bishop R. that I had been mistaken in my opinion of your sentiments, that you had answered some of my questions, but that you had declined answering others, and that I could not in conscience support your election.

This, as far as I recollect, is the substance of what I wrote to Bishop R.

I kept no duplicate, and do not remember the precise terms which I used. Instead of saying "declined answering," I may have said you "evaded my other questions." For in my communication to Bishop R., I went not into detail, nor has he any other knowledge of our correspondence than that above noticed, as he has neither seen me, or our letters. The idea of your having been guilty of "disingenuous evasions" never entered my head, was not *designed* to be conveyed by my letter, and if my language admitted such a construction, I am truly sorry for it; for, the purity of your motives, I never had the remotest idea of questioning or impeaching. And that Bishop R. should have expressed himself to this effect, and that indeed he should have uttered a single syllable as to our correspondence, on his way or in the Convention, I deeply regret. He probably forgot that I had written *expressly* in confidence, and *if* I used the term "evade," he interpreted it differently from my intention, for we may evade an answer from a sufficient and worthy, as well as from an insufficient and unworthy motive.

Permit me, however, in frankness to remark, that when I thanked you for the candor with which you expressed your sentiments, I could not mean to say that you gave a candid answer to ALL my inquiries. You gave a direct, or implied answer on three points. At all the others you seemed displeased, and waived them, by referring me to other sources for information. But, considering that you are, on principle, opposed to this questioning and answering, in the case of candidates for office, I thought you were very candid and kind to me in communicating your sentiments as freely and as extensively as you did. For this I expressed my gratitude.

You say that many condemn me for acquainting Bishop R. with our correspondence. The preceding account, I trust, shows that they are hasty in their censures. At all events, my own conscience acquits me of all offence towards God and man. After all that had passed between Bishop R. and myself, I could not in propriety do otherwise than acquaint him with the result of my letter to you; and should similar circumstances again occur, I should feel myself in duty bound to pursue substantially the same course. Experience would teach me only to use greater circumspection.

I may be permitted to hope that, as an act of justice and of brotherly kindness, when you see or write to those who censure me in this matter, you will briefly state the whole truth, as now exhibited.

For your kind prayers and good wishes, Right Reverend and dear sir, accept my hearty thanks. God's Providence has now made you my Bishop, and rest assured, nothing shall occur on my part to disturb our harmony, or impede our usefulness.

May the great Head of the Church multiply grace, mercy and peace upon you and yours.

Sincerely and affectionately, Your Brother in Christ,

A. EMPIE.

Bishop MEADE continued for some years to officiate as the rector of Frederick Parish, and now to the charge of this congregation, which, as the reports to the Convention indicate, still prospered under his ministry; he superadded the care of all the churches of the Diocese.

His first Episcopal service was the consecration of the new church in Winchester. "Seven brethren from Mary-"land and Virginia were present. The season was solemn "and interesting. On the two following days and nights "religious services were continued. Sacrament on Sun-"day."

For some weeks he was engaged visiting the churches in Frederick, and the neighboring counties. On the 1st of December, he commenced a tour which occupied him eight weeks, during which he visited the counties of Augusta, Rockbridge, Roanoke, Bedford, Campbell, Pittsylvania, Halifax, Mecklenburg, Amherst, Nelson, Cumberland, Albemarle, Orange, Culpeper, and Fauquier. On this visitation he preached fifty-four times, held two ordinations, administered baptism nine times, and confirmed one hundred and sixty-eight persons. His private record of these Episcopal services commenced with this preface:

"It having pleased Almighty God to call me in the thirty-ninth year of my life, and the eighteenth of my ministry, to the high and holy office of Bishop in His Church, it is meet that I should keep a record of those acts which I shall perform in this new character, and therefore I have obtained this book, and on this 19th of September, 1829, I write on this first page my humble hope and earnest prayer that I may never record anything which my own heart, or God, who is greater than my own heart, may condemn."

He closes the record of this visitation with these lines: "Reached home last night after eight weeks' absence, in some measure, I trust, sensible of the great honor conferred on me by God, in permitting me to labor in His service and perform such holy duties—and thankful to Him for preserving me in health and safety—giving me such favorable weather, and restoring me again to my beloved family and friends and people."

This journal, which is merely a memorandum of official services, from which he made his annual report to the Convention, was discontinued in 1831, with the note, "Kept elsewhere until the death of Bishop Moore in 1841."

(*General Missionary Society.*)—A general revival of pure and undefiled religion invariably produces a desire, that its privileges may be extended to others, and this desire, in its efforts to accomplish its object, recognizes no geographical lines, and is limited only by known destitution, and ability, and opportunity to render relief. A missionary spirit existed in the Protestant Episcopal Church, some time previous to any organization to provide for its efficient action in the foreign field. The contribution of its members in this direction were appropriated through the agency of other denominations, to whose periodicals, chiefly, they were indebted for the missionary intelligence by which their interest was sustained and increased. The first concerted movement in the Protestant Episcopal Church in America was made, not in the General, or any Diocesan Convention, but by an understanding amongst such persons, as, on this subject, were very naturally brought into communication, by being of one mind and one heart. A voluntary Association was formed, comprising clergy and laity of different dioceses. In this Society Mr. MEADE took a lively interest, and both before, and after his consecration, was active in its support and management. With the exception of the vast missionary district embracing the dominion of the Sultan, and having its beginning in Constantinople, all the foreign stations of the Society were supplied with laborers from the Virginia Seminary. This was early pervaded by a missionary spirit, which was in every way encouraged by the professors and bishops.

Never was there a special call from the foreign field that did not find a ready response from this favored school, which furnished the laborers in Greece, Africa and China, several of whom continued their canonical connection with the diocese of Virginia. When the Church at the two stations last named had so increased as to require the supervision of a bishop, in each case, the worthy brother appointed, was an Alumnus of the Alexandria Seminary. These facts, apart from other considerations, account for Bishop MEADE's intimate connection, and warm sympathy with the operations of the Society. Its voluntary character continued until 1835, when some of the most active friends, desirous to enlarge the number of its supporters and extend its influence, and supposing that their object would be effected by its organic connection with the General Convention, exerted themselves to bring about this result. Some persons who had hitherto stood aloof on the ground of its irresponsibility, expressed a willingness to sustain it if it were made a Church institution. The proposal met with general favor. The arrangements for accomplishing the change which, when the General Convention met in Philadelphia in 1835, had for some time been in progress, were then completed. By a majority of the voluntary Society it was transferred to the General Convention, and the transfer received by that body, which formally resolved the Church it represented into a grand missionary society, of which all baptized persons were declared to be members. At the same time, the field was defined to be "the world." The distinction between foreign and domestic was to be abolished, and the terms used only to facilitate division of labor, and secure systematic and accurate operation. The Board of Directors was to be elected triennially by the General Convention, and by two committees, a foreign and domestic, to manage the business of the Society and report to the General Convention. Provision was made for the designation of missionary districts, and the election of missionary bishops, by the House of Clerical and Lay Deputies, on nomination by the House of Bishops.

This arrangement, effected by many who were generally on opposite sides in Church matters, was hailed as very significant of a happy unity of spirit, and as giving promise of growing agreement in faith and practice. Bishop MEADE thus alludes to it: "I was not at the opening of this General Convention, being detained several days in Virginia. All things were agreed upon before my arrival, between some of those who, from their location and other circumstances, took a more active part in the conduct of the Society. On reaching Philadelphia, a number of brethren whose lead I was always ready to follow in regard to such matters, and some of whom are yet alive, informed me, that a most happy agreement had taken place among the active friends of missions, that all party distinctions were to be done away, and that, in proof of the liberal feeling toward those of our way of thinking, one Bishop should be chosen for China, and two for the domestic field—one of the latter, together with the former, should be such as we would designate. Of course this was very acceptable to one who had never professed to be indifferent to the distinctions which prevailed in the Church. It seemed to promise well. On conversing with that wise and good man, Bishop Griswold, I found that he was not at all carried away with the new plan; that he would rather it would assume more, than less, of the voluntary system, referring to the two successful Societies in England—the Church Missionary Society, and the Society for propagating the Gospel—which had always acted on the voluntary principle. When the proposed change came before the whole Society for discussion, there was, I thought, a disposition on the part of some to underrate the character and success of the old organization, and I took the liberty to object to such strictures, and to refer to what it had done, and especially to the great increase of its funds for the last year or two, at the same time declaring my intention, to act with those who understood the operation of the Society better than myself. All things were settled on the new platform, and some of us continued until the last night of the Convention under the pleasing expectation of having two missionary Bishops of our own choice; but it so happened that two of the other side were chosen for the domestic field, and the election of one for the foreign field was indefinitely postponed. This, among other things, may help to account for the fact that some of us are rather fearful of what are called compromises." (Old Church of Virginia, p. 379).

If this breach of good faith—for on the statement of Bishop MEADE it was nothing else—had determined those who had been overreached to withdraw at once, and on this ground, from the Society, and to reorganize the late Association, which, from mistaken views of expediency, had been dissolved, no one could have justly censured the manly move. It now needs no great discernment to perceive that the cause of missions would not have suffered by an early retrogradation. They concluded, however, as the alliance had been formed, to submit to the wrong, and not to allow their disappointment and mortification to interfere with their honest support of the Church institution. "In many addresses throughout Virginia," says Bishop MEADE, "I advocated it, even as though it had commended itself entirely to my choice and judgment." And such was generally the generous policy of those whose confidence had been abused by the first act of the new Society. That it accomplished good, though its machinery was in several respects objectionable, and its workmen not always of the stamp that "need not to be ashamed," is not to be questioned. But both departments, and more especially the domestic, failed to give satisfaction to the Church at large. The diminished contributions indicated, not abating zeal in the cause, but declining confidence in its management. Various expedients were resorted to, but with only temporary effect. The result was, that after a fair experiment, and no prospect of permanent improvement, "an Episcopal Missionary Society for the West was established in Philadelphia, which afforded a channel for the conveyance of funds to those missionaries, and those only, who are believed by the donors to disseminate the true doctrines of the Gospel and the Church." This Association established a connection with the Church Institution, but was really independent in its means and measures. Subsequently to this, a movement was made to form a general Society on the voluntary plan, which was countenanced and sustained by some of all orders of the Church. Bishop MEADE describes his own course in reference to each of the three organizations: "At first, and for some time, I gave my annual contributions to domestic missions (*i. e.:* directly through the General Society), but such were the accounts received in various ways, and such the most unsatisfactory reports of the missionaries, that I could not continue them with a good conscience." He therefore availed himself of the agency of the Philadelphia Association, and gladly contributed to its support. In the *foreign* operations of the Church Society he continued to be much interested, and though not always concurring in the policy of that committee, his influence and his means were generously bestowed to advance its great object. With the new independent enterprise he did not see his way clear to connect himself. On this subject he writes:—"Though hoping that the time would soon come, when, under favorable auspices, some voluntary society might by general consent be formed, I have hitherto discouraged all suggestions or proposals, either public or private, which looked toward a new society antagonistic to that already established." He was, from the first, unfavorable to its connection with the General Convention. There was, as has been related, enough in the action of that body, during the session at which the union was consummated, to increase this feeling of aversion to the ill-judged connection. Of one of the provisions he decidedly disapproved—that which devolved upon the House of Bishops the nomination, and on the other House the election, of the missionary bishops. He regarded this *as wrong in itself*—inasmuch as the election of a bishop should be by the clergy and laity over whom he is to be placed, and should be deferred until the Church, in that particular district, is capable of choosing for itself—and very *disturbing* in its influence on the Convention, as it furnished occasion for most exciting contention, and with it, very questionable management, and, as an unavoidable consequence, unchristian feelings—all of which are discreditable anywhere, but especially in an ecclesiastical assembly. A faithful history of the elections which have taken place under this ill-judged provision would be sufficient for its condemnation. But there is slender hope of its abandonment by any majority whose ascendancy it serves to perpetuate. The Bishop's views on this subject are embodied in a document relating to matters of more recent date, which will be found in its proper place.

(*Bible Society*).—At an early period of his ministry, Bishop MEADE was very sensible of the importance of the press, as an auxiliary, in the diffusion of religious knowledge, and before the existence of any formal organization for this purpose in the American Church, he diligently availed himself of this instrumentality, and engaged the co-operation of others, in publishing original works, and in reproducing such treatises as he found to be useful. When the American and Foreign Bible Society was formed, he became at once one of its most efficient supporters. Though he never appeared on its platform, or attended its anniversary meetings, he contributed systematically and liberally to its support, and often and earnestly commended it to the generous patronage of the people of Virginia. On his death-bed his heart was with the enterprise, then in progress, to organize a similar institution in the Confederate States. He directed a telegram to be sent to the delegates assembled at Augusta, Georgia, requesting to be enrolled as a life-member, and expressed the hope that it would receive the cordial support of the Bishops, and other clergy and laity, of the Protestant Episcopal Church.

The American Tract Society, formed by an union of the different evangelical denominations, to print and circulate tracts on those great doctrines and duties in reference to which they were all agreed, he regarded with like interest and sustained with similar zeal. Many doubt the feasibility of such a plan. He did not. For many years, its admirable management and great usefulness signally sustained his judgment, and compensated his confidence. After long and harmonious action, however, an attempt was made to introduce the leaven of New England fanaticism, in the form of tracts, not touching the lawfulness of slavery —any such intention was disavowed—but setting forth the duty, and mode of imparting religious instruction to persons held in bondage. The proposal was resisted by the Board of Managers, as in violation of the constitution of the Society, and sure to alienate from it all its friends in the South, among whom were many of its most influential and active patrons. At last the pressure became so strong, and the threat of secession became so loud, that the Board deemed it expedient to convene the Society, and submit the matter to their determination. On this call a meeting was held in the city of New York. Delegates were there from every State in the Union. The assemblage was said to be the most imposing of the kind ever convened in that city. The Bishop of Virginia, though intensely concerned, was not able to be present, but he communicated fully by letter with those who were, and though absent in person, his wise counsel was heard, and his salutary influence felt in that grave and momentous discussion. The result was, the triumph of conservatism, and a new guarantee that the constitution should be maintained. Christians and patriots, throughout the length and breadth of the land, were cheered by the announcement that the mischievous measure proposed was rejected by a vote of two-thirds. The action was regarded as happily significant of the decisive judgment of the religious community, that the institution of slavery was to be left entirely to the wisdom and conscience of those among whom it existed, and who, it might be presumed, best understood its relation and their duties. *O si sic semper ubique et ab omnibus!*

(*Episcopal Sunday School Union*).—The issues of the American Tract Society were, from the nature of the Union, confined to doctrines, and duties, in reference to which the different denominations of which it was composed, were agreed. But each denomination is distinguished by certain peculiarities, which, though not essential to salvation, are, by those who hold them, considered as important in their bearing on the integrity and efficiency of the Church, and on their influence in promoting the personal piety of those who profess, and call themselves Christians. To neglect their timely and distinct exhibition, with the reasons for their adoption and practice, would be a culpable delinquency in the cause of truth, and a want of charity to our fellow men. In publications of this description, none could be expected to co-operate, but those of the same communion. Many of the clergy and laity of the Church were desirous to form a Society for this purpose, and the meeting of the General Convention in 1826, was selected as the occasion most favorable for its accomplishment. The movement, however, was embarrassed by serious difficulties. Some proposed that the Society should be created by the General Convention, and managed by a Board elected by that body, and responsible to it for all their publications. But it was objected that this would be to give to them the imprimatur of the Church, and thus, by placing them on a level with the Book of Common Prayer, to add to the standards of the Church, in violation of its constitution. If such a Society were formed, it must therefore, from the object it proposed, be a voluntary association.

Again: On several points of doctrine, discipline and worship, the standards of the Church were so framed, as to allow within certain limits, a diversity of opinion and practice, and it was well known that under this wise allowance, her clergy, though differing in some of their views and policy, could, and did minister together in unity of spirit, and the bond of peace. It would not be easy to frame the Society's publications so as not to trench upon this latitude, and by thus interfering with the liberty sanctioned by the Church, to offend those brethren whose views were disapproved. The whole subject was beset by practical and serious difficulties, but candor and conciliation were in the ascendant, and the conference resulted in the formation of a voluntary Society, styled the Protestant Episcopal Sunday School and Tract Society, and with a distinct understanding that it should be conducted with a full regard to the diversity of sentiment known to exist among the clergy. But it was easier to promise with honest purpose to perform, than to execute accordingly. The only effectual security—a provision that the different parties should be represented in the Board, or Executive Committee, and unanimous consent required to authorize any publication, was neglected. What was commenced with so much expectation was not long in losing the confidence, and with it the support, of a large portion of the Church. Its history is best furnished in the language of Bishop Meade, who soon found it necessary to remonstrate with those by whom it was conducted, and ultimately to expose its errors, and withdraw his recommendation. :

"The Episcopal Sunday School Union was established at the General Convention of 1826. Nothing of its formation appears on the journal, for it was not even proposed to the House. It was the wish of some, to make it an institution of the Convention, and such a proposition was talked of; but the whole history of the action of the General Convention was against it. On more than one occasion, individuals had applied to the Convention, or to the House of Bishops, to adopt or recommend certain Church books, but were refused on the ground that the General Convention was formed for other purposes, and that the precedent would be bad. In that very year, 1826, the Rev. Mr. Barlow brought forward a scheme for a Church book-establishment, and was permitted to occupy many hours in the explanation, and advocacy of it. The following resolution was adopted in regard to it:

"*Resolved*, As the opinion of this House, that, without entering at all into the merits of the plan noticed in the report of the committee, it is inexpedient to legislate on the subject."

"On another occasion an effort was made to form a General Education Society under the patronage of the General Convention. This, also, after being considered for some time, was postponed, and never resumed. In truth, the only institutions which have been brought under the General Convention are, the General Seminary, and the Missionary Society; and whether they give any encouragement for the trial of others, all may judge for themselves. The Episcopal Sunday School Union was therefore, as has since been publicly and formally admitted by itself, a voluntary institution. Several attempts were made at different General Conventions to have it enrolled, and recognized, among the general institutions of the Church; but they failed—the Convention being reminded that it was only a voluntary Society. The determination of the Church not to embarrass itself, and produce discord, by adopting any such institution, was further manifested by the failure of an effort made in 1847 by Bishop Henshaw, who proposed to have a committee of both Houses to prepare a few catechetical books for the children of the Church, with a view to uniformity and harmony. It was opposed by Bishops Delancey, Whittingham, Hopkins and myself. After a discussion during a part of several days, the question being taken, the mover of the resolution was the only one who voted for it.

"There was, however, from the time of its formation a general disposition to encourage the Episcopal Sunday School Union as a voluntary society. The American Sunday School Union, and the American Tract Society, were noble institutions, and furnished many excellent and suitable works for individuals, families and Sunday Schools; but they could not supply certain books setting forth the peculiarities of the different denominations, in connection with the Gospel. It was therefore desirable that Episcopalians, as well as others, should have some organization for supplying such. It was distinctly understood at the establishment of ours in 1826, that it should assume no party character, but be conducted on liberal, comprehensive principles, setting forth only those common truths about which Episcopalians are agreed—which platform has been repeatedly declared since then. Accordingly, the Diocese of Virginia, at the first Convention after its organization, earnestly recommended it to the patronage of the Episcopalians of the State. A few months only, however, had elapsed, when some of its publications contained sentiments very different from what was expected, and which were calculated to dissatisfy many of us. I immediately wrote to the chief manager of it, the present Bishop of Maryland, making complaints. In reply, I was assured that the greatest pains should be taken in the future to avoid giving offence; that the book most objected to should be withdrawn from circulation; and that henceforth books favoring both parties in the Church should be published. I did not question the sincerity of the promise, and the intention, but saw the impracticability of the plan proposed. Thus disappointed, I did not take any particular concern in the operations of the Society after that. I only saw that from time to time some things came out which were criticized, and which I could not approve, though there were many good little books published for children, chiefly from the pens of pious writers in England." (Old Churches, pp. 375–6.)

Such of the letters alluded to in the preceding statement as are extant and available are here inserted as illustrative of the liberality, vigilance and fidelity of their author. The first is a fragment, without date, endorsed, "Extract from a letter to the Secretary of the Episcopal Sunday School Union Society":

"It would be uncandid in me, when writing concerning the affairs of this institution, not to express my fears arising from the adoption of one or two books which I perceive to be contained in the system of instruction, that it may not produce the desired effect of a general union through the Church. The books alluded to are the Baltimore edition of Mrs. Sherwood's Stories, and Bishop Hobart's Catechism. You are well aware of the controversy which has taken place in relation to the former, and how impracticable it will be to get those who are opposed to the altered edition to adopt it. Was it expedient, therefore, to introduce this into a system which, it was hoped, would unite the Church in the greatest possible degree of harmony? Excellent as the work is, would it not have been better to omit it altogether, than to have produced collision at the very outset? I have never seen the altered edition, but if I understand the changes aright, they make the work express sentiments on the subject of baptism, different from those of a large and respectable portion of the Episcopal clergy of England and America. I, for one, therefore, could not adopt or recommend it, especially when the author's own unaltered work is to be had. As to the other, Bishop Hobart's Catechism, I cannot speak so certainly, but I think I saw it once, and that one of the answers put into the mouth of the child was a passage of Ignatius or Jerome—"He that does anything without the privity of the Bishop, serves the devil." However properly such a sentiment might be used in an argument concerning the testimony of the Fathers, I cannot think it suitable for a child's constant use. If books of this description must be used in the schools belonging to the Union, if the children must be trained in what are called High Church principles, do you not perceive at once how you separate from your Society all those who cannot agree with you on such points? Unanimous as we were in the Virginia Convention in recommending this institution, I feel confident that we should have been almost as unanimous in rejecting the proposition, if it had been understood, that we were thereby to bind ourselves to teach our children principles which we disapproved. I feel confident that distrust is at once created, and that many are now crying, "We know not what is yet to come!" The institution cannot be generally received unless it be conducted in that mild catholic spirit which has ever breathed through the Church, and made it avoid as much as possible dictating on points wherein the members differed. If those who have the management of the institution cannot conscientiously conduct it otherwise, then there is no help; but they cannot expect the cordial co-operation of those who differ from them."

In his reply, the Secretary of the Protestant Episcopal Sunday School Society courteously expresses the "great pleasure" afforded "him by the spirit of candor and forbearance which pervades" the communication, and in a letter which covers six and a-half pages, endeavors in a very respectful manner to remove the objections urged:

1. Bishop Kemp's edition of Mrs. Sherwood's book is not contained in *any part* of the System of Instruction. It is merely on a blank page of the printed copy of the System, in a list of books recommended for "*premium* library books." "It is merely a recommendation which every one is at liberty to receive, or reject, without interfering in the least with his adherence *to our* other recommendations."

2. The alterations, in a vast majority of instances, improve the work by substituting plain English words for Indian terms, which need the use of a glossary to render them intelligible."

3. In a number of instances Mrs. Sherwood has *very strong* expressions respecting the corruption of human nature; for which, in every instance, Bishop Kemp substitutes the language of the Articles, or Liturgy of our Church itself.

4. Respecting *baptism*, the alterations (with one exception) are not (in the opinion of the Secretary) "improvements," but he sees not "how they can be objected to, by any person who conscientiously uses the catechism of our Church."

5. What purports to be "the entire difference" between Mrs. Sherwood's book, and the edition as altered by Bishop Kemp, on the subject of baptism, is exhibited in parallel columns.

6. A correction of misapprehension with regard to the testimony of St. Ignatius, as quoted in Bishop Hobart's Catechism—with the statement of a precedent for the introduction of "patristical testimony in a catechism designed for the higher classes in our schools," furnished in a Brief Explanation of the Church Catechism, by the Rev. Basil Wood, "an English clergyman, who is deservedly in high estimation among those of our brethren who would be most disposed to object to Bishop Hobart's Catechism."

The reply closes with an earnest disavowal of any wish or intention, "either to *force* or entice others to dereliction of any of their principles, or even prejudices"—a distinct assurance that the Society shall be managed so that neither "set of opinions" "can have reason to complain"—an expression of hearty thanks "for the candor with which" the Secretary had been made acquainted with the objections alleged; thereby affording "an opportunity of removing them, or taking warning from them, as the case may be"—and a solicitation of a portion "of his correspondent's influence in favor of the infant and important institution."

Both the reply, and the communication which called it forth, are eminently characterized by Christian frankness and courtesy. And the same excellent spirit, worthy of all imitation, pervades the rest of the correspondence.

The Secretary states in his reply, that in the edition of Mrs. Sherwood's book recommended by the system, the verbal changes amounted to the rejection "of nearly two thousand barbarous and unintelligible words from the text of a work designed for children," and this he regards as quite justifying these, and other alterations. Yet, even if this were a benefit, it has nothing to do with the question as to the morality of the liberty taken in making the changes. Besides, the author may with design, and good reason, have retained what others have assumed to displace. She may have justly concluded, that the words which the Secretary repudiates as "barbarous and unintelligible," are not capable of being substituted by English words conveying the same idea, and could only be translated by a periphrasis, which would hinder the narrative and mar the effect, and which had better appear (if at all), in the approved form of a glossary. She may further have supposed, that those very oriental words would invite the reader to such inquiry, as would lead to useful information relative to the peculiar customs of the country.

Any person with less reverence than the Secretary for the English version of the Bible might, with his views, pronounce many of its words barbarous and unintelligible, and publish a new edition in which they were displaced by vernacular terms, supposed to be of like import. The wise and learned translators adopted a different course, and the general Church has ever since approved their policy. The same judgment has been rendered in favor of the diction of Mrs. Sherwood's stories.

It will be recollected that Bishop MEADE, in alluding to Bishop Hobart's Catechism, had written, "I cannot speak so certainly, but I think I saw it once, and that one of the answers put in the mouth of a child, was a passage of Ignatius or Jerome, 'He that does anything without the privity of the Bishop, serves the Devil.'" He adds, "However properly such a passage might be used in an argument concerning the testimony of the fathers, I cannot think it suitable for a child's constant use."

To this the Secretary replied: "I trust, sir, it will be long before the G. P. E. S. convey their instructions to the rising generation with so little discrimination. Bishop Hobart's Catechism (New York ed., 1826, p. 68; our own being not quite through the press, I cannot quote the page) says, 'St. Ignatius, the disciple of St. John, and all the succeeding fathers, bear decided testimony to the superior power of Bishops. *Ques.* State the testimony of Ignatius. *Ans.* Ignatius says, Let no man do anything, of what belongs to the Church, without the Bishop.' This is all the patristical testimony given in that Catechism. I do not believe that you will entertain any objection to its being contained in a catechism designed for the higher classes in our schools."

The Bishop replies: "It is equally a pleasure, and a duty, to acknowledge the mistake under which I labored in relation to a passage in Bishop Hobart's Catechism. I had confounded the substance of Ignatius' testimony, with the offensive words in which it was expressed. It has been fifteen years since I saw it, as well as I can recollect. I will endeavor to examine it without prejudice when I see it again."

If the Bishop ever examined it, he found both expressions within a few lines of each other in the Epistle of Ignatius to the Smyrneans. The first, as translated by Archbishop Wake, reads:

"Let no man do anything of what belongs to the Church, without the Bishop." (§8.)

The second occurs in the next section:

"But he that does anything without his (the Bishop's) knowledge, ministers unto the devil."

The first, it is presumed, furnished the quotation in Bishop Hobart's Catechism, and was, after not being seen for fifteen years, confounded in Bishop MEADE's recollection with its offensive counterpart.

Bishop MEADE related his impressions as a matter about which he was not "certain," and it was not very remarkable that he should, after so long an interval, have mistaken a sentence which, in its unqualified form, is very extravagant, for another of like import, in more offensive words.

MILLWOOD, Sept. 20, 1827.

Rev. and Dear Sir :

I take the first moment of leisure from more indispensable duties to acknowledge the receipt of your last communication, and make a few remarks upon some parts of it. It is equally a pleasure, and a duty, to acknowledge the mistake under which I have labored in relation to a passage in Bishop Hobart's Catechism. I had confounded the substance of Ignatius' testimony, with the offensive words in which it was expressed. It has been fifteen years since I saw it, as well as I can recollect. I will endeavor to examine it without prejudice when I see it again. When I have an opportunity, I will, in like manner, endeavor to estimate the comparative merit of the Baltimore edition of Mrs. Sherwood's stories. I fear, however, that nothing can alter my opinion as to the inexpediency of recommending that edition of the work.

In the conclusion of your letter, you say in very strong terms, that it is the fixed determination of all concerned with the management of the institution, to conduct it on the most catholic, and comprehensive principles, that you wish neither to force, or entice any persons into a dereliction of their peculiar views or principles, that, "though you may sometimes sanction works which all the brethren may not cordially approve," yet if you "do this in favor of one set of opinions, it will also be done in favor of another, so that both can be supplied and suited, and neither have reason to complain."

Now, my dear sir, I cannot but think the committee have lost the first and fairest opportunity of exhibiting this determination before the public, when they chose the altered edition of Mrs. Sherwood's stories, as the one to be exclusively recommended. This book, in its original, expressed one set of opinions — in its altered state another set of opinions, each of which are adopted by different members and ministers of the Church. Had nothing been said about any edition, or had it been positively declared that either might be used at the discretion of the members, it would have assumed a very different aspect. As it is, and considering the angry controversy which had existed in regard to this work, the recommendation of the one edition was well calculated to provoke the jealousy of all who were opposed to it, and induce them to regard the measure, as a full proof of a determination to permit but one view of the disputed points to be seen by the rising generation. From the representation you give of the alterations, it appears that the most material relate to the much disputed subject of human depravity, that the expressions of Mrs. Sherwood are only moderated, and made to resemble the expressions of the Book of Common Prayer. I am well aware that there have been, and still are, philosophers and divines, and many private individuals, whose writings and opinions on this subject are foolish and wicked, and most dishonorable to God and man. I am aware of the impossibility of fixing with mathematical, philosophical or theological accuracy the exact degree of man's depravity; we cannot measure the height from which, or the abyss into which, he has fallen; but then, when I consider the language of God's Word on this subject, the many and strong expressions which abound in Scripture, concerning the sinfulness of man; when I consider how reluctant we are to admit the extent of our corruption, how prone we are to think more highly of ourselves than we ought to think, I confess that I feel bound to regard with the utmost jealousy, any softenings or modifications on this point. "If any man speak, let him speak as the oracles of God." The only question with me is, "Does Mrs. Sherwood use stronger expressions than the inspired writers?" If not, I would not alter them to suit the views of any persons, or Churches, in Christendom.

I see not, however, that they could be altered so as to speak a moderated language, if certain expressions of our Prayer Book were substituted: for instance, "there is no health in us." We are very far gone from original righteousness, as explained by the words "*quam longessime*," which shows that our forefathers were anxious to exhaust the strength of language in the cause, and indeed, which even Calvinists, except such as are lost to reason, must understand with some limitation; for none but such, would maintain that man might not be more depraved than he is, although so deeply, and universally stained with sin. I know not what the alterations are on this point; but any, however slight, would be received with the most fearful suspicion, and therefore should not be presented to the Church for universal acceptance. It is true, as you say, they are only recommended, we may adopt the recommendation or not at pleasure, but, if these are to be the only books in the depositories, there is no choice, and the institution cannot suit those who differ in sentiment. Moreover, the whole institution will be opposed, as having the effect of disseminating principles believed to be at variance with the Word of God. Dissatisfied as I still am with this step, I will still, with all the candor I can bring to the examination, carefully consider the different books which compose the system, as soon as you shall send them.

I must beg you to excuse this unworthy scrawl in consideration of the haste in which it is necessarily written. With best wishes and prayers, I remain

Your friend and brother in the Gospel,

W MEADE.

Some six months later, the Secretary resumed the correspondence, as follows:

NEW YORK, April 2, 1828.

Rev. and Dear Sir:

Not wishing to trouble you, or to trespass upon your valuable time, I have hitherto refrained from answering your reply to my communication of July, 1827. But the receipt of a communication from the Rev. Mr. Smith, of Middleburg, Vt., containing remarks of a nature very similar to those by yourself in your first letter, reminds me, that I ought to make acknowledgment for your frank, and liberal advice.

The Executive Committee have taken no formal measures as to Mrs. Sherwood's Stories in Bishop Kemp's edition, but the book has been left out of all their printed lists published since the reception of your communication, and no further measures have been taken for its circulation. For my own part, I am free to confess that after a careful examination of both editions, I cannot think any of Bishop Kemp's alterations liable to serious objection from *any* members of our Church, and very many, I am sure, (those which substitute intelligible expressions for Mrs. Sherwood's numerous Indian words) materially improve the book, and will render it much more useful. But, far be it from me (and I believe the sentiment to be that of every individual in the Executive Committee) to force upon the acceptance, or even the notice of others, what they may deem seriously objectionable, however different may be my own opinion. I think I may safely pledge myself that you will hear no more of "Sherwood's Stories on the Catechism" from the Sunday School Union. With the sentiments you express concerning the depravity of human nature, as limited by yourself, I entirely agree, and it will, I trust, be the stndy of my life to present these, and the other fundamental doctrines of the scheme of redemption, in all their strength and importance, to the notice of my fellow sinners. I think you will have discerned that they are recognized in the publications of the Union in all their extent, and with the prominence which is so absolutely necessary. To request your opinion on such of our books as have been forwarded to you (those now publishing will be sent, as soon as out) is the object of my writing now. I cannot help thinking that they have met with your approbation, and it is in the pleasing hope that I shall receive an expression of it, from yourself, and that it will induce you to lend us your aid in our important (for our sphere of usefulness is daily extending far and near) work, that I remain Yours, with the profoundest respect,

W. R. WHITTINGHAM.

Rev. Dr. MEADE.

To this the following answer was sent:

MILLWOOD, April 18, 1828.

Rev. and Dear Sir:

Yours of the 2d inst. came to hand in due course of mail. The Sunday School books of which you asked my opinion had been received not very long before, having been delayed on the road. Since the arrival of your letter I have given some time and attention to those which seemed to require it. Scougal's Life of God in the Soul of Man needed no examination. It was one of the first religious books I read after religion became a principal consideration with me, and

I rejoice much that it is set forth by a Society of our Church. A more accurate, and at the same time warm exhibition of the religion of the heart, is not to be found. A glance at all the other books except the Catechisms, was sufficient to assure me that they must be good. The Catechisms alone were the subjects of more careful perusal. On these I would offer a few criticisms.

As I am about to make some objections to them, I feel it but justice to the authors and promoters of them to make some remarks on the difficulty of such compositions. It was said by an admirer of Dr. Watts that, much as he esteemed all his writings, there was none he wondered at so much as his "Divine Songs for Children," on account of the great difficulty of writing for children. I have been all my life reading everything of the kind that I could meet with, and have felt very sensibly the truth of the above remark. When Mrs. Sherwood's Stories appeared, I pronounced them worth all the other explanatory catechisms in the world beside Children require to be interested. They are interested by the Bible because of the affecting narratives, striking parables, beautiful poetry, and impassioned eloquence contained in it. These charms cannot be introduced into catechisms. They must ever be comparatively dull, and a mere exercise of memory. The experience of parents, pastors and teachers, I am sure, will testify to this. I have long since come to the conclusion that much will never be done toward the pious education of youth by catechisms, especially long ones, which weary and disgust. Hymns and well-chosen Scriptures, and interesting illustrations of piety, are the great instruments for turning the thoughts and feelings of the young into a religious channel, and leading their souls to God. The remark which I have always made on the catechisms which have come under my notice, is, I think, true of those which have been issued from the Episcopal Society. I think they attempt to explain things which need no explanation, or which one remark from the teacher would do, so as not to require anything further. I wish you would read over the 2nd Catechism, or only the first two or three pages, and see if the explanations are anything more than the Catechism itself, and therefore a mere burthen on the memory.

As to all the Catechisms, it appears to me that they attempt and inculcate some things comparatively unimportant, and not likely to interest. The larger catechism is swollen to a formidable size in this way, and will, I fear, be a terror to those young minds which we would lead into the "ways of pleasantness" and "paths of peace." Upon the whole, there appears to me to be an inherent difficulty in the thing itself. In this species of composition, language has not a fair opportunity of exerting its magic power over the heart.

But I must now make an objection of another kind to two of the catechisms; one which relates not to the manner, but the matter. First let me observe, that this Society stands candidate for the favor of the whole Church, and was designed for all our people. That favor cannot be obtained, nor that design accomplished, if opinions are introduced conflicting with those which by many are believed to be the doctrines of the Bible and of the Church. Now it appears to me that such is the case with the catechisms in question, to such an extent, as to forbid the cordial reception of them by all the members and ministers of the Church. There are two subjects introduced into them which have ever divided the Church, and will, probably, to the end of time. The effects of baptism, and the divine right of Episcopacy, are those to which I allude. As to the former, there are, I believe, three leading opinions, with several modifications thereof. I might specify them as the views of Bishop Hopkins, of Mant, and of his opponent, Mr. Scott. Each of these writers, with their followers, appeal to the Scriptures and the Prayer Book as maintaining their views, and, as we all know, long and angry have been the controversies waged. Now these catechisms, if I understand them aright, espouse the doctrine of Bishop Hopkins, with some additions. But there are those in our Church who prefer the other two opinions, as being more Scriptural and Episcopal, and cannot be easily satisfied with this decision of the disputed points. The other subject is that of Episcopacy, which is rather forcibly drawn out of our brief summary of Christian doctrine, as contained in the catechism. There are two leading sentiments, with some modifications, on this subject. Some think Episcopal ordination divinely appointed, so that any deviation from it is a departure from the Church of God, and an exclusion from covenanted blessings. Others, that because the Apostles adopted this mode, and the primitive Church followed it, we ought to adhere to it, as having this divine sanction besides its other recommendations but undertake not to deny the validity of other ordinations differing a little from our own. Now these catechisms seem to assume the former, and, of course, teach a doctrine, which all cannot inculcate on their flocks. It appears to me, that our Church has most carefully avoided to assert the former opinion, and, as these catechisms are designed to set forth the doctrines of the Church, those who think the Church holds other views, must object. If any think that the Scriptures teach stronger doctrine on the subject, let them maintain it, but, not in catechisms setting forth the views of the whole Church. As true members of the Church, we ought to be most careful how we propose anything to be believed by others, which may not clearly be proved from Scripture, and is not plainly written therein.

While this rule should be observed in all our discourses and writings for the most intelligent, matured and aged Christians, how particularly, how scrupulously, should it be observed in what we write for children! There is a credulity implanted in the infant breast by our great Creator, which inclines them at once, and without inquiry, to receive. believe, and do whatever is taught and commanded them. What a talent, this, in the hand of parents and ministers, and what an account must they render of its use, or abuse, on the great day when God shall require at their hands those souls whose education was entrusted to them. See the effect of this principle, this credulity of the young, in all ages and religions. See the abuse of it, in the bigoted attachment to all the follies and false religions, that disgrace mankind and dishonor God. See how the Catholics have abused it to the corruption of our pure and holy religion. indelibly impressing upon the minds of children, opinions which will lead them to hate all others; and, when opportunity offers, to persecute even unto death, those who differ from their way of thinking, or worshipping. See how this very abuse of the docility of youth paved the way for the insidious proposition of Rousseau, that the mind be left a blank as to religion, till reason was matured, and the young immortals be permitted to walk forth in the dignity of freemen, and choose for themselves. 'Tis melancholy to think how many have fallen into the snare of the devil; how, while neglecting to write truth upon the blank of the human mind, supposing that it would remain blank, the wicked one has engraved falsehood in characters too deep to be effaced. Christian ministers and parents cannot be too fearful of this snare, nor too early in writing truth upon the impressible minds of their children. Neither can we be too careful to write nothing but truth, clear, revealed, essential truth. We have to answer to the God of truth, to our children in both worlds, and to mankind, for what we teach. Let the truths we inculcate be few, simple, practical, such as reach the heart, promote love to God, good-will to man, and let those matters which have divided even the most wise and pious into parties, and been subjects of bitter controversy, be deferred to a later period, and examined in those writings which treat more fully of them.

You will perhaps say that we have already a catechism, articles and offices in which these things are introduced, and they require explanation. To this I reply, that although these matters are introduced, it is in so very brief, modest and inoffensive a way, as to avoid the mischief spoken of. It is somewhat remarkable, and not a little to the credit of the Church, that persons differing on all these points, yet agree in their approbation of what the Prayer-Book teaches, just in the same way as all the contending parties in Christendom agree in approving of the Bible. But where is there any commentary or explanation of the Bible that suits them all? As soon as explanations begin, they must be multiplied far beyond the number of sects in order to satisfy all. So it is with our Catechism and Prayer-Book, at least with some parts of them. All agree to take them as they are, and think that the passages which contain the disputed points, either favor their own views, or admit of a double signification; but the moment it is attempted to explain them, so as to favor one view rather than another, dissension arises, and we split into parties.

I do not therefore see any other plan of proceeding, than to let the Catechism remain as it is, and serve as a text for each individual minister to expatiate upon before his little flock. As to the difficult and disputed points, he must say what he believes, or nothing at all As to the other parts, if he takes the pains which he should, he can make them plainer and more interesting than any catechism, because he can enlarge upon them, and illustrate them by anecdotes and Scripture quotations. This was plainly the design of the Catechism, as the Canons in the English Church and in our own Church show, for they direct the minister to instruct the children in it before the congregation — a plan which I have pursued for many years, endeavoring to interest both parents and children, either by explanations of my own, or by reading some affecting pieces from the publications of the day, which enforce the doctrines and duties taught in the Catechism. If I am told that this view of the subject narrows the ground of any Episcopal Society, by excluding things which are peculiar to our Church, I reply that there is ground enough left for genius and piety to exercise itself upon, for the benefit of the Church. Interesting tracts or stories, it seems to me, might be written on the subject of baptism, confirmation, the Lord's Supper, on the excellency and apostolic origin of the three orders in the Church, on the daily service of the Church, and even on the catechism, without agitating their inflammable materials, which are deep hidden in a great measure from view. It appears to me, there never was a time when more, and important considerations required us to let these matters alone, and attend to things which make for peace among ourselves, and are necessary to recommend our Church, to the esteem of the more wise, and pious, of our own and other communions. If we continue to bite and devour one another, we may expect to be consumed one of another.

I am not much given to nice speculations in doctrines which have always been discussed in the Christian world, having neither heart nor head for them, but in one thing I am immoveably fixed, to do my utmost to resist, and hold up to public odium, anything like intolerance towards opinions and practices (although I may neither hold the one nor observe the other,) which pious and sensible men have believed to be promotive of true religion. From such a spirit as this, I think our Church, is in more danger than from anything else which is supposed to threaten her peace and unity. I doubt not, that there are in both of the parties which now divide the Church, a number of pious and discreet men, lovers of peace, both clergy and laity, who feel and think alike on this subject, and whose influence, if felt as it deserves, will yet make us to dwell together in unity.

I have thus freely, my dear sir, expressed to you, as you requested, my opinions as to the merits of the compositions which the agent was so good as to send for my examination. So far as I can conscientiously promote the circulation of any books issued from a society of our Church, I hold it a duty, and shall feel it a pleasure, so to do. But I am constrained to say, that no society can receive general support, which ventures upon these topics, which are so disputed among us. If I have taken any wrong views of the books in question, I shall be glad to have them corrected, and will candidly acknowledge my error. I thank you for the promise contained in your letter, of transmitting the other publications as soon as they are issued. In rather more than two weeks from this time, I shall set out for our State Convention, and do not expect to return home before the month of August, as I have undertaken to spend some months in making collections for our Seminary, in the lower part of Virginia. A letter, written immediately, will reach me before my departure, or, at a later period, might be addressed to me at Petersburg, where I shall be from the 15th to the 20th of May.

With best wishes and prayers for your usefulness and happiness
I remain your friend and brother,

W. Meade.

P. S.—On the 20th page of the second Catechism, I find an explanation of the term "generally necessary to salvation" different from that which I have been accustomed in my own mind to attach to it. I have always supposed that "generally" was a qualifying phrase, in opposition to the doctrine that baptism was absolutely essential to salvation. As the explanation now stands in this Catechism, it appears to me that the Church is made to speak a language and declare a doctrine, which, I think, must be disowned by all its members and ministers. I should like to have some explanation of this.

Thus terminated a correspondence conducted in the best spirit, and with a result, which authorized the hope that the Society would be carefully managed, in accordance with the impartial policy to which it was pledged. Its direction, however, passed into other hands, and, with the introduction of the novelties which began seriously to disturb the Church, it was charged with favoring views which were regarded by many as essentially Romish. The dissatisfaction became so extensive and decided, that, in 1846, when a number of Bishops were assembled in New York at a meeting of the General Missionary Society, a meeting of the Executive Committee of the Sunday School Union was called by special request. The complaints alluded to were fully stated, and an order was passed, that a set of all the books of the society, should be sent to each Bishop for examination. In those sent to Bishop Meade he found so much to object to that, as he says, "I felt it my duty to spread the same before the Church. This was done in an octavo pamphlet of more than sixty pages. For so doing, I received much severe censure from the press, and elsewhere. My charges were pronounced to be false. The books were declared to be worthy of all praise, and to have no unsound doctrine in them. The Church was solemnly and repeatedly called on to sustain it just as it was." To repel those assaults, correct the misrepresentations by which they were accompanied, and vindicate his course, he addressed the following letter to the Board of Managers and Executive Committee of the Sunday School Union:

Millwood, Sept. 17, 1851.

Brethren:

I have received, and this day read, the last report of the institution under your care, and which is especially directed to be sent to each Bishop, Standing Committee, and Diocesan Convention, in order to receive their early and favorable attention. In that report I find myself not only alluded to in a way not to be misunderstood, but twice mentioned by name in connection with quotations from letter or letters, written in the year 1827, on the subject of the union. The object of adducing those passages in which; at that early period, I approve the object of the Society, must be manifest to those who are aware of the position I have taken in regard to it, of late years, viz.: to fix the imputation of inconsistency, or contradiction upon me. As not merely the Executive Committee, but those of my brethren in the Episcopate who were present, united in approving and sending forth this report, I must beg leave to offer a brief history of my conduct in relation to the institution.

Although I took no part in its formation, yet, when adopted, I determined to give it a fair trial, and therefore, at the approaching Diocesan Convention of Virginia, united with the Rev. Dr. Wilmer in supporting it in opposition to the doubts and fears of some of its members, which were expressed on the occasion. It was at this time I wrote the favorable sentiment quoted in the Report. I must, however, add that my own fears were soon awakened, by the appearance of some book, in which the author's views of regeneration were either suppressed or changed, so as to dissatisfy myself, and others in the Church with whom I agreed. I at once wrote to the person having then the chief management of the Society, complaining that its declared principle had been violated. A most friendly answer was received, assuring me that such was not intended, and that great care should be taken to avoid it in future. From that time forward I paid little attention to the operation of the Union, neither opposing or promoting it, until my attention was called, some few years since, by one or two of my brother Bishops, at a meeting in New York, to some of its publications which seemed to savor of the false doctrines and practices, which Tractarians, in England, and America, were seeking to introduce into our Church. A meeting of some of the Bishops, with members of the Executive Committee was held on the subject, and the result was, that a copy of all the publications of the Society was ordered to be sent to each Bishop, to be examined by him. I at once entered upon such examination, and soon discovered not only that there were many and serious errors in them, but that a gradual change had been for some years taking place in the character of the books, and that up to that time, they were becoming more and more assimilated, in language and doctrine, to the writings of the Tractarians. So numerous were those objectionable passages, so serions the errors, so widely circulated were the books through the Church, and, above all, so little had they been noticed, that I felt myself bound, not to deliver a caution to the Executive Committee in a private letter, but to address the whole Church in two printed ones, warning it of the danger to which it was exposed. That a private letter would have been of no avail, is evident from the fact, that the managers of the Society have repeatedly published to the world, a denial of any deviation from the principles of its organization and of the Church, and challenged proof of the reverse. I refer my brethren to my two printed letters for the decision of that question.

I have written the above, in order briefly to exhibit the consistency of my course, from the first establishment of the Sunday School Union, to the present time. As a minister and Bishop of the Church, I have desired to promote, as far as my judgment and conscience would allow, an institution which, though not under the patronage of the General Convention (for that was pointedly objected to at the time of its formation), was yet agreed upon, by some of the Bishops and clergy, as an experiment for supplying the Church with a great desideratum. I will only add one remark in relation to the support sought to be obtained in behalf of the Society from the names of White, Hobart, Griswold, and Moore. That they did assent to the Society at its formation, and wish it well afterwards, is doubtless true, but that this can be adduced as favoring the changes which took place in the progress of the Society, is untrue. Their writings on many points bear testimony to the contrary. Most of them had gone to their rest before the objectionable features were introduced into the Society's publications. It is perfectly fair to adduce their names as consenting to the establishment of the Society, and even to add my humble one to the same, but unfair, to use any of them so as to countenance errors which they did not hold. That one or two things which I have criticised in my letters, may have been held by one or two of those above mentioned, may be true, but that they can be adduced as sustaining the Society as to the others, is untrue.

(Signature omitted).

On the subject matter of the correspondence it may be remarked: *First:* In placing the altered edition of Mrs. Sherwood's Stories on the list of premium books, and ignoring altogether the genuine book, the Society certainly did all in their power to secure the circulation and use of the mutilated edition, with its *vast* changes, as the Secretary styles them. True, it was only a *recommendation*, but what more *could* they do? It certainly gave the spurious edition all the advantage possessed even by their own original publications, for these they do but commend, not force upon the Church. The only force supposable in the case is the force of circumstances, and if these were not determined by the Society so as to favor the exclusive currency of the obnoxious volume (which had already been the occasion of sharp controversy in the Diocese of Maryland), it would be difficult to suggest anything, within the limits of their authority, which would be more efficient for the purpose. To have merely named the book, without specifying any edition, would have been to act impartially, and this is precisely what Bishop MEADE suggests in his next letter.

Secondly: To alter the work of an author without his knowledge and approval, even though the changes be inconsiderable, and really contribute to its improvement, is a liberty which, it is to be hoped, few would justify. The Secretary of the Executive Committee very properly pursued a different course. Alluding in his letter to "Bishop Hobart's Catechism," he writes: "We have chosen it, slightly altered, at our request, by the Right Rev. author." Their own action in this case, where the change desired was *slight,* is a reliable exponent of their conviction of right, and commits their judgment in condemnation of the liberty taken with Mrs. Sherwood's Stories. And yet, when they adopted and recommended, exclusively too, the work seriously changed, without any reference to the author, they became virtually implicated in an offence, which their own recorded conduct, in a similar, but very much lighter case, decidedly disallowed.

(*Evangelical Knowledge Society*).—The hopeless perversion of the Sunday School Union to party purposes was now apparent. The only alternative left to the friends of evangelical truth and primitive order were, to leave the Church to be flooded by publications of strong Romish tendency, or, to counteract these, by providing and circulating others, in harmony with the teachings of the Reformers, and the doctrine of the Articles and Homilies. The election was soon decidedly made. The important movement, in its origin and successful progress, is thus recorded by Bishop MEADE, who was chosen its President:

"Seeing there was no promise or hope of amendment, a

number of those who believed that better books and tracts might be procured, determined to form another voluntary Society, in which those who agreed in sentiment, might, with more harmony and efficiency, benefit the Church by the press, and resist that torrent of evil which was pouring itself over our own, and mother Church. Wherefore a number of Bishops, clergy and laity, who met together at the Convention of 1847 in New York, united in forming what is called the "Evangelical Knowledge Society." For so doing they have been stigmatized by many of the friends of the other Society as the promoters of division, schism and discord, and as slandering that Society, whose publications are still defended as sound and useful. God has nevertheless been pleased to bless our efforts, and to extend the sphere of our operations beyond our first hopes. Under these circumstances, at the last General Convention, a most unexpected and extraordinary call was made upon us to cease from our work, and unite with the elder Society under a somewhat new organization, which disavowed all former claims by its friends of being other than a voluntary society, and made fresh pledges of the avoidance of all which could offend any serious and pious Episcopalian. Had the regular officers and members of the Society, after due consideration, formally proposed to those of the Evangelical Knowledge Society, a conference for the purpose of enquiring whether there might not be a union of effort on some liberal basis, and, having agreed on the same, called upon the Church generally to sustain such a union, there would have been something worthy the name of compromise, though I do not believe such union practicable or likely to satisfy long. Or, had the managers of the elder Society been content to discard such of their books as were at length found to be unworthy, and made, even on the ground of expediency, certain changes in others, and resolved on the most comprehensive and conciliatory mode of action for the future, and left the other society to do its own work in its own way, there would have been nothing to complain of. All must have desired to see the work of reformation go on. But, instead of this, as though it were the only society having a right to exist, having resolved on certain changes and certain promises, and forgetful of past failures, it calls upon all the clergy and congregations of the Church to rally round its banner, and it only, under pain of being regarded as wanting in true attachment to the Church, and devoid of Christian charity. If such is not the position which the old society (under an altered name) has assumed toward the Evangelical Knowledge Society, consisting of a large number of the Bishops, clergy and laity of the Church, I have mistaken its movement. So have I understood the language of its managers, its committees, and its active friends, as spoken throughout the land. As to the probability of success in making it answer all the wants of the whole Church, it is not in place to discuss the question. It is sufficient to say that the Evangelical Knowledge Society has seen no cause to relinquish its work. That work is not the division of the Church (as has been falsely charged upon it), either as designed, or as the natural or probable consequence. On the contrary, the best method of preventing division, is to allow a reasonable liberty of thought and action. By attempting hermetically to seal the minds and lips of men, there may be a swelling and an explosion. In our mother Church, different societies, having the same great object in view, but using somewhat different means, are not considered as interfering with the unity and welfare of the Church. Many there are, both among clergy and laity, who actively co-operate with different societies. I sincerely hope that both of our societies may be worthy of such general patronage." (Old Chs., p. 377–8).

Error is generally more restless under contradiction than truth. It could not have been expected that the Evangelical Knowledge Society would be permitted to take its defined position, and attempt the accomplishment of its avowed purpose, without encountering decided opposition. By some of the devotees of the Sunday School Union, it was rudely and magisterially assailed, as an invasion of a field which belonged exclusively to that institution. The only attack which moved Bishop MEADE, was made by an unanticipated antagonist, and even this disturbed him, not by its real formidableness, but because of its author, with whom his personal relations were always most friendly; and on account of the offensiveness of the language employed. Bishop Otey, in his annual address to the Convention of Mississippi, then under his provisional charge, had deemed it his duty to warn the Diocese against the Evangelical Knowledge Society, as having been formed with an avoidance of those modes of publication which are usual in such cases, and therefore justly liable to the stigma of being concocted in suspicious concealment—adding his testimony against it, as not only unnecessary and inexpedient, but an action inevitably detrimental to the peace and unity of the Church. This official denunciation impelled Bishop MEADE, who was the President of the Evangelical Knowledge Society, to address the following letter to its Episcopal assailant:

MILLWOOD, July 22, 1848.

My Dear Brother:

On my recent visitation a "Banner of the Cross" was presented to me, containing an extract from your address to the Mississippi Convention, which surprised and grieved me not a little. I need not say it was that which referred to the Evangelical Knowledge Society. My determination was immediately taken to address you a brotherly letter, such as our past relations not only justify, but call for; but sore eyes, and a disordered head, utterly unfitted me for the task until the present moment. When I read at the same time that your health was very bad, I could not but remember, how, on a former occasion, a diseased body had made you to take gloomy views of your own state with God, and to hope that the same cause had influenced your judgment, your feelings, and your language, in regard to the conduct of some of your brethren, in the matter alluded to. Whatever be the cause, you cannot be surprised that myself and others feel that you must think very differently of us, and our conduct, from what we had a right to suppose you would do, from all our past intercourse, especially that of the last few years. It is true you give me credit for intelligence and piety, but it must be rather of a doubtful character, when it not only could not prevent us from deliberately engaging in so evil a work, but did not even forbid our seeking concealment from yourself, and doing the work in secret; whereas, we should, in an open and manly way, have proposed it in general convention.

Such, my dear brother, is the construction put upon your language by those of both sides of this question. None of those agreeing with you, having gone so far as yourself, in the charge of cowardly concealed action, though indulging in very abusive language as to the motives and designs of the Society. Supposing that you must labor under some mistake on the subject of concealment, or you surely could not have permitted such language to escape you, in a public document, I will mention that not only was the proposition to form such a society the subject of discussion in the papers beforehand, but that we had four or five meetings during the Convention, at which from thirty to one hundred were present, with open doors; so that I never doubted but that it was universally known, and I did know that it was freely spoken of, being approved by some and condemned by others, according to their different religious views. You may perhaps ask why I myself did not invite you to unite with us in a special manner, over and above the general invitation to all the Bishops, given in our articles of association. I will tell you, candidly, why I did not. I believed that for certain reasons you would not wish to be forward in the organization of such a society, though you would be well pleased to see one formed, and if it were conducted in such a way as to meet your approbation, would promote its welfare. The same impression I formed as to Bishop Cobb, who had by letter expressed to me his thanks for my reviews of the books of the Episcopal Sunday School Union, of New York. I therefore said nothing to either of you, thinking it best to wait your own decision, after the subject was determined on. It never, however, entered into my mind that either of you were ignorant of what I supposed was so generally known, and so much talked of. That any Bishop in the Church should condemn the principle on which the Society was based, and the lawfulness of it, except Bishop Henshaw, I could not suppose, after the full discussion which took place on Bishop H's proposition, against which you and all of us voted. This is the reason I did not converse with you; why other Bishops who were present at our meetings did not, I am not competent to say.

And now, as to your strong denunciation of our Society, let me remind you of what I once heard you say, and what I have heard others say of you, viz: that you had never read one of the Oxford Tracts, and of course, could express no opinion about them. If such has been the case in relation to the numerous works, which, together with them, and of the same spirit and tendency, have been been issued from the press in this country; or, if you have not given a full examination to those books, whether from our Sunday School Union, New York Tract Society, or individuals have published, and which have been charged with false doctrine, let me ask, are you justified in pronouncing such a judgment on your brethren who have read them, and feel bound to adopt some measure to prevent the full influence thereof? Surely, my dear brother, you are not prepared to say that many of those sentiments, and views, and practices which have of late been advocated and introduced amongst us, are mere differences of opinion, which must not be opposed? If so, I have greatly mistaken your theological sentiments, and we are wide asunder on some important points.

But, even supposing that the differences of opinion be not so great, are you prepared to say, that those on the one side shall have all liberty granted them to organize and publish them, and the other be denied it? Shall some in New York be allowed to have a Sunday School society, and elect nominal managers from other dioceses, keeping the executive of it in their own hands, and impose itself on the public as a general Church institution, and set forth the views of one party, and those differing from them be forbidden to organize in the same way, to present their views? Or, if those called Evangelical or Low Church had happened to form the first one, would he have denounced the other for forming another? You must certainly remember that some years since, some of the Bishops—the Bishops of New Jersey and New York, (I certainly remember, were concerned,) formed an union for publishing tracts of a certain kind, to set forth the views of the Church, calling it the *Churchman's Library*, and endeavoring to circulate it through the Church. How long it lasted, and how far succeeded, I do not know.

And now let me point you to the organization of similar institutions in our mother Church of England. The Christian Knowledge Society was formed for the same purpose, by those agreeing in sentiment; the Church Missionary Society was formed by persons holding the same views as to Missions—both of them voluntary institutions, always opposed by some, and sustained by others, and yet doing immense good, and never producing schism in the Church, as you apprehend from ours. So far, indeed, from such institutions producing schism, I believe the effort to repress them, and denounce them, is far more likely to lead to separations in our Church. Let each freely set forth their opinions, by books and tracts, within the bounds of that liberty so freely granted by our Church, and we shall be much more likely to promote truth and love, than by any attempts to establish unity in the way some are so desirous to try.

I have thus written, my dear brother, because I really think that when some eight or nine Bishops were ever present or approved—that some of them have publicly recommended Diocesan auxiliaries—that one, Bishop

Elliot, contributed one hundred dollars annually, and myself am President of the society, and mean to do all in my power to promote it — that your public denunciation of it is not marked by that brotherly kindness, which we had a right to expect at your hands. As such are the thoughts of my mind, I considered that the relation which has ever existed between us, calls for such an expression of my regret and dissatisfaction at the manner in which you have denounced our proceedings.

(In his handwriting, but without signature).

Bishop Otey's reply, closely written, covers sixteen pages of letter-paper. To Bishop MEADE personally it is most respectful and affectionate. Thus he writes: "I do, and shall always, love you very dearly, and I hope through God's great mercy, in Christ, to occupy a place with you in Heaven, though I am sure it will be far below the height on which I expect to see you standing in that world of glory."

The general tone of the letter is one of sadness and dissatisfaction. Of his address to the Mississippi Convention he says, "It was penned under the pressure of incessant occupation, and during the intervals, very short, afforded for writing during a hurried visitation." His "mental state" at this time, he describes as "one of deep and abasing humiliation before God, under a sense of recent and overwhelming afflictions, aud of deep sorrow for the course which you (Bishop MEADE) and others had pursued." He adverts to his deep mortification on finding that he was not included in the invitation to attend the meetings preliminary to the formation of the Evangelical Knowledge Society, regarding what he considered, designed neglect as a want of that appreciation and confidence to which, from previous intimate intercourse, he felt himself entitled. "Every man," he writes, "is surely at liberty to choose his own associates, and select the objects of his benevolence, and determine the sphere which shall bound his virtuous efforts. And if we sometimes imagine that we have a place in the hearts and affections of our brethren, and rest upon it as a sort of staff, or stay under the burden of this weary world's calamities and afflictions, and find to our sorrow that our hopes have misled us, it may best remind us of the Psalmist's bitter experience: 'It is better to trust in the Lord, than to put any confidence in man. It is better to trust in the Lord, than to put any confidence in princes.'"

That there was no designed slight in the omission of which he complains, but rather a studious regard for what was supposed would be most agreeable to himself, and that the same reticence was considerately observed in reference to another esteemed brother, whilst the hope was cherished that "if the Society were conducted in a way to meet their approval, they would both promote its welfare," is expressly declared in the letter of Bishop MEADE.

For concealment, there was no conceivable motive, and if there had been, it would have been impossible in a movement which had been publicly discussed in the papers, and freely talked of by those specially interested in its accomplishment.

How far the mortification which Bishop Otey experienced from the fancied slight may have influenced his views, and suggested his language in relation to the Evangelical Knowledge Society, no one can decide. It did not, however, prevent his prompt disavowal of any intention of giving offence, and the declaration, "I am heartily sorry for having used language in my address which you (Bishop MEADE) deem uncharitable, and ask your forgiveness. This I am willing to say to you, and to all others who may feel as you do, and to say it as publicly as may be desired, to heal the wounds which I have undesignedly inflicted" —nothing could be more manly and Christian. Yet, on the fifth page, the influence of his unhappy prepossessions is again in the ascendancy, and without perceiving that he was virtually repeating the offence for which he had so becomingly apologized, he writes: "The word *conceal* may then be stricken from my address, and the manner and objects of the organization be described by any terms which will convey a just and truthful impression of the transaction, and I shall be perfectly satisfied. But I am greatly deceived, if the common judgment of mankind do not pronounce of the action in the meeting, so far as action can speak, that it entered not into wishes or contemplation to have the time, place, or purposes, of their assemblage known to the ministers and members of the Church then in New York." This assumption as to the verdict of mankind is, after all, only the repetition of his own offensive judgment, with a vain attempt to give it the sanction of universal concurrence. The whole reply shows that the communication of Bishop MEADE had effected no change in his impressions as to the character of the preliminary meetings, or his convictions with regard to the Society itself. He still considered the one censurably clandestine, and the other schismatic in its spirit, and "fraught with mischief and danger to the peace and welfare of the Church, to an extent which can scarcely be overestimated." This is the burden of his letter, and he labors to sustain it by a skillful and earnest exhibition of arguments and objections, which have been so often published in various forms, as to render their reproduction here as unnecessary, as it would now be useless. The experiment has been made for seventeen years. Both Societies are in active operation, and the Church, at the expiration of that time, was undivided, and less disturbed, and more prosperous, than before the denounced institution was organized. The result fairly proved that not the Bishop of Tennessee, but the Bishop of Virginia was the true prophet.

The views of Bishop Otey, as recorded near the close of his reply, will be gratifying to many who cherish his memory with warm affection. Bishop MEADE had written:— "And now, as to your strong denunciation of our society, let me remind you of what I once heard you say, 'that you had never read one of the Oxford tracts, and of course could express no opinion about them.' If such has been the case in relation to the numerous works which, together with them, and of the same tendency, have been issued from the press in this country, or, if you have not given a full examination to those books from our Sunday School Union, New York Tract Society, or which individuals have published, and which have been charged with false doctrine, let me ask, are you justified in pronouncing such a judgment on your brethren who have read them, and feel bound to adopt some measure to prevent the full influence thereof?"

Bishop Otey answers: "You refer to my acquaintance with the Oxford tracts, and kindred publications. I never read but one of them—'No. 90.' I happened to be in New York when that tract came out. I read it, and immediately wrote to Dr. Seabury, expressing my unqualified disapprobation of its views and principles. This is all I have had to do with Tractarianism. It is true that I have three volumes of the Oxford tracts in my library, but I have never had time and opportunity to peruse them." "I never expect to read them, as I look forward to no time of leisure, or rest, in this world."

"You would know whether I regard the views, sentiments and practices lately introduced amongst us, as mere differences of opinion. I wish you had been more specific, for I do not know with sufficient precision to what you allude, to enable me to answer. If you refer to the practices, so variant in different places, about wearing the surplice or the gown, about lectures and pulpits, communion tables on two or four legs, and desks, and crosses, in our churches, &c., &c., I hold them as matters of indifference, except that neither the one practice, or the other, should be insisted on, to the destruction of charity. We have never had any trouble about any of these things." (His trouble in this line, however, did come, and he met it manfully.) "The clergy preach in the surplice or gown, as convenience, or necessity, may require; only we strive, as the Apostle directs, that 'all things be done decently and in order.' We keep as near to the rubrics, in all cases, as we can. But we sometimes have to officiate without any clerical vestments, and I have even converted my hat into a desk, from which to read prayers and preach. I do think that it is an abominable shame, that questions giving rise to unprofitable strife and debate about such things, should be introduced among Christian people, or those professing godliness."

"If your remarks have reference to another, and, as I consider, a far more important topic, I can speak with definiteness and precision. If you mean, in short, to ask whether I regard those views which have sometimes been presented among us, upon the great and vital doctrine of justification by faith, going to deprive the Saviour of the glory of His work, and the poor sinner of his only ground of hope, I reply unhesitatingly, that I utterly, and wholly reject and repudiate them. I do not regard them as matters of indifference. I hold, without qualification, limitation, subtraction or addition, the doctrine set forth in our thirty-first Article, and distinctly recognized in the Communion office. I entirely condemn the notion, and every approach to the notion, or idea, that any work of man whatever, however done, can add one iota, jot or tittle to the perfect and alone meritorious righteousness of the Lord Jesus Christ, by which, and which alone, the sinner is justified—that there is not one particle of inherent or inwrought righteousness in the sinner, which he can plead for justification. I hold that justification is the act of God—that faith, the only instrument of justification, is the gift of God, and applies the merits of Christ to the sin-sick and condemned soul for pardon—that the sinner is justified by faith only—that baptism, the Lord's Supper—in short, all other means of grace, when properly used, add nothing whatever towards procuring the sinner's justification, which proceeds from the free mercy of God in Christ—that they are channels for grace, given for the sanctification of the believer in soul, body and spirit, to fit and qualify him for Heaven. These are the things which I constantly affirm and teach—these are the things in which I find comfort and hope to my own poor afflicted soul, and in faithful adherence to these, I trust to live and die." A full and feeling exposition of Luther's "*Articulus stantis vel cadentis ecclesiæ*"—the very life-blood of the whole Evangelical system, which it pervades to its very extremities, imparting vitality and nutriment to every member, and securing the power, and symmetry of the body, in its completeness. Can it for a moment be supposed that one who so clearly and cordially embraced this blessed faith, could willingly be indifferent to the diffusion of errors tending to adulterate and neutralize it? If the good Bishop of Tennessee had taken time to examine, as did his brother of Virginia, they would not only have been one in heart, but have stood shoulder to shoulder in conflict, in resisting the unscriptural teachings of the Oxford Tracts, and kindred publications.

The correspondence produced no change in the affectionate relations of the parties. Some six months afterwards, in a letter on another subject, Bishop Otey writes: "I am sure, it is not in my heart, to add one single care or anxiety to the many that oppress you under the increasing infirmities of age, the pains of sickness, and the weight of official duty." "I shall never forget your counsel, your advice, your prayers, and your many acts of friendly regard. I never fail to remember you in my prayers every Sunday morning, according to a mutual agreement of nearly sixteen years' standing. I shall never cease to revere and love you, and should esteem it the highest consummation of any earthly ambition I might properly cherish, to reach the measure of your labors, influence and zeal in the cause of Christ."

The "mutual agreement" alluded to in this extract, was formed in Cincinnati in 1838, where several of the Bishops were convened, to consecrate the Rev. Leonidas Polk as Bishop of the Diocese of Louisiana. Among the private devotional exercises of Bishop MEADE, the following prayer and superscription are found in his own handwriting:

"The following is the joint composition of Bishop Otey and myself, the result of an agreement between Bishops McIlvaine, Otey, Polk and myself, to pray specially for each other every Sabbath morning:

"O God, who art pleased not merely to receive the intercessions of thy son Jesus Christ in behalf of Thy poor sinful creatures, but dost command them to pray one for another, and promise that the effectual fervent prayer of the righteous shall much avail, favorably regard the prayers of Thy servants for themselves and each other, which we desire to offer up, trusting that our great Advocate will intercede mightily for us with Thee.

"And oh, that the Holy Spirit may intercede within us, with groanings not to be uttered, making us all deeply to feel our corruptions and weaknesses, and earnestly to desire what we pray for, assured that none but God can help us. O that we may come unto God with strong faith, verily believing, that He will reward those who diligently seek Him through His Son, asking his best spiritual gifts.

"O God! who knowest our needs, Thou knowest that ours is no common office, but the highest in Thy glorious Church on earth, and that the honor of Thy Son, and the salvation of immortal souls are connected with it. O why didst Thou put such a trust into such unworthy and feeble hands, and expose such great interests to such imminent hazard. Were it not enough that we have to answer for our own souls, and run the fearful risk of their eternal perdition? Must we in some degree be accountable for others also, and for such numbers too? And oh! awful thought, must we be responsible to Heaven not merely for our little flock given us to tend, but, in a measure, for all those numerous ones scattered over the hills and valleys which we are appointed to survey, and not merely for our ministry, but for the ministers of those over whom Thou hast placed us, giving us the oversight thereof. Great God! who is sufficient for this? Which of us can be saved? O God! Thou must have great compassion on us, and deal very gently with us, and remember the infirmities whereof we are made—that we are only earthen vessels—weak things, and foolish things which Thou hast chosen to magnify, that in them Thou mightest show to the world that the work is Thine, and Thine the glory.

"But still, O Lord, we cannot but tremble at the thought of the work we have undertaken, and sometimes greatly to fear, that though we have solemnly declared that we believed Thy Spirit called us to it, it was our own foolish vanity which led us to do it. But it is now too late to draw back, for that would be to our own perdition. The most solemn vows are upon us to do all that in us lieth, to fulfil the great duties of our office, and to whom shall we go but to Thee for strength to perform them? O God! if there be any upon this earth who need a double portion to enlighten, to sanctify, to strengthen and to comfort them, are not we the very persons? And hast Thou not promised grace according to our day, and that Thou wilt not put on man more than Thou wilt make him able to bear? O, then, unto us be the spirit of Thy servant Moses, ruler over the Jews, yet meek above all men—the spirit of Joshua, fearless of man, and trusting in the Lord—the spirit of David, man after Thine own heart, full of holy zeal and deep contrition—the spirit of Abraham, interceding for the cities of the plain—the spirit of Apostles, and Prophets, and Martyrs, and holy men of God in every age. Above all, oh! for the heart, the tender heart of the holy Jesus weeping over the city of God, and making ready to die for sinful man!"

So far, Bishop MEADE; the following is Bishop Otey's:

"Almighty and everlasting God, mercifully hear and graciously answer the prayers which Thy servants have covenanted to offer for each other at this time, through the intercession of Thy dear Son. Grant, oh Lord, that we may never lose sight of the weighty responsibility resting upon us. May we ever realize an abiding and deep sense of the value of souls, and never relax our exertions to win them to Christ. May we always have such views of the dreadful nature and danger of sin, and be so affected with the love of Christ in dying for sinners, that we may esteem no toil too great, no hardship too severe to endure, in warning the ungodly, in reclaiming the erring, that they may be saved through Christ Jesus. Be with us in all our journeyings, protect us in all our dangers, assist us in all our difficulties, support us under all our trials; enlighten our understandings with heavenly wisdom, establish our hearts with grace, and so replenish us with the truth of Thy doctrine, and adorn us with innocency of life, that, by word and deed, we may faithfully serve before Thee, to the glory of Thy name, and to the edifying and well governing of Thy Church and people.

"Bless us in all our labors this day, and grant that we may rejoice in every opportunity of spreading abroad the truth of Thy gospel, and proclaiming the glad tidings of reconciliation with Thee. Bless Thy ministers and people everywhere, and grant that 'Thy ways may be known upon earth, and Thy saving health among all nations.'

"Hear us in these our prayers, answer us as shall be most expedient for us, and grant us all needful blessings, according to Thy will in Christ Jesus our Saviour, to whom, with Thee, O Father, and Thee, O Holy Ghost, be glory everlasting. Amen."

In the reply of Bishop Otey to Bishop MEADE, allusion is made to the use of gown and surplice. The views of the Bishop of Virginia on the subject are expressed under the heading, "Of the use of clerical vestments," in the first volume of "Old Churches of Virginia," pp. 47, 48, 49:

"It is well known that the controversy in our mother Church concerning the use of the surplice, was a long and bitter, and most injurious one; was, indeed, considered by some of her ablest Bishops and clergy as that which was the main point which caused the final secession; that if the obligation to use it had been removed, the Church would, for at least a much longer period, have been undivided. Various attempts were made to abolish the canon or rubric enforcing it, but it was thought improper to humor the dissenters by so doing, and alleged that if this were done, other demands would be made. At the revision of the Prayer Book by our American fathers, this and other changes, which had long been desired by many in England, and still are, were at once made, and the dress of the clergy left to their own good-sense, it being only required that it should be decent. I believe it has never been attempted but once, to renew the law enforcing clerical habits. Soon after I entered the House of Bishops, some one in the other House proposed such a canon. A warm but short discussion ensued, which ended in the withdrawal of what found but little favor. During the discussion the subject was mentioned among the Bishops, who seemed all opposed to it, and one of whom, more disposed, perhaps, to such things than any other, cried out, '*De minimis non curat lex.*'

"The Clergy of Virginia, from the first efforts at resuscitating the Church, have been charged by some with being too indifferent to clerical garments; nor have they been very careful to repel the charge, thinking it better to err in this way, than in the opposite. Bishop Hobart once taunted me with this, though at the same time he acknowledged that there were times and places when it would be folly to think of using the clerical garments, saying that in his visitations, especially to Western New

York, he sometimes dispensed not only with the Episcopal robes, but even with the black gown. The Bishops of Virginia have sometimes been condemned for not requiring the candidates to be dressed in surplices at the time of their admission to deacons' orders, although there is no canon or rubric looking to such a thing. They are at least as good Churchmen, in this respect, as the English Bishops. When in England, some years since, I witnessed the ordination of fifty deacons by the present Archbishop of Canterbury, in Durham Cathedral, not one of whom was surpliced; some of them, as well as I remember, having on their college gowns, answering to our black gowns, and others only their common garments. There is, I think, less disposition to form and parade there than is sometimes seen in our own country. I only add that Bishop Moore, in his visitations, always took his seat in the chancel in his ordinary dress, except when about to perform some official act, and thus addressed the congregation after the sermon. I have seen no cause to depart from his example."

In 1841 the subject of clerical vestments was agitated in Western Virginia, and a memorial, praying that their use might be rendered obligatory, was prepared and forwarded to Bishop MEADE, to be laid before the General Convention, then sitting in New York. To this communication he replied in the following letter:

NEW YORK, Oct. 11, 1841.

To the Ministers and Vestry of the Episcopal Church at Wheeling.

Dear Brethren:—Your letter touching the difference of sentiment prevailing in the congregation, concerning the use of the surplice, was duly received, and has been the subject of consideration. Not willing to trust to my own judgment, I referred the letter to Bishop Moore, whose age, experience, and authority in the Church, demanded this reference. On consulting together, we have agreed that it would be better not to present the memorial to the General Convention, but to address this letter to you from ourselves. We are sure that you will consider it as a sufficient reason for not complying with your request, that at the last general Convention a proposition was made merely to recommend the use of the surplice in all

11

the churches, but so great was the opposition made to it, that the resolution was withdrawn. The objection to any act of the General Convention on this subject is, that the circumstances of many of the churches through our widely extended country are so different, that it would not be expedient to attempt to enforce any general rule as to the dress of the ministers, but rather to leave it to the discretion of each minister to decide what is most proper. Had the memorial been presented, it would probably, through the pressure of more important business, have been laid on the table, or else been the subject of an unpleasant discussion, of which we do not think you would wish to have been the occasion.

While we thus decline presenting the petition, we cannot forbear adding our decided opinion that this is one of those questions which ought to be left to the decision of each minister of the Church, and that every congregation should be willing to acquiesce in the judgment of their minister.

We would therefore most affectionately recommend it to the congregation of Wheeling, to allow their minister to determine what is most expedient to be done, and that those who may differ from him, would, in a spirit of Christian love, yield up their own private desires for the welfare of the whole.

The matter of ecclesiastical vestments incidentally introduced in connexion with the language of Bishop Otey's letter, being disposed of, the notice of the Sunday School Union and Evangelical Knowledge Society may be concluded by mentioning an attempt which was made, in 1855, to have a depository of the Sunday School Union established at the Theological Seminary near Alexandria. The overture was made, not to the Professors, but to the students, and was accompanied by the assurance that, through its agency, they would be furnished with facilities in procuring professional books. Before acting on the proposal, the students very properly applied to Bishop MEADE, the President of the Institution, for advice. The following letter is his reply:

MILLWOOD, March 9, 1855.

To Mr. JOSEPH JONES,

My Young Friend:

Yours of the 7th reached me last evening. I know not how I can present my views of the subject of which it treats, so well, as by a brief statement of my connection with the Society of which you speak, and of my separation from it.

I was a member of the General Convention of 1826, at which it was formed. It was purely a voluntary Society. Some wished to have it under the auspices of the General Convention, but that was objected to. Some of the Bishops took part in it; others did not. The founders of it chose to make all the Bishops members and officers of it, as they have done ever since, without their consent, in order to give it the aspect of a general institution. The strongest assurances were given that it should in nowise be a party institution. I was pleased with the prospect, and took a leading part in causing it to be recommended, the following Spring, by the Convention of Virginia.

A few months only elapsed, before I discovered that the pledge was violated, in the most palpable way, by some of its issues. I immediately remonstrated with the Secretary and prime agent, the present Bishop of Maryland He replied that one obnoxious work should not be republished or recommended any more, and that as an offset to others, some of an opposite character should be put forth. The first part may have been fulfilled, the latter never has. The present Bishop of Kentucky made a similar remonstrance.

Since thas time, and more especially as Tractarianism progressed, its issues have been more objectionable, although assurances have been given to the public in their annual Reports, that only such books were, and should be issued as "*presented in their integrity those, and only those great truths, which are plainly recognized in all the authorized standards of the Church.* Dissatisfaction, however, still increased, and in the year 1846, a number of Bishops being in New York, convened the Executive officers of the Society, made known their complaints, and directed a set of all their publications to be sent to each of the Bishops for examination. Some of the Bishops did receive them. I carefully examined those sent to me, and in two letters made known to my brother Bishops, and some others, my objections. A reply was made to this by the Secretary, Rev. Mr. Tenbroeck, and, it is believed, with the approbation of those acting with him, in which my criticisms, which were couched in respectful language, were treated with scorn and derision, and charged with falsehood. I then republished my letter, with notes and an appendix, in a pamphlet of sixty octavo pages, and gave it more extensive circulation. For this I received the thanks of the Church in Virginia, which rescinded its former vote of approbation. The pamphlet has ever since been assailed in certain Church papers, one or more of which published in full Mr. Tenbroeck's reply. It has also been repeatedly declared in reference to the objection made in it, by the Reports of the society, and by its defenders, that the charges were false, and that the society's publications were sound. As the Tractarian tendency advanced, Bishop Chase, their senior and presiding Bishop, wrote a public letter of remonstrance to its present Secretary, which was as publicly answered in a most disrespectful tone, and the charge denied.

Seeing that there was no prospect of obtaining what we desired, in the year 1847 a number of the Bishops and clergy, after much deliberation, formed the Evangelical Knowledge Society, which has continued to increase in public favor, though violently assailed by the friends of the other, who for a time claimed for it the character of an institution of the General Convention, though that has been entirely abandoned.

At the last General Convention a great change took place in the policy of its friends, who, though they would not acknowledge that there was unsoundness in the books, determined as a matter of expediency, that there should be a revision and expurgation. A committee was appointed for the purpose, which sent forth a statement and appeal, declaring their determination to make such changes as would remove all objection, and ought to satisfy and receive the patronage of all the true members of the Church.

Had the committee and others been satisfied to make these changes in a spirit of moderation, all would have rejoiced; but they have, in a manner too plain to be misunderstood, made an assault upon the Evangelical Knowledge Society, and called upon all to abandon that, and unite with them in the only society which the friends of unity ought to support. Our destruction is their evident object.

Their statement and appeal has been sent to all the bishops and clergy of the Church, and to I know not how many of the laity, calling for pecuniary aid and other patronage. This was sent to me with a request that I would patronize its object, one part of which was, to break down the society of which I am president. This, of course, I declined to do. More recently I have been called upon to express my opinion as to the merits of a doubtful tract, "The Sacrament of Responsibility." To this I replied, that I did not purpose to take any part in the affairs of that society. I am now called on to approve the establishment of a society auxiliary to it, and of a depository for its books in the bosom of a Seminary of which I am president and professor, and all of whose professors are of the same mind with me on the subject.

I am confident that I might safely leave the decision of the question to those who have proposed it, only asking them, in view of the above statement, to place themselves in my circumstances and situation.

Although the foregoing statement should be a sufficient reason for my course, yet, as you have mentioned certain considerations in favor of the plan proposed, it is due to yourself and those agreeing with you, that I should briefly notice them.

First: The great change promised, and begun in the character of the books of the society. But it is a fact that they have never dared to condemn any of them, but merely on the ground of expediency to discontinue some and make slight alterations in others, if the Provisional Bishop of New York agree. Expediency is a very changeable thing. It may, in time, become expedient to change back again. In proof of the uncertainty resting upon the whole matter, I mention their recent action in the case of the tract on Baptism—"Sacrament of Responsibility," as it is called. In it, some very high views of baptismal regeneration are set forth. The committee being divided as to its rejection, it was left to the decision of the Bishops. It appears from the Church Journal that nearly all the Bishops advised its rejection, though only upon the ground of expediency, it being much objected to by some persons. The Journal states that the high doctrine of baptismal regeneration is thus most triumphantly established by the Bishops, and that the same doctrine is found in other books of the society, which have not been complained of. It is only inexpedient to publish it in this tract. On what is our confidence to be placed?

Secondly: You speak of the advantages to be derived through this society, from the venerable Christian Knowledge Society of England. That society, once venerable, has for some time past lost the confidence of a most respectable portion of the Church. It has fallen into the hands of High Churchmen and Tractarians, and has issued books different from those of an earlier period, and even mutilated some of its first issues, making them teach a different doctrine. I wish to have nothing to do with it.

Thirdly: You speak of the advantage of being able to get such works as those of Hooker, etc., through this connection. But, Hooker's works are in all the large book stores of the land, and can be gotten by any one who wants them. And, as to all the publications of the society in New York, they can be readily gotten, and I think it probable for asking, by any who desire to examine them, without the establishment of a depot at the Seminary. Depots are for large cities and booksellers, and the publications of the Society have been freely sent to various cities and booksellers in Virginia, some to Alexandria, I think which is so near at hand. They have no room in the Seminary for a depot, and if there was, the trustees would not be disposed to open it for the reception of the books of the society in question.*

It is clear, then, that whatever consideration may have been presented to your minds in favor of this measure, that it cannot otherwise than wear the aspect of a mere party movement in some quarter, in order to effect something of a triumph for the managers and champions of a society which ought to be put on trial for a longer period, after the unfaithfulness of twenty-eight years, during which period it has so often been complained of, and as often promised better things from the seat of its establishment, without performing them.

At my approaching visit, I can, if necessary, be yet more full and particular, if it be desired. I am sorry that I have not a copy of my pamph-

---

* This sentence was in a note in the original.

let, and of Mr. Tenbroeck's reply, to send you. Perhaps you can get one from some of the professors. I refer you also to a defence of the Evangelical Knowledge Society, more recently put forth by the Rev. Mr. Andrews.

Commending you, and all our young friends, to the guidance of the great Bishop of souls, I remain

Very truly yours in Christ,

WILLIAM MEADE.

P. S.—I add that, besides the society's own publications, it has a set of approved books, which amounted to three hundred when I wrote my pamphlet. I saw a very few of them, but found some most objectionable things, of which I wrote in my pamphlet."

When this reply was received, the students, at a meeting called for the purpose, passed the following resolutions, which, with the note from the secretary, were transmitted by him to the Bishop.

RESOLUTIONS ADOPTED BY THE STUDENTS.

THURSDAY NIGHT, March 15, 1855.

On motion, *Resolved*, That we cheerfully acquiesce in the wishes of the Rt. Rev. the Bishop of the Diocese, and at once abandon all idea of founding a Seminary auxiliary of the Gen. Prot. Epis. S. S. Union, and Church Book Society.

Resolved, That we tender the Rt. Rev. the Bishop of the Diocese, our hearty thanks, for his kind and paternal treatment of our letter of inquiry, and that we heartily concur in the arguments expressed in his answer.

Resolved, That the secretary of this meeting be requested to acquaint the Rt. Rev. the Bishop of the Diocese, and the Rev. Dr. May, with the resolutions of this meeting.

THEO. SEMINARY, March 16, 1855.

My Dear Bishop :

Enclosed, with the copy of the letter which you were so kind as to write me, are these resolutions, unanimously passed at a meeting of some of the brethren, who originally were in favor of the object proposed. I am certain that there is not one who does not heartily acquiesce in the course you recommend. I myself, indeed all, were ignorant of many of the statements in your letter. Had it been otherwise, I for one, would not have thought of troubling you on the subject. Praying earnestly that your valuable life may yet long be spared to preside over us and the Church to which we belong, I remain,

Your son in the faith,

JOSEPH JONES, *Sect.*

The violent abuse, and gross insults experienced by Bishop MEADE, and his co-laborers, for their vigilance and fidelity in the cause of evangelical truth, harmed their hot-spirited authors, but hindered not the movement which they so fiercely opposed. The society became a power in the Church, productive of positive good in diffusing sound scriptural views of truth, and also, if the statement be allowable, exercising a salutary influence in the interests and usefulness of the institution of which it was denounced as the rival.

The only question of any especial interest which brought out a difference of opinion, related to the propriety of publishing works of fiction. The question was concisely and clearly stated by the Rev. C. W. Andrews, D. D., to whose indefatigable activity, and intelligent zeal, the society is, under God's blessing, largely indebted for its reputation and usefulness. "Is it lawful to use fiction as a vehicle of religious truth?" and he argued in favor of the negative with earnestness and ability. The majority, however, did not adopt his view, and the course which had been commenced, though more carefully regulated, was not discontinued. Pending the discussion, some one wrote to the president to obtain the benefit of his judgment in the case. His reply, a copy of which he retained, does not contain the name of the person to whom it was sent.

WESTERN VIRGINIA, NOV., 1854.

Reverend and Dear Sir:

Your letter asking my opinion about the admission of any fictitious works into our Society's publications, has overtaken me in the woods of

Western Virginia. My reply must be just such as I can make in the midst of duty, and on the wing. I have thought seriously of it before, and my mind is made up. I should be very sorry to have our hands bound up, so that we could not publish any little books, interesting and useful to children and young persons, because they are not actual history, biography, or purely didactic. I think we should thereby, give other societies the advantage over us in that respect. At the same time, I should be sorry to see our Society going as far in the way of fiction as the American Sunday School Union, and the Episcopal Sunday School Union once did. As to larger works of fiction, for older persons, designed to recommend sound doctrines and expose false ones, I would rather let the booksellers fulfil that department.

I would say a few words on the subject of fiction in general.

1st. I think it is sanctioned by the figurative language of Scripture, by the parables, by the book of Job, etc., which, though having truth for their basis, are yet not the plain manner of stating facts and truths.

2nd. I think that our Lord and His apostles sanctioned it when they held up a perfect pattern and standard of duty which no man ever reached. Our Lord says, "Be ye perfect, even as God is perfect." Perfection in holiness is ever enjoined. God could not require less without sanctioning sin. A well written story, holding up a lovely pattern of piety, though not affirming that the character is perfect, is only a picture of the perfect law of God, or an example of it, which we are called on to imitate and get as near to as possible, just as we are called on to obey the law of God as nearly as possible. Our Lord as man, was a perfect pattern which we are called on to follow. We are also called on to follow the example of others of the highest sort. Why not discribe some high example? It is said that they are beyond the truth—beyond reality of life, but still, they are not beyond the requirements of the divine law.

Blair, I think it is, who says that novels are good for elevating the minds and characters of men, by placing the noble deeds, and high virtues, of the heroes and heroines before the reader, thus exalting the reader. This may be true of some few heroes and heroines of novels, but, for the most part, mere human virtues are exalted, not the graces of the Spirit. It is not the gospel hero, but the mere moral man of the earth, and all the scenes are extravagant, and the tendency of the books to lead away from religion; religion is either absent or caricatured, and weaknesses are ridiculed. Such is eminently the character of Walter Scott's novels and poems. Now religious novels are written as antidotes to these, to commend piety, to present the Christian graces of humility, meekness, forgiveness, love, zeal, etc., and sometimes do it most effectually. That they sometimes go beyond what we see, even among the pious, though not beyond the requirements of God's perfect law, may be true, but then they are intended to set forth what we should all seek to attain, and to stimulate us to the same. I believe that some biographies are as much in fault by overstating the character of their subjects, as some of those fictions, because the latter are put forth as fiction, though representing truth in the most favorable form.

I think, on the whole, that religious novels have done good by prejudicing the minds of many readers in favor of sound doctrine. But they have been too numerous, especially for the young, in comparison with other kinds of reading, or books to be studied. Let this error of excess be corrected, but let not the good be rejected. Such is my hastily written but well considered opinion.

Yours truly,

WILLIAM MEADE.

The history of Bishop MEADE's connection with the societies of his day will be completed by a statement of his relation to the organized efforts to promote the cause of temperance. These, under the original pledge, which was restricted to abstinence from alcoholic liquor as a beverage, had his cordial approbation, and received his zealous support. But when the pledge was so enlarged as to prohibit wine, though he had long abstained from its habitual use, he felt that the authority of Scripture, and other considerations, forbade his advocating the new measure.

His views are expressed in his reply to a letter addressed to him by the Rev. Alonzo Potter, D. D.,* now Bishop of Pennsylvania, an early and able advocate of the temperance cause:

NORFOLK, March 3, 1835.

Reverend and Dear Brother :

Your esteemed favor of the 17th ultimo came to hand yesterday, and though you do not ask a reply, I take up my pen to give you a brief, though free exposition of my sentiments on the subject. I am sorry that I should seem to any of the worthy laborers in the cause of temperance to entertain any sentiments which oppose the most complete success thereof. I am aware, however, that such is the case, and that some regret that I cannot go with them to the full extent of their condemnation of wine, and

* Written in 1864.

all fermented drinks. I feel assured, however, from the tenor of your letter that you and I differ very little, if at all, and so you will perceive when I shall state my sentiments and practice on the subject.

And first, that you may be sure my practice does not bias my judgment, let me state that though I have been a housekeeper for four and twenty years, and have had many friends to visit me during that period, I have never even had a wine-glass in my house, (except for the purpose of measuring medicine,) and of course have never invited my friends to sit around the wine table. I have, however, generally had a little currant wine made at home without a drop of ardent spirits, which, mingled with water I have sometimes offered to the older guests, in the place of something stronger, to which they had been accustomed. As to my own habits when dining where wine is used and offered, I sometimes decline altogether, and sometimes take a glass, or half a glass, not because I love it, but because I have never yet seen the propriety of passing such a total condemnation upon it, as I think distilled spirits most justly deserve. I never, however, invite any one to drink with me. As to other fermented liquors, although I should think it wrong to attempt to bring them within the temperance pledge, yet I never have them in my house. Such being my practice, long since adopted, and which I have never seen cause to change, of course I could wish that my Christian friends regarded the matter in the same light, and would go at least as far as I do. More especially do I wish, for their sakes, and for the sake of the holy calling, that all my dear brethren in the gospel ministry accorded in such sentiment and practice. I am sure that the habit of using wine as a common drink at table, of inviting and being invited to drink according to the custom, at dinner, which tempts to the freer use of it; and the practice of tarrrying at wine after dinner, cannot be necessary or good for health, but is often injurious to it, can never raise a minister of God in the esteem of any, but often lowers him, sometimes leads to sad consequences, and is surely not the best way in which he can spread his own or his neighbor's time and money. Wine, even in its purest state, cannot, I think, be used as freely and as constantly as some do who are considered temperate men, without injury; but the wicked and most dishonest method of adulterating and poisoning it with alcohol and drugs, renders it far more necessary to observe the strictest caution in regard to it. So great is the adulteration indeed, that I am not surprised at the perplexity which it has occasioned among the friends of temperance, as to the proper course to be pursued in regard to it in some places I undertake not to dictate as to the best method of correcting this evil, but am afraid that some are disposed to adopt rash measures. I feel confident that the attempt to embrace wine, even when adulterated, within the temperance pledge in our Southern country, would be injurious to the cause. The fact is, wine and all fermented liquors are but little used among us, at any rate, far less than with you. Whiskey, brandy, and rum, are the great authors of mischief. My impression is, that if all the drunkenness, and the evils thereof, in Virginia, were divided into an hundred parts, not more than one of those parts would be found to proceed from wine, and other fermented liquors. Is there, then, a sufficient reason for waging an equal and indiscriminate warfare against things so unequal in their effects? Would it be well to array against the cause, or at any rate to neutralize the influence of many worthy persons who would heartily unite against ardent spirits as a common and dreadful foe, but who cannot regard wine in the same light, because they consider it as having the sanction of God's word and the Saviour's example. We have quite enough on our hands, I think, without undertaking this vexed question. When we shall have grappled with the monster in his own native form, and, under his own acknowledged name, and slain him, or driven him to some other device of mischief, it will be time enough to vary our attack, and endeavor to strip him of his disguise and slay him.

I am not, I assure you, for avoiding a contest with the real author of evil, in whatever shape he may present himself. Though Satan come to deceive in the garb of an angel of light, I would assail him, and endeavor to trample him under foot. This I would endeavor to do without showing any disrespect, however, to the order of angels. If ardent spirits should come in the garb and color of wine, I would not be deceived thereby, but endeavor to expose it, without confounding it with the substance into which it has insinuated himself, and whose form and appearance it has assumed.

Let us in this delicate, difficult and most important work, combine all the wisdom of the serpent with the harmlessness of the dove. We should beware, lest, either by word or deed, we seem to cast a censure on the practice or institution of our Lord and Master. We may do much harm to the best of causes by taking improper liberty with the word of God, and trying to draw from it a condemnation of that, whose temperate use was plainly allowed. We may teach the enemies of religion and temperance an evil lesson, when they perceive us torturing the word of God in order to find out something which will support our peculiar views. I have occasionally been surprised and grieved at meeting with essays on this subject, whose spirit was not kind, and whose arguments from Scripture were far from being sound. Let us not injure so good a cause by any indiscretion.

My own view of the subject is this: That the use of wine, in great moderation, of course, is generally allowed in Scripture, but by no means commanded as a duty, All may abstain. Some, in all ages, have abstained, even from the purest wine, as John the Baptist, Samson, the Nazarites, the Rechabites, the priests when officiating in their order. Some of these were enjoined so to do, others did it voluntarily, and all must be commended for doing what was either enjoined, or for other reasons seemed right to them. Occasions may now arise, and causes occur, which may make such abstinence expedient. The very discovery of ardent spirits may make the use of wine less proper, if it shall lead us into the jaws of this devourer. The great adulteration of wine may be another reason, why that which is called wine, ought to be more carefully avoided. Certain descriptions of persons, as young men, and the ministers of religion, ought to use it very carefully, if at all. Children, and those who have once been enslaved by any kind of strong drink, ought never to touch, taste, or handle it. Thus far I am willing to go. But let us beware how in word or deed, we put it on a level with that fell poison which is extracted by a most labored process from the best fruits of the earth, and whose pernicious effects on the souls and bodies of men, I am inclined to believe, have been during the last fifty years, an hundred fold greater than those of wine, in any past age of the world. Let us also be very careful, not to pass too severe a condemnation on those who differ from us, either in opinion or practice, lest we be found to go beyond the word of God. By a steady example of self-denial, and by appeals to the good sense and good feelings of our fellow men, we shall effect far more than by denunciation or forced interpretation of God's word. We have already seen much success attending our endeavors in the present plan, and I trust shall see much more.

Your very affectionate friend and brother,

W. MEADE.

(*Oxford Tracts*).—These remarkable publications were issued by clergymen of the Church of England, most of them connected with the University of Oxford, who associated, avowedly, for the purpose of strengthening the establishment against the violent assaults of dissenters, by exhibiting its claim to divine right, and its standards in their proper construction. The real object, however, afterwards admitted, was to unprotestanize the Church, by so explaining away the distinctive doctrines of the Reformation as to assimilate them as nearly as possible, to the teachings of the Council of Trent. The plot was skilfully arranged, and conducted with great caution, and with no little display of patristical and other learning. On some points, its authors were, at first, unmeasured in their denunciations of the papacy and a certain class of its corruptions, so providing against the suspicion of any Romish proclivity. Under the confidence thus conciliated, with proclamation of unbounded deference to episcopal authority, which their subsequent practice did not warrant, and many pretensions of clerical power and prerogative for the other orders of the ministry, something of architecture, and vestments, and posture, to please the exquisite and the pietist, they so operated by their tracts, and other publications on the Articles of the Church, as to leave little, save the supremacy of the Pope, to determine a choice between them and the Tridentine doctrines. As the nature and design of the movement were perceived, faithful prelates, and other good men and true, sounded the alarm, and came to the rescue of the great truths so insidiously assailed. In the controversy which ensued, some of the leading Tractarians, unable to sustain themselves in the position they had assumed, apostatized to Rome, and carried with them not a few of the misguided laity. The agitation in England can scarcely be said to have entirely subsided. Its lamentable effects will, it is to be feared, be slow in disappearing.

Such are the relation and intercourse of the churches of England and America, that it is not surprising that the Oxford tracts found sympathizers and abettors in this country. Their endeavors were promptly and firmly met by some of the ablest bishops and presbyters of the Church, who, from the pulpit, through the press, by their own writings, and by republishing the most approved works of English divines connected with the controversy, exerted themselves diligently to banish and drive away from the Church the erroneous and strange doctrines, contrary to God's Word, which so seriously threatened her peace and purity.

The venerable presiding Bishop, the Rt. Rev. Alex. V. Griswold, was fully aware of the importance, and deeply interested in the result, of the controversy. In a letter addressed to Bishop MEADE, he writes:

"Yours of April 29th is, on my return from a journey, "received, as also the pamphlet, which I hope will have a "good effect in the Church. I think it well adapted to the "present gloomy times, and return you my thanks for the "favor. Had I not become too advanced in age; were my "other duties less arduous, and my health not too precari-"ous to engage in controversy, I should write something "in opposition to the Popish corruptions which so many "of our Church are introducing among us. What will be "the end, the Lord only knows."

This introduction is necessary to prepare the way for noticing the action upon the subject in the Diocese of Virginia, and the course pursued by Bishop MEADE. He was at this time the Assistant Bishop. He had a very delicate perception of the proprieties of official relation, and was most studious to avoid everything which might have even the appearance of interfering with what pertained to the Diocesan. In his annual address to the Convention, he confined himself strictly to the statement of those services with which he was formerly entrusted.

During the life of Bishop Moore they contain no allusion to the great controversy by which the general Church was agitated. The natural temperament and lovely Christian spirit of Bishop Moore inclined him to maintain and set forward quietness, peace and love among all Christian people, and especially among them that were committed to his charge. But, there were crises, when even his gentle spirit could not refrain from that official and public testimony against error, which charity itself demanded; and when he did speak, it was with earnestness and power, which were increased by the habitual reluctance which had to be overcome. Such precisely was the case in May, 1839, when he delivered to the Convention, which met in Norfolk, the annual address, from which an extract is here given:

"Having heard much said on the subject of a late publication in England, distinguished by the name of the Oxford Tracts, it would be improper for me to pass over them in silence, especially as one of the English bishops, and several of the most eminent clergymen of that Church, have expressed in most decided manner, their disapprobation of some of the principles and views they contain. The Bishop of Chester, alive to the consideration of those dangers resulting from the tracts in question, has thus addressed the clergy of his diocese: 'Many subjects present themselves, towards which I might be tempted to direct your thoughts. One more especially concerns the Church at present, because it is daily assuming a more serious and alarming aspect, and threatens a revival of the worst evils of the Romish system. Under the specious pretext of deference for antiquity, and respect for primitive models, the foundations of our Protestant Church are undermined by men who dwell within her walls, and those who sit in the Reformers' seats are traducing the Reformers.' 'It is again,' continues the Bishop, 'becoming matter of question whether the Bible is sufficient to make man wise unto salvation. The main article of our national confession, *Justification by Faith*, is both openly and covertly assailed, and the stewards of God are instructed *to reserve* the truths which they have been ordained to dispense, and to hide under a bushel those doctrines which the Apostles were commanded to preach to every creature.'

"To be reserved, my brethren, when discoursing on the atonement made by the Lord Jesus Christ, would be a departure from duty, of the most unpardonable character, and would subject any clergyman who should attempt it, to the charge of a denial of that Being who has bought us with the price of His most precious blood. It was the object of St. Paul to bring forward the Redeemer, in bold relief, to the view of all Christians to whom his epistles are directed; for, 'God forbid,' said that venerable Apostle, 'that I should glory save in the cross of our Lord Jesus Christ.' Nay, so deeply was his mind impressed with the importance of that principle, that he again declares, 'I am determined to know nothing among you, save Jesus Christ and Him crucified.'

"The tracts are also charged with erroneous views on the subject of the justification of penitent man in the sight of God. Our Church declares in language the most explicit, that 'we are counted righteous before God, only for the merits of our Lord and Saviour Jesus Christ, by faith, and not for our own works or deservings;' and the Apostle declares that our 'justification is not of works, lest any man should boast.'

"The clergy of this diocese, I have always considered, and do now consider them, decidedly pure and correct on the subject of the atonement made on the cross for the sin of the world, and also in their views of the justification of the returning offender in the sight of God; and I trust, my beloved brethren, while we live, and are permitted to exercise our official duties, we shall keep in view the cross of the Lord Jesus Christ, and proclaim to penitent sinners that 'by grace they are saved through faith.'

"It is under the banner of the Redeemer that we have enlisted. It is under this banner that we have succeeded in our ministry, and our labors have been blessed. It is by preaching the doctrine of the cross, that the Church in Virginia has been resuscitated, and that it now holds a conspicuous place in our communion; but should the awful period ever arrive, when we should be reserved on the doctrine of the atonement, or teach poor fallen man to trust his own merits for salvation, the blessing of Almighty God would be withdrawn from us, Ichabod would be written on the doors of our sacred temples, and we should be left to grope our way in midnight darkness. Let me entreat you, then, my clerical brethren, to hold fast to the faith once delivered to the saints, and so fully expressed in the Articles and Liturgy of our holy and apostolic Church. It was on the cross that the covenant of peace and reconciliation with God was made—it was on the cross that the fountain for sin and uncleanness was opened—and it is on that sacrifice once made on Calvary, that we are to depend for our present and eternal happiness. To withhold from the view of the believer the principle of the atonement, would be, to remove from beneath his feet the foundation upon which he has erected the superstructure of all his hopes—his support in every difficulty—the rock of his dependence in death—his only ark of safety when the heavens shall be rolled up like a scroll, and the elements melt with fervent heat. Be steadfast then, my beloved brethren, I beseech you, in the discharge of your duties—suffer not your minds to be influenced by any novel doctrines which may be presented to your view by restless and speculative men—be immovable—always abounding in the work of the Lord—forasmuch as ye know that your labor is not in vain in the Lord." (Con. Journal, 1839).

The Committee on the State of the Church, to which this address was referred, and of which the Rev. Adam Empie was chairman, reported:

"In reference to the excellent address of our Diocesan, referred to us, we remark, that we deem well-timed the effort made therein to place the members of our Church on their guard against the influence of error. To resist the first beginning of evil—to espy temptations at a distance, in order the better to guard against them—and to give warning of approaching danger, are common duties of God's ministers and people. And he knows little of the weakness and depravity of our nature, who thinks, either that the orthodoxy of all the members of our Church is a proof against heresy, or that the holy wisdom of our people is superior to a'l the wiles of the arch-adversary. As to those who publish such works in our country, without most amply exposing the poison, and placing the antidote close by its side, they are engaged in a work of very questionable morality and expediency. And those whom God has placed upon the watch-towers of Zion cannot, without guilt, see the enemy coming, and neglect to give the warning. Should the press introduce and facilitate the progress of this enemy over the country, may the providence, the spirit, and the people of God, lift up their standards against him. All of which is respectfully submitted.

A. EMPIE, *Chairman*."

The Convention of 1840 passed without any reference to the existing controversy, but in the Convention of 1841 (the last one over which Bishop Moore presided), though neither of the Episcopal addresses contained an allusion to the Oxford publications, the subject was again noticed by the Committee on the State of the Church:

"Lastly, that 'in the midst of judgment, God remembers mercy,' your committee think sufficiently evinced by the fact, that, though as a punishment for her religious declension, and a warning to 'repent and do her first works,' He has seen fit to permit the spirit of error and popery, under the guise of suitable 'tracts for the times,' to array itself against the Church, yet He has been graciously pleased to save the Church of Virginia from the infection of this plague. For, though a few may have been in doubt as to the dangerous tendency of Oxfordism, it has now, by the good providence of God, been so fully developed, that the ignorant and unguarded are no longer in much danger of being caught in the enemy's snare.

"In this we cannot but see the hand of Heaven, and the distinguishing goodness of God to our Zion; and this calls upon us for gratitude, while it warns us to exercise increased vigilance against the wiles of the adversary. And, as some around us may look for our 'halting,' and stand ready to reproach us with secret leanings towards popery, and with having departed from the genuine principles of the Protestant faith, your committee think it proper, in self-defence, and due to the cause of Protestant truth, and real godliness, to say, distinctly, that the Church in Virginia disclaims all sympathy with the Oxford Tract system, and denounces it as containing some of the worst doctrinal errors of Popery. We are obviously called upon, too, with increased fidelity and zeal, to rally round our standards to study more thoroughly the principles of the glorious Reformation, to exercise redoubled vigilance against the prevailing errors of the age, and to make ourselves more fully acquainted with the hydra heresies, superstitions and abominations of that corrupt Church from which we have been happily delivered, and with whose worse than 'beggarly elements,' some who call themselves Protestants have recently become so much enamored."

The report having been read, and a motion being made and seconded, that the same be adopted, a discussion ensued which continued till 3 P. M., when a motion for a recess prevailed, and the Convention adjourned until half past 4 o'clock.

The Convention reassembled agreeably to adjournment, Right Rev. Assistant Bishop presiding.

The report from the committee on the State of the Church being under consideration, it was moved and seconded, to recommit said report, with instructions to strike out so much thereof as relates to the Oxford Tracts. This motion produced an animated discussion, which lasted until near night, when the question to recommit was taken, and determined in the negative by a very large majority. The question on the adoption was then put, and carried by a corresponding vote.—[*Convention Journal*, 1841.]

From those who were present, and who participated in the discussion, it is ascertained that the objection to the report was based on the assumption, that the members of the Convention had not examined the Tracts with such care as to be competent to sit in judgment upon them. And again, that they contained good things, whereas the condemnation proposed was unqualified. To the first it might be said in homely sort, that to ascertain that venison is tainted, does not require one to masticate the whole haunch. Besides, tastes would differ, after all. Epicures prefer it when it is "*high*."

To the second it would be sufficient to say, that if valid, it would protect the Church of Rome, for "Satan's masterpiece," as Cecil styles it, is not so unwarily contrived as to be all and only evil.

In the Convention of 1842, Bishop MEADE presided as the Diocesan, and under a deep sense of his responsibility, now, for the first time in his address, expresses his opinion of the Oxford Tracts.

After alluding to the general revival of religion in the Church of England, during the latter part of the last century, he proceeds:

"Such has been the acknowledgment of the candid and pious of every name in England; and the traveller from our land, however prejudiced by birth and education, has been forced to admit its truth. It is, however, to be lamented, that within the last few years some have sprung up within the bosom of the Church, who, while acknowledging the glorious improvement in her character by means of the faithful and zealous exhibition of truths hitherto neglected, have nevertheless sought, by a very serious change in the manner of preaching, and by giving undue prominence to things of less importance to bring about something like another reformation, professing itself to be more allied to the Church in primitive times. It is deeply to be lamented that while God has so signally blessed the ministry and preaching of the last fifty years, under which the Church of England and America have been so wonderfully improving, any of our ministers, not content with pursuing more and more zealously the same, should strike out into some other path, venturing on an experiment which, so far as it had been hitherto tried, had proved fatal to true piety. The result thus far has been truly unhappy, though we trust the kind providence of God will bring good even out of this evil. The tendency of the system to which I allude, in some of its doctrines and usages is evidently toward some things in the Church of Rome, which our reformers most clearly renounced. The enemies of our Church have always delighted to ascribe such a tendency to her. Many pious persons of other denominations, not examining its truth for themselves, were induced to believe that such was actually the case. This, which has ever been an obstacle to the conversion and return of numbers to our Church, has been gradually passing away from the minds of the candid, and an acknowledgment becoming general, that our reformers established between the Church of England and of Rome a line so broad and deep that fellowship was impossible; a line stained with the blood of thousands of martyrs, who died the most cruel deaths rather than for a moment assent to doctrines and practices of the Church of Rome, which some would now have us believe differ little from our own. It is one of the evils of this new movement that it has again revived fears and prejudices in the minds of many truly sincere and pious persons, as to the affinity between the Church of Rome and our own, emboldening those who ought to know and speak otherwise, to use it in a spirit of party, against our Church. We may, however, now as of old, boldly affirm that no Church in Protestant Christendom more fearlessly contended for the faith once delivered to the saints, and more thoroughly renounced all the unchristian doctrines and practices of Rome, and it becomes both our ministers and people, more carefully to review the bloody contest, and know for what our forefathers fought, seeing, there are those within our own communion who are disposed to make light of some of the causes of the reformation, and even to regret some of the changes effected thereby; and seeing also, that Rome herself, as if waking up from sleep, is now in our own and mother country, putting forth more vigorous efforts to recover what she had lost.

I cannot, while on this subject, but commend to the notice of my brethren some short and well written essays now in the course of publication in some of our religious papers, by our venerable Presiding Bishop, (Bishop Griswold), and which I hope will be republished in some form better calculated to perpetuate them. In these numbers, while the differences between our Church and that of Rome, in many important particulars, are very truly and forcibly set forth, the peculiar opinions and practices of the tractarians receive their merited condemnation. I dismiss this painful subject with only one other remark. It is the most frequent and plausible praise bestowed upon the leaders of this party, and used even as an excuse for their errors by those who cannot but condemn much of their doctrine, that the state of things in the Church of England called for some new and stronger exhibition of certain peculiarities in her polity, which distinguished her from the Christian churches; that those who for the last fifty years had been the instruments of reviving true piety within her pale, by insisting upon the true doctrines of the gospel, and the holy observance of its precepts, had been too negligent of those external arrangements of Christ's kingdom, which, though of minor importance by comparison with the great doctrines of life, are, nevertheless, of great importance, by reason of their use in the preservation of order and unity, and their value in many other respects.

It has, moreover, been affirmed, that by reason of their agreement with pious dissenters in the leading doctrines of revelation, and in the promotion of various pious and benevolent works, that there was danger of greater neglect of the distinctive principles of the Church. That such was in some measure the case with some of the members and ministers of the establishment, is not to be denied, but the evil was undergoing correction without the help of that extravagance into which the leaders of this new school were hurried, even in their views as to church polity and sacerdotal authority, to say nothing of their heretical opinion and Romanistic tendencies. The Protestant dissenters in England, with the exception of the followers of Mr. Wesley, have, for many years, been more and more clearly uniting, together with the Romanists, Radicals and Infidels, in a steady and organized opposition against the established Church, so as to make the most truly catholic and charitable of her communion, feel the necessity of guarding themselves, and her, most effectually against assault. This, with many other causes, was operating so as effectually to prevent the evil apprehended, and it was surely unnecessary to bring in another and worse error, other and more injurious extreme, to correct what was only apprehended. Still less were such writings, and their extravagant doctrines, needed in our own country and church, where so many circumstances had, from the first, combined to place the defence of our principles on the ground of Scripture and primitive practice, rather than any human establishment, and where works containing such arguments in its behalf, have ever been so freely used. And as to the danger of too much intercommunion with our Christian brethren of other denominations, unfortunately, too many circumstances attending the efforts to build up our churches, not only serve as an effectual antidote to that, but strongly tempt our frail nature to the indulgence of feelings which we would fain suppress, as contrary to that charity, which should ever rejoice to hope all things.

I trust this notice of one of those "erroneous and strange doctrines, which, from time to time, in all ages, have assailed the peace of the Christian church, and which the Bishops are solemnly sworn to "banish and drive away," as far as they can, while seeking to promote love and peace among all Christian people, will not appear improper for one, who has endeavored to give the subject a full and impartial examination, and has been since we parted, in the country where it originated, and in circumstances enabling him to form a more correct judgment of its merits. Let us pray the great Head of the Church may bring good out of this evil also, and by the examination into which it has led, only ground us the more deeply in the faith once delivered to the Saints, and again revived by wise and pious reformers of our branch thereof."—[*Convention Journal of* 1842.]

But his conscience was not satisfied with this testimony against a system "fraught with evil to the Church, which could not be over-estimated." He was a member of the House of Bishops, and had a duty to perform in his official relation to the General Convention, and the Church of which he was the representative. In anticipation of the meeting of that body, he prepared a paper and a series of resolutions which exhibit his well matured views of the obligation which devolved on it, and of the action proper to be taken, and though they may not have been offered for adoption, they are both presented as they have been preserved in his own handwriting:

"SOME THOUGHTS AS TO THE DUTY OF THE EPISCOPAL CHURCH IN AMERICA, IN ONE OR BOTH BRANCHES OF THE GENERAL CONVENTION, IN RELATION TO TRACTARIAN ERRORS.

Firstly. There is a general impression both within and without our Church, at home and abroad, that the approaching Gen ral Convention will, in some form or other, take up this subject, and that the result will show the general sentiment. Even silence will be regarded as very expressive. It becomes those composing that body to feel the heavy responsibility resting upon them, considering well the effects which may be produced by the course pursued.

Secondly. It has ever been the wise policy of the General Convention to confine its *legislation* to great points of doctrine, discipline and order, avoiding smaller and more doubtful things. It will be an evil day for the Church when this principle shall be abandoned, and legislation, or action, be conducted by the majority, without due reference to the condition of all parts of our country, and a proper regard to what should be left to the different dioceses.

Thirdly. There are, however, some things proper to be considered and determined by general councils, and though the management of them may be painful and difficult, the duty should be faithfully performed in the fear of God. From the time of the blessed apostles, when certain matters in dispute were considered in council, and decrees made, or advice given, there ever have been councils of the Church, before which certain points of doctrine or discipline have been brought for establishment or correction.

Although much of human infirmity has doubtless attended them, and false decisions have been sometimes made, yet their continuance to the present, and their use in all parts of the Christian Church, show that they are necessary.

Fourthly. Although they are fallible, and our great reliance for the promotion of true religion must be on the truth of God's Word, faithfully, fearlessly and diligently set forth from the pulpit and press, yet there is weight and efficacy in the deliberate decision of a body of wise and holy men, assembled in the fear and love of God, which ought to be used for the condemnation of error.

Individual bishops, and other ministers, are sometimes restrained, by various considerations, from expressing themselves as fully and strongly in the condemnation of error, as it deserves. Sometimes bishops may not feel the necessity or expediency of special addresses to their own dioceses. And yet, all these, when met together, might feel it a duty to the general cause of religion, to unite in a remonstrance against what are believed to be pernicious errors.

Fifthly. Doubtless all the bishops and clergy have not only formed, but in some way expressed an opinion on the matters now in dispute; but there would seem to be a propriety in answer to the general call now made upon them, to do it publicly and in concert, so that no doubt may exist in regard to their sentiments. A refusal must subject them either to the charge of approving or lightly regarding, or even, under favor of the Church's silence, wishing to propagate the opinions, or introduce the practices complained of.

The English bishops and clergy cannot do it in concert, there being now no convocations in their Church, but with every inducement to forbearance, and after having postponed to the latest hour, hoping there might be no necessity for it, they have, nearly all of them, been compelled to come out with the most solemn protest against the peculiar opinions and practices of this school. Surely none are more competent than they to judge of the true character and effects of the same, and none less tempted to magnify their errors, than the English bishops, for every effort has been made by the Tractarians to secure their favor; all their peculiar views being calculated to magnify the Episcopal office.

Sixthly. The very important nature of the subjects in dispute call for action. Though some, in a spirit of charity, try to think and argue that it is more a verbal than actual difference, and though in all disputes between large bodies of men, there be those, who, on some points, do not widely differ, yet it is vain to hope that there is not a wide division here, and it would be dangerous to the truth to act on such a supposition. The wisest and best men on both sides, after many years of examination and free discussion, declare that the difference is great; and it is throwing contempt on the understandings of the first men on both sides, to say that it is only a war of words.

If it be only a verbal controversy, who introduced it? and how great must be the guilt of those who have thrown this firebrand amongst us, who, for the sake of introducing only new terms, have thus disturbed the peace of our Zion, and exposed us to the derision of the world. It cannot be that the great body of the English bishops, with every inducement to the contrary, should have come forth in such condemning and warning words, if it were only an idle logomachy. It is confessedly a movement, weighty and widespread, by which the Church of England is agitated to its centre. Since the Reformation, no such has been felt, as to degree and intensity, though there may have been as to kind.

Seventhly. A proposition to protest against the supposed errors, is not bringing those who prefer silence into such a position that they must needs declare themselves by saying yea or nay. The bishops and other ministers are in such a dilemma already. If the matters complained of be wrong, or so esteemed by us, we must either say so, or assign reasons for not doing so. Shall we give as a reason, that we fear to offend those who hold and practice them? This would be not only an acknowledgment that they are wrong, but that they prevail to such an extent, that we fear to assail them; or else, perhaps, that the persons holding and practising them, are those who will not bear to be censured by the Church.

Eighthly. But what is to be feared? The persons supposed to be in error, are those who claim for themselves, and their system, the most profound reverence for the decisions of the Church. If their claim be just, then they would most readily acquiesce in the same. An expression of disapprobation would surely not drive them out of the

Church, or diminish their zeal for it. They would be indignant at such a suspicion. On the other hand, as it regards those who are sometimes charged with being less attached to the Church, such a course might serve to increase their attachment, by inspiring greater confidence, while members of the community at large would be relieved from some serious doubts as to our soundness, and the mouths of some enemies be in a great measure stopped. If it be said, that alienation of the brethren would be the result, we reply that it is not likely this would be increased. If an expression of condemnation would be regarded as a triumph by one party, silence would be regarded by all as a triumph of the other. It would be so used before the whole world, and boasted of. Those who hold to certain views, and incline to certain practices, would feel emboldened to proclaim the one, and pursue the other more openly and actively, and the disputes of those within our pale, and the railings of those without, only increase more and more.

Ninthly. What is the fairest and most proper method of proceeding in relation to matters of such general notoriety, interest, and acknowledged importance? If the majority of the bishops, clergy and laity do, in their hearts, lament and condemn certain extreme opinions which have been introduced, and some new or obsolete usages which seem to assimilate us to the Church of Rome, and wish that certain books had never come among us, why not permit them, in answer to the general demand, to say so, in proper language, to the whole world? If all the bishops, clergy and laity present, were to be called on solemnly to say what they believe to be the sentiments of those whom they leave behind—that is, the great body of ministers and members—we entertain not the shadow of a doubt, that they would declare that the general sentiment was one of regret, and condemnation. Let the members of the Convention therefore, consider well what is due to the general sentiment of the Church, and how its character will be affected by those into whose hands have been confided its most important interests.

Tenthly. That a great majority of the bishops and clergy disapprove of many things of which some are suspected, and with which others are positively charged, it is firmly believed, and they owe it to themselves and the Church to express themselves plainly, and those who hold other views ought not to wish them to keep silence. The most suitable vehicle for such expressions is the pastoral letter which is prepared by the Bishops, read to the other House, and ordered to be printed and distributed through the Church.

Unless the pastoral letters treat of some subjects about which different sentiments prevail, they must soon be given up, or else be so general as to have neither interest or effect. Greater latitude may be allowed to the Bishops in a pastoral address than to the General Convention in their legislation; the one being only advisory, without the force and penalty of law, the other under certain pains and penalties, being obligatory in practice.

Eleventhly. The course proposed is in accordance with the practice of the Church in all ages, and particularly so with that of the bishops of the Episcopal Church in this country in their pastoral letters. Whoever will examine the canons and decrees of the different Churches during the earlier ages, will find them frequently re-enacting laws and creeds previously adopted, but which, having been either neglected or disputed, required to be re-affirmed and pressed on the attention and observance of the ministers and people.

The same may be said of the English Church, in the course of whose history we find that it was deemed proper at different times, and under certain circumstances, to enjoin a strict adherence to the doctrines established at the Reformation, and not by any evasion, do away or depart from them. So, also, as to certain matters of outward observance laid aside at the Reformation, as favoring the superstitions or false doctrines of Rome; when a disposition was sometimes shown to restore them, it was not thought sufficient that they were once abolished, but they were again forbidden.

But what bears especially on the present question is, the uniform practice of our bishops in using their triennial addresses for the purpose not merely of enforcing things about which we are agreed, but also warning against supposed errors in opinion or practice which were coming, or had come into the Church, notwithstanding some difference of opinion, not only among the people, but among the Bishops themselves. Some instances of this are here presented:

In the pastoral letters of 1808, 1811, 1820, we find the Bishops speaking in very strong language of condemnation concerning some who were disposed in any degree to vary from the prescribed service of the Church. In each of these they call on the laity to unite with them in opposing any such deviations of their pastors, thus endangering the array of the laity against the clergy.

Again, in the year when the question of the obligation to use a certain part of the service was much discussed, and the practice was various, the House of Bishops, in their pastoral, expressed a very decided opinion on the subject, condemning those who differed from them.

In the letter of 1814 we find the bishops expressing no doubtful opinion on the subject of revivals, about which diversity of sentiment and practice has ever prevailed among the Bishops, ministers and members of the Church. In the same letter we find the Bishops expressing themselves in the strongest terms of approbation of the British and Foreign Bible Society, and the concurrence of Americans in it. In another, it is believed the American Bible Society is commended.

In the pastoral of 1820, we find them, at the request of

the other house, expressing their opinion on the rubric enjoining public baptism, and on the qualifications of sponsors; on which subjects no little diversity of sentiment and practice existed, and does exist. Their sentiments were by no means acceptable to all.

In the pastoral of 1823 we find them engaged on the then exciting topic of Theological Seminaries, and, though the right of single dioceses to such Seminaries was fully declared by the General Convention, and such were, by many, much preferred, the Bishops decidedly argue in favor of the General Seminary, giving it the weight of their influence over others, although there were Bishops present having diocesan institutions.

In the letter of 1832 the Bishops felt it to be their duty to warn the Church against any combinations of Christians, which should undertake to interfere with political elections, by means of societies for the promotion of morals and religion. There must have been here a reference to those temperance societies which refused to vote for such persons as were politically opposed to them. In the same letter, there is a warning against any institutions which, like the American Sunday School Union and Tract Society (which were doubtless alluded to), proposed to promote religion by avoiding all the peculiarities of denomination, and confining their operation to books and works in which all might agree.

In various letters, we find them speaking of other denominations in terms different from those which some would have preferred.

Our attention should be particularly directed to the pastoral of 1835. It was the last from the pen of Bishop White, and much of it would answer well our present need. It was written when the Tractarian movement had but just begun, and yet, probably, after it had displayed enough of its character to excite his apprehensions, and lead him to the selection of a subject, whose sober exhibition by his pen forms such a contrast to the extravagance of the Oxford divines. The topic is, the right use of the Fathers, as made by the Episcopal Church, in which there are set forth the benefits which have been derived from a proper estimate of their authority, with a decided protest against that over-valuation of them, which has led to the elevation of tradition to a co-ordinate rank with Scripture, as a rule of faith—to the invocation of saints—to the doctrine of purgatory—the power of pardon vested in the Gospel ministry, and, finally, to transubstantiation.

Against all these doctrines, the pastoral of 1835 enters its protest, as if to meet them on their first entrance into our Church with a solemn condemnation. By a reference to all the pastoral letters, some of which are not at hand, other instances might doubtless be found. The above are sufficient to show what has been the practice of the bishops in time past. On some of the topics introduced, very different sentiments and practices prevailed among some of the truest ministers and members of the Church. The censure was, however, submitted to by those on whom it was cast, and no rebellion or alienation took place. Many, no doubt, continued to think and act as before on some subjects, on which they had a right to think and act for themselves—the Bishops not assuming the right to control, but only to warn and advise. But if they had a right to warn and advise on all these topics, some of which were comparatively unimportant, how much more ought they to speak in a decided, though calm and temperate manner, as to principles and practices renounced at the Reformation, but now sought to be re-introduced to the injury of the Protestant faith. It is to be urged that each Bishop, in his own diocese, may deliver his opinion, and thus the mind of the majority be ascertained. It is replied that the same might have been done as to all of the above-mentioned subjects, and may in the future, as to all others that shall arise, and so the pastoral letters be altogether superseded.

If it is to be questioned whether the majority do condemn, as has been supposed, then let it be so declared, and the honest truth be made known to the world, and all of us will better understand our duty.

Twelfthly. If it be asked, against what the censure is to be directed, it is answered, surely there can be no hesitation, after the manner of the English bishops, to condemn any language that speaks slightingly of our glorious Reformation—any lamentations over changes then made—any desire to restore things then renounced, or any disposition to change our title or character as a Protestant Church. Surely, there can be none to re-affirm the Articles of our Church, in their plain meaning, as established by the Reformers, and to protest against any interpretation of them, such as is seen in one of the tracts, which identifies them with the decrees of the Council of Trent.

As to the corruption of the doctrine of justification, and the extreme views of tradition, and of the sacraments as seen in some of their writings, can there be hesitation about censuring them, and referring for the sense of the Church to the Articles, Homilies, and Liturgy, of the Church? Could any otherwise than approve a warning against all changes in dress, postures, furniture, pulpit arrangements, which may even seem to favor the once renounced doctrines of the Church of Rome?

As to the invocation of saints, prayers for the dead, purgatory, and such like things, it would indeed seem most useless to refer to them, had not even these found apologists, and were not the Church reproached for either holding, or allowing them.

Finally. Can any object, in this time of renewed contest with the Church of Rome, and when some of the ministers of the mother Church have actually been seduced into her ranks, others found pleading her cause, and some in our own Church are charged with making light of our difference with Rome,—to a solemn, expressed determination on the part of her Bishops, to be most faithful in requiring of all candidates for the ministry, that they be not only well informed as to the points in dispute, but most decided in their adoption of Protestant doctrines, and resolved to maintain them? To this, let there be added a solemn injunction to all who are concerned in the preparation and examination of candidates, that they do likewise; and then, if any shall charge the Church with favoring these false doctrines, now so freely imputed, the pastoral letter will stand as a public testimony to the contrary.

Resolutions or Opinions of the House of Bishops concerning certain Controversies now agitating the Church.

The Bishops of the American branch of the Episcopal Church, mindful of the solemn vows resting upon them, to endeavor as much as in them lies to banish and drive away from it all erroneous and strange doctrines, feel called on at this time, to declare their united sentiments concerning some differences of opinion, and practice, which have in some measure interrupted the harmony of our Church.

They have perceived with deep regret how their mother Church has, of late years, been agitated by certain publications issuing chiefly from Oxford, containing some things contrary to the doctrines of our Reformed Church, and liable to the charge of assimilating us again to the Church of Rome, in some points of doctrine, and practice, which had been renounced.

They have seen, with pain, not only that such things were imputed, but that the effect of these writings had been to lead back some of her ministers and people to the communion of Rome, whereby great reproach has been cast upon her. As might be expected, these publications have found their way into our country, and some of them been reprinted, and freely circulated. We undertake not to judge, or say how far their errors may have found favor in the minds of any of our ministers or people, but certain it is, that the charge of entertaining them is freely made against many in our Church, so that it becomes our duty to declare our sentiments on the subject. We deeply regret that such books or tracts should ever have been issued, and such opinions entertained, though we may hope, that in the good providence of God, some good may be brought even out of this evil.

We feel it our duty to declare our entire disapprobation of any parts of such writings, which speak slightingly of our glorious reformation; which lament any change thereby made in doctrine, discipline, or worship; which favor the restoration of any terms, forms, or usages, abolished at that time. More especially do we here solemnly re-affirm the articles of religion then set forth, to be understood in their plain meaning as intended by their framers, and those enjoining them; and we do protest against that interpretation which would make them differ but little from the decrees of the council of Trent. We do especially protest against any view of the doctrine of justification, which shall remove it from the ground on which it is placed in our articles on that subject — against the elevation of tradition to an equality with Scripture, either as a joint rule of faith — as an interpreter of Scripture, or as a teacher of the truth, coming down in a stream separate from Scripture, from our Lord, and the Apostles.

We warn against certain extravagant views of the sacraments, and of the succession of apostolic grace through the ministry, which are found in some of their writings, and refer you for the doctrines of the Church on these subjects, to the articles and offices thereof, understood as the Scriptures themselves are, by a faithful comparison of their different parts.

We would also warn you, as most inexpedient at this time especially, against all changes in dress, postures, furniture, the places of preaching, or performing the different services which have been, or may now seem to be, promotive of doctrines once renounced. Even some things not forbidden, but which have become obsolete, and thus virtually renounced, should be cautiously introduced, and not without general agreement, lest evil should result. We hope it is unnecessary to enter our protest against such Romish corruptions as the veneration of relics, the invocation of saints, prayers for the dead and purgatory, which have of late found some apologists among the descendants of those who died in their condemnation.

We will only add, that while it is our duty as far as candidates for the ministry come under our instructions and examination, to see that they be well acquainted with those points which separate us from the Romish communion, and that they do most unhesitatingly adopt the Protestant views of them; we also enjoin it on all professors in our Seminaries, and others having any part in their preparation and examination, to be faithful in this respect, that neither Romanists on the one hand may have cause to boast; nor any Protestant on the other, to suspect that we have in the slightest degree departed from the spirit and principles of the Reformation."

These documents leave nothing to be added to render perfectly obvious his mind and position in reference to a movement which had agitated the Church in England and America, more unhappily than either the thunders of Rome, or the violence of sectarianism.

Bishop MEADE published but little in connection with this controversy. He was satisfied with securing the reprint of such English treatises on the subject as particularly recommended themselves to his judgment. To his zeal and liberality the Church is indebted for American editions of the invaluable works of his learned friend, the very Rev. Dr. Goode, Dean of Ripon; works which have not been, and never will be, *answered.*

(*Discipline*).—Government is a Divine ordinance, founded on the instincts and necessities of our nature. Without it, the social relations and individual rights of men cannot be maintained. Its earliest action is in the domestic circle, and, when duly exercised there, it is a salutary schooling for its support and efficiency in the more enlarged relations of civil and ecclesiastical life. Without authoritive rules of action, enforced by penalty in case of violation, government is a mere name, not a reality. However admirable the polity and excellent the laws, all are nugatory, unless sustained by wholesome discipline.

Bishop MEADE was born when discipline was something more than theory. Like the father of his country, he learned from the lips of an intelligent and devoted mother the moral precepts by which he was to be controlled, and when occasion called for it, received from her gentle but firm hand, the correction which his own improvement and the order of the household required. In these days of laxity and self-indulgence, when parental authority is almost antiquated, and filial subordination deemed scarcely compatible with youthful independence, such control would find few advocates among young, or old. Many are the plausible arguments to prove that its effect is to alienate children from parents—to break the spirit, and prevent the formation of manliness of character. It may be necessary to notice such arguments, when adifferent policy produces more devoted sons, and nobler patriots than George Washington, and WILLIAM MEADE, and when the dreams of doating parents are more reliable than the inspiration of God.

The mature convictions of Bishop MEADE's own mind were in accordance with the teaching and the training of his childhood, and gave direction and character to his course in the various positions in which he was placed. It was part of his creed, that discipline constituted one of the marks of a true Church, and is essential to its purity. As a parish minister he was diligent to minister the discipline of Christ, as he believed the Lord had commanded, and as the Church hath received the same. The record of his proceedings in this respect in the congregations committed to his charge has been already made, and need not here be repeated. It sufficiently evinces his vigilance and fidelity in reference to those evils to which some of his communicants were liable — the judgment and gentleness with which he interposed his official authority, and the happy result in the improvement of their consistency, the elevated tone of their piety, and the many hopeful additions to the churches which he served. But his sense of responsibility was not satisfied by seeking the amendment of his own immediate cure. As a Presbyter of Virginia, he felt it his duty to unite with others in correcting abuses which then lamentably prevailed, and by which the reputation of the Church was seriously suffering. His own account of the measures adopted is as follows:

"In the Spring of 1815, the first Convention under his (Bishop Moore's) Episcopate, assembled in Richmond. It must be evident to all, from the accounts given of the past history of the Church in Virginia, that much prejudice must have existed against it, and that the reputation of both clergy and people for true piety, must have been low; and that it was most proper to take some early occasion of setting forth the principles on which it was proposed to attempt its resuscitation. The last Convention, which was held under Bishop Madison, and which was followed by an intermission of seven years, had prepared the way for this by declaring the necessity of a reform in the manners of both clergy and laity, and by establishing rules for the trial of both. Wherefore, among the first things which engaged the consideration of the Convention of 1815, was the establishing a code of discipline. The Diocese of Maryland, from which two of our brethren, the Rev. Messrs. Wilmer and Norris, came, had already been engaged in the same work, and we did little else than copy the regulations there adopted. But although they were only the grosser vices of gaming, extortion, etcetera, which it was proposed to condemn, yet great opposition was made. The hue and cry of priestly usurpation and oppression was raised. It was said that the clergy only wanted the power, and fire and fagot would soon be used again — that we were establishing a Methodist Church, and that the new Church needed reformation already. The opposition, indeed, was such at this and the ensuing Convention, that we had to content ourselves with renewing the general resolution of the Convention of 1805, under Bishop Madison. In two years after this, however, in the Convention held in Winchester, when the number of the clergy and the piety of the laymen had increased, the subject was again brought up, and the condemnation of those things which brought reproach on the Church was extended to theatres, horse racing, and public balls, by an overwhelming majority. The same has been renewed and enforced at a more recent one."—[*Old Churches, vol.* 1, *p*. 39.]

To complete the history of this canon, it must be added, that in the Convention of 1847, when a revision of the canons was ordered, the chairman of the Committee appointed for that purpose, had introduced into his draft and submitted for the approval of the Committee, a canon on lay discipline, in substance, as it now stands, though with less detail. This, however, was objected to by the other members, and therefore laid aside, when the report was presented to the Convention of 1848. The canon as it now stands, was proposed by the Rev. Dr. Norwood of St. Paul's Church, Richmond, and pressed with much earnestness and ability. Though some questioned the propriety of attempting to be more specific than the language of the rubric prefixed to the order for the administration of the Lord's supper, and denied the right of the Convention to include among offences justifying repulsion from the communion, any not forbidden in express terms by the word of God, yet no one, it is believed, advocated any one of the practices which the proposed canon was designed to declare unlawful. The discussion was continued in the Conventions of 1849 and 1850. At the close of the debate, Bishop MEADE delivered his views, with great clearness and force, in favor of the canon. On taking the vote by orders, it was adopted by a large majority, especially in the lay vote, and yet stands unaltered as the law of Virginia concerning "Lay Discipline."

Among the Bishop's papers there are two manuscripts, one in his own hand—the other an exact copy by an amanuensis, designed to state accurately certain treatment which he experienced from one of the opponents of the canon. It was evidently his wish that the memorandum should be preserved:

"When the canon on 'Lay Discipline' came up, Mr. B. B. Minor took the floor, and spoke for nearly three hours against it. Holding in his hand my charge on Ecclesiastical Law and Discipline, he criticised it during his speech, saying several times that he had intended to digest his objections to it more systematically before he came to the Convention, but was hindered by other business.

On opening his speech, he adverted to the fact that had embarrassed him, that unlike judges in civil courts, to whom lawyers addressed themselves, the judges in this case were committed, and against him. His remarks seemed so personal to the Bishops, especially myself, that he was called to order. During his speech he made great use of Bingham's Antiquities, and quoted him as affirming, that the Primitive Church condemned theatres and such places, only on account of the idolatry of them, in direct opposition to the affirmation and quotation of my charge. I interrupted him for a moment to correct this statement. In arguing from the fact that the General Convention declined legislating on such subjects, he drew the conclusion that it was opposed to any legislation on the part of the Dioceses, and then, in opposition to the views of Bishop Johns and myself, adduced the conduct and opinion of Bishop Otey, of whose character he spoke in high terms, though not stronger than it deserved. He said that Bishoy Otey opposed legislation on such subjects when the General Convention proposed so to do, and therefore was opposed to all legislation. I rose, and said, that I felt it a duty to my esteemed brother, Bishop Otey, to correct an erroneous statement, which might make a false impression as to his opinion of the subject in question—that in the first place, he was not even in the ministry until some years after the canon was proposed in the general Convention, and that, so far from being opposed to my views as set forth in the charge, and which were criticised and condemned by the speaker, I had only a few days before received a letter from him, thanking me for it, and expressing his unreserved approbation of its contents, and that he was entirely opposed to all those fashionable amusements mentioned in the canon and the charge.

At the close of Mr. B. B. Minor's remarks, he alluded to myself as being the main speaker on the side of the question to which he was opposed. I rose, and said, that such was a very improper remark, and that the Chair had been the party assailed throughout the speech: that I had, however, no objection to the sentiments of the charge being duly considered, and opposed.

William Meade.

P. S.—I also mentioned, either in Convention, or afterwards in private, to Mr. Minor, that on the subject of special legislation on the part of dioceses, against which he spoke, that Bishop Otey was not opposed: that I was present as visiting Bishop at the introduction of a code of laws into the Tennessee Convention, when special legislation as to some matters in dispute was proposed, and that Bishop Otey, then a Presbyter, was in favor of it. I alluded either to some canon about lay delegates or communicants, which was opposed and prevented, I believe."

The letter alluded to in the manuscript is a reply to one from Bishop MEADE, enclosing a donation to the Diocesan Male School, of Tennessee, and dated April 16, 1850. In it Bishop Otey writes: "As to the condition which you make, that your contribution shall not go to any establishment which gives encouragement to *dancing*, &c., I say amen! heartily. I join with you, heart and soul, in the condemnation of all that class of worldly amusements, which are the opprobrium of many calling themselves Christians, and an abomination of this age. I resisted this thing firmly when our Tennessee school was founded." Again, "I have read your charge with great interest, and while there is a great deal to which I give my cordial approval, there is nothing, which I now remember, as exceptionable."

Certainly Bishop MEADE had good authority to pronounce the statement of the speaker to be erroneous. It appears that Mr. Minor thought proper to appeal to Bishop Otey on the subject, from whom he received a letter, the substance of which he embodied in one addressed to Bishop MEADE, dated July 1st, 1850. The purport of both may be sufficiently learned from the ample quotations furnished in Bishop MEADE's reply:

MILLWOOD, July 15, 1850.

Dear Sir:

Yours of the 1st inst. came to hand while I was engaged in the engrossing duties of my office at the close of the Seminary and High School. My first employment, after reaching home, is to reply to its contents. I have not only carefully read it, but revised Bishop Otey's letter to which it refers, and so far from being convinced of any misstatement on my part, find that the language of his letter is stronger than as represented by me from memory in the Convention. If any misunderstanding of his views has taken place, it is not to be ascribed to myself, but to the strong and unqualified language of his letter, and the introduction of his authority and sentiments by yourself. No one can read his letter without being impressed with the conviction that he had examined the whole of the charge carefully, and endorsed it thoroughly.

You quote a passage from his letter to you, which says that he had read only to the 41st page, and that he wrote to me tha the approved it, *as far as he had read it.* Of this there is nothing in his letter to me. Now the first 41 pages contain only a third of the matter of the charge, and yet, the Bishop, besides uniting with me in the condemnation of all the fashionable amusements reprobated in the charge, says, "*I have read your charge with great interest, and while there is a great deal to which I give my cordial approval, there is nothing, which I now remember, as exceptionable.*" Who could otherwise than suppose that the whole, and not merely a third part, had been read, and approved? Moreover, the very spirit and object of the charge was to show the propriety of special legislation, and of including fashionable amusements in that legislation. This runs through the whole —through the first 41 pages as well as the remainder. Was I not justified, then, in supposing, nay constrained to suppose, that Bishop Otey approved the main design of the charge in regard to legislation and discipline, as well as my condemnation of certain amusements?

And now in relation to the part you took in the matter. You say, "you will recollect that I only alluded to Bishop Otey because he had recently put forth a very decided letter against worldly amusements, and yet was opposed to diocesan enactments." To this I reply that your allusion to Bishop Otey (his name was not mentioned) was of such a kind that no one could mistake, and his authority was adduced in opposition to that of Bishop Johns and myself. As to the reason for your introducing him, viz., that he had recently put forth a pastoral against worldly amusements, I certainly have no recollection whatever, nor indeed, till your letter, have I ever heard of such pastoral, although he always sends me his publications. So far from my recollecting that you adduced this as a reason for introducing him, I stated to the Convention that I feared my brother of Tennessee would be misunderstood on this subject, and that I had received a letter expressive of entire condemnation of them, which I should not have done, had you prefaced your remarks by referring to some recent pastoral "of as strong and lofty tone as my own," to use your own language. You were arguing from the fact that the General Convention refused to legislate on the subject, and therefore, that our Convention ought not, and then stated that a Bishop with whom you were connected, and on whom you bestowed high praise, was amongst those who opposed it in the General Convention. It was then I corrected your error. If Bishop Otey is dissatisfied with the introduction of his name, I am not to blame. If the letter made a false impression, that must not be laid to my charge; for, as I have said, it was stronger than my statement. I never thought of introducing his name and letter, till forced to do so in self-defence, and in defence of himself, who I saw would be misunderstood. Not to have done it, would have deserved censure from him for being silent when I had just received such a letter. I think it proper to state that without such a statement on my part, Bishop Otey would have been identified with you yet more, as to the general strain of your speech. You labored hard to prove that the Primitive Church only condemned theatres because of the idolatry set forth in them, and it was understood that, though not attending the theatre in Virginia, you had done so out of the State since you were a communicant, and at no remote period, and that you had even encouraged by your presence, though under the plea of visiting them as statuary, those shameless persons of both sexes who in a state of nudity, have been going through our land, tempting the citizens to a lewd exhibition,—who had been excluded from some of the towns, and against whom even the gates of New Orleans were closed.

Having thus noticed the manner of the introduction of Bishop Otey's opinion into the discussion, and the reason of my referring to his letter, I shall notice briefly what you quote from his letter to you, as to the propriety of the legislation of the General Convention, and the impropriety of diocesan legislation.

You quote thus from his letter: "It has been attempted at several General Conventions when I was present, to pass canons making judicial proceedings uniform throughout the Union;" and you add, "I believe from his letter, that he would be in favor of some further legislation *by the General Convention*, on the subject of worldly amusements."

Being one of the three bishops who for a number of years have been on the Committee of Canons, in conjunction with clergy and laity from the other house, I can speak understandingly on the subject. One of our Bishops, whom I have always understood to be alone in his views on the subject of a uniform code of laws for all the dioceses, and who has, once or twice, I think, expressed himself in favor of it, though without proposing anything to the Bishops, did at length offer to our committee, at the last General Convention, something on the subject, but it was disapproved of by every other member present, and so roughly handled by one or two, that the said Bishop withdrew from the committee, and could with difficulty be persuaded by myself to let his name continue on the committee. There is not the least probability of the General Convention's going one step further in the way of specifying offences for which a layman is to be tried, or providing any uniform mode of trial. The probability of this is less and less every year. If any advance is made, it must be by the diocesan conventions, not in contradiction to what has been done in the General Convention, but in the same direction.

You quote Bishop Otey as saying, "If Virginia may pass a canon declaratory and explanatory of rubrics, making certain things specific offences, calling for discipline, there can be no question, I apprehend, that Maryland or any other diocese, in the exercise of equal rights and powers, may pass a canon declaring that precisely the same things are not matters of discipline." And let us suppose that some such discrepancies should actually occur, of which there is no probability, would it not be better that some dioceses should condemn certain evils, though others refuse so to do, than that all by their silence should consent to them, as is much the case now, for silence is pleaded as consent, and acted on.

In some of our civil codes, certain things are forbidden by law, and punished, as lotteries, faro bank, etc.; in others they are not. In some of them these things are legalized. There may be reasons, in such a widely-extended country, for legislation in one State or diocese which do not exist in another, so that general legislation would not answer for all. That such has ever been the view of Churchmen in America as to many subjects of legislation, is to be seen from the course of many of the dioceses, especially the older ones. I have carefully examined some of them, and found that ever since the confederation, they have legislated on special subjects without contradicting the constitution and canons of the General Convention. Virginia has done so since the very first convention after the confederation, for the present canon is only an enlargement of one then adopted. Forty years since, at least, Maryland passed a canon just like the one Virginia has adopted, specifying offences, and enjoining it positively on ministers to exercise discipline. A few years since she revised her code, and renewed this same canon. I have never heard an objection raised against it, as interfering with the General Convention.

You also quote Bishop Otey as saying, that "Another objection is, that specific legislation is an endless thing, and generally, if not inevitably, leads to the assumption of unauthorized power, to say nothing of the evils of excessive legislation." To this I reply, that special legislation has always been resorted to for the purpose of preventing the assumption of unauthorized power. Laws are made to guide rulers and judges, so that they may not be left to their own arbitrary will, and unaided judgment, to determine what are sins, and how they should be punished. Neither Bishops, or clergy, should wish to have it entirely in their hands to determine what is evil living. Canons should, as far as practicable, do this. The Church of God in all its branches, and civil governments in every age, have done so.

You also quote him as saying, "The things aimed at by the Virginia Convention have been pointedly reprobated by the Bishops in their pastoral letters to the whole Church. Now, it does seem to me that a minister, in exercising discipline, requires no higher authority to sustain him than the clearly-expressed opinion of the House of Bishops. The superior authority of the House of Bishops (I speak of moral power) can scarcely gain any strength from the act of a diocesan convention." To this I reply: More than thirty years ago, the Bishops did in one pastoral letter, and one only, censure some of the things reprobated in the Virginia canon, and called upon the ministers merely to warn the people of their cures against them, but expressed no opinion as to the exercise of discipline. The House of Bishops has ever protested against the doctrine that the expression of their opinion should have the force of law. The opinion of the Bishops, and a canon of either General or State Conventions, are very different. The former is designed to influence by moral suasion; the latter to justify discipline. I have thus briefly expressed my dissent from Bishop Otey's objection to the Canon.

In conclusion, I have only to say that if you have used Bishop Otey's letter in order to contradict my statement at the Convention, you will do me the justice to use this in order to the true understanding of the case. I particularly request this to be done in regard to Mr. Macfarland, who heard my statement, and to Dr. Empie, with whom you have doubtless conferred. I shall send a copy of this to Bishop Otey.

Sincerely praying that God would enlighten our minds with a knowledge of His truth, on these and all other subjects pertaining to the honor and purity of His kingdom, and lead us in the right way, I remain

Your friend and servant,

W. MEADE.

P. S.—The concluding sentence of your letter demands a brief reply. You complain that "freedom of opinion, and in the expression of that opinion," was "in a measure denied you." To this I reply, that you were allowed to speak for nearly three hours, while those who followed were restricted to twenty minutes; that you occupied more time, I believe, than all who followed you put together, though they were not less than ten in number. You had, therefore, full time for any explanation which you desired to make then, and also on the following day, when you asked leave to explain, and were allowed to do so. The Convention and the audience, I am sure, believed that full latitude was allowed you. Your insinuations that the Convention wanted the independence that you possessed, and which you repeated to me the next day in a very offensive manner, was such as I have never before heard made against the clergy and laity of Virginia, assembled in convention.

What you say also as to my reading you only a part of Bishop Otey's remarks on the subject (the whole of which was sent you by letter from Charlottesville), is a mistake. My own recollections are most distinct, viz., that after carefully examining the letter, I read you every word which was transmitted to yourself and Bishop Otey.

(*Lay Deputies*).—Another very important reform in which Bishop MEADE was deeply interested and took an active part, finds its proper place in this connection. He relates it thus: "We now refer to the method adopted, after a considerable time had elapsed, for the purification of our conventions from unworthy lay delegates, by requiring that they be in full communion with the Church, and not merely baptized members, or professed friends, whether baptized or not. No law, either of the General or State Conventions, forbade an infidel or the most immoral man from being the deputy from a parish in a diocesan convention, although questions might come before them touching the creed and articles and worship of the Church, or the trial of bishops, clergy, and laymen. The strange anomaly of persons legislating for others, and not being themselves subject to such legislation, was allowed in the Church, when it would have been resisted in any and every other society. The consequence resulted, that, although there was a great improvement in the general character of the Church, and the respectability of the lay delegation to our conventions, we were still distressed and mortified at the occasional appearance of one or more unworthy members, who were a scandal to the Church, the scandal being the greater because of the number of the attendants. The frequenters of the race-ground, and the card-table, and the lovers of the intoxicating cup, sometimes found their way through this unguarded door into the legislative hall. It was proposed to close it, but strenuous opposition was made by some, as to a measure assailing individual and congregational rights. It was discussed for three successive years, and though a considerable majority was always ready to pass the proposed canon, that majority yielded so far to the minority as to allow of delay and further consideration, which only resulted in the final passage of it by increased and overwhelming numbers. An incident occurred, during one of the discussions, showing how the consciences of even those who are not in full communion with the Church approve of wholesome legislation and discipline. A worthy clergyman who was opposing the canon, referred to his own lay delegate as a proof of what excellent men might be sent to the Convention, who were, nevertheless, not communicants. When he was seated, the lay delegate, a very humble and good man, who had never spoken before in convention, rose and expressed his entire dissent from his minister, and, as it was proposed to postpone the question until the next day, begged that there might be no delay, as he should sleep more quietly that night after having given his vote in favor of so necessary a regulation. He lived to appear in our body once more, in full communion with the Church. We have never, since the adoption of this rule, had cause to repent of our legislation, or to blush for the scandal cast upon us by unworthy members.—[*Old Churches*, vol. 1, pp. 44–5.]

(*Clerical Discipline*).— The character of the Colonial clergy has been candidly exhibited by Bishop MEADE in his "History of the Old Churches, &c., of Virginia," and adverted to in the previous part of this memoir. He further remarks, "That the ministers then in the colony were men of zeal, can scarce be supposed; as a law was required enjoining it upon them to preach every Sabbath, and administer the sacrament at least twice every year." "As to the unworthy and hireling clergy of the colony, there was no ecclesiastical discipline to correct and punish their irregularities and vices. The authority of a commissary was a very insufficient substitute for the superintendence of a faithful Bishop. The better part of the clergy, and some of the laity, long and earnestly petitioned for a faithful resident bishop, as the Bishop of London was, of necessity, only the nominal bishop. For about two hundred years did the Episcopal Church of Virginia try the experiment of a system whose constitution required such a head, but was actually without it. No such officer was there to watch over the conduct and punish the vices of the clergy. It must be evident that the Episcopal Church without such an officer, is more likely to suffer from the want of godly discipline than any other society of Christians, because all others have some substitute, whereas our Church makes this office indispensable to some important parts of ecclesiastical government and discipline."

The first Convention of the Protestant Episcopal Church which met in Richmond, May 16, 1785, addressed itself at once to remedy these evils. Rules were adopted as to the offences for which a clergyman might be tried; the constitution of the court, and the manner in which the trial should be conducted. From time to time, as experience suggested, these rules have been revised. After the revival of the Church consequent on the election of Bishop Moore to the Episcopate, they were systematized and revised with still greater care, and now, with no material change, are found among the canons of the diocese. In giving them their present form, which differs in no important particulars from that of other dioceses, Bishop Meade and the early associates whom he names, were prominent. His general views on "Clerical Discipline" are recorded in a manuscript with that superscription, prepared for some one who had asked for information on the subject:

"Being asked what was the practice of the Primitive Church in relation to clerical discipline, that is, who exercised the same, I have looked over several books in my possession, such as the abridgement of Bingham, the book of Apostolic canons, so-called, and Lord Ring's treatise. The following is the result of such brief examination.

The government of all the clergy, and the exercise of

discipline both over the clergy and laity, seems to have been in the bishops. They usually commissioned the presbyters to aid them in the exercise of discipline over the laity, and sometimes, probably, took the voice of all the congregation on certain cases.

As to the trial and punishment of the higher clergy, it does not appear, I think, that any court of presbyters was required for the trial of a clergyman, but, as the presbyters were considered as the senate and counsellors of the bishop, he consulted with them on this and all important cases. As the dioceses were very small, the bishops numerous, and near to each other, any bishop having cause of complaint against a presbyter or deacon, would call upon some of the adjoining bishops to aid him in the trial and punishment of such person, forming something like the ecclesiastical court of presbyters in our Church at this time. But it is evident from the canons and history of the earlier ages, that an appeal might be taken, and often was taken, to a synod or council, by one who thought himself oppressed.

The experience of those ages, and the history of denominations more modern, who have adopted that mode of appeal, having shown how vexatious and injurious in many ways it is, our Church has provided none such, except it be the privilege of a new trial, if it shall be asked, and shall seem reasonable. Such being the case, and bishops being liable to err through rashness or mistake, it is the more important, since there is no appeal, that the bishop should have the best counsel beforehand, lest he should do injustice.

It is also desirable that too heavy a responsibility should not rest upon the episcopal office in this painful department of duty, lest some bishops should neglect discipline altogether, or reduce the penalty too low for the offence.

I have therefore always preferred that the court should not merely examine the facts, and report the offence, but also express their opinion as to the proper penalty, leaving it to the bishop to inflict a lesser.

W. MEADE."

To the credit of the clergy of Virginia, it is proper to state that clerical trials have been almost unknown in the diocese. The paternal supervision, and, when occasion required, the "private remonstrance," of Bishops Moore and MEADE, obviated the necessity and avoided the scandal of public prosecution, only two instances of which, it is believed, have occurred within the last fifty years. The more recent of these deserves notice, not as of any general interest, but simply as involving a question concerning episcopal power, and illustrating the spirit of the bishop by whom it was directed.

A young man who had been a student of theology in a Presbyterian seminary, applied to be received as a candidate in the diocese of Virginia. His testimonials were from most respectable persons, and exceeded the requisitions of the canons. After the usual probation, he was admitted to the diaconate by Bishop MEADE, who, in the exercise of that discretion with which the ordination service recognized the bishop as invested, licensed him to preach the Gospel, and also sent him to minister in one of the vacant parishes. He had not been there long before his conduct gave such offence, that an appeal was made to the Bishop and Standing Committee to have him removed. The Standing Committee regarded the offences alleged as of so grave a character, that they formally advised the Bishop to remove him at once, and withdraw his license to preach. Bishop MEADE doubted his right to withdraw the license. Whether authority to grant, necessarily involved authority to revoke; whether, having given the license, he had not *fulfilled all the agency* contemplated by the language of the ordinal; whether, as the revocation would be a public censure seriously affecting the character of the deacon, it ought to be left to the discretion of one man. The course recommended would have been a short and easy mode of disposing of the case. But the exercise of doubtful power found no favor with Bishop MEADE. He therefore suspended action, and, as was his custom, sought such counsel as might aid him to a just determination. The opinion of the Assistant Bishop of Virginia was adverse to the recommendation of the Standing Committee, and in favor of allowing the accused the benefit of a trial. The views of other bishops were solicited. The following replies were received and preserved:

HARTFORD, May 6, 1860.

Rt. Rev. and Dear Sir:

Being somewhat indisposed when your letter came to hand, I took the liberty of sending it to Bishop Williams, asking his opinion, and that of the Rev. Dr. Coit (who I knew to be with him), in the case to which your communication refers.

Entirely concurring with them in their statements and reasoning in regard to the points at issue, I beg leave to forward their letter for your consideration.

Very truly, your friend and brother,

T. C. BROWNELL.

Rt. Rev. Bishop MEADE.

MIDDLETOWN, May 3, 1860.

My Dear Bishop:

Dr. Coit and I are quite agreed as to the question asked by Bishop MEADE, and I send you the conclusion, hoping it may meet with your approval.

1. The right to preach, in the case of a deacon, is not communicated to him by the mere act of ordination, *i. e.*, laying on hands. It forms the single exception to the list of powers "appertaining to the office," mentioned in the fifth question in the ordinal.

2. Not inhering in the ordination itself, it is a power in the will of the bishop to grant or not, as he may choose.

3. A power thus granted can, of course, be revoked by the grantor; since it is, in this case, his individual act.

4. But cause should undoubtedly be alleged and shown; and it should be either "*error in religion or viciousness of life,*" the two things, either of which would disqualify the deacon for a letter dimissory.

How *practical* a result this may be for Bishop MEADE's particular cases and purposes, I suppose *we need not inquire.* It leaves, after all, the responsibility on his shoulders.

Coit joins me in most affectionate remembrances; and I am, dear Bishop,

Your affect. son and servant,

JNO. WILLIAMS.

PHILADELPHIA, April 25, 1860.

My Dear Bishop:

Canon 6 of Title I. seems to place deacons entirely under the bishop's regulation (see Sec. 1); permits him to officiate in no case without the assent of the bishop (see Sec. 2); and by saying that when he officiates in a parish or congregation, he shall be entirely subject to the direction of the rector in *all* his ministrations (Sec. 3), implies nothing less of his subjection to the bishop.

I should suppose that the provision of the canon, added to what is said in the ordinal, places the deacon's preaching or not, at the discretion of the bishop.

Still, withdrawing a license might, under some circumstances, be an act of *discipline*, or *might be so regarded*, and, in that case, would be of more doubtful expediency.

I have generally protected myself, in doubtful cases, by giving a qualified or limited license.

Yours, faithfully,

ALONZO POTTER.

WILMINGTON, April 26, 1860.

My Dear Bishop:

You are more likely to know than myself what has been the practice in regard to the withdrawal of a deacon's license to preach. It would seem from the ordinal that it was revocable. But if it has not been done, I do not think a bishop could safely venture upon it without precedent. The jealousy of mere prerogative is very great, and would probably excite a great deal of clamor against such an attempt. Even in England, we have lately seen the Bishop of London severely assailed, and, I believe, prosecuted, for withdrawing Mr. Poole's license as curate; an act which I suppose to be of a parallel nature.

Whatever, therefore, might be the abstract right of the bishop, or the original theory of the diaconate, I should not think it expedient to exercise it. If there were sufficient ground for a trial, you might give the deacon himself the option as to which course you should practice; which would, of course, preclude any subsequent complaint on his part.

Hoping that you continue as well as when we last met, I remain,

Affectionately, your brother in Christ,

Bishop MEADE. ALFRED LEE.

It will be observed that Bishop Williams expressed the opinion, in which Bishop Brownell concurs, that "the license may be revoked by the grantor," for cause, which should be either "error in religion or viciousness of life." Thus adding to his opinion as to *the power*, a *caution* as to the only occasions for its *just* use.

The reply of Bishop A. Potter is very *non-committal*. He uses the canon which places deacons entirely under the Bishop's regulation, to interpret the language of the ordinal, and "supposes" that the two "place the Deacon's preaching or not preaching at the discretion of the bishop." The canon to which he alludes authorizes the Bishop "to *regulate* the Deacon"—"to *direct* the places" in which *he shall officiate*," which imply the *continued* exercise of his proper functions, and have no reference to their *revocation*.

If the withdrawal of the license be regarded as an "act of discipline," (Bishops Brownell and Williams held it must be so), then according to Bishop A. Potter, it would be of more doubtful expediency." To protect himself in licensing a person who has not his full confidence, his custom is "to give a qualified or limited license, an expedient which neither the ordinal or canon contemplated, and necessarily invidious in practice — a protection to the Bishop it may be, but an indignity to the Deacon, in which proper self-respect would determine him not to acquiesce, but rather to wait till he could secure the usual unqualified license to preach the gospel. It has the appearance of taking a liberty with the ordinal at the Deacon's expense, to save the Bishop the painful duty of declining to license doubtful cases, or the necessity of an act of discipline, when confidence has been abused.

To Bishop Lee, of Delaware, the ordinal seemed to recognize the power in question, but as there is no precedent for its exercise, he thought it could not be ventured in safety, by reason of the great jealousy with which mere prerogative is regarded, and advised, if there is sufficient ground for a trial, that it should be left to the deacon to choose which course should be pursued.

Bishop Whittingham, misled by a rumor that Bishop MEADE was consulting with some other members of the Episcopate about the practicability of deposing a deacon without form of trial, and by other erroneous impressions, at last gave utterance to his indignant censure in a letter to Bishop MEADE, which will presently be in place.

The correspondence with his Episcopal brethren afforded no relief to the Bishop's mind. In a letter of a subsequent date he says: "I wrote to several of the bishops on the subject. My doubts are confirmed by reflection. All the bishops generally think otherwise. In the case before me I determined not to act on the suggestion of the standing committee." Under these circumstances, judicial proceeding was unavoidable. The court canonically constituted for the purpose so far sustained the charges as to deem suspension for one year the proper penalty for the offense proven, and so informed the Bishop. What his opinion was as to the proceedings and judgment of the court, need not be stated. It is plain, however, that he considered the award disproportionate to the offences of which the accused was found guilty, for, in the exercise of his official authority, to "mitigate" a sentence, "if he see cause," he immediately reduced the suspension from twelve to six months.

The able counsel of the accused, in a letter to him after the trial, expressed his "profound respect for the intelligence, candor, and firmness" of the court, adding, "You are more indebted under God, to the high character in every respect of the gentlemen who tried you, than to my poor abilities, for the result. And again: he declares his "unmixed admiration for the firmness and impartiality of those gentlemen who disregarded all influence from without, as much as men could do, and tried your case with an eye single, as I believe, to justice and truth. May they, and may we all, when we act in a spirit like theirs, have fulfilled to us the promise, 'with what judgment ye judge, ye shall be judged.'"

In reply to the Bishop's letter, informing the party concerned of the judgment and award of the court, and of the mitigation, he writes: "I assure you that I firmly believe that both the court and yourself were actuated by the purest motives in your respective decisions." "Assuring you that for the mitigation of punishment which you have already been pleased to bestow, you have my inexpressible thanks, and that in all your dealings with me I recognize the stern but nevertheless well-meant dealings of a father, and that my reverence for you, and admiration for your character as a bishop in the Church of God, remain unaltered."

Although the canons require the bishop who pronounces sentence to give notice thereof to all the bishops of the Church, only in case of "degradation," Bishop MEADE deemed it proper to observe this formality in the present instance. As the notice is merely for information, not for approval or disapproval, no response is needed or expected, and none was received except the one already alluded to, from the Bishop of Maryland, who, from the beginning, seems to have been plied with plausible misrepresentations which produced a total misapprehension of the case, and prejudiced him strongly against the whole proceeding.

His letter is hypothetical, but indignant. If half the hypotheses could have been resolved into facts, double indignation would have been less than would have been demanded by such cruel, unjust and tyrannous oppression.

BALTIMORE, Sept. 8, 1860.

Rt. Rev. and Dear Sir:

I am in receipt this day of your notice of the suspension of the Rev. ——— ——— for six months, after trial.

If it is true that that clergyman had, before trial, humbly apologized for the offence for which he was tried, declared his true sorrow for it, as a grievous fault, and his determination to offend no more in like manner;

If it is true that having done so, he went to seek work elsewhere with your allowance:

If it is true that he was denied letters dimissory, in any form, after he had found work elsewhere, and a bishop, who, on his humble profession of his sorrow for his past fault, was willing to receive him on trial with any letter dimissory which he might be able to obtain:

If it is true that when asked for letters dimissory, his bishop, without trial, advised him to renounce the holy ministry:

If it is true (as rumored) that the same bishop, having reference (as is presumed) to the case of this deacon, actually consulted with his brethren about the practicability of deposing a deacon without formal trial:

If it is true that the trial of the deacon was only gotten up after he had been privately and publicly reprimanded, and had obtained offer of reception in another diocese with any statement that the ecclesiastical authority might think fit to make concerning him:

If it is true that on his trial, party grounds were openly taken before the court by his accusers:

If these things, and others concerning the origin and conduct of the trial, of which I have less certain knowledge, be true: I can only regard the sentence of which you notify me, as a cruelly unjust and tyrannous oppression, and express my deep regret that there is no mode by which, on appeal, the case could be brought to new trial before an impartial tribunal; and my wish that it were in my power by any means to bring to account those who have thus pressed to a ruinous result the persecution of an unwise, erring but simple-minded, earnest, and, as I believe, truly devout brother in the ministry of Christ.

I am, Right Reverend sir, very faithfully,

Your friend and brother,

William Rollinson Whittingham,
Bishop of Maryland.

To Rt. Rev. William Meade, D. D., Bishop of Virginia.

Bishop Meade had learned to "show out of a good conversation his works with meekness of wisdom." To the offensive implications of this letter, he replied with dignified composure and happy effect:

Millwood, Sept. 11, 1860.

Rt. Rev. and Dear Sir:

Yours of the 8th was received by the last mail. From the spirit of it, I might be excused a reply, and some may blame me for making any; but on consideration, I think it best to furnish you with the following information on the subjects treated of."

The letter is a plain narrative of the case, showing clearly that all the hypotheses of his correspondent were utterly vain and contrary to fact, both in relation to the course of Bishop MEADE and the conduct of the court. It did not change entirely the views of Bishop Whittingham, but it occasioned a prompt apology for the offensive insinuations, and a very modified tone in the reply.

BALTIMORE, Sept. 17, 1861.

Rt. Rev. and Dear Sir:

I beg leave to tender my sincere and respectful acknowledgment of the condescension with which you have labored to put me in possession of your view of the case of the Rev. ——— ———.

While, unhappily, I find myself still unable to agree in that view, it is with much gratification that I learn from your statement the untruth of one of the suppositions that had most force to move me to the expression of my opinion in the case. I learn with great pleasure that you did not consult with some other members of the Episcopate concerning the power of *inflicting deposition*, but only concerning the very different question, whether license to preach might be withdrawn. The very proposition of which question was a proof of moderation, rather than the contrary.

When I last wrote, I had not heard Mr. ———'s statement of his case, or seen the charges against him. I am still as far as ever from justifying his conduct, or endeavoring to secure him from the charge of grave error in that conduct; but the more I hear concerning the course pursued with him, the more painfully I am impressed with the conviction that he has not been wisely or justly dealt with, to say nothing of charity or mercy.

Of course, my opinion on the subject is of no legal consequence. It may be worth very little, or of no weight at all, with those whom it affects. Certainly it is not expressed as having any claim on their respect, beyond that due to the honest judgment of any Christian man. It would not have been expressed at all, but for the peculiar relations with Mr. ———, and the ecclesiastical authority to which he is amenable, into which I have been brought by no seeking of my own.

Very respectfully and truly,

Your friend and brother,

WILLIAM ROLLINSON WHITTINGHAM.

Rt. Rev. WILLIAM MEADE, D. D., Bishop of Virginia.

The persistent convictions which the Bishop of Maryland thus frankly stated, are in decided contrast with the "inexpressible thanks" of the condemned party, and the "unmingled admiration" of his able counsel. The condemned man respects the motives of the jurors who pronounced him guilty and awarded the penalty he is suffering. His counsel rises superior to the prejudices almost inseparable from his professional stand-point, and honors and eulogizes the court which has withstood his earnest pleadings, and convicted his client; but in an intelligent bystander, who has no responsibility or personal interest in the case, the strong impulses of compassion prevent the conviction that the condemned has been "wisely or justly dealt with, to say nothing of charity or mercy."

The most painful cases of clerical discipline with which Bishop Meade was connected, were those which affected some of his brethren in the Episcopate. It is not intended to introduce into this memoir a record of the several proceedings, so distressing and humiliating in their nature and results. Every friend of pure and undefiled religion would desire their early and absolute oblivion, especially as those involved have long since finished their ministry on earth, and passed into His presence who, without respect of persons, judgeth every man's work. Unhappily, however, the course which Bishop Meade felt it incumbent on him to pursue in reference to the alleged offenders, and the motives by which he was influenced, have been scandalously misrepresented, and his character violently assailed, not only in the columns of some of the Church papers, but also in several anonymous pamphlets. One of these, signed by "A Member of the Church," and known to be the product of Horace Binney, Esq., of Philadelphia, is marked by the distinguished professional skill of its author, which is only surpassed by the bitterness and malignity of the assaults in which it abounds, and the inexcusable errors as to facts which the obviously extraordinary prepossessions of the writer determined him to publish.* These harsh and reproachful accusations may be reproduced at a future day, when the facilities for exposing their injustice and falsehood might not be available. It is due to the memory of Bishop MEADE that they should be considered and corrected here, and that his true mind and action in those lamentable cases should be satisfactorily ascertained. If, in accomplishing this, there shall be found any statement unfavorable to others, it is hoped that their introduction will not be imputed to the odious purpose of clouding their character, but to the obligation which truth and justice impose, to vindicate the course of the subject of this memoir.

1. With the case of Bishop Henry U. Onderdonk, of Pennsylvania, Bishop MEADE had nothing to do till it was before the House of Bishops for final adjudication. This will appear from his own printed statements, from which the following representation is derived:

"In the year 1844, the Bishops were grieved to find from the public papers, that the rumors which had been afloat for some years, had assumed so serious a character as to have led the clergy of the Diocese (Pennsylvania), to the number of sixty-eight, at the annual Convention, to confer with their bishop on the subject; and that in consequence of it, he had tendered the resignation of his diocese. After the resignation had been accepted by the Convention, leave was asked to withdraw it. This was refused by a vote of fifty-one of the clergy and fifty-five of the laity in the negative, and thirteen of the clergy and five of the laity in the affirmative. The Bishops read with pain his account and excuse for a habit which had occasioned so much unhappiness and scandal. They read also his endeavor to withdraw the proffered resignation. In a

* Extract of a letter from Bishop MEADE to Dr. Anthon, dated "Millwood, Dec. 12, 1854": "Mr. Binney is out again in a huge pamphlet, of his usual acerbity. I shall not reply to the part devoted to myself, especially as he intimates that he will not notice me further."

short time they came together in General Convention distressed and perplexed. There was no canon for the trial of a bishop, except one or two short sections, hastily drawn up at the last General Convention, and which could only be regarded as setting forth the main principles on which one should be hereafter framed. Neither three Bishops nor any Diocesan Convention could think of making a presentation under such a canon, destitute, as it was, of any directions or provisions for carrying it into execution. It was, however, soon understood that Bishop Onderdonk would not only resign his Diocese, but submit himself to such sentence as the Bishops should think fit to inflict. Two or more of the Bishops had friendly conference with him of their own accord, and not by any direction from the rest. After some time, three letters were agreed on between them, and were presented to the House of Bishops. In the first of them, dated October 4th, he declares that the Convention of his Diocese having failed to investigate or present under the canon then existing, though invited so to do on a certain contingency, he was free, and that, in honor and morals, no others could present—evidently denying that three bishops could, after that, present him for trial; and, in the close of his letter, he calls for an investigation of the question whether he had resigned or not. In the second letter, dated 4th of October, he makes a certain acknowledgment, and submits himself to the judgment of the Bishops. In the third, of October 19th, he resigns his diocese. The Bishops were pleased to think that a mode of action was thus proposed to them which might answer the end of discipline without trial, viz., by accepting the resignation of his Diocese, and inflicting such penalty as should seem proper to them."

On the journal of the House of Bishops (1844, October 19th) the following record is found:

"Bishop Ives presented to the House certain communications from the Bishop of Pennsylvania;" whereupon, on motion of Bishop DeLancey,

"*Resolved*, That the said communications be referred to Bishops Chase, Brownell, MEADE, Ives and Hopkins." In the Journal of the 21st, the report of the committee is recorded.

"The committee appointed upon the resignation of the Right Rev. H. U. Onderdonk, D. D., Bishop of the Diocese of Pennsylvania, recommend the adoption of the following resolutions:

Whereas, the Right Rev. Henry Ustick Onderdonk, D. D., Bishop of the Diocese of Pennsylvania, has made known in writing to the House of Bishops his desire to resign his jurisdiction of the said Diocese, with the reasons moving him thereto, and has tendered to this House his resignation of the said Diocese; *and whereas*, the House of Bishops having made investigation of the said reasons, and of the facts and circumstances of the case, deem it expedient to accept the said resignation; therefore,

Resolved, That the House of Bishops accept the resignation of the Episcopal Jurisdiction of the Diocese of Pennsylvania, made by the Right Rev. Henry Ustick Onderdonk, D. D., and hereby declare that from and after this 21st day of October, in the year of our Lord one thousand eight hundred and forty-four, he is no longer Bishop of said Diocese. And further

Resolved, That the foregoing resolutions be duly recorded on the journal of this House, and that information of the same be communicated to the House of Clerical and Lay Deputies."

The documents connected with the case of the Right Rev. Henry Ustick Onderdonk, D. D., having been called up, the following preamble and resolutions were proposed, considered and adopted:

Whereas, This House has heard with pain and sorrow of heart, the communication addressed to it by the Right

Reverend Henry Ustick Onderdonk, D. D., in which he acknowledges the habitual use of spiritous liquor as a remedy for disease, to a degree which has been the occasion of unfavorable imputations upon the Church, and brought upon him an evil report among men.

And whereas, This House, as well by the tenor of the communications of the said Right Rev. Henry Ustick Onderdonk, D. D., as by the investigation of the facts and circumstances of his case, which have now been made, is well assured that the usefulness of the said Right Rev. Henry Ustick Onderdonk, D. D., in the office and work of the ministry has ceased, and that the reproach and injury which he has been the means of bringing upon the Church of Christ require the administration of discipline in the premises;

And whereas, The said Right Rev. Henry Ustick Onderdonk, D. D., has requested of this House such an act of discipline as, in the judgment of the said House, is proper; therefore,

Resolved, That the Right Reverend Henry Ustick Onderdonk, D. D., having made to this House a written acknowledgment of his unworthiness, this House does now determine that he be suspended from his office, and that the Presiding Bishop, in the presence of this House, shall pronounce the following sentence, viz.:

Sentence: The Right Reverend Henry Ustick Onderdonk, Doctor in Divinity, having acknowledged himself the cause of reproach and injury to the Church, and having submitted himself to the judgment of the House of Bishops, in General Convention assembled, the said House does hereby adjudge that the said Henry Ustick Onderdonk, Doctor in Divinity, be suspended from all public exercise of the offices and functions of the sacred ministry, and in particular from all exercise whatever of the office and work of a Bishop in the Church of God; and does accordingly so suspend the said Henry Ustick Onderdonk,

Doctor in Divinity, and declare him suspended from and after this twenty-first day of October, in the year of our Lord one thousand eight hundred and forty-four, from all public exercise of the office and functions of the sacred ministry, and from all exercise whatsoever of the office and work of a Bishop in the Church of God; in the name of the Father, and of the Son, and of the Holy Ghost, Amen.

The Presiding Bishop then, in the presence of the Bishops, pronounced the above sentence.

On motion of Bishop DeLancey, seconded by Bishop Whittingham,

Resolved, That the documents connected with the case of the Right Rev. Henry Ustick Onderdonk, D. D., be placed on file."—*Journal General Convention*, 1844.

Among the documents in the case there is one in the keeping of the Registrar of the Church, and which, in a letter on the subject to Bishop MEADE, he designates "No. 4, A communication from several clergymen to the House of Bishops, 19th October, 1844, enclosing a printed statement." The following is the communication from several clergymen:

"*To the Right Rev. Bishop Chase, Presiding Bishop.*

October 19, 1844.

Rt. Rev. Sir:

We, the undersigned, a committee of the clergy of the Diocese of Pennsylvania, beg leave to transmit to the House of Bishops, through you, the document enclosed, with the respectful request that it be laid before them forthwith, and read at such time as they may think proper. Its authenticity rests upon the responsibility of our names.

Most respectfully and affectionately,

Your sons in the Gospel,

J. BOWMAN,
J. C. CLAY,
H. W. DUCACHET,
JOHN COLEMAN.

The "printed statement" sets forth the offences with

which the Bishop was charged, consisting not only of those which came under the head of intemperate use of spirituous liquors, but also of others of a different character, and causing even greater scandal; and further, that evidence to sustain the charges was ready to be furnished if wanted.

At the date of the letter from the clergy, great anxiety and painful suspense existed in the minds of some as to the issue of the negotiations which were going on. It was apprehended that the Bishop might, after all, decline tendering his resignation to the House of Bishops, and, as the Church's consent was necessary to its consummation, he would still be the Bishop of Pennsylvania. For such exigency the printed statement was intended to provide, by furnishing information which would leave no alternative but presentment and trial. A copy of the statement was sent for each Bishop. None seems to have been received except that which was transmitted to the Presiding Bishop, and this not until the proceedings in the case had advanced so far as to render it inexpedient to have it read. It was simply consigned with the other documents to the keeping of the registrar. Had it reached the Bishops, as was designed, it must have determined their action differently, by showing the necessity of a thorough judicial investigation.

Such is a brief representation of Bishop MEADE's agency in the case of the Bishop of Pennsylvania. In one of his pamphlets, after mentioning a conversation on the subject with Bishops Griswold, Ives and Whittingham, in Richmond, at the consecration of Bishop Johns, October, 1842, he writes: "I am confident, also, that from that time until the whole matter was proclaimed to the world by the action of the Bishop and Convention of Pennsylvania, I never made any communication to, or received any communication from any Bishop in the Church. During all that time — eighteen months—I continued silent and inactive, when, perhaps, I ought not to have been. Nor when the General Convention met, did I become a leader in the work. On the contrary, I was rather a silent and passive spectator, the whole matter being taken in hand and managed by those whom Bishop O. regarded as his friends, and who, from time to time, communicated with him. At the close of the negotiations, I was put on a committee with Bishops Brownell, Chase, Ives and Hopkins, to which was afterwards added Bishop Whittingham, for the purpose of considering the documents and bringing in resolutions and a sentence in proper form."—*Bishop* MEADE'S *2nd Pamphlet, p.* 9, 10.

These statements are important in connection with certain proceedings at subsequent Conventions, and for the vindication of Bishop MEADE against the violent assault to be hereafter noticed.

2. The Right Rev. B. T. Onderdonk, D. D.

Offences similar to those imputed to the Bishop of Pennsylvania, by the clergy of his Diocese, were, by common fame ascribed to the Bishop of New York. Such rumors had been in circulation for several years. At the General Convention of 1844, they had become so definite and loud that the purity of the Church would not permit any further delay of their formal investigation. This unacceptable service was undertaken by Bishops Otey, Elliott, and a third, whose place Bishop MEADE was afterwards induced to take, for a reason which will be duly noticed. Not satisfied to rely on the information communicated to them by persons attending the General Convention, they went, after its adjournment, to New York, and spent much time in carefully tracing the reports to those with whom they originated, ascertaining precisely what they were prepared to testify, and in satisfying themselves as to the character of the witnesses. This investigation determined them to present "to their brother Bishops the Right Rev. Benjamin T. Onderdonk, D. D., as guilty of immorality and impurity," and solemnly to demand a trial of the said

Benjamin T. Onderdonk, pursuant to the provision of the canons of the General Convention of the said Church, in such case made and provided."

For the concise and inadequate canon of 1841, "of the trial of a Bishop," the General Convention of 1844 had adopted a substitute, making suitable provision for the accomplishment of its object, and indicating, with reasonable clearness, the manner in which the prosecution should be conducted.

The Court was organized in St. John's Church, in the city of New York. It continued its sessions from day to day for about three weeks, laboriously engaged in the painful process of examining the witnesses — deciding such points as were submitted by the prosecution or defence, listening to the arguments of counsel, and finally, in giving form and effect to the judgment of the majority of the Court, on the charges contained in the presentment.

By that judgment the accused was declared "*guilty*," and the penalty of "*suspension*" was awarded.

The suspended Bishop was very naturally exceedingly dissatisfied with the course which had been pursued by the presenters. He was not prepared to submit silently to the wrongs which he conceived they had inflicted upon an unoffending brother, with whom their relations had always been those of Christian courtesy. He could not forbear giving loud utterance to his complaints through the press, in a pamphlet purporting to be "a statement of facts and circumstances connected with his trial." In this pamphlet he assailed his prosecutors in terms of strong reprobation. As Bishop MEADE came in for a large share of the odious charges and indignant censure, upon him devolved the vindication of his brethren and himself. This he managed with his habitual moderation, relying upon a calm recital of what they had actually done, as all sufficient to expose the mistakes, and counteract the criminations of the excited complainant. The reply contains such copious quotations from the statement, particularly in reference to the grievances charged to Bishop MEADE, that nothing more can be needed to form a correct judgment.

In the first part of his statement, Bishop Onderdonk thus writes of my participation in the steps leading to his presentment. "Some six or seven days after the opening of the Convention, (the late General Convention in Philadelphia), when the House of Bishops was about coming to order, Bishop MEADE approached me, and suggested that I had better leave the house. I expressed my surprise, and asked why he made the suggestion. He said he could not explain the reasons, but again urged me to absent myself. On my repeating my surprise at a proposition so dark and suspicious, and so little comporting with the courtesy of a gentleman, the duty of a friend and brother, and the proprieties of a Christian, he said that if I continued in the House, my feelings might be hurt. This increased my surprise, and I demanded of him his reasons for so strange a procedure. He hesitated about giving any explanation. I warmly expostulated with him on the injustice and wickedness of the course he was pursuing. At length, as if reluctantly compelled, he said that there were reports unfavorable to my character, respecting which he wished to take counsel of the Bishops. I felt what I trust was just indignation, and expressed myself to this effect: 'Now my course is clear. I will not shrink. I will remain at my post. If any man has aught against me, let him look me in the face and say what it is.' I also spoke strongly of his unworthy design of inducing me to withdraw, that he might, in my absence, make my character and conduct the subject of discussion in the House of Bishops. He replied, not in the House of Bishops, but before the Bishops, informally. This unholy evasion was the subject of severe remarks, but not more severe than they deserved. I asked what were the charges against me. He said he was not at liberty to tell. There our conversation ended. This was all I ever heard from the brother of his having aught against me, until he was about to become one of my Presenters for trial. Yet I have good evidence that Bishop MEADE had, for years, been speaking against me, and contributing towards public rumor to my prejudice. After some time, Bishop MEADE came to me again, and said in substance, you were right. I will have nothing more to do with the matter. They must attend to their own business. These last words satisfied me that he had been acting in concert with others. And when we consider the darkness and secrecy with which he acted his part, how can an honorable and Christian man think otherwise, than that he was connected with a conspiracy against me."

To the same effect, in his letters to the Presenters, he says: "I assume that a clear case of malicious motive may be made out; that other views than regard for the purity of the Church may be shown as lying at the foundation of this movement; and that a well defined conspiracy, not, it is to be feared, falling short of our own House, (the House of Bishops), in its comprehensiveness may be made manifest." In the same letter he also writes: "Of Bishop MEADE, I was asked two or three days since whether I considered him my friend. The question was put by one who had been in Virginia, and who said that his doubts on the subject were the result of what he had there heard, I think from the Bishop himself. I cannot but connect this with his present position, and particularly with his effort at the late General Convention, to get rid of me, that he might, in my absence, make my character the subject of remark among my brethren."

"Having made these extracts from the statement of Bishop Onderdonk, no apology is needed for the following narrative in explanation of the part I have taken in this unhappy transaction. The reader must judge how far I am justly liable to the charges made against me."

"It is, I think, about four or five years ago, last August, since a worthy Presbyter of our Church mentioned to me that the Bishop of New York brought great reproach upon religion, by the intemperate use of intoxicating drink; that on two occasions, at the meeting of a Missionary Committee, he had greatly distressed the same by coming thither in a state of inebriety. Shortly after this, in passing through Philadelphia, another Presbyter asked me how it was that our House of Bishops was so secret as to their admonition of Bishop Onderdonk for his intemperance, adding, that at their last meeting it was understood such admonition was administered. I replied, that "no such thing had occurred, so far as I knew;" for I had never heard of the transgression until a few weeks before, nor did I mention to the Presbyter having heard it then. A year or two after that, perhaps, I heard something, though not very particularly, about his misconduct to Mrs. B. On my return from England, three years since, to the General Convention in New York, I heard two of the Bishops, one of whom was very intimate with Bishop Onderdonk, and much attached to him, and the other on the most friendly terms, say, that "the Bishop of New York was slumbering over a volcano, which might break forth at any moment." I did not ask the cause. The next fall, at the consecration of Bishop Johns, in the city of Richmond, I met with Bishop Griswold, Bishop Ives, and Bishop Whittingham. By this time the intemperance of the Bishop of Pennsylvania had become the subject of much conversation, and I mentioned it to Bishop Ives as a matter which ought to be inquired into, requesting him to confer with Bishop Whittingham. I also mentioned it to Bishop Griswold, who said that he would make it his duty to attend to it; but he died soon after. Bishop Ives has since mentioned to me, that he did inquire into the aggravated case that was stated, but found that it was unsustained.

I also alluded to the case of the Bishop of New York, and stated that I had heard as to his intemperance, and the question asked me as to the admonition of the Bishops. Bishop Ives informed me that it was true. He had been guilty in that respect, and that several of the Bishops had spoken to him on the subject, that he had promised amendment, and, as he believed, fulfilled the promise. I asked him if I was at liberty to mention the fact of the admonition, and the belief that amendment had taken place. He told me that he wished me so to do. We also spoke of the other evil report, and Bishop Ives assured me, that though he believed he had been imprudent, yet he was satisfied there was no evil design; that one of the other Bishops had made inquiry concerning reports in Western New York, and found that there had been great exaggerations. This statement of Bishop Ives, I have repeatedly made, when the subject has been mentioned. In the month of July last, I met with Bishop Whittingham, in Alexandria, at which time, while conversing with him about the unhappy course of the Bishop of Pennsylvania, I asked him how it was now with the Bishop of New York. He replied, "All right now." Knowing that he was intimate with him, and well acquainted in New York, and taking his opinion in connection with that of Bishop Ives, I was satisfied that whatever may have been the transgression of this brother six or seven years ago, when the charges were first made, that there was no ground now for them. This I repeatedly said, on the authority of the brethren above mentioned.

I remember stating this my conviction to a Presbyter of Maryland, on my way to Philadelphia, last fall. Not only then, but for some days after leaving Philadelphia, such continued to be my conviction as to both of the faults imputed to the Bishop, and such was declared to others when the first rumors of an inquiry were brought to my ears. It was not, until from day to day, I heard it asserted most positively that one of these evil habits, at least, had continued to a much later period than I had supposed, and might not then be abandoned; that proof could be adduced of the fact; and that the members of the Convention, from various and even distant parts of the land, had brought with them this evil report; that I began to think I might be mistaken. I heard rumors that an impeachment was threatened by some visitors of the General Seminary. On one occasion I met a clergyman in the street, who proposed to communicate something in confidence, and left him rather abruptly, as he will remember. At length I became satisfied that something ought to be done. On the night preceding the day on which I attempted to bring the matter before the Bishops, I seriously considered what was my duty, not, I trust, without sincere prayer to God for direction. The result was, a determination on the ensuing morning, without conference with any human being, wishing to implicate no one in the act, to seek an occasion of proposing to the Bishops, not as a House of Bishops, but as individuals, informally, to confer together as to the course of duty. And now, before I proceed to state my mode of proceeding, and what occurred, I must beg of the reader just to look over again that part of Bishop Onderdonk's statement which refers to it, and which is at the head of this paper, in order that he may the better see wherein we differ, and also what additional matter I present. It was as he has said, just before the opening of the House, that I proposed to him that he should retire. I had previously asked one of the Bishops to do it, but he declined. I did not state my particular object to that Bishop, I believe. Most of the bishops were in the room, and some of them near us. In an undertone of voice I asked Bishop O. to retire for a short time, as I had a communication to make, at which he might not wish to be present. He immediately asked whether it related to himself or his brother, whose case was expected daily to come before the House. Of course, I replied that it related to himself. He asked what it was. I replied, I did not wish to state it then, but that he would know in due time. On being again requested to inform him, I said it related to some evil reports concerning himself, about which I wished to consult the Bishops. He then replied that he would not leave the House, adding that he knew more about this subject than I did; alluding, I suppose, to charges and threats in his own Diocese at a previous period, or to what was then going on. He then remonstrated against the method I proposed for the first consideration of the case as improper and uncanonical, saying that if any persons had charges against him, let them be brought forward, duly proved and presented as the canon provides. All this was said, according to my recollection and firm conviction, not in the style of severe and indignant condemnation of myself, as an artful and wicked conspirator, but in a respectful manner, as toward one who he believed was doing what he conceived to be his duty, but was about to adopt an improper mode of effecting his object. He seemed as one expecting something of this kind, and ready to meet it in the way most likely to prevent its prosecution. Such was the impression made on my mind at the time, and immediately conveyed to some of my brethren. On his refusal to leave the House, and his remonstrance against the proposed method of bringing the subject before the Bishops, I desisted, and immediately communicated to Bishop Whittingham, whom I took into the church-yard, what had occurred. He united with Bishop Onderdonk in his objections to the proposed method of proceeding. I assented to the force of the objections, so far as to resolve not to proceed any further at that time, and in that way.

Immediately on closing the conference with Bishop Whittingham, I saw at a little distance in the church-yard a clergyman who had spoken to me in strong terms on the subject a day or two before, expressing his firm belief of the Bishop's guilt. I went to him and told him that I had communicated to the Bishop these evil reports against him; that his reply was, let those who make them come forward with the same duly proved in the canonical form. I then said to the clergyman, "there has been much on this subject in the way of evil report; it is time that the matter be settled. The Bishop should either be proved to be guilty, or else the persons speaking of him be silenced, and regarded as false witnesses." The clergyman's answer was: "A regular memorial is now preparing, or has been prepared, to be signed by a number of respectable ministers and laymen, and sent to the House of Bishops, requesting them to inquire into the case." I forthwith left him, and communicated to Bishop Whittingham what had passed. I afterwards spoke to Bishop Onderdonk, saying that I believed I was in error as to the proposed method of introducing this subject; that I had stated what had occurred between us to a gentleman who was acquainted with what was going on, requesting him to say to those who were making complaints, that they must make them in a regular canonical way; that I had endeavored to do my duty, and should proceed no further in the way I had intended to adopt.

Thus my action ceased until a day or two afterwards, when the memorial of five gentlemen was sent in to the House of Bishops. During the discussion whether this memorial should be even read, which was earnestly and effectually opposed by the Bishop's most particular friends as an uncanonical procedure, although a precedent was in its favor, I rose and stated to the House what I had attempted to do a day or two before, my reasons for the attempt, and also for relinquishing it. My statement was briefly this: that in consequence of the numerous and scandalous reports in circulation among the members of the Convention, in the private and public houses of the city, and in the country at large, I had, during many sleepless hours of the night, many of which had of late years fallen to my lot, and which admonished me that my life was more uncertain than that of perhaps any of them, seriously inquired as to my duty in this instance; that I had come to the conclusion, that it was proper to take counsel of the Bishops on the subject, but without conferring in the first instance with any of them; that, being aware how the canon provided that three Bishops might present a brother Bishop for trial, I knew that the Bishops as a House were not the proper body for originating the trial; but yet, as they were all assembled together, there might be a peculiar propriety in conferring in an informal manner as to the duty and expediency of having an investigation, that each one might state what he knew or had heard on the subject, and thus all the information which could be obtained would be before us, and there would be less liability to mistake as to the responsible step of making a presentment. I stated the possibility of three Bishops being led to make a presentment of an innocent person, not only through some misrepresentation, but, in some measure, through prejudice; but that where all were convened together, as at that time, it seemed the safest and most proper course for them as brethren to communicate the knowledge of the facts of the case, and their opinion as to the propriety of an investigation grounded either on the probability of the guilt, or the extent and nature of the evil report requiring correction. I further stated, that in conversing with Bishop Onderdonk and Bishop Whittingham, I had been so far satisfied as to the impropriety of an individual bringing it forward, as I proposed to do, that I had desisted from my purpose. Several of the bishops, the warmest friends of Bishop O., most solemnly remonstrated against any such preliminary conference, saying that it would be a previous trial; that the matter must be commenced by three Bishops acting on their own responsibility, and I was called on most earnestly to take part in it, if I thought there was sufficient reason.

Such is the simple narrative of what I have heard said and proposed in relation to the case of Bishop O., up to the period of its agitation in the House of Bishops. So far from being engaged in a secret conspiracy with those who have been charged with such a mode of action in this case, it may not be amiss to state that I saw Mr. Trapier but once, I think, during the Convention, and then, after the memorial was presented, and for a few moments only, at the church door; that I was not even introduced to Mr. Gallagher until the memorial was sent in; that I was introduced to Mr. Memminger only the day before the memorial was handed to me by himself, and had no conversation with him on the subject; that at the time he gave me the memorial, our meeting was accidental, in the church-yard, as I was going into the street; that with Dr. Dubois I had not the slightest acquaintance until some time after the memorial was sent, and then, only an introduction in company; that with Mr. Morris I had a brief conversation on the subject of Bishop O., along the street one Sunday morning, as we fell in together on our way to church, whether before or after the presentment I do not recollect. With Dr. Hawks, who has been considered by some as a chief mover in the business, I spoke a few passing words on two occasions, once in the church-yard, and again along the street, on subjects entirely foreign to this matter. Not a word did I exchange with him on the subject while in Philadelphia. While thus contradicting the charge of acting in concert with these or any other persons in bringing on the trial of Bishop Onderdonk, I beg not to be understood as casting any censure on those worthy persons who did confer together for the purpose of investigating the truth of reports so injurious to religion, and of bringing the supposed guilty person to trial. It is impossible to exercise godly discipline on the Bishops of the Church without such conference, and the Bishops are the last persons who should attempt to load with obloquy those who are faithful to their duty in this respect, lest they subject themselves to the suspicion of preventing discipline in their case.

My only object in the foregoing is to state the real facts of the case, and that, neither directly or indirectly, by word or epistle, did I have any intercourse with these or any other persons in the incipient steps leading to the trial. My action, or effort at action, was entirely independent, as stated above, and without conference with any being on this earth."

To the next complaint of their (the presenters') want of honor and generosity in not showing him all the affidavits, and having a personal brotherly interview with him before the presentment, thus affording an opportunity to make explanations which might have prevented the trial, Bishop MEADE replies:

"As no new affidavits on which the presentment was formed, had been obtained in New York, and the former ones had been read to three of the Bishop's friends, with a request that they would state the contents to him, which contents were of such a character as could not easily be forgotten, and might readily be stated; we had, therefore, nothing new to communicate. In requesting to hear from the Bishop the next morning, we did not positively limit him to that time, but I must say that we did not think he would desire more, as we believed he had nothing to offer in delay or hindrance of the presentment. When, however, on the following day, more time was asked by his friends, we at once postponed it for twenty-four hours longer, at the end of which time we were informed that though there was dissatisfaction at the manner of our proceedings, yet no further delay was asked. In relation to the complaint that we did not personally appear before the Bishop, and receive his explanations and rebutting statements, it is sufficient to say that the charges were such as to admit of no explanation that would satisfy. So did they appear to the court and counsel on both sides. They must be either true or false. They came to us sworn to by most respectable members and ministers of the Church. Bishop Onderdonk could only deny them—as he has done since. We wished to avoid the painful refusal to admit his denial against the oaths of so many excellent persons, to which we might have subjected ourselves by a brotherly visit, such as was indeed spoken of amongst us."

To the complaint "of our delay of the presentment for two weeks, perhaps, after the General Convention, as affording opportunity and encouragement to his enemies, to injure him by false reports," Bishop MEADE remarks: "Having undertaken so painful and responsible a task as that of inquiring whether a presentment should be made, and if so, of doing it in the most unexceptionable way, it became our duty to proceed in the most cautious and deliberate manner, and to be sure that the charges made should be properly sustained. We felt, indeed, from the peculiar nature of the case, and the difficulty of obtaining information as to all the rumors afloat, and the complaints made, that months rather than weeks were required to do ample justice to the subject. The fact that more than three weeks were required for the trial, on the comparatively few cases adduced, is one proof of this." "Another and most sufficient reason did we have for delay. Besides the cases on which affidavits were given, we heard while in Philadelphia, and New York, of numerous other instances of similar misconduct imputed to the Bishop, and measures were in operation for ascertaining their truth, and the practicability of obtaining evidence of the same for the trial; on which account it was proper to keep the presentment open. There was reason to believe that in several most important ones, witnesses might be induced to furnish affidavits. This expectation, however, was disappointed. And I must here remark, that if the Bishop and his friends had reason to complain of certain disadvantages from the lapse of time and the nature of the charges, much more had the presenters to complain of the difficulty of obtaining testimony, from the nature of the crime charged, and from the obstacles thrown in the way of either affidavits, or an appearance of the insulted females before the court. Efforts most likely to succeed, were made to dissuade even those whose affidavits had been given, and who had consented to appear, to relinquish their purpose. Letters anonymous, and letters with the signature of friends, were written to them, entreating and warning them not to appear.* The terrors of examination before a court were set forth. Ruin to the reputation of young females thus coming before the public, was declared to be inevitable, however true their testimony. A young minister of the gospel was told that he might as well give up his ministry at once, as appear against the Bishop on trial. Although these failed, yet the opposition of friends in other instances prevailed to prevent the attendance of witnesses. And when we consider the shrinking modesty of the sex, and think upon the severity of examination to which the witnesses were subjected, our wonder now is, that so many were induced to come forward. In the fact of their coming, we see the hand of an overruling Providence, and in the manner in which they were enabled to bear their testimony, we see the power of truth to sustain the most timid of the sex, under circumstances most overwhelming. In this great difficulty of obtaining witnesses to facts which came to our ears in

---

* Attempts were made to intimidate the Presenters. The following, addressed to Bishop MEADE, may serve as a specimen: "Sir, one who hates you has his eye on you. You are pursuing to the death one who has done no wrong. Charges are now in preparation against you in a quarter of which you little think. Your hateful race is nearly run."

such a manner as greatly to increase our conviction of the certainty and frequency of the Bishop's misconduct, we surely had a very sufficient reason for the delay complained of. To this may be added a consideration which had weight with us, in desiring to obtain an additional number of cases well substantiated, viz., that it would make the trial less difficult, and perhaps supersede it altogether by a confession of guilt."

In reference to the last complaint in "the statement," Bishop MEADE remarks: "It is that which states that besides the foregoing specified cases, there were sundry others, which, for want of power to compel the attendance of witnesses, the presenters were unable to state as particularly as the others, but that the names of the persons who could testify, and who had been summoned, were placed in the hands of the accused. In the statement made of the difficulty and failure in obtaining affidavits, and promise of attendance in different cases reported to us, may be found one reason and our justification for this article. There were some cases which we still hoped might be witnessed to, when the court should meet, but whose particulars as to time, place, and circumstances, we had not been able to ascertain, through the unwillingness of the persons concerned. There were others, which we hoped the authority of the court might enable us to obtain. We designed to say to the court, and to the accused, if it is wished to have the fullest investigation of the whole matter, we ask leave to enlarge the number of cases, and to introduce others which have contributed no little to the evil report against the accused. Lest he should complain of being taken by surprise, we had, at the time of the presentment, furnished him with the names of the additional witnesses, and if more time were required to adduce rebutting testimony, the court would grant what was asked. Such was our motive and object in this last article of the presentment. The Bishop and his friends being entirely opposed to this, although there were those of the court who thought it would conduce to the most satisfactory examination of the case, it was stricken out; nor did the presenters object. They always meant to leave it to the Bishop himself. The court, however, did not dismiss it without ordering that the names of those who, being summoned, had refused to testify, whether clergy or laity, should be reported to the Bishop, or ecclesiastical authority of the Diocese to which they belong."

Rarely have men, for the conscientious discharge of a painful duty, been more abundantly and abominably abused than these three faithful and fearless presenters. Their compensation was found in a full and firm persuasion, that they had done only what was *right and requisite*, in which comfortable consciousness they were confirmed by the numerous communications which they received from various quarters, thanking them for the good service they had done to the cause of pure and undefiled religion, and the credit of the Church, by the abatement of the scandal from which both were seriously suffering. Of these extracts, a letter from the rector of St. Stephen's Church, Philadelphia, must suffice as a specimen:

PHILADELPHIA, Feb. 22, 1845.

My Dear Bishop:

I feel that the Church, and every individual member of it, owes you a large debt of gratitude for the moral courage you have manifested in bringing a most unworthy man to justice. For one, I feel that I ought to acknowledge the obligation. I cannot but regret that the unhappy Diocese of New York is left in so perplexing a situation, but hope that Providence will open a way for speedy relief. The Bishop's friends, or at least some of them—Bishop Ives, Bishop Doane, Bishop Kemper, Prof. Moore, and Mr. Ogden, his counsel, have advised him to resign. Had he done so at once, how much trouble and pain would have been saved. But he holds on in the vain hope that the sentence may be rescinded, or at least declared void by his Diocese. So long as he remains, we shall have trouble. Already have there been about a dozen pamphlets published, besides daily newspaper paragraphs, and the end is not yet.'' I understand that the almost universal feeling is *now* against him in New York. The "trial" has changed everybody. So much so, that a meeting that was to have been held, to raise an annuity of $3000 for him, that he might retire comfortably, *failed* entirely after its publication. And the Trustees of the Episcopal Fund have refused to pay his salary, being advised by counsel, that his claim upon it is so doubtful, that they pay, (if they do pay,) on their personal liability. It is a most unfortunate business, but I really consider the most injurious circumstance in the whole affair, to be the fact that six bishops should have been found to declare him "not guilty." That is doing more harm than anything else, and that in many ways, and it gives him and his "friends" boldness to resist and fight it out, somewhat longer.

We now see what loud professions about "the Church," "ecclesiastical authority," "submission," etcetera, are worth. What a difference there is sometimes between "*tweedle dum and tweedle dee!*" But a certain dynasty is now at an end, and I thank God for the downfall. I regret that it should have been accomplished in that way, but I trust it is gone forever. It has done the Church great, very great harm. But I am prosing, and must check the freedom of my pen. Renewing the assurances of my cordial admiration of your noble conduct, and my thanks for the good service you have done the Church, by your resolute integrity, I am, Right Rev. Sir, most affectionately,

Your friend and son in the gospel,

HENRY W. DUCACHET.

---

3. *Right Rev. George W. Doane, D. D.*—In the Convention of the Diocese of New Jersey, which met in St. Mary's Church, Burlington, May, 1849, at half past six o'clock, P. M., of the last day's session, the following resolution was offered by Wm. Halstead Esq., of Trenton:

Whereas, A Bishop should be blameless, and should have a good report of those who are without, lest he fall into reproach; *and whereas*, public rumor as well as newspaper publications, have made serious charges against our Bishop, impeaching his moral character, tending to impair his usefulness, and to bring the Church of which he is a Bishop into disrepute; therefore,

Resolved, That a committee be appointed, consisting of three clergymen and three laymen, who, or a majority of them, shall make such inquiries as shall satisfy them of the innocency of the accused, or of the sufficiency of ground for presentment and trial, and that they do make report to this Convention at the present session, or at such other time as this Convention shall designate."

Charles H. King, Esq., (President of Columbia College,) then a deputy in that Convention, reported so much of its proceedings as related to the charges against the Bishop. From this report, which was published on a fly-leaf of the Journal of the Convention, the following extracts are made:

"Previous to presenting the resolution, Mr. H. said that, inasmuch as the proposition he was about to submit nearly concerned the character of the presiding officer, he desired the courtesy to that distinguished gentleman, to give him an opportunity of vacating the chair, by going into committee of the whole."

"This being quite an unusual course in the Convention, and the Bishop indicating no wish to shrink from any duty as presiding officer, the motion was not "pressed, and the resolution was presented."

"Mr. Halstead prefaced the resolution with a few remarks, in calm and measured language, disclaiming any unkind feeling towards the Bishop, or any purpose other than one of enabling him to place formally and officially before the diocese, such explanation as he might be disposed to give of the charges, which, in the shape of rumors, newspaper publications, and placards in our chief cities, were calculated so injuriously to affect his reputation."

An earnest debate ensued on this resolution. It was opposed by Mr. A. Gifford, Judge Dayton Ogden, Charles King, the Rev. Mr. Phillips, and the Rev. Mr. Ogilby, and supported by the mover, Mr. Halstead.

"By the first two gentlemen it was shown that the Convention could not lawfully pass the resolution presented to them; that it was wholly uncanonical, and unconstitutional; but those gentlemen, and all others who spoke in opposition to the resolution, unreservedly declared, that if charges specifying, with reasonable precision, the offences imputed by rumor, or any offence cognizable by the Convention, should be presented, they would oppose no obstacle to the receiving, referring, and investigation of such charges; but that in no other way could the Convention lawfully reach or touch the subject.*

At about nine o'clock, the Bishop rose to put the question on the passage of the resolution. "When, after a few brief, touching, steadily-uttered sentences upon the extraordinary and trying position in which he stood, the Bishop said, 'All who are in favor of this resolution will say *aye.*' A silence deep as death fell upon the assembly; the beating of each heart was audible, but not a word was

---

*The ground assumed was, that no inquiry could be instituted unless founded on specific charges, presented to the Convention. *Inquiry* seems to have been mistaken for *trial*. Specific charges must precede a *trial*, but inquiry must *precede* specific charges. The Convention is not a court, and cannot hold a trial. By the law of the Church, the Convention is an *inquest*, a body specially authorized to *inquire* into the conduct of her Bishop, and if it seems fit, to make and present to a court of Bishops specific charges against him. No person is especially appointed to present specific charges to the Convention, and no person can reasonably be expected to volunteer the performance of a task so odious, and so likely to excite the wrath of the Bishop and his friends. So far from being unlawful in the Convention to *inquire* into the truth of rumors adverse to the character of their Bishop, *such inquiry is their special function*, to be exercised with a sound discretion. It is for the Convention to judge whether the rumor, in its source and character, merits notice, and, if it does, then it is not only the right, but the duty of the Convention, to inquire into its truth.

The pretence that a Convention can only act on specific charges, virtually deprives it of the power of an inquest. A Bishop may be guilty of various crimes, and the proof of his guilt at hand, but the Convention cannot move, till some accuser comes before them, and then their powers of inquiry are limited to the particular charges which this accuser may adduce. No *rumors*, however rife, however all-pervading they may be, however crushing in their influence on the character and usefulness of the Bishop, and the good name of the Church, can attract the notice of the Convention. On this subject, that body is to be both blind and deaf, till some person shall volunteer to unstop their ears, and open their eyes, and, even then, they are to hear and see only just so much as this volunteer accuser may, in his discretion, deem expedient. Now if any thing more be needed to show the utter nonsense of the ground assumed, that it is wicked and unlawful to *inquire* into a *rumor*, it may be found in the 37th canon of 1838, which makes it the duty of a Bishop, if a minister "*be accused by public rumor, of crimes and offences,*" to see that *inquiry* be instituted as to the truth of such public rumors.

spoken. No solitary *aye* broke through this awful silence. The mover of the resolution himself was voiceless. After a due pause, the Bishop again spake: 'All opposed to this resolution will say *no*.' Then went up as with one breath and from one heart, such a negative as no one could mistake the import of. Its tone, its fervor, its sincerity were significant, even more than its unanimity. The work was done, and after finishing some formal business, the Convention adjourned." This report, prepared by one of the earnest speakers against the resolution, was at once extensively circulated in the *New York Courier and Enquirer*, and in many other papers, and, as already noted, was inserted by authority of some one, on a fly leaf of the Journal.

It was said that the decided vote was rather a *nemine contradicente*, than *unanimous*. Certainly the mover, though he refrained from voting, for a reason which will be assigned, was unchanged in his conviction, and whatever may have been the "fervor and sincerity" of the many within the walls of St. Mary's, there was a large and increasing number without, who concurred with the mover of the resolution, that the serious charges so publicly and extensively circulated demanded formal *inquiry*.

The undismayed, though unsupported author of the motion for such inquiry, is entitled to be heard in reference to the circumstances and considerations which determined him to offer a resolution which, (according to Mr. King's report,) was rejected by "such a negative as no one could mistake the import of." Who was Mr. Halstead, and how came he to commit himself to a course so unpopular, and apparently impolitic?

About two years later, he had occasion to answer these inquiries in a communication to certain Bishops, whose action he and others invoked in furtherance of an investigation which they deemed more than ever imperative, and which they believed the majority of the Convention of New Jersey were determined to evade. From that letter, the following extracts will furnish the appropriate information, and help forward the necessary narrative.

"It is due to you as well as to myself, that I should state fully and frankly the manner in which I have been brought into the attitude of an accuser of the Bishop of this Diocese. I reside in Trenton, in a county contiguous to that in which the Bishop resides. I practice law in that and the adjacent counties. My central position, my professional business, as well as the public offices I have held for some years in this State, have given me an extensive acquaintance throughout New Jersey. When, in the Fall of 1848, and the Spring of 1849, rumors derogatory to the character of Bishop Doane became rife through the counties in which I practiced law, I could not fail to hear them. As a member of the Episcopal Church, I could not but feel deep regret and mortification. I was asked if it was possible these rumors could be true. I could not deny them, for many of them came from sources entitled to credit. They became topics of public and newspaper discussion. They were used to cast odium upon the Church, and to operate injuriously to her interests. I asked myself what ought to be done, and I reasoned thus: 'These rumors and charges against the Bishop are true, or false. If true, then he is unworthy to preside over a Christian Church; if false, then it is due to the Church, to religion, to the person unjustly accused, that their falsity should be exposed, and the public mind disabused.' Soon after my mind had reached this conclusion, I was on my way to attend the Convention at Burlington, in May, 1849, in company with two clerical and two or three lay delegates, when the subject of these rumors again became the topic of conversation, and it appeared to be the unanimous opinion of those present, that the Convention would or should take some action in relation to them, and I then remarked, that if nobody else would introduce a resolution in regard to them, that I would do it myself. It was not a great while after I arrived at Burlington, before I was unexpectedly approached by a friend, (with whom I had never previously exchanged a word on the subject,) who said he had been informed that I intended to offer to the Convention a resolution in regard to the rumors against Bishop Doane. I replied that I had said, that I thought such a resolution should be offered, and that if nobody else would do it, I would do it myself. He then entered into a course of reasoning to dissuade me from it, the substance of which was, that an inquiry into the conduct of the Bishop would have a tendency to injure the schools and college, to diminish the revenues to be derived therefrom, and render the Bishop less able to pay his debts. These arguments were not satisfactory to my mind. While I regretted the position in which the schools and college might be placed, I could not think it right that they should flourish at the expense of the Church, or that religion should languish in order that learning might increase. I waited patiently, therefore, all the first day of the Convention, and until near the close of the second day, to see if nobody else would introduce any resolution on the subject, and while waiting, I cast my eyes round the Convention to see if there was any one there, upon whom this disagreeable duty could more appropriately devolve than myself. But though I found many members older than myself, (with the exception of two lawyers,) they had not been accustomed to public speaking. The lawyers older than myself in the Convention, were both infirm in health, (both have since departed this life). They were, besides, members and attendants upon the Bishop's Church, in Burlington, and their social relations were such, with the Bishop and his family, that I felt I had no right to ask either of these gentlemen to assume the performance of an unpleasant duty, to relieve myself from it. I therefore offered a resolution of inquiry into the Bishop's conduct. That resolution, and the action, or rather want of action upon it, will be found in the Journal of the Convention for that year. I will not go into the argument by which I supported my resolution, nor the argument by which it was answered. The gentleman to whom had previously been committed the task of answering my argument, in replying to it, stated, and stated truly, that what I had said in support of my resolution, was said in the "most guarded and measured terms." I was unwilling to go one step beyond what I conceived to be my duty, and I did not intend to fall one step behind it. I had no hostility to gratify; I had no private interest to subserve. I felt that I was acting under a solemn responsibility to Christian character, and I desired not to overstep the bounds of Christian charity. When the vote was taken on the resolution, I confess I was mortified to find not a single voice in its favor, and as I thought it might look more like bravado than Christian humility to give a solitary vote for my own resolution, I remained silent."

After the emphatic repudiation of Mr. Halstead's resolution, and before the adjournment of the Convention, the treasurer's accounts were under consideration, and the Episcopal Fund became a matter of inquiry. Mr. Halstead writes: "Then, for the first time, it was disclosed that the treasurer had, without the knowledge or consent of the Convention, sold out the stocks and mortgages in which that fund had been invested, and loaned the proceeds thereof to the Bishop, without taking any security therefor, other than the Bishop's individual notes. The Bishop then said that he intended to secure the amount borrowed of the Episcopal Fund 'very soon,' or words to that effect. I rose and said I was glad he had made the statement, and that I hoped the security would be speedily given."

Those who had complained against the Bishop were led

by the stand taken by Mr. Halstead, to communicate to him the grounds of their dissatisfaction. "These," he says, "came to me from such sources and in such forms, as would not allow me to doubt that there was too much foundation for many of them." The recollection of the complete failure of the effort for inquiry at the last Convention, indisposed him to renew the attempt, and the pressure of his professional business reconciled his conscience to leaving further interference to others. The state of the Episcopal Fund, however, gave him much concern, and he attended the Convention in May, 1850, chiefly to see that matter promptly adjusted. It had been given to a committee the day before he reached Newark. His account of the proceedings in the case is, that "when, subsequently, the committee made their report, I called for the reading of the report, but I was told that the report was not in writing, but verbal, and that I was out of order. I said, "I desired to know what the securities were, which had been accepted by the committee." Of this very reasonable request, no notice was taken at the time.

Soon after this, some remarks of the Rev. Mr. Sherman, upon the finances of the Church, preliminary to a resolution which he proposed to offer, brought the Bishop to his feet, when, as Mr. Halstead represents, "he went out of his way to refer to me as Mr. Sherman's counsellor, and to say that he had understood the gentleman from Trenton, (meaning me,) had said he intended to come to the Convention to see that the Episcopal Fund was made secure. This was said in what I considered, a sneering, uncourteous, undignified, and unparliamentary manner. I rose and replied that it was true — that I had said so — and that I meant to have it secured."

The avowed determination of the "gentleman from Trenton," was not without its effect. "Shortly after this, one of the friends of the Bishop came to me and said, that if I wished to see the securities, they were in the hands of Mr. Ryall, the chairman of the committee, and I could examine them. I then left my seat, and went to the other side of the Church to look for Mr. Ryall, but before I could find him, the Bishop gave out a hymn, which was sung, a prayer immediately followed, and before I could examine the securities, the Convention adjourned. I did, however, examine them, and found them entirely insufficient."

The treatment of Mr. Halstead was, to say the least, impolitic. To persons of a suspicious disposition it would have the appearance of a manœuvre to keep them in ignorance of the character of the securities, till too late to object to them in Convention, and yet to put him in possession of them a few minutes before adjournment, so as to escape the charge of unwillingness to have them inspected.

No doubt this was the construction given by Mr. Halstead and his friends, and perhaps by many beyond the Convention, whom the unhappy failure of the Bishop, and consequent assignment of his property, had predisposed to unfavorable conclusions.

And now follows a recital of the special occurence which determined Mr. Halstead and others to appeal to certain Bishops to enter upon an inquiry which they were canonically competent to institute, and which the petitioners deemed indispensable to the vindication of the Church. An inquiry which the Convention of New Jersey had been urged to institute, and had only declined because, as they alleged, it was not duly presented for their action, but which the petitioners were persuaded that Convention had evaded.

Thus matters remained until a few days previous to the Convention which was held in Burlington, in May last, (1851,) when Michael Hays, one of the creditors of Bishop Doane, called upon me to consult me professionally in regard to the recovery of his debt, and then stated to me the transactions he had had with the Bishop, and also that he had called upon the Bishop a few days previous, and told him that if he did not comply with his promise to him, that he should present a memorial to the Convention, and that the Bishop replied, "if he did, he should put himself on his defense, and that he (Hays) should get nothing." Hays then made up his mind to present a memorial of his grievances to the Convention, stating the Bishop's conduct towards him; and he actually drew up such a memorial, and handed it to me, and desired me to present it to the Convention. I consulted with several members of the Convention upon the propriety of presenting the memorial, and gave it to a gentleman who designed presenting it, and it was determined that I should speak on the presentation of the memorial. I, with the other gentleman, attended the Convention on the first day of its sitting, and as it had always been the practice of the Convention to sit two days, and as, by the canon of the Convention, the treasurer's accounts could not be presented on the first day of the Convention, and as it had been given out in the morning that there would be divine service in the evening, it was fully believed that no business of importance would be done that evening. I therefore left Burlington in company with several other members of the Convention, and returned home, supposing there would be ample time next day to have the memorial presented. When, however, I returned to Burlington the next morning, I learned to my surprise, that the Convention had dispensed with the evening service, had hurried through busness, and without waiting to receive, or act on the treasurer's accounts, had adjourned.

I have not the least doubt that this sudden adjournment of the Convention was brought about by the Bishop and his friends, for the purpose of preventing the memorial of Mr. Hays from being presented to the Convention. It would extend this already too long epistle beyond reasonable bounds to give my reasons for such belief. It is sufficient to say that the same opinion is entertained by other members of the Convention. This unworthy trick, perpetrated for the purpose of avoiding investigation into the conduct of a minister of the gospel, ought not, in my opinion, to be allowed to attain its object, and I have felt that the proper way to counteract it was to present the memorial which has been transmitted to you."

The memorial was signed by William Halstead, Caleb Perkins, Peter V. Coppuck, and Bennington Gill, and was addressed to the Right Rev. WILLIAM MEADE, D.D., Bishop of the Diocese of Virginia; Right Rev. Manton Eastburn, D. D., Bishop of Maine. It stated the considerations which determined the subscribers to make this appeal; sets forth nineteen formal charges, with specifications of fraud and falsehood, against the Bishop of New Jersey, which, the subscribers add, "we believe can be sustained by proof, and we therefore present them to you, that you may take such measures, in accordance with the canons of the Church, as your official duty and your well known devotion to the welfare of the Church may seem to you to require."

Annexed to the charges and specifications is an affidavit of Michael Hays, in reference to the false pretences by which, as he alleged, Bishop Doane had obtained from him large sums of money — the rough treatment he had experienced, when insisting on payment, and the manner in which the memorial he had prepared to be presented to the Convention had been frustrated by its extraordinarily early and sudden adjournment.

The consideration to which the document from the four gentlemen of New Jersey was entitled, depended on their character and position. On these points the Bishops applied to would need satisfactory information, before committing themselves to a procedure of so much delicacy, and difficulty. A certificate from the Rev. Mr. Sherman, and the Rev. Mr. Starr, furnished the requisite assurance.

NEW JERSEY, Aug. 18, 1851.

Rt. Rev. and Dear Sir:

The undersigned, Presbyters of the Diocese of New Jersey, herewith transmit to you a document signed by sundry persons, strangers to yourself; and to the intent that our evidence may be accorded them in the premises, take this method of vouching to you for their respectable position as communicants in the Church, and we would hereby assure you, that from our personal knowledge of those gentlemen, their statements are entitled to the fullest confidence. It may be well also to state in this connection, that they are all resident in the immediate vicinity of Burlington, and that each of them is a member of the vestry in their several parishes, to wit: Hon. Wm. Halstead, Trenton; Mr. Perkins, Beverly; Mr. Coppuck, Mt. Holly; and Mr. Gill, Allantown. As it is desirable, on several accounts, that at this stage of the business our names should not appear as acting in the premises, we beg that you will consider this as confidential, and merely as your voucher for a favorable consideration of the individuals of whom we have testified. We are, Rt. Rev. Sir,

Your obedient servants,

HENRY B. SHERMAN,
Rector of Christ Church, Belleville.
SAMUEL STARR,
Rector of St. Michael's Church, Trenton.

At an early period, some of the complainants in New Jersey solicited the views of Bishop MEADE as to the proper mode of proceeding. They are clearly expressed in the following reply:

"It is not, as many suppose, the duty of the Bishops to forward and take the first steps in a presentment. It is evidently the province of the Diocesan Convention to enquire into any evil reports of a Bishop, and present him for trial, should there be cause. In the event of neglect on the part of the Convention, then, any individual or individuals, believing that there is sufficient cause, are bound to present to three bishops whom they may select, and such bishops, without sufficient excuse, are bound in duty to act, if there appear to be justifiable grounds for a presentment."

When he was informed by a letter from a clergyman in New Jersey that he would be applied to as one of three Bishops to take canonical action in the case of Bishop Doane, his answer was just what those who knew him would have predicted—the expression of strong aversion, and earnest desire to be excused from the painful service proposed, enforced by a reference to his recent laborious and distressing duties in connection with a similar case, and yet no decision to avoid by a positive refusal what he knew must prove a toilsome, sorrowful and invidious undertaking. If the offences alleged were of a character calling for such inquiry, and were properly brought to his notice, his conscience would not permit him to withhold himself from the office proposed.

MILLWOOD, Feb. 18, 1851.

Rev. and Dear Sir:

Yours of the 12th reached me by the last mail, and I have, I hope, in the fear of God and with a desire to do my duty, considered its contents. You intimate that I will be called on as one of three Bishops, to confer as to the propriety of presenting Bishop Doane. If there be any of the Bishops who, on account of past action and sacrifice of time and means in such a painful duty, ought to be excused, and who, for various reasons, might wish to be excused, it is surely myself, and I hope the gentlemen about to move in this business will find enough without me who are better qualified for it. Nevertheless, when I consider the great distance of many of the Bishops from your Diocese, the youth of others, and the relations of some of them to Bishop Doane, and the difficulty of inducing any to engage in so painful a work, I do not feel at liberty positively to refuse. If, therefore, respectable persons, as in the case of Bishop Onderdonk of New York, call on myself and others to examine into such charges as those mentioned in your published defence, and such as have been set forth in the public papers, and otherwise, concerning business transactions, and shall promise them aid in the investigation, in such manner as shall be necessary to its proper execution, I shall feel bound to meet with such of my brother Bishops as shall be selected, at Philadelphia, New York, or such place in New Jersey, as may seem best, and inquire into the matter which shall be presented to us. The probability of getting Bishops to act will doubtless depend much on the matter contained in the letter which shall be addressed to them.

Praying that God may guide all who are engaged in this most distressing business, into the most proper way of doing it, I remain,

Yours in Christ,

W. MEADE.

The bishops who at first agreed to act in the application were Bishops MEADE, Eastburn and Burgess. Their distance from each other made it necessary to confer chiefly by correspondence. The first conclusion to which they came is indicated by the following extracts:

Bishop Eastburn to Bishop Meade.

(Boston, Sept. 4, 1851.)—"You will hear from Bishop Burgess the result of our conference here on Tuesday last in relation to the dreadful business laid before us." "What would you think of a communication addressed by us to Doane, urging upon him to ask from his Convention a committee of investigation? What are the objections which strike you? Would it not, if unregarded, place us in a favorable attitude before the Church and the community? and if attended to, what more could be desired?"

From Bishop Burgess to Bishop Meade.

(Gardner, Sept. 9, 1851.)—"I went up to Boston on purpose to see Bishop Eastburn, and we made the subject one of very anxious conference, and consulted two laymen of the highest Christian character; one a mercantile man, the other a lawyer. The result of our reflections, so far as we arrived at any, was favorable to the course of communicating with Bishop Doane, and calling on him to present the charges to his own Diocese for a fair investigation. I am clearly in favor of this course, after having studied the question of my duty with most earnest attention and continued prayer." * * "Should he refuse to seek or permit a full and fair investigation, the matter would still be in our power; and we should then stand before the public free from all obloquy, and *compelled* either to pronounce the charges inadequately sustained, or to act. In such a matter I should wish to act only under compulsion of one kind or another.

"Should this course be satisfactory to you, much trouble will be spared us, and I suppose that it would be sufficient for you to communicate with Mr. Halstead, and then to prepare a document addressed to Bishop Doane, which we all might sign. But I should wish, in such a document, very clearly to express our sense of the conduct imputed by these charges, and even of that part which has long been made public and not denied, and to show that no general vote of a Convention, without an ample and honest inquiry, would be viewed by us as withdrawing the subject from our hands."

Concurring with the views of Bishops Eastburn and Burgess, Bishop MEADE prepared a letter in conformity to their suggestions, signed it and forwarded it for their signatures, and then to be sent to Bishop Doane.

In a letter to Bishop MEADE from Bishop Burgess (Bath, Sept. 17, 1851), he writes:

"The letter strikes me as admirably worded, and in the very tone which I would have desired, and which is best adapted to its purpose. That it will lead Bishop Doane to ask the investigation, I am by no means confident. But, whatever be the result, this course is satisfactory to my conscience, as one, which, while it is faithful to the discipline of the Church, is the kindest towards him, and it approves itself to my judgment as adapted to take away all cause of resentment on the part of his Diocese, and to show to all the Church, that, if compelled to institute inquiry, we did it not from any motive of theological or ecclesiastical opposition, but only from the plainest compulsion of duty, and after every other resource had been exhausted.

Would to God that our brother would, first in his own secret chamber, and then before his Diocese, offer that full and humble acknowledgment of all which has been wrong, as much, be it more or less, must have been, which might bring peace to him, and them, and all of us, through our Lord and Saviour! I am, with great respect and affection,

Your brother in the Lord,

GEORGE BURGESS."

The next letter from Bishop Eastburn simply signified his resolve to take no part in the proceeding:

BOSTON, Sept. 29, 1851.

Rt. Rev. and Dear Sir:

Your communications have all been received safely. I write this, however, to let you know that I have determined, after the most careful reflection, to take no steps in the matter of the charges against Bishop Doane, sent to us from New Jersey.

I have also written this day to Bishop Burgess, communicating to him the above. I am,

Your faithful brother,

MANTON EASTBURN.

The Rt. Rev. WM. MEADE, D. D.

This sudden abandonment of the Bishop of Massachusetts necessarily occasioned embarrassment and delay. At length, however, the vacancy was supplied by the accession of the Bishop of Ohio, who, after much hesitation arising from personal considerations, concluded to co-operate with the Bishops of Virginia and Maine, and affixed his name to the letter bearing the date, September 22, 1851, the day on which it was signed by Bishop Burgess. This letter was delivered by a special messenger at Bishop Doane's house, to one of his domestics (who said the Bishop was at dinner), on the 2d instant:

Sept. 22, 1851.

To the Rt. Rev. George Washington Doane.

Rt. Rev. and Dear Sir:

We, the undersigned, your brethren in the Episcopate, have recently received from certain lay members of our Church in the Diocese of New Jersey, a communication* calling upon us to perform the painful duty of making inquiry into the truth of reports in relation to yourself, which have been in circulation for some years past. This we are requested to do, in order that we may determine whether it may not be proper to institute a trial according to the Canon of the General Convention provided for that purpose. Such is the character, and so great is the number of the charges specified in that document, that we do not feel ourselves at liberty to decline the call thus made upon us, unless the object thereof can be attained in some other way, which shall satisfy the reasonable demands of complainants in your Diocese, and in the Church at large.

In order to relieve ourselves from a most distressing duty, we have determined to appeal to you, in the hope that you will take prompt and effectual measures for carrying into operation what must have been the expectation of the Church in her canon for the trial of a Bishop, viz: That action shall first take place in Diocesan Conventions.

It appears to us, that it is only when a Diocesan Convention refuses to institute inquiry, or neglects to do it for too long a period, or performs the duty unfaithfully, that the Bishops can be reasonably expected to interfere. It is true, that in the present case, as the above mentioned document sets forth, and as has been otherwise made known to us, it has been wished and attempted to induce the Convention of New Jersey to take this subject into consideration, and that the effort has been resisted and prevented; never-

* The communication of Mr. Halstead and others, including charges and specifications, accompanied the above letter.

15

theless, so reluctant are we to engage in a task so painful as that set before us, that we have resolved to advise and urge you to have, without delay, a Special Convention for the purpose of a full investigation of all that has been, or may be, laid to your charge, whether in the document we transmit to you, or otherwise. It is also our duty, as your brethren, and as Bishops of the Church, most earnestly to impress it on your mind, that such is the nature of the charges made against you in that document, and of the same and similar reports, which for years have been in circulation, to the great grief of many, and the injury of religion, that nothing else can satisfy others, and relieve yourself from the suspicion of great guilt, but the appointment by the Convention of an impartial and intelligent committee, in whom great confidence will be reposed — with instructions to make the fullest investigation of the evil reports which are, and have been assailing your character and conduct. We feel bound to say, that no mere report of a committee, or vote of a Convention, declaring a belief of your innocency, and that an inquiry is unnecessary, will suffice for your reputation or give satisfaction to the public. We are persuaded that nothing but such an investigation as that which we have described and recommended, can either satisfy those whom you may deem unfriendly to you, or relieve the minds of many anxious and distressed friends. Should such a course as we have pointed out be pursued by you, and either a presentment made, or sufficient reason be assigned why it is not merited — we, your brethren, who have been sought out for the purpose, and have most reluctantly consented to take any part in it, will be rejoiced to be relieved from the most trying duty which could possibly be laid upon us.

Sincerely praying that you may be able to disprove, or satisfactorily to explain, the things laid to your charge, or else have grace from God to acknowledge whatever has been done amiss — we remain your friends and brethren in the ministry of Christ,

WILLIAM MEADE,
Bishop of the P. E. C. of Va.

GEORGE BURGESS,
Bishop of the Prot. Epis. Church in Maine.

CHAS. P. MCILVAINE,
Bishop of the Prot. Epis. Church in Ohio."

The private response to this letter was significant, though short :—

"Bishop Doane sends his 'determination' to Bishop MEADE by the mail, which bears this note.

"*Riverside*, 16 *Feb.*, 1852."

The "determination" of Bishop Doane appears in a pamphlet of fifty-two pages, entitled "Bishop Doane's Protest, Appeal and Reply." It contains, 1st. The letter of the three Bishops transmitting the charges and specifications as furnished by the four gentlemen of New Jersey, and counseling the Bishop to adopt the only course which, in their opinion, would satisfactorily dispose of the complaints.

2nd. A document with a superscription to the three Bishops by name, and signed simply—"G. W. Doane, Bishop of New Jersey." This document speaks *of*, but not *to* the three Bishops, and seems really not to be addressed to them, but to others whom it may concern. It complains of their taking "action against a Bishop on the shewing of four persons." They were credibly informed that many others could easily be procured, but the four, from their personal character and position, were deemed sufficient to justify inquiry. It complains of their presuming to dictate to him under the menace of a presentment, the calling of a special meeting of the Convention—"its object"—"how it shall be sought"—"the character of the committee," &c.

Although the Bishop mistakes what was meant merely as fraternal counsel, to present a deeply-to-be-deprecated, but otherwise unavoidable alternative, for dictation and menace, which would have been both sinful and silly, yet, it must be admitted, the minuteness of detail with which the advice was given might be viewed as not very complimentary to the perception and principles of the Bishop and his Convention. One cannot suppress the wish that the particularity of suggestion, which was liable to be misapprehended, and when misapprehended, to irritate a mind already disquieted, could have been avoided. But, no doubt, the particularity was deemed necessary, in consequence of the previous proceedings of the Convention, the members of which had so decidedly expressed their opinion of the entire innocence of their Bishop, that it was fair to conclude, they would not, if left to themselves, regard farther action in the case, either requisite or proper. They had, moreover, by the vote which "no one could mistake the import of," committed themselves to the position taken by Mr. A. Gifford, Judge Ogden, and the Rev. Mr. Ogilby, that for the Convention to attempt to touch or reach the subject by any action of its own, without specific and precise charges presented by some responsible accuser, would be "wholly uncanonical, unconstitutional and iniquitous." It was therefore deemed necessary by the three Bishops to be both particular and emphatic in advising the agency of the Convention in making inquiry, as the only inquest by which they could be relieved from the painful duty—and also, as the confidence of the Convention in the innocency of their Bishop had been loudly declared, that the committee of inquiry should be carefully so constituted as to avoid the possibility of being suspected of personal partiality, or of any improper bias, if their finding should be favorable.

The Bishop reviles them as the triumviral papacy of Virginia, Maine, and Ohio—treats their advice as insulting, and their professions as insincere, more than insinuating that, all the while, the real secret of their earnestness to have the presentment made by the Convention, might be their anxiety "to save their votes for use upon the trial." The closing paragraph proclaims—"the three Bishops have mistaken their man. The undersigned has not asked their advice, and will not submit to their urgency. Least of all will he listen to their advice or endure their urgency under the enforcement of a threat. No such special Convention will be called by him," &c.

Bishop Doane must have strangely "mistaken his men," if he allowed himself to suppose that either of them would be deterred from the alternative which they had indicated, by the utterances of "surprise, heated to indignation"—or by scornful defiance.

The second document in the pamphlet, which is as remarkable as the first, is his "Protest," as aggrieved by the three Bishops. To this is annexed his "Appeal" to the Diocesan and Missionary Bishops of the Protestant Episcopal Church in the United States, each one being named with his title, and also to all and singular, the Bishops of the "Reformed Catholic Church in all the world."

The "Protest" is against "the procedure in regard to him, as heretofore set forth in the document bearing their signatures"—which procedure he denounces as *uncanonical, unchristian*, and *inhuman*.

1st. Uncanonical being an unauthorized intrusion into his Diocese, contrary to the canons of the ancient Church, and the constitution of the Protestant Episcopal Church in the United States, which ordain that every Bishop of the Church shall confine the exercise of his Episcopal office to his proper Diocese, and further, being an invasion of the rights of the Convention of New Jersey, to whom primarily it pertained, to proceed against their Bishop, and who, having declined such proceeding as unnecessary, precluded all action on the part of any three Bishops.

It is preposterous to represent the action of the three Bishops as an *uncanonical intrusion*, when the canon "of the Trial of a Bishop," expressly provides that a "presentment may be made by "three Bishops," which certainly involves the right to take such preliminary steps as may be requisite to enable them to judge if a presentment be necessary. And where can such inquiry be so properly made as in the Diocese and in the localities where the offences are said to have been committed, and the reputed witnesses are to be found. Unless authorized to make such investigation, no three Bishops would ever presume to venture on making a presentment for crime and immorality.

As to the prior *right* of the Convention, it is unrecognized by the canon, which simply provides "Said presentment may be made by the *Convention of the Diocese*," and it may also be made by "*any three Bishops of this Church*." They are concurrent inquests, each authorized to make a presentment; of course, if not already *made* by the other. Not, if not already considered—or considered and deemed necessary by the other, but if not *made*. Nothing short of positive action by one inquest can be a bar to the action of the other, or, it would be in the power of a Convention, by a hasty resolution, that "no presentment was necessary," to preclude all action by "any three Bishops," and so shelter a Bishop from trial, and defeat the very purpose of the provision of an alternate presenting power. The Convention of New Jersey had made no presentment—had declined originating inquiry—had prejudged the case, by pronouncing their Bishop innocent, and three years had so elapsed, when, on the complaint of the four gentlemen from New Jersey, the three Bishops concluded that an inquiry was indispensable, and resolved that if the Convention, by whom it could be most advantageously conducted, could not be induced so to proceed—they must perform the painful duty themselves. Only a vision so disturbed as to see things which are not, could, in such action, see anything to be denounced as *uncanonical*.

2nd. But the Bishop further protests that the action of the three Bishops was *unchristian*, being contrary to our Lord's injunction—"If thy brother shall trespass against thee, go and tell him his fault between thee and him alone, and if he shall hear thee, thou hast gained thy brother. But if he will not hear thee, take with thee one or two more, that in the mouth of two or three witnesses, every word may be established. And if he neglect to hear them, tell it unto the Church." Yet, though some of the reports had been in circulation several years, "no one of the three Bishops ever told him his fault alone, or came with two or three to tell him"—"or uttered a word or addressed a line to him of admonition or expostulation, or even of inquiry."

The misapplication of our Lord's injunction is palpable. The offences charged were not personal wrongs to each of the three Bishops, and of which each was cognizant. They professed to know of these offences only by public rumor, and the representations of persons entitled to consideration. They were not prepared to say that they believed those representations, for they had not yet heard the testimony on which they were said to rest. They could not go to the Bishop to "tell him of his fault." There is no parallel between the case contemplated by our Lord, and the one now in view. But the true spirit of the injunction was regarded. Though they did not go to him alone, they did what, under the circumstances, was more judicious, and calculated, as most would suppose, to be more agreeable. They wrote to him a private letter, "between them and him alone," and which, but for his own action, might have remained unknown except to the parties themselves. When he allowed himself to misapprehend the intent and spirit of the communication, and forthwith published it to the world, denouncing them as a "triumviral papacy," it is not difficult to determine where the charge of *unchristian* action justly belongs.

3rd. The action of the three Bishops is protested against as *inhuman*, because they chose for it a time when they knew he was suffering from pecuniary embarrassment and severe domestic bereavement. But, very evidently, the three Bishops were not responsible for determining the time. They could not act till complaint was made to them by the four gentlemen of New Jersey, and, when thus formally addressed, they acted with as much promptness as the nature of the case, and the delay occasioned by their distance from each other, permitted. In the baseless imputation to them of a deliberate design to strike him in his sorrow, that the stroke might be more severe, there is as little humanity as there would have been in the cruel course ascribed to the three Bishops.

Such were the points of the Protest, which, "as in the immediate presence of the judgment," Bishop Doane "deliberately subscribed" on the 5th of February, 1852.

In his Appeal, he speaks as one "in whom the sacred order of Bishops had been insulted, and the first principles of our Diocesan Episcopacy, as handed down to us by Jesus Christ, have been disregarded, the sovereignty of Dioceses invaded, and the independence of Diocesan Conventions laid under dictation." In this appeal to his "brethren in the Episcopate," he professes to ask nothing for himself—it is for the "House of God, and the officers thereof." If the action against him is warranted, "What Bishop can be safe, what Diocese secure?" He "would rouse his brethren all" to the alarming inroad which is now attempted on the peace, the freedom, and the order of the Church," through a "triumvirate of tyrants." He "could never rest on his pillow, nor go in hope to his grave, nor look for mercy at that day, did he not call on his brethren in the Episcopate, to see to it, on the peril of their consecration vows, that this high-handed undertaking be frowned down." In closing, he declares, "as under the immediate eye of God," "his entire and perfect integrity and innocence, as to all and singular, the charges made against him."

But for the preceding narrative, no reader would be prepared to admit that the Protest and Appeal, and all the hot blasts with which they abound, could have been occasioned by a professedly fraternal letter from three of his brethren in the Episcopate, informing him that charges with specifications had been laid before them by four respectable gentlemen of his Diocese, that they might inquire concerning them, and take such canonical action as they might think necessary, and further, that the three Bishops advised him to relieve them from the painful process, by having the inquiry properly made by his own Convention.

The reply to what are styled "the false, calumnious and malignant charges of William Halstead, Caleb Perkins, Peter V. Coppuck and Bennington Gill," occupies thirty-two of the fifty-two pages of the pamphlet. In the introductory paragraph, the four laymen are defamed as having desperately plunged into the depth and darkness of a flood of falsehood, calumny and malignity," and "the writer" is lauded as occupying "the ground of perfect honesty of purpose, and unreserved and ruinous self-sacrifice," from which he "might challenge the world."

"The writer" then gives a history of his Episcopate, with its fruits, and of his enterprises for Christian education, with the trials and ultimate failure in which they involved him, and which furnished occasion for many of the grave charges which the four laymen had brought before the three Bishops for canonical inquiry. These charges and specifications are noticed in order, with such answers as the Bishop thought proper to make, but without documentary or other proof of the correctness of his explanations.

The last page of the answer is devoted to the four laymen and the three Bishops. The parting words for the laymen are: "They have distilled in secret the poison of their hearts, and they now commend the chalice to his lips with the astounding declaration, 'We are actuated by no motives of personal hostility against the Bishop.'"

Of the three Bishops, for relying on the authority of the four laymen, he says: "Fearful indeed the reckoning they will have to meet." "For interfering with him in his various duties, disturbing the peace and quiet of the Church, for their aggression in the Diocese of New Jersey"—"for the whole amount and all the shapes, and every incident and consequence of this enormous wrong, the undersigned holds as responsible the Bishops of Virginia, Maine, and Ohio, accuses them before Christendom, and summons them, in all solemnity and sorrow, before the judgment-seat of God."

GEORGE W. DOANE,
Bishop of New Jersey.

Riverside, 9 *February*, 1852.

The Bishop of New Jersey, alluding to the advice of the three Bishops in reference to calling a special Convention to investigate the charges which they had transmitted to him, had declared very emphatically, "No such special Convention shall be called by him." A special Convention, however, he did forthwith call, to be held in St. Mary's Church, Burlington, on the 17th of March, not indeed to examine into the nineteen charges with specifications, but "to consider and express their judgment on the official conduct of the Bishops of Virginia, Ohio, and Maine, as touching the rights of the Bishops and the Diocese in dictating a course of action to be pursued by them.

The special Convention met at the time and place designated. Diocesan independence and its invasion by the three Bishops formed the burden of the Bishop's address. To this the Convention responded by resolving that they approved the refusal of the Bishop to call a special Convention to examine the charges against him; "that the official action of those Right Reverend Bishops (the three), is, in the judgment of this body, unwarranted by any canon law or usage of the Church;" "that in reference to the subject matter of the alleged charges against our Bishop, this Convention has entire confidence in the uprightness of character and purity of intention, which have actuated him during his Episcopate;" "that whilst the Bishop has ever avowed his willingness," "and the Convention ever been ready for an "investigation of any charges duly made and presented," yet the best interests of the diocese, and of the Church at large, require no such proceedings.

When it is recollected that this Convention had on its table nineteen charges, with twenty-nine specifications, preferred by four communicants of the Church, with the declaration of their belief that these charges could be sustained by proof, and, when it is recollected that these had been forwarded by three Bishops, with their urgent advice that they should be fully investigated, then the resolutions of the Convention would seem to justify any measure of surprise and regret.

The Bishop and Convention, willing and ready to investigate any charges duly made and presented, and yet, with nineteen charges, and twenty-nine specifications, formally offered for this purpose, no action had, and no notice of them taken! If a canon of the diocese restricted the action of the special Convention to the object for which it was called, "to consider and express their judgment on the conduct" of the three Bishops, then why, without any investigation of the charges, introduce the resolution concerning their entire confidence in the integrity and purity of intention of the Bishop of the Diocese? If they could resolve that he and they were willing and ready to investigate any charges duly presented, why not at least notice the grave charges actually on their table? And above all, why the inconsistency of proclaiming their readiness to do what they solemnly declare "neither the interest of the Diocese nor the Church at large require."

Whatever the confidence of the Church at large in the integrity of the Bishop, it certainly could not have been much increased by this extraordinary proceeding of the special Convention, nor were they entitled to claim for themselves, after such action, that confidence in their judgment which would give weight to their resolutions.

It was quite a stroke of policy in the Bishop to endeavor to change the positions of the parties, becoming himself the accuser of those connected with the charges, and to divert attention from the complaints against the Bishop of New Jersey by the hue and cry to be raised against the Bishops of Virginia, Maine, and Ohio! But they were not the men to be disconcerted by manœuvre, or dismayed by the indignant repulse and clamorous invective which resulted from their fraternal overture.

Nothing now remained for the three Bishops but to prosecute the inquiry so as to determine whether a presentment was necessary. This required time, labor, and care, and these were conscientiously bestowed on the painful undertaking. They placed themselves in communication with those said to be cognizant of the facts alleged; examined them — in several instances obtaining affidavits, and also other pertinent documentary testimony. The conclusion to which they were thus led was, that the character of the accused and the honor of the Church demanded a trial. In this conclusion they were unanimous. They drew up a presentment in twenty-seven specifications containing charges of crime and immorality, signed it on the thirtieth of March, 1852, (this was addressed to "the Bishops of the Protestant Episcopal Church in the United States,") and forwarded it to the Right Rev. Philander Chase, D. D., who was the presiding Bishop, who sent copies of the same to the several Bishops, and caused a copy to be served on the accused. At the same time, notice was given to all concerned, appointing the 24th of June as the time, and Camden, New Jersey, as the place, for the bishops to assemble and constitute a court for the trial.

On the 17th of May, 1852, the Presiding Bishop gave notice to the several Bishops as follows: "By request of a number of Bishops of the Protestant Episcopal Church in the United States, and also of the counsel of the Right Rev. G. W. Doane, I hereby postpone the trial of the said Bishop from the 24th of June until the 7th of October, 1852, the place not being changed."

The request was conveyed to the Presiding Bishop by

Bishop McCoskry, one of two selected by certain Bishops who had met in New York, to send, informally, a deputation to be present at the Church jubilee, soon to be observed in England, and this they could not attend without being absent from the court, unless the latter was postponed. "Without the knowledge and against the wishes" of the three presenting Bishops, the request was granted, and, unfortunately, the preceeding notice given. *Unfortunately*, because the Presiding Bishop had no such authority. The proceeding was uncanonical, and void. Whilst the effect would be to prevent the Bishops from assembling under the authority of the notice for the 24th of June, it could communicate none to meet on the 7th of October, so that when the first named day actually passed without a court being constituted for trying the Bishop of New Jersey under the presentment of March 30th, there was no legal authority for the Bishops to convene for that purpose at any other time. The irregularity vitiated the proceeding, so that unless the presentment should be abandoned, it must be recommenced. Of this necessity, the counsel of the Presenters apprised them, with instructions how to proceed. They prepared another presentment, dated July 22, including all the contents of the first, with some additional specifications, which had been omitted either accidentally, or from doubts of the availability of the evidence. Without formally withdrawing the first, this was forwarded to the Presiding Bishop, who sent it to the several Bishops and the accused, summoning the court for its trial on the 7th of October, the day to which he had assumed the right of previously adjourning the former court.

On the 26th of May, the Convention of New Jersey held its regular session. They were informed by the Bishop, that since the special meeting on the 17th of March, he had been served with a formal presentment, (dated March 30th,) made by three Bishops, and had been summoned to appear and answer before the Court of Bishops, to be held at Camden, on the 24th of June. In his address he said: "I have perfect confidence that the Diocese whose representatives at the special Convention filled the hearts of Christendom with grateful admiration, will look well to its own rights and responsibilities."

It has been a wonder to many, how, between the 17th of March and the 26th of May, intelligence of the action of the New Jersey Convention could have spread over Christendom, and tidings of the "grateful admiration" it caused have been conveyed from all parts to Riverside! The encouraging report was not lost on the Convention. It animated them to re-enact, with variations suggested by a change of circumstances, the proceedings which had gained them world-wide applause.

The Convention resolved that the presentment by the three Bishops, "furnishes the first and only occasion in which any Convention of New Jersey has had an opportunity of exercising its solemn duty and clear right, under the canon, for the trial of Bishops, to investigate on the first instance, accusations against the Bishop." Why such an opportunity was not afforded by the nineteen charges, and twenty-nine specifications, endorsed by the four New Jersey gentlemen, and forwarded by the three Bishops, with the earnest request that they might be investigated by the Convention, would, perhaps, puzzle parts of Christendom to explain.

Before availing themselves of the first opportunity now, at last, furnished, they respectfully re-affirm their "entire confidence in the purity and integrity of the Bishop," and with this significant preface to their service as an official inquest, appoint a committee to make full investigation, and adjourn to the 14th of July, to receive their report.

The question very naturally suggests itself, what can have occurred since the special meeting in March to have revolutionized so completely the views of the Convention?

Then, they resolved that "the best interests of the Diocese, and of the Church at large, require no such proceedings" as investigation would involve. Now, they appoint a committee for the express purpose. They had not then, it is true, the presentment of March 30th before them, but they had almost its equivalent in the charges of the four gentlemen of New Jersey, presented and pressed for investigation by the three Bishops. In moral force, and in particularity of specification, the difference between the two documents is scarcely worth estimating. But there is a difference, and a very striking one, between the two documents. The first is not official in its bearing; it is no part of a judicial proceeding. The other is both. The one is not certainly connected with investigation, but may be balked by a bold blast, and its object frustrated. The other makes its next move into court, and insists upon trial. The one may be hazarded yet longer; the other must be headed off at once, or, who can predict consequences? At the special Convention in March, this formidable arraignment was not known; now, it is on their table, and to prevent the trial to which it might otherwise lead, the Convention must change its course, must itself proceed to investigate those very charges, and try to oust the three Bishops from the investigation, on the plea of prior right, and so retain the inquiry and its results entirely in their own hands. In this explanation there can be no want of charity, because this is precisely what the Convention now commenced to do, under the quickening power of the presentment. They appointed a committee to make a "full investigation" of the charges in the presentment, and adjourned till the 14th of July, to receive the report.

It was not necessary for this committee to notify the Presenters. It was fair to presume that they would not in any way participate in that investigation. It might, however, have been well to have applied to them for a list of the witnesses on whose testimony they relied to sustain the charges, though if such list had been obtained, it would, as the sequel showed, have been to no purpose. The time and place for the meeting of the committee were fixed. Notice was given to the four New Jersey laymen, out of whose hands the matter had now passed, for the Convention had always ignored their charges, and now acted entirely in reference to the presentment. Notice was given to every one named in the presentment.* The Bishop was also invited to attend. The presence of an accused person at his trial, to confront his accusers, is right, but at a preliminary inquiry it is obviously inexpedient and inadmissible.

Neither of the four laymen attended the investigation. One of them furnished the committee with the names of thirty-eight persons, and specified charges to which they could testify. These were all notified, and requested to attend. Only five complied, and their testimony was imperfect, and just as much as they thought proper to express, for the committee had no power to compel witnesses to attend, or to say more than they chose. Those who had anything to communicate favorable to the Bishop could have no difficulty in appearing, and imparting what they knew, whilst adverse witnesses would not care to be connected with an inquiry ordered by a Convention which had, in advance, resolved that the accused was innocent, or to be examined by a committee, each of whom had, by his vote, sustained the resolutions.

On the 14th of July, the Convention met according to adjournment, to receive the report of the committee, which, with the testimony taken, occupied 146 pages. The following resolution was adopted: "That the result of this investigation, and the evidence now laid before the

*Named, not necessarily as witnesses, but merely as persons connected with the transactions referred to. In many of the charges, no individuals were named.

Convention, renew and strengthen the confidence heretofore expressed, in the integrity of the Right Reverend, the Bishop of this Diocese, and in our opinion, fully exculpate him from any charge of crime or immorality made against him." The Convention appointed a committee to appear before the Court of Bishops to urge them "to consider whether it will be wise, just, or for the peace of God's Church to proceed further on the charges laid before them."

Of the proceedings of the Bishops who assembled at Camden, New Jersey, on the 7th of October, 1852, for the trial of Bishop Doane, the following manuscript, written by Bishop MEADE at the time, furnishes as particular an account as can now be procured.

"Fourteen Bishops, besides the Presenters and Respondents, met on the day and at the place. A dispute at once arose, originating with Bishop Whittingham, whether the Bishops present were at once *ipso facto* a Court, or House of Bishops. He maintained that they were not a Court until organized into one by some previous steps, viz: The election of President, Secretary, etcetera, and that this could only be done by electing a President, *pro tem.*, and proceeding to choose a permanent one by ballot. This was done, and Bishop Hopkins called to the Chair. Bishops Hopkins and Kemper were put in nomination. Bishop Hopkins was elected. Bishop Hopkins then offered the resignation of his seat as Judge, in consequence of some difference between himself and the accused, many years since, when associate ministers in Boston. Resignation not accepted; the Respondent said he did not object to his sitting. Bishop Delancey offered a resolution, that in the opinion of this Court, no one who had ever been, as a parish minister, or Bishop, at variance with an accused Bishop, and no Bishop who was an assistant to a presenting Bishop, ought to have place among the Judges, thus meaning to reflect on Bishop Hopkins and Bishop

Johns. Bishop Johns made some strong remarks in reply, as to the unworthiness of such an indirect way of reaching his object, and said that it should also be added, that no one who had already committed himself in favor of the Respondent, should sit in the Court.* This settled the matter, it being capable of proof, that some had declared positively in favor of the accused. Bishop Whittingham, afterwards, in the Court, declared himself perfectly satisfied of his innocence, and that it was a malicious proceeding, issuing from the foul hearts of usurers."

Bishop Delancey's proposition was either not passed to a vote or negatived. Dr. Wainwright was then proposed as Secretary. He was chosen. On coming in he nominated the son of Bishop Hopkins as assistant Secretary."

"It was now proposed to remove the court to Burlington. Bishop Doane urged in favor of it that *it was impossible* to get some of his witnesses anywhere else; that the expenses of others he had not the means of defraying, and that domestic affliction required him to be at home; that the heart might have too much put upon it, and might break. This proposition was opposed by the presenters on the ground that there was so much excitement at Burlington that it would be wrong to place the Judges under its influence; that judges in civil courts always avoided the houses of persons interested. Bishop Burgess referred to the scandal brought on the Church by the fact that one of the Bishops staid at Bishop Onderdonk's house during his trial, and hoped it would never be so again. Bishop Doane, in reply, said he presumed that Bishop Burgess was

---

* Bishop Johns remarked further, that though he would not regard any such unbecoming expression of opinion as that proposed by the Bishop of New York, yet, that if the respondent supposed that Bishop Johns' official relations as assistant to one of the Presenters ought to prevent him from acting as a Judge in the case, he would promptly ask his brethren to excuse him from a service in which he had no desire to participate. Bishop Doane immediately said, "that he had no such thought, and hoped the Assistant Bishop of Virginia would retain his seat."

not aware that he himself was the bishop who staid at Bishop Onderdonk's house during his trial, or he would not have spoken thus. Bishop Burgess replied that he did know it. Bishop Doane said, "then I have done with the Bishop of Maine." Quite a speech has been put in the mouth of Bishop Doane by some one, in the papers, which he never made. He did, however, say that it had never entered into his mind that there was the least impropriety in his staying at Bishop Onderdonk's, or that any one would so consider it. *Credat Judæus apella.*"

"On Bishop Doane's solemn declaration that he could not get his witnesses at Camden, and therefore that justice could not be done him there, the Court agreed to adjourn to Burlington. It was publicly declared by him in the Court that accommodation would be provided for the Bishops in Burlington, and immediately after the Court rose, written invitations were delivered to all the Bishops except the Presenters. The Judges had all been assigned suitable places in the families devoted to Bishop Doane and his cause. But few of them, however, did more than dine with them. They went to Philadelphia each evening."

"On Friday morning we met at Burlington. The Court received a letter handed in by Bishop McCoskry, who said he knew nothing of its contents, or where it came from; that some one put it into his hands. Bishop Hopkins opened it, and said it was from a committee of the New Jersey Convention, asking to be heard by the Court. A debate then arose as to the propriety of receiving any such communication. It was maintained that such a course was unheard of in courts of justice; that those gentlemen might come in as witnesses on the trial; that on the strength of their memorial offered as testimony, it might be moved to quash the presentment after it was read and the trial commenced. On the other hand, it was contended that the inherent undefined power of Bishops prior to and independent of all canons, and laws and courts of justice, justified their receiving the memorial. After a long debate it was decided by a majority of one (Bishop Greene being absent, having missed the boat), that the committee from New Jersey be admitted to a hearing after the presentment had been read.

"On Saturday morning, before the presentment was read, various objections were raised. Bishops Delancey, Chase and Whittingham, and perhaps others, spoke of their having received two presentments, and did not know which was the one, and whether they did not destroy each other. Bishop Whittingham said that he had never received the last; that he found its envelope at his house, but no enclosed document. It was determined, however, to let the presentment proceed. We then began to read a few explanatory remarks as to the two presentments, stating the reasons for the same, and some circumstances occasioning the delay of the last, and that the first was never withdrawn, though the last included all the first, with something additional. We were not permitted to read them.

"Having read the second presentment and taken a recess for dinner, the New Jersey committee were admitted, and read their memorial which had been previously printed.*

* The purport of the memorial might be anticipated from the resolutions of the Convention which it represented. It claimed for the Convention the leading, controlling, presenting power, stating that having ever been ready to investigate whenever any responsible persons would affix their names to written charges involving criminality, and having actually done so as soon as the presentment of March 10th by the three Bishops was before them—"having pronounced a verdict of acquittal in reference to those charges—the Convention now stands before you to plead that verdict in all its canonical force and moral weight." It contended that the refusal of the Convention to present the Bishop after this open and fair investigation into the truth of these charges, is equivalent to a dismissal of a presentment by a lawful court. As for the few new charges in the second presentment, they were part of the same case which the Diocese had already taken in hand, and which the Diocese alone should complete. After a pledge that the Churchmen of New Jersey would address themselves to the discharge of their duty, the Court is invoked in the name of the Diocese, "to forbear."

This read, the presenting Bishops asked leave to be heard in reply, and were allowed until Monday morning. On that evening (Saturday), they with their counsel met in Philadelphia, and determined generally on the facts and arguments to be introduced.

"To Bishop McIlvaine was committed the introductory statement covering the first six pages of the printed presentment, and to Mr. Davis the legal argument, occupying the remaining twenty pages. On Monday morning we met at an early hour and revised it, and at twelve o'clock were ready to deliver it. We introduced into it a reference to Bishop McCoskry's proposition made immediately after the New Jersey memorial on Saturday, viz., that the case should be dismissed, among other reasons, because of the postponement which vitiated the presentment. We referred to the part Bishop McCoskry took in procuring the postponement, and to the impropriety of his taking advantage of it. This led to a defense of himself. He declared that he had no part in procuring the postponement; that he only carried a letter to himself from Mr. Wharton, Bishop Doane's counsel, expressing a wish that a postponement might take place, and saying that he was authorized to promise that Bishop Doane would take no advantage of it; that he (Bishop McCoskry) told Bishop Chase that he would express no opinion about it; moreover, that he told Bishop Chase that the Bishops who met in New York declined asking a postponement on the ground of its illegality, but that Bishop Chase said he did not care a snap of his finger for their opinion, and should, therefore, postpone it. (It is difficult to reconcile all this with Bishop Chase's circular postponing the trial, wherein he says it was done at the desire of one of Bishop Doane's counsel and of several Bishops.) Bishop McCoskry and others objected to this part of our reply, and Bishop McCoskry withdrew his proposition, saying it would be misunderstood, and he be charged with first procuring the postponement, and then making it a plea for dismissing the presentment. His resolutions being withdrawn, our notice of them was also withdrawn.

"Bishop Whittingham, after the reading of the presentment, moved that the Secretary furnish to the presenting Bishops and to the respondent a copy of an order passed at his motion, to the effect that in the opinion of the Court it would be wrong that either the memorial from New Jersey or the reply of the presenting Bishops should be published without the other should be furnished to the presenting Bishops and the respondent. This first brought to the presenting Bishops the knowledge of the fact of such a resolution by the Court. Two at least, if not all of them, were absent at the time it was passed. If one were present, he did not hear it on account of the feebleness of Bishop Whittingham's voice, and the great difficulty of hearing any one in the room where we met. Immediately, when it was known, the presenting Bishops made themselves heard, and remonstrated against so unfair a proceeding. The New Jersey memorial had already been printed and circulated; a large portion of it had already appeared in one circular paper, and it was impossible to say for how many other papers, secular and religious, it was now in type, and yet the presenters were to be prevented from giving publicity to their's, unless they first republished the other. So monstrous a proposition was only adhered to by Bishop Whittingham himself.

"Bishop Upfold now took Bishop McCoskry's place and renewed those resolutions, which were finally adopted. The discussion was continued from this time, (Monday afternoon,) till Friday morning. On Thursday afternoon all were ready for the question, but Bishop Greene, who said that he had not been able to make up his mind, and asked that it might be postponed until the next day. This was agreed to. On the next morning he read an opinion in favor of dismissing the case. The written opinions of

Bishops Hopkins, Potter and Eastburn were also read on Friday morning. Others had been read the day before. They will appear on the minutes of the Court.

"Bishop Doane was allowed, as the representative of the committee, or Diocese, or both, to reply to the argument of the presenters. He said, as he had often done before, that he appeared in two characters, as Bishop Doane and as the defender of the rights of his Diocese; that as Bishop Doane he said nothing to prevent the trial, but as the defender of the rights of his Diocese, as speaking for God and His Church, he would say and do everything to prevent the trial; that he would insist upon every technicality which might upset the presentment, (and he acted accordingly); that the Court had no right whatever to try him, and once, in thundering tones, he commanded the Bishops to go home, and leave the matter where it properly belonged. He condemned the canon; said he wished to make the trial of a Bishop hard, instead of easy; appealed to the Church of England and of Rome in favor of this, and declared and repeated it when charged with the same; that he would rather be guilty of all the offences charged against him in the presentment, than not to defend to the uttermost the position taken by his Diocese; for the latter he said, would be treachery to the spouse of Christ—as if the crimes and immoralities alleged in the presentment were not the greatest treachery to the spouse of Christ. He said the same thing with regard to the crimes for which Bishop Onderdonk was condemned, that they were nothing compared with the evils of his condemnation. (Such is the language of many others who seem to have lost sight of the importance of godly discipline.)"

"In reply to that part of our argument wherein we say that out of fifty-nine parishes having a right to representation in the Convention of New Jersey, less than half were there by delegates, and only nineteen voted for the appointment of a Committee;* he replied that a number of them were only nominal parishes, having no vitality in them, having neither priest nor people. Hitherto he had ever been boasting of the number of parishes which had sprung up under his Episcopal labor, never lessening their number, never speaking of any as dead ones; but now, when it suits him, he finds that a number of them have *only a name and are dead.* Still he wound up his last speech by an enumeration of all his labors and great successes as a parish minister, as Bishop, as President of St. Mary's Hall and College; of his universal popularity throughout the land; not of this land only, but as he said, "In Europe, also, where I am well known, there I am esteemed; yes, at their largest meetings, when my name is mentioned, the loudest acclamations were heard uttered upon the same." This finished, he bade the Bishops dismiss the presentment and "*go home, go home.*"

"When the presenting Bishops heard such declarations concerning the charges in the presentment against Bishop Doane, and those against Bishop O., making so light of them, they determined to call the attention of the Court to the nature of the offences charged upon the respondent. Bishop Burgess spoke, recapitulating the chief things in the presentment, and referring to the fact that some of them were indictable offences by the civil law. In reply to this, Bishop Doane said it was an atrocious libel. Hitherto he had said, and not without effect, that he believed the presenters were misled by some two or three evil persons — his enemies. This was calculated to

* The Canon of "the Trial of a Bishop," whilst it authorizes a Diocese to present its Bishop, provides that "two-thirds of each order present concur, and that two-thirds of the clergy entitled to seats in the Convention be present, and that two-thirds of the parishes canonically in union with said Convention, be represented therein." The presenters maintained that the Convention of New Jersey from which this memorial emanated, was not thus canonically constituted, as the journal shows, and therefore had no right to make a presentment, or a preliminary investigation.

impress the Court in his favor, inducing the belief that we had not examined with proper lights the things charged in our presentment."

"When the presentment, which was read, had been disposed of, the senior presenter, in the name of the others, rose and stated that previous to the offering of it, we had wished to read some explanatory statements as to the two presentments, but were not allowed; that we should then have stated that by advice of counsel, we had never withdrawn the first presentment, and had cautioned Bishop Chase not to do so, which caution he had observed in his circular; that we had purposed to leave them both with the Court, as is done in civil courts, when two presentments or indictments are made, the latter containing some additional matter. In such case the Court may use both of them, or only the latter. We said that as in the course of the discussion several of the Bishops had objected to the last presentment, saying that they came to try the first; we now offered the first presentment, and were ready to go into the trial on that, although it did not contain several of the charges made in the other.

"A great clamor was immediately made against this, though no argument used, till it was alleged that the Court was summoned to receive a presentment on the 7th of October, and this old presentment was not offered until the 15th. This seemed quite conclusive to some. But little was said, and the proposition was negatived. It should be added, that, whereas Bishop Doane sometimes declared that he himself wished for a trial and considered it a misfortune that it could not take place, so that in our reply to the memorial from New Jersey, we speak of his expressed wish for it; yet, at the close, when Bishops Johns and Hopkins introduced the same into their written opinions, he publicly declared that they had mistaken him — that he never had expressed such a desire, so that they have either stricken the same out of their opinions, or corrected them in a note. That he did repeatedly speak as desiring a trial, is as certain as that he spoke at all. At the last he said that he only contemplated or expected a trial. Surely his most partial friends cannot vindicate him from such contradiction and falsehood."

[HERE THE "NOTITIA" ENDS.]

The preamble and resolutions offered by Bishop Upfold were as follows:

" *Whereas,* Previous to the making the presentment now before this Court, the Convention of New Jersey had investigated most of the matters contained therein, and had determined that there was no ground for presentment, therefore,

Resolved, That, as to the matters thus acted upon by said Convention, this Court is not called upon to proceed further."

"*Whereas,* The Diocese of New Jersey stands pledged to investigate any charges against its Bishop that may be presented from any responsible source, and, whereas, a special Convention has been called, shortly to meet in reference to the new matters contained in the presentment now before this Court, therefore,

Resolved, That this Court, relying on said pledge, do not now proceed to any further action in the premises."

On the eighth day of its session, the Court came to a decision. Eight Bishops gave their opinions in favor of the resolution to dismiss the presentment, and six against it. The opinions in its favor were those of Bishops Kemper, McCoskry, DeLancey, Whittingham, Chase of New Hampshire, Upfold, Green, and Rutledge.

Against it were those of Bishops Hopkins, Smith, Lee, Johns, Eastburn, and Potter.

The presenters, in their brief notice of the proceedings, say: "The result is, therefore, that when the charges, made in strict accordance with the canons, have been dismissed, it has been without the slightest consideration of their merits.

"They have not been refuted; they have not been tried; and they are not retracted.

"The undersigned, having discharged their duty fully, without fear or favor, and to the utmost of their ability, rely with confidence on the moral feeling and correct judgment of the Church for the approval of their conduct. The remaining responsibility rests on their brethren."

Thus the scheme of the New Jersey Convention proved a success. On the plea of prior right, their committee were permitted to interpose themselves between the presenters and the Court, and on the assurance that the Convention had investigated most of the charges against their Bishop, as set forth in the presentment, and found him innocent, and pledged themselves fully to investigate the remainder—a majority of the Court determined that in reference to the charges said to have been investigated, "it is not called upon to proceed further," and that in reference to the "new matters contained in the presentment, relying on said pledge, it do not now proceed to any further action in the premises."

"Not called upon to proceed;" and yet they were literally and loudly called upon by the presenters who had firmly resisted the claim of the New Jersey Convention, and the admittance of their committee to a hearing—as not being a party in the case—and who now distinctly declared that they were *full-handed with proof of the allegations of the presentment*, and ready to produce it. But, unaffected by this earnest declaration, and not regarding the course of proceeding indicated by the canon, under which the Court was constituted, the majority refused to move except to put the presentment in the pocket of the Committee to be conveyed to the Convention, with an expressive nod of approval of their past conduct, and a significant hint to do likewise with the new matters of the presentment. And so the Court became a competitor with the Convention for "the grateful admiration of Christendom!"

The Bishop of New Jersey had already called a special Convention with a reference to what "purports to be a new presentment of the Bishop of the Diocese." Meeting on this call at Newark on the 27th of October, they were soon ready for action. The Bishop in his address assured them of his "sincere conviction" that the decision of the Court was "attained under the guidance of the *Holy Spirit*, whose presence in the Court had been invoked at a thousand altars, and by ten thousand firesides."

The questions before the Convention were, the reception of the report of the Committee appointed to appear before the Court to urge them not to proceed to trial—and, the reference of the new matters in the second presentment to the same Committee that had passed upon the other charges it contained.

The debates were stormy. Mr. Halstead was no longer solitary in openly resisting the policy of the Convention. Walter Rutherford, Esq., Mr. Cortland Parker, Hon. Jas. Parkis, Mr. Archer Gifford, the Rev. Mr. Sherman, and Rev. Mr. Lowell spoke in the opposition. Walter Rutherford, Esq., offered a resolution, stating that, as it appears from a report of the investigating committee, that only a portion of the witnesses had been examined before them, and scarcely any on whose evidence the presentment rested, and, as the presenters had declared that they stood "full-handed with the proof" of their charges—that the Bishop be earnestly solicited to demand from his peers a trial of these charges, that public opinion may be satisfied, and his character sustained in the Church.

This resolution the Bishop refused to put, and, as to his demanding a trial of his peers, he said: "I shall do no such thing. It is too absurd to talk about."

Mr. C. Parker moved that in "the opinion of this Convention the fair fame of the Bishop cannot be effectually rescued from the accusations against it by any *ex parte* inquiry, however thorough, nor without a canonical trial."

This the Bishop pronounced to be worse than the other, adding, "I'll put no such resolution," &c.

Mr. Archer Gifford, who in the Convention of 1849 opposed Mr. Halstead's resolution for a committee of investigation "as wholly uncanonical and unconstitutional," in his speech in this Convention thus expressed himself:

"The committee have embodied a matter in their report, which they were not charged with by the Convention; and, however I may feel bound to accept the report of the committee, I cannot agree to accept it with that part included which relates to the pledge *further to investigate.* Neither can I believe that the House of Bishops have been constituted with any power to recommend to this Convention such a course. Their business was and is, to *try.* This Convention can only *present.* These last charges are before the House of Bishops on a presentment made by three of the Bishops, according to the canon. And what power can they have to recommend to us to do what it is their peculiar duty to perform, as directed by the Canon?

"As to the appointment of the same committee, there would appear to be some indelicacy in committing another and distinct set of charges to them for investigation, especially if they are to proceed as they have done with the first charges. They have acted the part of a jury to *try,* and (to use their own language) '*found a verdict.*' For this they had no commission. And now, as it were, without going out of the jury-box, they are to proceed upon an unauthorized recommendation of the Bishops—one for which no precedent or direction can be found—and, as it were, afraid to select any other men with whom to trust our Bishop's character. Whatever respect we may entertain for these gentlemen of the Committee, it may be looked on with suspicion. The public have to be satisfied. This is the great ordeal at last; and we must act with proper deference to it."

The Convention re-appointed the Committee by whom the previous investigation was made, and adjourned.

Dec. 21st.—The Convention met again and received from the investigating Committee their report that "the evidence in this case has produced on their minds no diminution in their confidence in the integrity and purity of your Bishop; on the contrary, increased love and respect for him; but has presented to them and the world, drawn from their modest hiding-places, habitual and beautiful examples in him of that virtue greater than all other—*charity.* [The testimony which led to this special commendation was given by Dr. Joseph Parrish, the Bishop's physician, who said, 'When I was first employed at the Schools, I was told by Bishop Doane to consider his wines and liquors always under my command for the use of such persons at the School and for all needy persons, in town and country. I have always acted upon this permission, and have made *large* drafts upon it.' "]

After hearing the report of the Committee, the Convention passed the following resolution:

Resolved, That the evidence now laid before the Convention renews and strengthens the confidence heretofore expressed in the integrity of the Rt. Rev., the Bishop of this Diocese, and, in our opinion fully exculpates him from any charge of crime or immorality made against him."

The policy of the New Jersey Convention had prevailed, and they might congratulate each other on having avoided making a presentment themselves, and on arresting the action of the Court on the presentment of the Bishops of Virginia, Ohio, and Maine. But, the end was not yet. Great dissatisfaction existed in the Diocese. This was formerly expressed by two memorials addressed to the Bishops of Virginia, Ohio, and Maine. The first in November, 1852, with more than a hundred signatures, after a preamble referring to what had been done, proceeds: "We, the undersigned, laymen of the Protestant

Episcopal Church in New Jersey, do most respectfully entreat the Bishops of Virginia, Ohio, and Maine to take such further action as will give the Bishop of New Jersey an opportunity to refute the charges, in order that he may be blameless and have a good report of them which are without."

The second, dated Dec., 1852, and with nineteen signatures, is as follows:

"The undersigned laymen of the Protestant Episcopal Church in the Diocese of New Jersey, believing that the reputation of the Bishop can only be sufficiently vindicated, and the peace and welfare of the Church maintained and preserved by a judicial investigation of the charges which have been preferred against him, are desirous that such further action should be taken in the premises, as may bring the matter to a final adjudication."

Very evidently the resolutions of the Court of Bishops did not acquit the accused or entirely dispose of the presentment. Though uncanonically placed in other hands, it could be remanded for final consideration.

But the presenters having seen enough of the disposition of certain members of the Court to raise technical difficulties, determined to avoid, as far as possible, all occasion for such objection. With this view they notified the presiding Bishop that they withdrew the former presentments, and then made another embracing the same charges, which they asked that the Bishops should be summoned to try.

The Court assembled at Camden, New Jersey, Sept. 1st, 1853.

On an application from Bishop Doane, earnestly claiming the immediate adjournment of the Court to Burlington, "no action was taken." The Court continued at Camden.

The presentment was read.

On the second day, the Bishop Respondent read a letter

from a committee of the New Jersey Convention, asking to be heard before any action was taken on the presentment.

The Bishop Respondent offered, with preambles, two orders for adoption by the Court. 1st. That this Court will now hear the statement which the Committee of the New Jersey Convention desired to make. 2nd. That the Court will not proceed to any further action in reference to the presentment, and that the same be dismissed.

The Bishop Respondent, and the Presenting Bishops were respectfully heard on the first order, and the ayes and noes being called, it was rejected by the following vote: Ayes, Bishops of Wisconsin, Michigan, W. New York, Maryland, New Hampshire, Indiana, Mississippi, Florida, and Provisional Bishop of New York—9. Noes, the Bishops of Connecticut, Vermont, Kentucky, Tennessee, Louisiana, Georgia, Delaware, Assistant Bishop of Virginia, Massachusetts, Missionary Bishop for the South West, Pennsylvania, and Assistant Bishop of Connecticut—12.

The Court expressed its willingness to hear, through the Bishop Respondent, the results of the proceeding of his Convention, that he might have all the advantage which he could derive thereby, at the same time "distinctly declaring that by this action it does not recognize any right of the Diocese of New Jersey to appear as a party before the Court." From this declaration the Bishops of Wisconsin, Michigan, Western New York, and Mississippi dissented. Thus the Court embraced the opportunity, both by deed and declaration, to manifest its disapproval of that act of the previous Court which prepared the way for the other irregularities by which the proceedings were embarrassed.

On the second order proposed by the Bishop Respondent, both the Respondent and the Presenting Bishops addressed the Court.

On the eleventh day the Bishop of Pennsylvania moved that the seven Bishops present, who were not on the last Court, be a Committee to take legal advice as to the effect which the action of the former Court should have, in determining the decisions of the present Court, and to confer with the presenters and the respondent to ascertain whether they cannot come to some understanding mutually satisfactory, and fully subserving the purposes of justice.

This order was unanimously adopted. In the discharge of their duty, the Committee had conferences with the presenters, pressing upon them a first, and then a second and stronger admission which the accused was prepared to make, and, as these were not accepted by the presenters, inquiring of them what kind of an acknowledgment would be satisfactory.

Bishop MEADE has left a manuscript account of the intervention so far as the presenters were concerned.

[This was drawn up by Bishop MEADE and approved by the other Presenting Bishops, and read to seven or eight of the other Bishops who wished them to enter into a compromise.]

"(*Proposed Compromise.*)—On Friday, the 19th of September, I was asked by one of the Bishops in the Court, (Bishop Greene,) if the case of Bishop Doane could not be settled without a trial, or further proceedings. He proposed and urged a plan, which, he said, he and some other Bishops were considering. I replied, that there appeared to me insuperable difficulties in the way of it. On the following day the subject was renewed, when he urged the same by various considerations, viz:—that we, the presenters, were suffering far and wide, both among our own and other denominations, from the impression that we were actuated by malice in renewing the presentment; that the Bishop of New Jersey was not only backed by his Diocese, but had an able counsel who might probably defeat his conviction, and that the motives of the presenters should be fully asserted in the compromise. I do not remember what else was said by way of inducement, which inducements, it will be seen, were addressed to our fears of censure and of failure, and to our desire of being exculpated from any improper motives in what we had done. My reply was still the same — that there appeared to the presenters insuperable objections to any plan of compromise, that another had been proposed some days before, which we at once rejected. The proposition alluded to is, that the Bishop should draw up an acknowledgment, or confession of a certain degree of guilt, or of great imprudences on the part of Bishop Doane, on the signing of which the presenters should withdraw their charges, and the whole subject be terminated. To this, the following objections are made.

1st. This confession is to be the only penalty; a principle, it will at once be seen, subversive of all discipline, since, no matter how many or grievous the charges made, all may be set aside and discipline escaped, by a confession when brought to trial.

2nd. What if a Presbyter were arraigned on similar charges, or less aggravated ones, and when the time of trial came, he should, at the instance of friends, sign some paper confessing a small measure of guilt, or great imprudences, and this were accepted as satisfactory, and he returned to his charge — or a communicant be thus dealt with; what has become of the godly discipline of the Church, which we promised to enforce?

3rd. It becomes us to look to the past for precedents, and to the future for consequences. When Bishop Onderdonk of Pennsylvania addressed a letter to the Bishops, containing a very dubious confession of intemperance, and submitted himself to their decision, they at once suspended him from office, and received his resignation of jurisdiction. Just before the presentment of Bishop Onderdonk of New York, two deputations came to the Presenting Bishops, asking them in the one case to relinquish their design and leave the work to the Diocese, and in the other to relinquish it in consequence of what he had already suffered, and because he was doubtless sorry for the past, and would offend thus no more. Each of these petitions was declined, and the public has approved the course which was pursued. After the examination of witnesses in the case of the Bishop of New York, in answer to the question, what he had to say why sentence should not be passed, in a very subdued reply he acknowledged error, but not to the extent charged upon him. This, however, did not arrest or modify the sentence.

If Bishop Doane, on such a slight confession as it is at all probable that he will make, is to be dismissed without trial, it will be difficult to see how a petition for the restoration of the two suspended Bishops can be rejected, should they make some imperfect acknowledgment of guilt, connected with their acknowledged reformation.

4th. In order to see what kind of confession Bishop Doane could assent to, without acknowledging that he has been uttering palpable falsehoods for the last ten years, and that his Diocese and friends have been endorsing the same, all of his and their declarations of his entire innocence, up to the present time, must be examined. To be unfortunately too sanguine, or even imprudent, is not the guilt to be confessed. But to come to him with any other confession, ought to be indignantly repelled by him and his friends, if he be innocent.

5th. On the other hand, to see what kind of confession could be accepted by us, even if the honor of the Church could be sustained without a trial, those who proposed a compromise should read over the charges made in the presentment, and in our reply of last Fall, and then frame a confession consistent therewith, and see whether Bishop Doane could sign it.

6th. There should be carefully considered the difference

between the case in hand and those where pecuniary and personal disputes are the subjects. In them, compromises may take place, and often do without sacrifice of truth and principle. Not so in this.

7th. Let it be remembered that the Respondent and his Diocese have for two years been spreading before the public his own statements, and *ex parte* examinations—that these remain, and will remain on record, though only partial exhibitions of the case, while the Presenters, representing the honor and purity of the Church, have no such documents except their arguments in reply to the Committee of the Diocese of New Jersey. If the compromise is made, they are precluded from any such advantage in defence of the Church and themselves. Silence must then in honor be bound upon all, though it is feared that it will often be broken, and peace not ensue.

8th. The Presenters are placed in a most responsible situation. It is difficult to conceive one more so. To them and to them alone the whole Church and country now look for the proper disposal of this case, until it is in the hands of the Court, and on trial. All the evils resulting from neglect, must be laid at their door, and be chargeable on their unfaithfulness. To ask them to compromise, especially at this late hour, and, while the Judges are on the bench, to come forward and withdraw the charges and dismiss the trial without any change of conviction on their part, is a most unreasonable proposition. Their rejection of this and a former proposition may be used by their opponents as grounds for the charge of a spirit opposed to the peace of the Church; but, by the grace of God, they will bear it, and do what seems to them their solemn duty. They believe that nothing but a trial can reveal the truth and lead to justice. But even an acquittal, no matter how deep the guilt of the accused, resulting from want of evidence or other like cause, would be less dishonorable to the Church than any compromise proposed by the Judges, and assented to by the Presenters and Respondent."

The following statement by Bishop MEADE was intended to be presented to the Court, if the request of the Presenters to be heard on the morning of the last day had not been objected to:

"I beg leave to offer a few remarks before the Court shall take the final step, which we are told it is likely to take, in dismissing this presentment on the ground of a confession or acknowledgment to be made by the accused.

"I say nothing of the legal question which has been so ably argued by my brother of Ohio in behalf of the Presenters. My objections are altogether of a moral character.

"1st. I object to the acceptance of any confession as the only penalty, because it opens a wide door for the escape of any offender, whether of the clergy or of the laity, who, when he sees no other mode of escape, will resort to this.

"2nd. Because both of the now suspended Bishops did make some confession before their sentence; and because if Bishop Doane be dismissed without trial or penalty, I see not how a petition for the restoration of the same can be refused, on such acknowledgment as they will probably be disposed to make, especially since their reformation is confidently believed.

"3rd. I cannot consent to take any part in the sin of holding out a temptation to a fellow-being in the circumstances in which Bishop Doane now is, to add to his other transgressions that of making a confession which is at variance with his repeated asseverations during the last two years, in order to escape a trial; and I do not see how the Bishops can consent to any participation therein.

"4th. I cannot see how either the Presenters or the Court can for one moment think of dismissing the accused, when, though one of the charges in the presentment is that of his excessive use of intoxicating drinks, the accused has presented himself before the Court, at an early, as well as later hour of the day, in such a condition as indicated by his countenance, his breath, and otherwise, that the charge was too true, so as to lead one of the Court to say that 'he was not himself on a certain day,' and another, that he was 'a ruined man,' and others, to complain of the offensiveness of his breath.

"With this protest, which I beg to be placed on the Record, I leave the responsibility with the Court."

"WILLIAM MEADE."

The result of the Committee's compromise with the accused appears in their report which was presented on the 12th day—Sept. 15th:

"The Committee appointed to confer with the Presenting Bishops and Respondent, to ascertain whether they cannot come to some understanding which shall be mutually satisfactory, and also fully answer the purpose of justice, beg leave to report, that upon consultation with the Presenting Bishops, they found that no understanding could be come to, of the sort contemplated by the Court, the Presenting Bishops feeling themselves unable to withdraw their presentment under any such acknowledgment of error as the Respondent would be willing to make. The Committee then conferred with the Respondent, who expressed himself quite ready to acknowledge, as he had already done, to some extent, in open Court, such errors as his conscience accused him of; the result of which conference was, the paper embodied in the preamble and orders now submitted as the basis of a settlement of this vexed and painful question.

"T. C. BROWNWELL,
"JAS. H. OTEY,
"LEONIDAS POLK,
"STEPHEN ELLIOTT, JR.,
"GEO. W. FREEMAN,
"JNO. WILLIAMS,
"JONA M. WAINWRIGHT.

"*Whereas*, Very serious embarrassments have been thrown in the way of the action of this Court, first, by the postponement of the trial of the original presentment, and afterwards, by the decree and orders of the Court of Bishops which assembled at Camden in October, 1852, and continued its session by adjournment at Burlington, to wit:—

"Whereupon it was decreed, that,

"*Whereas*, Previous to the making of the presentment now before this Court, the Convention of New Jersey had investigated most of the matters contained therein, and had determined that there was no ground for presentment, therefore,

"*Ordered*, That, as to the matters thus acted upon by said Convention, this Court is not called upon to proceed further.

"*Whereas*, The Diocese of New Jersey stands pledged to investigate any charges against its Bishop that may be presented from any responsible source; *and whereas*, a Special Convention has been called, shortly to meet, in reference to the new matters contained in the presentment now before this Court, therefore,

"*Ordered*, That this Court, relying upon the said pledge, do not now proceed to any further action in the premises."

Which decree and orders have been pleaded in bar to the trial of the presentment.

And, whereas, The Convention of the Diocese of New Jersey has, through a Committee of its most influential and honorable laymen, satisfied itself, that whatever may have been the imprudences in word and act of the Respondent, there was no intention of crime or immorality on his part.

And, whereas, The said Convention stands pledged to investigate any further charges which may be brought at any future time, from any quarter, against said Respondent, with fairness and impartiality.

And, whereas, The Diocese of the Respondent is now engaged in raising the sum of one hundred and thirty-five thousand dollars, for the release from all embarrassment of St. Mary's Hall, Burlington College and Riverside, the surplus income of such property, when thus released, is to be annually applied to the liquidation of the remaining debts of the Respondent.

And, whereas, The Respondent comes into Court and says:

"The undersigned in prosecuting his plans of Christian education in connection with St. Mary's Hall and Burlington College, found that the expenses of the enterprise greatly exceeded his calculations, while the assistance on which he confidently relied, perhaps too sanguinely, fell altogether short of what he deemed his reasonable expectations. In this condition of things, being entirely left alone, and without advice, every step which he advanced involved him more and more deeply in pecuniary embarrassments. In endeavoring to extricate himself from these embarrassments, he admits that he made representations, which, at the time, he believed to be correct, but many of which turned out in the event to be erroneous. He was also led by his too confident reliance on anticipated aid, to make promises which he fully expected to perform, but which experience has taught were far too strongly expressed. He was also induced, for the sake of obtaining money to meet his necessities, to resort to methods, by the payment of exorbitant interest on loans, which he did not suppose were in contravention of the law, and which common usage seemed to him to justify. He also, in entire confidence in his ability to replace them, made use of certain trust funds in a way which he deeply regrets; and, although they have long been perfectly secured, does not now justify.

"The embarrassments here referred to were followed by a long, and well nigh fatal illness, which, withdrawing him entirely from the business which he had carried on alone, was mainly instrumental in the entire failure in his pecuniary affairs. The perplexity arising from this failure, with the protracted infirmity which followed his sickness, made him liable to many errors and mistakes which might easily bear the appearance of intentional misrepresentations. In connection with the assignment of his property, he set his name, under oath, to an inventory of his goods, and also, to a list of his debts, which he believed to be correct; an act which, he grieves to find, has given rise to an impression in the minds of some that he exhibited an insensibility to the awful sanctions of the oath of a Christian man. But, while he laments the impression, he declares that this act was only done under legal advice, and in the firm conviction of its correctness.

"Some time after his recovery from the illness above alluded to, but while he was still in the midst of his perplexities, smarting under his heavy disappointments, and wounded by the imputations to which, in some quarters, he was subjected, the letter of the three Bishops came to him. He has no disposition to ascribe to them any other than just and proper motives in thus addressing him. But, at the time when he received the communication, he viewed it otherwise; and, under the strong excitement of the moment, penned a pamphlet, parts of which he does not now justify; and expressions in which, in regard to those brethren, he deeply regrets.

"In reference to his indebtedness, he now renews the declaration of intention which he has constantly made, and acted on, to the utmost of his ability, thus far, to devote his means, efforts, and influence, in dependence on God's blessing, to the payment, principal and interest, of every just demand against him—an expectation which there is reasonable hope of having fulfilled, since a committee of the trustees and friends of Burlington College, by whom both institutions are now carried on, have undertaken an enterprise which is nearly accomplished, to discharge the whole mortgage debt; and thus secure the property at Riverside and St. Mary's Hall, with that of Burlington College, to the Church forever, for the purposes of Christian education. And, this done, the trustees have further agreed to appropriate, during his life, the surplus income of both institutions to the liquidation of all his other debts incurred by him in carrying on said institutions.

"That in the course of all these transactions human infirmity may have led him into many errors, he deeply feels. He does not wish to justify or excuse them. If scandal to the Church, or injury to the cause of Christ, have arisen from them, they are occasions to him of mortification and regret. For these things, in all humanity and sorrow, before God and man, he has always felt himself liable to, and willing to receive, the friendly reproofs of his brethren in Christ Jesus, and especially of the Bishops of this Church.

"G. W. Doane,
"Bishop of New Jersey."

Ordered, Therefore, That the presentment before this Court be dismissed, and the Respondent be discharged without day.

The Committee likewise recommended the adoption of the following orders:

1. That no order or decree of the Court in October, 1852, or this Court, shall be taken to admit the right of any Diocese to come between a Court of Bishops and the Responding Bishop, after canonical presentment first made by three Bishops.

2. That this Court believes the Presenters to have acted in good faith, and in the desire and determination to carry out the law of this Church in such case made and provided, in the painful duty which they have felt themselves called upon to perform.

The following communication was received from the Presenters, and ordered to be entered on the Minutes:

To the Court of Bishops:

The Presenting Bishops, having been informed by a Committee of the Court, that a proposal is now under consideration to dismiss the presentment upon several grounds stated in a report of the said Committee, the chief of which is a certain acknowledgment on the part of the Respondent, do represent to the Court, that the exclusive right of withdrawing the presentment, is with the presenters; that the only legal mode of disposing of these charges, by the Court, is to try them by the evidence; that the Presenters stand ready with their evidence to enter on the trial which they have contended for; and they feel themselves bound to ask that the Court will call on the Respondent to plead guilty, or not guilty, to the presentment. With this statement of the legal position of the Presenters as representing the executive of the Church in this case, the undersigned are prepared to abide by such action as the Court may take in the premises.

Wm. Meade,
Chas. P. McIlvaine,
George Burgess.

Camden, Sept. 15, 1859.

"The question being taken upon the acceptance of the report of the Committee, and the adoption of the preamble and orders annexed, the report was accepted, and the preamble and orders adopted by the unanimous vote of the Court, all the members being present and voting."

"Record of the Proceedings."

In reviewing, at the distance of twelve years, this determination of the New Jersey case, it does appear most unprecedented, uncanonical, inconsistent, unaccountable.

1st. That a Court constituted to try for crime, should

permit itself to tamper with the accusers and the accused, and so unavoidably unfit itself for further proceeding if the intervention should fail, is, in our judiciary, something novel.

2nd. That a Court, acting under a statute, should assume an office unrecognized by it, and counteractive of its end, is uncanonical.

3rd. That a Court should pronounce the order of a previous Court illegal, and yet profess itself embarrassed to decide how far it ought to be influenced and controlled in its decisions, by such illegal order, is inconsistent.

4th. To permit a person indicted for crime to excuse himself on the plea that the action was error of judgment, and without criminal intent, is to mistake an explanatory vindication for confession. And to accept such admission as sufficient for discipline, is—unaccountable!

A Court may receive a confession of guilt from the accused, but then it must be a confession of guilt in the offenses charged, and not merely an acknowledgment of well-meaning infirmity. The charges in this case were crime and immorality. The Bishop makes no such admission. His promises he intended to perform. His loans he hoped to return. Whatever he did, he did at the time in good faith, though afterwards he discovered that, in some instances, he had been too sanguine, and trustful. Such errors he "deeply feels." There is no confession of the offences charged in the presentment. The Bishop had no idea of making it such. The Committee did not pretend so to name it. One of the counsel for the Presenters styled it "a confession of innocence," and it cannot be more aptly described. That it was felt by the Court to be no more, is apparent from the fact that it ordered that "The presentment be dismissed, and the Respondent be discharged without day." No punishment—not even a word of gentle admonition! And all this with the remonstrance of the Presenters—their declaration that they were ready with their evidence to enter upon trial—and their earnest petition that the Respondent be required to plead guilty or not guilty to the presentment now in the hands of the Court.

The grave earnestness and steadfast purpose of the three Bishops left no room to doubt the honesty of their convictions, or the conscientiousness of their course. Neither the gross insults heaped upon them on one hand, nor the disappointment which they experienced on the other, provoked them to resent the affronts, or to abandon the prosecution in disgust. The manly manner and Christian spirit in which, to the last, they stood up to the painful duty which they felt themselves called upon to perform, rendered the order of the Court, declaring the belief that the "Presenters had acted in good faith and in the desire and determination to carry out the law of this Church!" mere surplusage. How far the Presenters could reciprocate the compliment, they were not afforded the opportunity to affirm.

It is but justice to the Bishop Respondent to record that his bearing was bold—often defiant. His management of the case was very able, and in close keeping with his avowed purpose to maintain "the rights of his Diocese," and to protect his order, by "making the trial of a Bishop hard." Notwithstanding the violence into which, under the exciting matters involved he was too often betrayed, even those who did not sympathize with his aim and policy, saw much to admire in his address, and to strengthen their wish that he would face his accusers, and clear himself of the charges in the presentment. His firmness never even seemed to falter, till he was meddled with by the compromising Committee. The character of the motives which they vainly tried upon the Presenters, is disclosed in the paper prepared and read to them by Bishop MEADE. What inducements they offered to influence the Bishop Respondent no one has revealed. A second and a third application were requisite, before he conceded the minimum which would be available as a pretext for dismissing the presentment—a concession which, though in fact it scarcely stirs him from the spot on which he stood and "challenged the world," yet, under the circumstances, might be regarded by some, as a slight yielding to pressure, that the Court might be able to let the presentment pass away smoothly without discredit to themselves or detriment to the Respondent.

Throughout this sketch, the conduct of the Bishop of New Jersey in resisting investigation by his Convention, and in his action in reference to the proceedings of the three Bishops has been freely censured; but, in regard to the rumors and charges not a line or a syllable has been penned expressive of a belief that all, or any of them, were true. The Presenters held them all to be true; but the proof on which their convictions were founded never passed from their possession, and even if it had, it might have failed to convince others. Less, should not be said; more, could not be asked.

With regard to the Court, it was irreproachable, until, perverted by a plausible spirit of compromise, it descended from the bench to negotiate between the accusers and the accused, and brought its business to a close by a determination more creditable to its sympathies than conducive to its judicial reputation. *Of this censure the writer appropriates to himself his full share.*

The Presenters came out of the embroilment unswayed and untarnished; and carried with them the comfortable consciousness that, though foiled by the delinquency of the Court, they had done their duty, their whole duty, and nothing but their duty.

On subsequent occasions, the Bishop of Virginia was placed in official positions which required him to ignore his honest convictions in connection with the New Jersey case, or else, to do what could not but be painful to himself, and offensive to Bishop Doane, and those by whom he was sustained. Under such circumstances he did not allow himself to hesitate, or to compromise. He often said to others " Stick to truth—it may get you into difficulty at first, but it will surely aud safely bring you out." His action on one of these occasions and the considerations by which he was governed, are stated in a manuscript which he wrote fifteen days after the event.

"Notice of an occurrence at a Missionary Meeting in Baltimore on the evening of the 13th of October, 1858, written in Lunenburg Co., Virginia, Oct. 28, being the first opportunity as to time after leaving Baltimore.

"At a late meeting of the General Missionary Society of our Church in Baltimore on the 13th of October, 1858, being the senior Bishop present and presiding, having appointed the committees that were called for, and, as usual on such occasions, having omitted the name of Bishop Doane on any of them, a brother Bishop arose, and after speaking of his worthiness to be placed on some committee on account of past services, moved that he be added to that on the Report of the Managers of the Domestic Department. I immediately arose, and expressed my regret that such motion had been made, as it imposed upon me the necessity of saying something in self-defence for the course I had pursued for some years in relation to this subject—that I must under the circumstances of the case, regard the motion as conveying a decided, though indirect censure on myself, and that I was prepared to enter as fully as might be required, upon a statement of the reasons for the course I had pursued. The Bishop making the motion rose, and declared that he had no design to cast any censure on me. I replied that after all that had transpired in relation to this matter, and which was well known to those present, it must bear that aspect, and, if carried, must have that effect.

"At this moment a lay member rose, and after some remarks called me to order, denying my right to do anything but put the question. I replied that I had for a great many years of my life been presiding over public meetings, and thought I knew something of the privileges of the Chair—and that I had never before heard the right of a Chairman to make some remarks before putting a motion, called in question; and as this had a bearing on myself, I should assert that right. The laymen then proposed to the mover to withdraw it, which was acceded to, and the Society immediately adjourned.

"The following is a brief history of my past action in this matter, and statement of my reasons for the same:

"The attempted trial of Bishop Doane for the second time, and the dismissal of the case, on the ground of some partial confession, took place just before the General Convention of 1853. It was hoped that after so humiliating a confession as he was obliged to make in order to escape a trial, and all that was injurious to the Church in what had occurred, and what had been published to the world, that he would not attend that Convention. The Presenters were told, in order to induce their acquiescence in the dismissal of the case, that he was humble and penitent, and would henceforth bear himself meekly and modestly, and retire from public notice. He did, however, attend that Convention, where not only the Bishops, clergy and laity of our Church were assembled in great numbers from all parts of our land, but to which Bishops and clergy of our mother Church from England and Canada had come on matters of deep concernment, and there was deep mortification felt that he should be present and prominent on some public occasions. In the absence of Bishop Brownwell from these meetings held on the evenings of certain days for missionary and other purposes, it fell to my lot to preside and appoint the committees that were required. I felt that to appoint Bishop Doane on any of them would be most offensive and distressing to the feelings of numbers of the best friends of religion and the Church, as there were so many other Bishops present worthy to fill the places to be supplied. I appointed them to the same in the exercise of that discretion which belongs to every presiding officer. For not appointing Bishop Doane, I was censured by some, and Bishop Doane himself, in open assembly, complained that I did not put him as Chairman of the Committee on Foreign Missions, as he had heretofore been. But, receiving the thanks of many whose judgment and character I highly esteem, and having no reason to believe that any change in the character of the Bishop required a change on my part, I have continued to act in the same manner in all those public meetings of the General Missionary Society which annually occur, and over which I have presided, there having always been Bishops enough present whom I deem more worthy to be on the committees, and whom I had a perfect right to select.

"I do not deny the right of any body over which I preside to adopt their own method of appointing committees, whether by ballot, by nomination, or by the Chair; nor, when the nomination is by the Chair, do I question the right of the body to add to the committee, or the propriety of so doing, when the committee stand in need of aid from one especially competent to render it; but when such addition is proposed under circumstances calculated to call in question the right discharge of duty by the presiding officer, and of course to reflect upon him as in the present instance, I affirm the right of defence on his part, in some explanatory remarks before putting the question. I also remark, that when an individual thus rises and nominates one to be added to a committee, he actually becomes the chairman; for such nomination is certainly an election; for it is so painful a thing to reject, that it will scarce ever be done, no matter how much opposed to the nomination the majority of the body may be. It is also well known that some take advantage of this unwillingness to object, in order to elevate some favorite, or effect some special object.

"If I am asked whether I do not by this conduct in the Chair cast some censure on my brother Bishops, who on a certain confession of Bishop Doane dismissed the charges, and left him in the position of a pardoned person, or of one who has suffered the penalty assigned by his judges, and has a right to all the privileges before possessed?—I reply, that such persons are not necessarily restored to all the honors and privileges formerly possessed. We may refuse to one whose previous guilt or present unworthiness we suspect or believe, our society or confidence and respect, though there be certain rights which belong to him. In like manner, one in office may use his discretion in the selection of such. The chairman of any body has no law but his own judgment and conscience to regulate his selection of committees, though he will doubtless pay a due regard to the opinions of others. I should be truly sorry, even to seem to cast censure on my brother Bishops, but I should incur the condemnation of my own heart, and of One infinitely greater, were I to act contrary to the convictions of my own mind, in order to avoid seeming to disapprove their course. In dismissing the charges against Bishop Doane, I have always considered and said, that they were worried and almost forced into a measure which was most painful to most of them at the time, and which some of them have deeply regretted since, and, though the Presenters objected to it to the last, they have never been disposed to severity in their complaints.

"Being subject to evil reports and having opposed and thwarted all attempts to investigate scandalous charges, instead of following the examples of high-minded and honorable men, who call for the strictest *investigation into their characters,* I cannot feel that I am bound to confer an office on him, which for the time being is in my gift, although in the performance of public services, I am bound to administer the Lord's Supper to him, and in some other respects to act towards him as to the other Bishops.

"In conclusion, I add, that in the course pursued under the circumstances in which Providence has placed me, and the responsibility resting on me as a presiding officer, I have acted as one bound to remove, as much as in me lay, some share of that heavy weight of odium which the individual in question has brought upon the Church, by withholding such honor from him, as I lawfully could, in the discharge of such office as has fallen to my lot—that it might not be said, that the Church in her highest assemblies and most important meetings, had lavished her choicest favors upon him."

MOVEMENTS FOR THE REMISSION OF THE SENTENCES OF SUSPENSION.

From the first there appears to have been a settled purpose on the part of certain Bishops in the minority to use every effort to procure the restoration of the suspended Bishops. This was to have been expected from their, no doubt, honest persuasion that in each case the penalty was either unlawfully imposed or unduly severe, or perhaps both. The Bishop of Maryland had announced that he "did not mean to cease his efforts until *both* the brothers are replaced in the positions in which they once were." (Letter from Rev. Paul Trapier to Bishop MEADE.)

A memorial from the Right Rev. B. T. Onderdonk, D. D., was addressed to the General Convention which met in New York in 1847. The Committee to whom it was referred, in their report, which furnished a brief reply to the considerations urged by the memorial, closes thus: "But while your committee sustain the proposition that the remission of that sentence is a possible event in contemplation of law, they deem it but justice to the memorialist, and to the Diocese of New York to add, that they consider the possibility of its occurrence so slender and remote, as scarcely to afford a reasonable basis for future action.

"In conclusion, your committee respectfully recommend the adoption of the following resolution:

"*Resolved,* That the memorialist have leave to withdraw his letter and memorial.

"All which is respectfully submitted.

"T. C. BROWNELL,
"JOHN H. HOPKINS,
"I. P. R. HENSHAW,
"GEO. W. FREEMAN."

Bishop McCoskry signed "as concurring in the resolutions without taking part in the argument of the Committee."

When the question was put, sixteen Bishops voted in the affirmative, six in the negative. The Bishop of New Hampshire did not vote.

With regard to the effort to effect the restoration of the other brother, a manuscript of Bishop MEADE furnishes the following account:

"*General Convention of* 1847.

"Immediately on the meeting of the Bishops, after the opening services in the Church were over, the first* memorial from Bishop Onderdonk of New York was read. That laid on the table, Bishop Whittingham proposed the restoration of Bishop Onderdonk of Pennsylvania, having prepared a regular sentence for the purpose. Bishop DeLancey seconded it, saying that he had intended to do it himself. Bishop DeLancey urged its immediate passage before we adjourned, saying that every moment's delay was injustice to Bishop Onderdonk.

"I rose and expressed my astonishment at this whole

* It was a letter to the Bishops. The memorial was not presented till the sixth day's session.

proceeding, especially the haste which was urged, expressed my fear that this was one of those mercies which might prove cruel to the object of its exercise and to the whole Church, that no evidence of confession or penitence was produced, and moved to lay the resolution on the table.

"On the following morning, Bishop Whittingham called up his resolution, stated that he had made it his business to go to Philadelphia to inquire into the case—that there could be no question of his repentance and reformation, that there was but one sentiment in the Church of Pennsylvania, and that was strongly in favor of his restoration.

"Bishops DeLancey, Kemper, Ives, and McCoskry followed, each declaring that they had visited Philadelphia and made special inquiry, and found that there was an universal desire for his restoration—the latter saying that the members of other denominations would, in the streets, express their astonishment that such a man was still kept under suspension. Bishop Brownell expressed his willingness, under such a representation, to restore him to the office of Presbyter. Bishop Whittingham expressed his readiness to accept this. In opposition to all this, I rose and still expressed my incredulity as to the main fact stated, viz.: the universal wish for his restoration—that I had seen two or three of the clergy of Pennsylvania, since our adjournment, who expressed their utter astonishment at the proposition, declared that it would come as a surprise on the whole Diocese, and give great dissatisfaction—that they scarcely knew of any who would not grieve at it. I moreover stated that I was informed sometime since, that in May last, various attempts were made by some few persons to get up a memorial in his behalf, but that it was an utter failure.

"Bishop Whittingham here interrupted me, saying that he knew much more of that meeting than I did—that there would have been an unanimous vote in favor of a memorial, but for the fear in the minds of some, that an act of justice to one brother might lead to an act of mercy to the other. I replied that it was most strange indeed that the Bishop's friends, met to ask an act of justice for him, should be driven from that, and desert him, lest it should lead to an act of mercy to another—that his friends at that meeting would indignantly have repelled such an imputation from themselves. I proceeded then to state that the Bishop of Pennsylvania had scarcely made any confession three years since, on which to ground a sentence. Môreover, that if all the information which ought to have been laid before the Bishops, in regard to his guilt, had been so done, he would have been tried and degraded, and not permitted to hope for restoration—that copies of a printed statement of charges, signed by other clergy of Pennsylvania, were put into the hands of one of the Bishops to be given to all the rest, and other documents were in readiness when called for—that such printed document was never seen by a number of the Bishops, and that in order to judge of the propriety of his restoration these documents should now be examined, in order that we might know the extent of the evil report against him, and reproach brought on the Church and religion. I therefore moved that a committee be appointed to examine into the propriety of his restoration, with power to call for documents, and summon witnesses as to the evidences of his repentance and reformation, and as to the general desire for his restoration.

"The motion was adopted, and Bishops Brownell, Ives and myself were appointed the committee.

"Other business and various causes prevented the meeting of the committee. Bishop Whittingham called for the report several times, and said he was prepared to meet any objections I could urge, and to rebut any documents which could be brought, and that he had not the least doubt as to the result. At length Bishop Brownell and Bishop Ives called me, one day, to a corner of the room and told me they had determined on the report which he held in his hand, which was in favor of his restoration to full Episcopal powers, and they read a sentence to this effect. I expressed to them my surprise at their mode of proceeding—that at my instance a committee of examination should have been appointed, myself being one of them, and that two of that committee should without calling me to a conference, agree on a report, and merely show it to me before its presentment, was altogether improper. They replied that of course they expected me to offer a minority report. I told them that was not enough, that the object of appointing a committee was, that we meet and examine documents and witnesses, and reason the matter, and see if we could not come to some agreement; but, since they did not choose that mode, I should draw up my own opinion and sustain it. I accordingly drew up a report against his restoration, stating six or seven objections at some length, to be sustained by documents and arguments. I presented this to them, and requested them to show it to Bishop Whittingham.

"On the morning when the report was to be presented, Bishop Brownell spoke to me, saying that Bishop Ives and himself had agreed that if I would unite with them we would report unanimously that 'it is inexpedient at this time to restore Bishop Onderdonk.' I replied that I objected to that, because it seemed to say that it might be expedient some time hence; whereas, I believed it never would be expedient. But, on being urged, I consented for the sake of peace, and to avoid unpleasant argument.

"Accordingly the report was thus presented, but it did not prevent discussion. Bishop Gadsden read a long written argument in favor of his restoration. Bishop DeLancey followed at some length. When he closed, I remarked that it was my hope that only my silent vote would be required, that I had been led to believe that by assenting to the report, all discussion would be avoided, and the whole matter dismissed—that I was opposed to the report first drawn up, and had drawn up a minority report, and that the committee had agreed to the present, on the supposition that it would pass without debate; but, as it was otherwise, I should now proceed to deliver my opinion, and as a basis would read my minority report. This being done, I proceeded to sustain it by documents in my hand, consisting of letters from different clergy in Pennsylvania, protesting against restoration as a measure unthought of, and unasked for, and, as they believed, contrary to the wishes of the great body of the clergy and laity; and also, by the printed document referred to above, and signed by sixty-eight of the clergy of Pennsylvania. I began with the latter, but no sooner had I taken it in hand, when Bishop Whittingham objected to its being read, as out of order, because referring to things occurring before his suspension. Bishop McCoskry said nobody knew that it was genuine—it might have been raked up from the streets. I maintained that it was in order, and the Chair decided that it was.

"Bishop Whittingham appealed to the House. I proceeded to show that it was in order, but before I had stated my reasons, a conference took place between Bishops Whittingham, Ives, and DeLancey, and the whole proposition to restore was withdrawn by the mover, Bishop Whittingham. Not, however, without his declaring that the treatment of Bishop Onderdonk was 'ungodly, unmerciful and unjust.' For this he was called to order; when he made some explanation, which, however, was to my mind, and to others also, I am sure, entirely unsatisfactory. He also moved that the whole matter be stricken from the Journal, which was agreed to."

MINORITY REPORT OF BISHOP MEADE, REFERRED TO IN THE PRECEDING STATEMENT.

"Report of the minority of the Committee on the proposition to restore the late Bishop of Pennsylvania."

"The undersigned is constrained to differ from the majority, and begs leave to state some of his reasons for so doing, and also to request that the same may be inserted on the Journal.

"He is opposed to the restoration—

"First. Because he has no evidence that, either at the time of the sentence, or since, Bishop Henry U. Onderdonk has ever made a proper confession of guilt, and been truly humbled on account of it.

"Secondly. Because he believes that Bishop Onderdonk was guilty in other respects besides that for which he was suspended, the proofs of which were not in the possession of the Bishops, as was designed by those who obtained them, and which, had they been known, would probably have led to his presentment and degradation.

"Thirdly. Because such scandal as had been resting on the Church for so many years on account of his intemperance, and his unbecoming conduct to ladies, cannot be removed by a suspension of three years. On the contrary, it is believed that such vices as those imputed to him, and of which, to a certain extent, he acknowledged himself guilty, are of such a nature as to debar the guilty person from the resumption of Episcopal or ministerial office.

"Fourthly. Because at the time of a meeting of the Convention of Pennsylvania, sixty-eight of the clergy thereof united in a printed statement of the great scandal produced throughout the Diocese by his misconduct, causing the same to be published, and because fifty-one of the clergy and fifty-five of the congregations of the Diocese, did, by their vote in Convention accepting his resignation, (although he endeavored to withdraw it,) show their full conviction of his guilt in the matters laid to his charge; thirteen clergymen and five parishes only being willing to allow him to withdraw it; and because there is no evidence that any change has taken place in their opinions and feelings which should induce us to believe that they would wish his restoration. On the contrary, from all the inquiries the undersigned has been able to make, and from letters in his possession, he believes that Bishop Onderdonk's restoration would not only occasion great surprise, but very general dissatisfaction among them.

"Fifthly. Because it would place the Bishop and clergy of Pennsylvania, or any other Diocese to which Bishop Onderdonk might remove, in a very embarrassing and painful situation, and might lead to very unhappy discord among the clergy and congregations, some of whom might feel bound by respect to the action of the Bishops in restoring him to admit him to their pulpits, while others would be restrained by conscience from so doing. And also, because in case of a vacancy in the Diocese of Pennsylvania, or the need of an assistant to the present Bishop, the undersigned is confident that the Diocese of Pennsylvania would not be willing to re-elect the restored Bishop as their Diocesan or assistant Bishop.

"And, Lastly. Because, without the fullest proof of a candid acknowledgment of guilt in the matters laid to his charge, and an expression of heartfelt penitence, and an humble petition from himself for restoration, the whole community would condemn the House of Bishops for such restoration, even if it could be brought to believe that restoration were proper, under any circumstances, after such continued and disgraceful deportment.

"For these and other reasons, the undersigned must dissent from the Report of the Majority."

In the General Convention which met in Cincinnati in 1850, the efforts for the restoration of the Right Rev. H. U. Onderdonk were renewed, and by the same parties and with unabated earnestness. They were again successfully resisted by Bishop Meade, for the following, among other reasons:

"Because, 1. After such offences as led to the suspension,

restoration would, under any circumstances, be of very questionable propriety.

2. It would certainly be inadmissible, without satisfactory evidence of repentance and reformation. No such assurance had been received from the suspended Bishop, and some who advocated his restoration stated none such would be given by him.

3. Even if he should—if he were to appear before his brethren and in the posture and with the language of a penitent pray for restoration—though all had confidence in his profession, and freely mingled their tears of joy with his tears of godly sorrow—*this alone* would not be sufficient to justify the termination of the sentence."

Discipline has other purposes besides the reformation of the offender. It must be so administered as to express the Church's abhorrence of the offence and her determination not to permit it to pass unpunished—that so her own purity may be vindicated—her members be deterred from evil living, and her sacred offices be conducted by an irreproachable ministry.

That these ends had been already answered by this case of discipline, there was no proof. The Diocese which had requested his resignation, and from which the pressure came for his suspension, neither originated nor countenanced the effort for his restoration. There was no mistaking this significant silence. To terminate the sentence against this virtual protest would be to trifle with discipline.

The efforts which signally failed in 1847 and in 1850, were successful in the Convention of 1853, which met in Philadelphia; for, though the Convention of the Diocese expressed no wish for the restoration, it was now zealously pressed by the Bishop of the Diocese and other residents of the city, whose opinions were certainly entitled to much consideration. A majority in favor of the proposal was secured. After a suspension of nine years the sentence was remitted, and the Right Rev. H. U. Onderdonk was restored to the exercise of the office and work of a Bishop in the Church of God. The minority, among whom was Bishop MEADE, would be greatly misunderstood if it were supposed they did not sympathize in the grateful relief afforded to a suffering brother, though effected by the act of others, in which they could not conscientiously concur.

In the General Convention at Richmond in 1859, the restoration of Bishop B. T. Onderdonk was proposed, but found little favor except with the Bishops who formed the minority of the Court by which the sentence was imposed.

The preceding pages are designed to set forth, with as much brevity as the nature of the case would admit, the part taken by Bishop MEADE in connection with the proceedings which have been narrated. For that agency, he was, as has been stated, violently assailed, not only by some of the Church papers of the time, but in a pamphlet signed "A member of the Church," written by Horace Binney, Esq., of Philadelphia. It is a very magisterial condemnation of the action of the Bishops in the suspension of Bishop H. U. Onderdonk, as unjust, uncanonical and illegal—a very bitter censure of the Bishops who declined granting the application for a remission of the sentence in 1847, and a specially sarcastic assault on Bishop MEADE as the ecclesiastical Jeffries of his day. To this "statement of the case of Bishop H. U. Onderdonk," Bishop MEADE published a counter-statement in which, with his habitual moderation, he corrects the offensive errors of his trained assailant by an unpretending recital of the facts of which he was personally cognizant, leaving the distinguished jurist and his legal arguments to be attended to by Bishop Hopkins, who it was understood was preparing a reply.

Of Bishop MEADE's "Counter-statement," Mr. Binney published a "Review," which certainly did not excel his

"Statement," either in accuracy or amiableness. He refuses to admit the Bishop's declaration that his personal relations with Bishop Onderdonk had always been of the most friendly character—asserts that the sole import of the declaration was "to enhance the justice of his reluctant severity," sneers at what he calls the Bishop's high-toned and sublimated notions upon the subject of discipline, of which he has given decisive evidence by being the foremost man in every instance of judicial discipline, either consummated or attempted in this quarter of the Church.

How utterly false this assertion is, the narrative renders perfectly palpable. There were altogether but three instances of judicial discipline consummated or attempted in "this quarter of the Church." 1st. Bishop H. U. Onderdonk's, with which Bishop MEADE had nothing to do, till placed on the committee to whom the matter was referred in the House of Bishops; and there is no evidence of his action on the committee, further than to concur in the report and resolution as submitted to the House.

2nd. Bishop B. T. Onderdonk's, in which, of the three presenting Bishops, Bishop MEADE was the *last* who agreed to engage in the inquiry which led to the trial. His name precedes the other two, simply because he was their senior.

3rd. Bishop Doane's, in which, as the correspondence shows, Bishop MEADE was neither foremost in the proceedings, nor did he yield to the canonical requisition made upon him, until he had endeavored, as far as allowable, to excuse himself from the disagreeable duty. A very little inquiry would have saved Mr. Binney from a misrepresentation as unworthy of himself, as it was calculated to prove injurious to the character of Bishop MEADE.

But the temper of the Reviewer will be better apprehended by the annexed quotation from the same paragraph:

"The psychological fact has been too often illustrated to admit of any doubt, that such minds have very little difficulty in driving the currents of the heart back to their fountains, or in drying them up by the heat of conscientious zeal, in a service which they deem to be their highest duty, and rightly, if they understood it rightly. But herein is the difficulty, that when the streams of mind and heart become disunited, which our beneficent Creator meant to run together to temper our feelings with wisdom and our judgment with gentleness and mercy, then our sharp and steel-edged minds, left to their own sway, without the tempering influence of their better companion, cut their way even to the bloodiest conclusions without remorse; for remorse is in general but the biting back of the heart's current into that untempered torrent that had swept on to the end alone. There is no necessity of referring to Calvin and Servetus. Calvin was both a great and good man. Luther, Knox, Cranmer had the same sharp dividing mind, and at times drove it up to the head in the bowels of humanity, with the same unrelenting stroke. It was in a great degree the fault of their age. It may be a personal fault in any age."

This extraordinary passage is cited, not because of any peculiar psychological truth or profundity which it exhibits. The fact so elaborately treated, may be conceded without adopting the philosophy by which it is cumbered. Neither is it commended by its rhetorical refinement, for from beginning to end it presents a tissue of mixed metaphor attributable to "the streams" of judgment and imagination becoming disunited, and so leaving "the untempered torrent" of the latter, "to sweep on to its end alone." But these are irrelevant and minor matters in comparison with the sad proof and illustration which the paragraph affords of the very theory which its author expounds. It is better dismissed, with the single remark that, its spirit is clear to impartial readers as the sun at noonday, obviating the necessity of a detailed notice of the harsh charges and tart reflections with which the Review abounds. The corrective of the mis-statements is amply provided in the brief history of the cases furnished with this view; and the arguments of the astute assailant of the Bishops will be found satisfactorily disposed of in "a Letter" addressed by Bishop Hopkins of Vermont, "to the clergy and laity of the Protestant Episcopal Church in the United States," and entitled "the True Church Principles of Restoration to the Episcopal Office." This remarkable letter appears to have settled the legal questions involved. No reply was attempted. It ends with an appropriate testimony to the character and course of Bishop MEADE, which will afford a pleasing close to the painful subject of ecclesiastical discipline.

"And now I close my humble labor in defence of the House of Bishops. Much might be added, if I were inclined to notice the many sharp thrusts of our adversary, and especially his severe attack on Bishop MEADE, my worthy and widely reverenced brother of Virginia. But on this field of remark, I shall not enter. My object is to vindicate *principles* rather than men, and men only as far as they maintain those principles which constitute the praise and glory of the Church throughout the world.

"Bishop MEADE stands in no need of defence from me. His life is his defence, and I would to God that we could all appeal to the same evidence with equal safety."

"Our learned antagonist, however, seems to think it matter of reproach, that this eminent man has been *the leader* in all the presentments against Bishops. But who has a right to impeach the honesty of his motives, or the utility of his labors, in this most thankless, and yet most important part of his official duty? Assuredly there are thousands in our land who have cordially approved it — while yet there might not be one amongst them all who would have undergone the odium, toil, and trouble, of the task. As to myself, I lay no claim to the Christian boldness and fearlessness which it required. But yet, I should esteem it an honor, far beyond any in my reach, if my epitaph could say, 'Here lies the body of a Bishop, who was distinguished beyond all his brethren for his zealous, sincere, and consistent support of pure Church discipline.'" (pp. 38–9.)

DOUBLE DUTIES, AS RECTOR AND BISHOP.

The duties which devolved upon Bishop MEADE in the double relationship which he sustained as Rector and Diocesan were arduous, and not unfrequently so conflicting in their claims as to render it questionable whether they could both be satisfactorily discharged by one and the same incumbent. If it could be accomplished by any one, Bishop MEADE, with his iron constitution, active habits, and indefatigable energy, must have succeeded. His heart was in both ministrations, and he was alike apt and meet to perform either to the honor of God, and the edifying of His Church. In one of the smaller Dioceses he would have had no difficulty, but with a territory of 61,352 square miles, and, at this period, few of the facilities for traveling which present internal improvements afford, even his herculean strength and unsurpassed diligence were inadequate to the combined services. With the increasing demands of the Diocese, the relinquishment of that office which could be resigned, was only a question of time, and in due season it became matter of fact. This may seem an inconsiderable change to be so seriously noted, and yet, if the testimony of those who have experienced it be listened to, it is just here that the most painful sacrifice is made by the minister of a congregation who loves the work which he leaves, to assume the responsibilities and devote himself exclusively to the peculiar functions of the Episcopate. Outside the divinely-instituted family-circle, there is no relation as sacred, refined, tender, and eventful as that which is formed and fostered by the parochial office and its various ministrations. The "good work" of a Bishop has strong attractions to one who rightly appreciates its high and holy services, of which none perhaps is more alluring than the privilege of proclaiming the precious gospel to the crowds who congregate at the different points of an Episcopal visitation, and under circumstances which open a great and effectual door to the ambassador of Christ. But even these special opportunities lack the lively and affecting interest which attends the parochial dispensation of the Word. If a Bishop preaches to the many, he is to most of them personally a stranger. He preaches, and passes on, ignorant of the reception given to his message. If any have been impressed, he must leave it to others to hear their anxious inquiries, and, with frequent prayer and faithful instruction, disperse their doubts, encourage their desires, and bring them to Jesus—a process of deep and delightful interest, and productive of a bond of most affectionate and enduring friendship. These hallowed ties are constantly forming between the faithful parish minister and his people; but if he becomes exclusively a Diocesan, he is unavoidably withdrawn from the sphere where they originate, and from the intercourse by which they are commenced and cherished. So, also, in reference to the pleasing and profitable services of the chancel—at the font, in connection with baptism, and the catechetical exercises for the young, preparatory for the renewal of their vows in confirmation; at the communion table, and in all the intimate and solemn converse which precedes, especially the first approach—and then, in the household visits to the sick, and the afflicted, and the dying—even more salutary to the pastor than to those to whom he ministers—all these blessed associations and services by which he becomes identified with the most sacred interests of his people, "rejoicing with those who rejoice, and weeping with those who weep"—he must, if he gives himself wholly to the Episcopate, for the future forego, and in doing so he sacrifices sources of religious and social improvement and happiness, not easily over-estimated, and to which, if he does not sometimes look back with troublesome desire, he must be better or worse than Bishops in general.

Twice during his Episcopate, occasions arose which rendered it expedient for the Bishop to resume the parochial relation. In each instance the arrangement was prompted solely by a desire to unite an important congregation, the members of which could not concur in the choice of any one else, but were unanimous in soliciting him to become their Rector. And in each instance he continued in charge until conflicting preferences were yielded, and the congregation united in inviting a minister whom he commended to their consideration.

Christ Church, Norfolk, and St. Paul's Church, Petersburg, were those favored with his faithful and very acceptable ministrations for a season, and relinquished only when the purpose for which he had accepted the rectorship was satisfactorily accomplished.

During his connection with Christ Church, Norfolk, the congregation was remarkably blessed—many became deeply interested on the subject of religion, and large numbers were at different times added to the Church. The tone of religious feeling was decidedly improved, and the standard of religious character elevated. The churches in Norfolk, and the Diocese at large, long rejoiced in the happy fruits of that genuine revival, and the Christian zeal and activity which it produced are still benefitting even some of the distant missions of our communion.

On his way to his new field of labor, he addressed a letter to Mrs. Meade, whose delicate health, and the inclemency of the season, made it necessary for her to remain for the present in Clarke County.

STEAMBOAT RELIEF, Thursday, ——— 14, 1835.

Dear Wife:

We left Baltimore this morning, and are now under way for Annapolis, where the Columbus is ready to convey us to Norfolk. This boat is called the Ice-Breaker, and plies between Baltimore and Annapolis during such a season as we now have. We hope to reach Norfolk some time to-morrow. I wrote to you from Washington, and this will go back in the boat to Baltimore, and thence, I hope, speedily to you. We are all well, and have met with no accidents. I cannot help wishing sometimes that you were along, since we get on so safely and comfortably. Last evening we spent our time agreeably in a private parlor at Barnum's great hotel, having Mr. Henshaw and Johns and Dale with us, for two hours after tea. * * * * * * I hope my dear wife prays for me more ardently than ever, now that I am about to engage in new and more arduous duties. My mind is still the same as it regards the propriety of the step I am taking, though I feel very deeply the pain of such a charge. I hope I am enabled to say "the will of God be done."

Yours, most tenderly,

W. MEADE.

In his annual address to the Convention of 1835, having reported his laborious visitation of the western part of the Diocese, and some of the parishes in the vicinity of his residence, he introduces a notice of his removal. "After this I remained at home in the discharge of parochial duties until the middle of January, when, in obedience to what appeared to my mind a call from Providence, I felt it to be my duty to accept the invitation of the large and interesting congregation of Christ Church, Norfolk, to become its pastor. In so doing I distinctly stated to the same, that I could not for a moment think of neglecting any previous or higher obligation to the Diocese, and that time and trial only could decide whether it be practicable to perform my duties to the Diocese and to that congregation, so as to satisfy the reasonable expectation of both. As to my prospects of usefulness in this new charge, I must refer you to my parochial report. As one evidence, however, that I am not a little encouraged to believe that the gracious smiles of our Emmanuel are vouchsafed to the people of this charge, let me mention that on Easter Sunday twenty-four persons were added to the communion, and on the second Monday in this month ten others were confirmed, with a view to the communion, when it shall next be administered." (Journal 1836, pp. 13–14.)

The same Journal contains his first report as Rector of Christ Church, Norfolk.

"The Rector entered upon his charge the middle of January last, and was soon encouraged to hope that an unusual seriousness was taking possession of the minds of a considerable number of his hearers. This was greatly increased, and in many instances brought to a happy conclusion, by some deeply interesting services, which were performed during five or six successive days, in the latter part of March. At that time the Rev. Mr. Mann, accompanied by two esteemed brethren from Baltimore, the Reverend Messrs. Henshaw and Johns, paid a visit to Norfolk with a view of making collections for our Theological Seminary at Alexandria. The Rector availed himself of the opportunity to have frequent religious services, with a view to the spiritual interests of his congregation. In this he was cordially supported by the Rev. Mr. Boyden, minister of St. Paul's Church, and the Rev. Mr. Wingfield, of Portsmouth, whose congregations shared in the services."

"Bishop Moore also came down from Richmond, and lent us much affectionate aid. Our services were continued for six successive days, and were divided among the three congregations. At an early hour of the morning, a goodly number met together with the ministers, in one of the churches, and by suitable services were prepared for the large assemblies at the hour of eleven and at night. At these meetings, besides the prayers and hymns, several short addresses were delivered, well calculated to make them interesting and profitable. The sermons, also, in the after part of the day, were usually followed by short and touching exhortations. An interest proportioned to the zeal and sound judgment which was put forth on the occasion, was soon awakened, and continued to increase to the conclusion of the services. All who were present at those exercises expressed themselves well pleased, and hoped for the frequent return of them. The fruits thereof have been such as to gratify the hearts of all the friends of the Church. Concerning thirty persons who have since made a public profession of religion, the minister, after much intercourse with most of them, entertains the pleasing hope that they have passed from death unto life. They appear determined to answer the description of God's people; that is, to be "a peculiar people, zealous of good works." The most happy effect seems also to have been produced upon the old professors of religion. They have been stirred up to more zeal, and been made to remember the time of their first love, and to do their first works."

"One evidence of an awakened interest in behalf of the kingdom of Christ was furnished before the close of our services, in the liberal subscriptions of four thousand dollars to our Seminary. The Rector has seen other evidences, in the readiness manifested by the congregation to engage in every good work recommended by him."

To all his other cares there was now added the painful solicitude on account of the declining health of Mrs. Meade, by which he had been delayed in his attendance at the General Convention, and prevented from making certain visitations which he had purposed.

In the Journal of 1836, after detailing the official services performed, he adds: "These labors being ended, it was now time for me to return to the duties of that pastoral relation which I had undertaken toward the congregation in Norfolk."

"On the first Sunday in November I entered anew on the discharge of parochial duties in Christ Church. During the winter and spring he was able to officiate several times in Portsmouth and at "Old Point Comfort." In reference to other visits which he should have made to "the neighboring congregations," he states, "but it pleased Providence to forbid it by the continued and increasing indisposition of my wife, whom I could not leave for the last few months, without a sacrifice of feeling which, I am sure, my brethren would not ask at my hands. My time, however, was fully occupied by the claims of the large congregation which has been cast on my care, and also by some services to the congregation of St. Paul's in Norfolk, whose hopes and zeal I have endeavored to cherish, until they can get some one to take the oversight of them."

To his impending domestic affliction he now alludes with most delicate tenderness and submissive faith. "In the midst of painful uncertainty as to the issue of that on which so much of my earthly happiness depends, I have been cheered not only by the unsurpassed kindness of the people of Norfolk, but by the hope that my labors among them have not been unblest. Since I have been there, between forty and fifty have been united to the Church, and, I trust, to the Lord; eighteen were confirmed on Easter Monday, all of whom then partook, and some of them had before partaken of, the Lord's Supper. I hope ere long to have the aid of a brother, who will shortly, if the Lord permit, be clothed after the forms of our Church with authority to minister among us.

"And now my brethren, as to the services which are to be expected of me during the season upon which we have entered, and which I have sacredly consecrated to Episcopal visitation, I am unable to say more, than that I am in the hands of God, to do with as He pleases. Perhaps, if we are permitted to meet together again, I may have very little to tell you of Episcopal duties performed during the present summer. There are claims of a private nature which may sometimes be permitted to take the place of more public duties. Such claims are now pressing heavily upon me, and I beg an interest in the prayers of all the brethren and friends here assembled, that I may be enabled, now and always, to do and suffer the will of God, in the spirit of our once suffering and now exalted Saviour."

His parochial report of the same year, records the happy effects of the recent revival. "During the past year a regular Missionary Society has been established, whose contributions are made four times a year. It is composed according to the recommendation of the General Convention, of all the baptized members of the Church, whether children or adults. There are between two and three hundred subscribers on this plan, and more than three hundred dollars have been the fruit of this happy arrangement. Nearly three hundred dollars have been collected by the agent of the Episcopal Sunday School Union, for the benefit of that institution. The Education Society and Theological Seminary still share the generosity of the members of the congregation. More than two hundred dollars are annually given to the former—and those who united in the subscription of nearly four thousand dollars last year to the Seminary, payable in annual instalments, have not, I am sure, repented of their engagement, but will, from year to year, cheerfully discharge their obligations."

"During the last spring a pious member of our communion, Miss Susan Boudoin, who departed this life in the triumphs of faith, bequeathed the sum of five hundred dollars to the Education Society, and the same sum to the Bible Society of Virginia, both of which bequests have been faithfully and cheerfully paid by the executor and heir, to the proper authorities. During the present spring, a generous donation of a lot suitable for a lecture and Sunday School room has been made to the Church, by a female member of the same. The value is estimated at three thousand dollars. The sum of six hundred dollars has already been raised for the purpose of its enlargement.

The Rector of this congregation has reason to hope that a better evidence than any above mentioned of the prevalence of a good spirit of piety in the members of the Church is to be found in their punctual attendance, their correct conduct, their love and harmony, their disposition to every good work, especially their zeal in behalf of the poor, and the children of the poor. For all this he desires to praise God, and give all the glory to Him." (Journal 1836, pp. 27–8.)

In about two months after the Convention of 1836, the prayers which he earnestly solicited in the close of the Address of that year, were especially needed. Mrs. Meade died on the 26th of July, at Edgewood, Hanover county, and the heart of her devoted husband, so full of sympathy in all the afflictions of his brethren, was again pierced by its own sorrows. To this he appropriately refers in the commencement of his Convention Address of the ensuing year. "In presenting you with a statement of such labors in the Lord's vineyard as I have been permitted and enabled to perform during the past year, I may be allowed, without improperly intruding domestic afflictions on your notice, to allude to an event which has deprived me of my best earthly friend, and the Church of one who was alive to everything which affected her welfare. But few among you are able to estimate the loss which I have sustained. But if through God's abounding grace the bereavement shall minister to my spiritual improvement, and to the increase of my labors for the advancement of His kingdom, I shall then be enabled the more truly to say, "God's will, and not mine be done." That such may be the happy result of my affliction, let me ask an interest in all your prayers." (Journal 1837, pp. 6–7.)

The same Journal contains a record of the satisfactory issue of his temporary connection with Christ Church, Norfolk,—of the effect upon his own mind of the experiment he there made, and of purposed policy for the future. "On my arrival in Norfolk, I soon became happily confirmed in the hope and belief which I had cherished for some time, that in the Rev. Mr. Parks, who had for some time been acting as my assistant, I had found a brother into whose hands I could safely confide the charge of a congregation which had been greatly endeared to my heart during a pastoral connection of the last two years. I had been becoming more and more convinced each year, that it was impossible for me, with comfort to my own mind, or satisfaction to others, to discharge those Episcopal duties which Bishop Moore and the Diocese wished at my hands, in connection with any pastoral charge, especially with one so large and responsible, as that of Christ Church, Norfolk. I therefore determined to avail myself of the present favorable opportunity and resign my rectorship, and henceforth give myself entirely to the Diocese at large. My resignation was immediately followed by the unanimous election of Mr. Parks, and subsequently by the choice of Mr. Atkinson as his assistant." * * * * * "It becomes me in drawing this communication to a close, to make some allusion to my future plans for the more effectual discharge of the duty of Assistant Bishop.

"On communicating to Bishop Moore my intention to decline any parochial charge in future, and requesting his advice as to the best disposal of my time, he expressed a wish that I would hereafter consider the whole Diocese as the field of my labors, leaving it to himself, of course, to re-visit, as he might think proper, any of those parts most convenient to him.

"On examining this extensive field by such lights as my previous experience afforded, I found that to visit each congregation in the Diocese and perform the Episcopal duties required, will occupy about twelve months of uninterrupted traveling and preaching. Of course, to visit one half of the Diocese each year will occupy six months, besides those occasional visits which particular cases may call for, and which may require two months more, leaving only four months for those private studies which are indispensable to prepare the mind for the right discharge of the very high and responsible duties of the Episcopate.

"It is my purpose, by God's blessing, to adopt this course for the future, and the congregations may henceforward expect an Episcopal visit every other year, while God shall give me ability to perform the service."

During the Bishop's sojourn in Norfolk the pressure upon mind and body must have been prodigious. But neither the magnitude nor the multiplicity of official services made him unmindful of the unobtrusive charities of private life, and the quiet offices of domestic and Christian relationship. It is most interesting to observe, that when the cares of the churches of the Diocese, and especially of one of the largest congregations, were claiming his attention, he had the heart, and made the time, to consider and discharge his duty as god-father, to children from whom he was separated by several hundred miles. The following letter, which may incite others to the performance of a much neglected duty, was addressed to children living in Frederick County:

NORFOLK, February 4, 1835.

To my dear god-children, Archy and Roberta Page :

Although I am now a great way off, yet I do not forget those I have left behind me in Frederick, not even the little children, particularly my god-children—whom I am bound to think of more than others. I send each of you a little book, which, though I have not read it myself, I am sure must be good. If God should spare my life, and permit me to see you again next Summer, I hope to hear you read in them. Now, my dear children, is the very time for you to learn everything that is good.

"'Tis easier far if we begin
To serve the Lord betimes,
For sinners who grow old in sin,
Are hardened in their crimes."

By trying to be good and praying to God every day to assist you, you will make your parents happy, and God Himself will love you, and take care of you. God has given you parents who care for your souls, and wish you to be happy forever in Heaven. Many poor children have no such parents to watch over them and keep them from sin. I hope that you will both be great comforts to your parents, by becoming better and better every year that you live. You must remember me and your cousin Thomasia very affectionately to your papa and mamma, and kiss my little namesake for me. Tell your papa I got my box safe and sound, and am much obliged to him for all the care and trouble he took about it. And now, as I have a great deal to do in this large congregation, I must finish my letter. And may God, our good Father in Heaven, be very gracious to you, my dear children, prays

Your affectionate god-father,

WILLIAM MEADE.

The same affectionate consideration for the young, with faithful vigilance in warning them of the perils to which they may be exposed, appears in a letter addressed to one who had just matriculated in the University of Virginia. It well deserves the serious attention of the college student. Though of later date than the letter to his god-children, it is in the same excellent spirit and finds its appropriate place in this connection.

MILLWOOD.

Dear T.:

By a letter from your mother I learn that you are a student in the University. I trust that you will prove yourself in all respects worthy of the benefit afforded. I never think of a young person in whom I am interested making his first entrance upon college life, without remembering my own feelings at such a time, and the peculiar dangers to which I was exposed, which, however, I was enabled to escape by reason of the blessing of God on a good education. As each of my sons went to college, I addressed them from my own experience, warning them against the evils of a college life, and seeking to improve the advantages thereof. A college life is either the making, or the ruining of youth; much oftener the latter, than the former. If he is idle, if his companions are irreligious and dissipated, he had far better be at the plough or the anvil. Instead of fitting himself for some useful and honorable profession, he is unfitting himself for any respectable position in society on earth, and preparing himself, soul and body, to be banished with dishonor from the presence of God and His angels hereafter.

Very much of the final and permanent result of a college life depends on the first few weeks or months of the same. If we idle at the start, we shall scarce ever begin to be diligent. On the same principle *Similis-simili gaudet*, the idle will gather around us, and idlers are never as corrupting as at colleges. Elsewhere, they may be comparatively harmless, but in college they must be wicked and mischievous, and more or less successful in corrupting others. Youth is too full of life, and energy, not to be doing something either good or ill. Hence, those who will not study books, are apt to study cards, and be given to wine or strong drink. I hope I need not warn you against ever looking at cards, or tasting anything intoxicating. "Touch not, taste not, handle not," is, I hope, your motto as to all such things.

But you are not safe by only avoiding such things; you must be active in pursuing the contrary. Some young men are beset with the weakness of wishing to magnify their talents, by studying as little as possible, or seeming so to do. Such never rise to any distinction in life. God blesses the diligent in all the departments of life, and never the idle. It is by the sweat of our brow that God makes us to earn our bread. It must be with us as with the painter, *Nulla dies sine lineæ*, as with him who runs in the race, *nec mora, nec requies. Sic itur ad astra.* I could fill many sheets with the testimonies of the wise and experienced on this subject. I hope you will ever act on this principle. During your scholastic year, when a kind of necessity was laid upon you to study, you have conducted yourself with credit, and I hope will continue so to do, when the necessity is removed, and you are at more liberty. Many who have done well at school under much restraint, have dishonored themselves at college, by neglecting their studies, and abusing the advantages bestowed on them by parents and friends, or some public institution.

I hope, dear T., that you will never by such neglect, or by any misconduct, reflect discredit on your father's memory, or give pain to your mother's heart. Above all, as you would secure the favor of that God whose favor is life itself, I hope you will be faithful to your Bible, to private prayer, to public worship, and to any duty which religion requires of us.

I hope you often see my son Richard, as your pastor and as your father's friend, who will, I am sure, take pleasure in rendering you any service in his power.

Very affectionately,

Your own and your father's and mother's friend,

William Meade.

DOMESTIC AFFLICTIONS.

It might safely be presumed, that one so eminent for personal piety, and distinguished for ministerial ability, was not a stranger to the divinely-instituted school where such attainments are made, or to the sharp but salutary discipline, by which they are nurtured. Shortly after one of his severest afflictions, he transcribed into a small blank-book which he had purchased for the loved one whose removal he mourned, but which her rapid decline had prevented her from using, those comforting lines from Cowper:

> "The path of sorrow — and that path alone —
> Leads to the Land where sorrow is unknown."

With that path he became painfully familiar. He had entered upon it early in life, and had been conversant with many of its trials. He had buried father, mother, brothers, sisters, and, though he was never bereaved of a child (his three sons survived him) yet he heavily mourned the loss of their beloved mother; and then, after the lapse of nineteen years of diversified experience, his heart was again lacerated by the death of that excellent lady, who had become a mother indeed to his boys, and to himself a devoted wife. The sacredness of this sorrow, and the delicacy of the relation with which it is connected, would retire them from general observation, and impose a limit to biographical notice. But in this instance, the afflicted has himself, from high considerations of usefulness to others, as well as to his own family, recorded his "Recollections of two Beloved Wives," and, in doing so, has unavoidably disclosed his own heart and bearing as a husband, and his experience under the pressure of his affliction. A notice of this peculiar narrative cannot, with propriety, be omitted in this Memoir of its author. Though printed, it was not for publication, but simply with a view to its being more conveniently distributed among relations, and those friends to whom it might prove profitable. The circulation was intentionally limited. The preface discloses the purpose of the writer in recording the recollections, and the considerations which, contrary to his original design, led him first to introduce into his will a permission to print what he had penned, and, subsequently, to have it printed during his own life. The preface is itself so characteristic, and of so much interest, that no apology for its insertion here will be required.

"When the following 'Recollections' were committed to paper—some of them more than thirty-seven years ago, the others more than twenty-one—the thought of their being seen by any eyes than those which followed the pen that traced them, and those of a few near relatives, never entered the mind of their author. During all the intervening years they have lain in my drawer unaltered, and just as they now appear, both as to language and sentiment, except that in transcribing, some passages have been omitted of too personal, too private and delicate a nature to be exposed to public view. Perhaps some may think that more of that character ought to have been erased; and I will not complain, if blamed for such an error. It has been some years since the thought arose in my mind, that not only my children, and children's children, but some others, might be gratified and benefitted by their publication, when I shall be quiet in the grave, and beyond the reach of criticism and censure. It was in an hour of sickness, and when life seemed most uncertain of continuance, that I introduced a clause into my will, leaving it optional with my children to publish them when I should be no more.

"But God has continued my life far beyond former expectation, and I hope has also made me somewhat less sensitive as to either the praises or censures of men, and more desirous of doing some good in such ways as are still open to me, since others have been closed. I am more and more satisfied of the obligations resting upon Christians to do good by the use of their property and every other talent, during life, instead of postponing it until after death, and leaving the uncertain execution of it to others. Some, who might be benefitted by the examples set forth in the following pages, may be beyond their reach by the time of my death. I therefore, in humble dependence upon God, determine to do at once what I find upon my hands ready to be done. I here present to the mothers and daughters of Virginia, two specimens of Christian character well known to some who are yet alive. I am especially moved to do it at this time from the apprehension that in too many instances it is much needed—that with the great increase of the female professors of religion, there has not been an increase of true piety; that on the contrary, there has been a manifest falling off from the pattern set by a number of those who, in the time of the first love of our reviving Church, were bright examples of a strict, zealous, and self-denying religion. I know that there are still many, among the young and the old, who are found faithful; but are there not many, also, who cause grief by their manifest disposition to be as much conformed to the world as may be tolerated in connection with the profession of religion? It is matter of lamentation that the love of dress, of fashionable parties, of light reading, and idle conversation, has increased among those who have professed to renounce all the pomps and vanities of this wicked world; and that there are so few who dare to be singular in relation to such things, and to be examples of a consistent and devoted piety. Female education is now cultivated, in all its branches at an expense unknown in former times; and yet, how few are the mothers who give to their children the benefit of what they have acquired at such great cost! I fear, also, that domestic economy and industry are not on the increase, though I acknowledge with pleasure, that after marriage, and becoming mothers and mistresses, many of the young and pleasure-loving exhibit a marked improvement.

"In this connection, let me acknowledge that, in the printing of these pages for private circulation, I have had my brethren of the clergy partly in view. I would point them to the deep experience of sin, and active practical piety as evinced in both of those whose characters have been sketched. I would ask whether we dwell sufficiently, in our public preaching and private intercourse, on the necessity of a deep sense of sin; whether we do not sometimes speak peace and encourage hope too soon, and thus draw the only half-convicted sinner into an open profession of religion too soon to show how superficial the work has been? Let me say to my brethren, on the authority of not only these two cases, but of many others, during a ministry of more than forty-six years, that our surest confidence of perseverance and consistency must rest on a deep, heart-felt conviction of sin, which may sometimes continue for a considerable time and be a heavy burden, before the Saviour is joy and peace to the soul; and yet I do not hold that the experience of all on this subject must be the same as to intensity and duration; nor do I confound these convictions of sin with those nervous affections with which some are afflicted, in connection with their religious exercises.

"If the following 'Recollections' of two beloved friends, whom I hope to meet in Heaven, shall rightly affect any of those to whom they are presented, I am willing for the sake of that good, to seem, in the eyes of some, to have improperly obtruded myself, my private joys and sorrows, upon the notice of the reader.

"W. M."

The early marriage of WILLIAM MEADE to Mary, daughter of Philip Nelson and Sarah his wife, has been already noted. It was a marriage which gave great satisfaction to all their friends, and, though both were younger than is usual in parties to so solemn a contract, yet their then bright hopes were not disappointed. "Few persons," he states in his "Recollections," "enjoyed more of this world's happiness than we did. It was indeed too much for us;

at least it was for me. I thought so then and have known so since."

Of Mrs. Meade's personal appearance he says, "She was not beautiful in the worldly acceptation of that term, but then she had a sweet and sensible and modest and loving countenance." Her intellectual character and acquirements were superior. "Her husband was never ashamed of her in any place or company, or to hear her speak on any subject lest she should betray ignorance or folly, as too many do."

"She had, while young, been very attentive to the improvement of her mind, under the direction of her parents and uncle; nor did she, after marriage, cease to add something to her stock of knowledge. Her historical and geographical information was very considerable. Her taste for the classics and poets was just and exquisite. Ah! how many happy moments have we spent together in reading and admiring good poetry, true eloquence, and fine composition, when these were exercised upon worthy themes. She was well acquainted with the French language, and at the time of our marriage (herself at the age of eighteen) she had advanced as far in Latin as most scholars do in the academies, being better acquainted with it, indeed, than the generality of those who are said to have learned it. An amiable motive first induced her to undertake the study of that language. Her father, being then in straightened circumstances, was unable to send her brother to school, and being much engaged on the farm, could not himself do justice to him at home, and Mary determined, by such assistance as her father and uncle could lend, to try and learn each lesson before him, so as to be able to instruct him in what she had first learned. Her genius and industry soon enabled her to progress rapidly in the study, and when we were married, she had begun Virgil, which we afterwards completed together, and read parts of Grotius, Horace and Buchanon. Such a knowledge of languages, and of almost all the branches of polite literature, was a great temptation to her. The wicked one sought to insinuate vanity into her mind, and sorely troubled her. She complained against herself before God, and her friends on earth, that she had been seeking that knowledge, not for the good of her soul, or the glory of her God, but from earthly-mindedness. She was deeply humbled under a sense of this, when she became enlightened by the Spirit of God to see the deceitfulness and wickedness of her heart. All this she learned to consider as loss, compared with the excellencies of the knowledge of Christ Jesus." * * * *

"And yet, my children, suppose not that your mother was vain, or pedantic, in her manners or conversation. None, I will venture to affirm, ever heard her quote a Latin sentence (though she could have done it so often and so well) except her husband. To but a few was it for a long time known that she had learned it. It was accident that discovered it to your father, a considerable time after his engagement to her."

"Nor let it be supposed that she was wholly taken up with literature. She was, from a child, trained up in the knowledge of the Scriptures. I never yet met with one so well versed in the Psalms and New Testament as she was. What a help was she to her husband in the composition of his sermons! I was scarcely ever at a loss for the chapter of any verse, but she could supply me with it immediately. The Psalms she could repeat throughout, for she had read them daily, almost from childhood. She was also the most humble and affectionate child and sister in the world. I remember, even after we were married, to have seen her take her station, as she was wont to do, at the head of her brothers and sisters, to repeat the catechism on the Sabbath morning to her father. Thus early, and thus constantly, was she instructed in the blessed truths of our holy religion."

Her exemplary devotion to her children, and her judicious and gentle manners with their servants are interestingly described.

Her experience as a Christian, as a member of the Church of God, to which the Bishop designed to give prominence in the narrative, is thus related:

"Shall I speak of her as a Christian, as a member of the Church of God? I have said she was trained in the knowledge of God, by the reading of the Scriptures, and in the worship of God, by the use of prayers. From my first acquaintance with her, or rather from the time of our marriage, I knew she was regular and conscientious in the observance of these means. Yet had I often to lament that she did not have views sufficiently deep, and feelings sufficiently strong in regard to the peculiar doctrines of the Gospel. I feared she had not known the desperate wickedness of the human heart, and the necessity of a greater change than she had experienced, to prepare her for heaven. Each year, however, and each good book which we read together, and each successive bereavement which afflicted herself and family, seemed to deepen her impressions, and to increase her endeavors after holiness. In her vigorous effort after the one thing needful, it pleased the Almighty to let darkness and wretchedness, and almost despair for a time rest on her soul. She underwent one of those dark dispensations, one of those severe tribulations, which God, in His wisdom, no doubt, sometimes sends to prepare and purify the sinful soul for heaven. She prayed always, and yet said she had no pleasure in prayer. She read, but found no comfort in the Word. Her soul was preyed upon by wicked thoughts. She would not as formerly, approach the sacramental table. She took no pleasure in the society of her husband, children, or friends. She ate and drank but little, and wasted away very much. On one thing only was she intent. Her husband reasoned with her out of the Scriptures, and from the experiences of those who had gone through similar exercises; her friends agreed to unite in prayer for her, but all seemed unavailing. My faith sometimes almost failed me. I feared, impiously feared, that the bruised reed would be broken, and the smoking flax be quenched. I watched over her with a fearful soul. I listened to her prayers and complainings when she knew not I was at hand. I have even taken her in my arms at the midnight hour, when she was prostrate on her knees, and borne her to her needful rest. Nothing but miracle could have supported her feeble frame under such exercises, for she never complained, and indeed was never sick. At length, that God who by degrees brought her to repentance, in like manner gradually soothed and comforted her soul. She returned to her duties as mother, mistress and wife, which had been in a measure neglected, and, to the last moment of her life was the humble, faithful, self-denying disciple of the crucified Jesus. She never had that perfect assurance, that rapturous foretaste of Heaven, which are granted to some, but she had a good hope, and a faith which overcame the world, and worked by love. The world was crucified to her, and she to the world. Its pomps and vanities had no charms for her. Higher objects were in her view. Duty was her happiness. She was humbled to the dust. She became more and more dear to him who witnessed all her sorrows, and who has thus recorded them."

Of their domestic recreation, a pleasing glimpse is given in the following passage:

"How often when the weather allowed, would we, with our two eldest boys playing round us, walk over our little farm, rejoicing in its richness and abundance, and admiring the woods and mountains which surrounded us! How often in our rambles would we pause to admire that piece of woodland in particular which adjoins the house, or our small fields, richly covered and beautifully blooming with clover! Her mind was formed for the most exquisite enjoyment of the beauties of nature, and I had just divided to her for flower beds a part of our garden, and we were tilling and planting and sowing it, when a messenger came to call her to the cultivation of a garden of perennial plants, and never fading flowers in Heaven."

After the account of Mrs. Meade's distress in connection with her religious experience, the Bishop states that he "did not see or know to what this violent and refining fire was made to possess her soul. It was not for him to know that it was sent to prepare her for an early death." Yet he remarks that, "I was often overwhelmed at the thought of the value of this beloved object—a thousand times have I said, 'what if Heaven should take her from me?' The thought was anguish at first, but it became habitual, for it often entered into my mind, being sent there by Heaven to prepare me for the event." In commencing the record of her decline and death, he writes: "Thou hast fulfilled all Thy warning, God of truth. Fulfil also, oh, God of mercy! all my hopes and desires of improvement. Fulfil all Thy will in me."

The affecting narrative proceeds: "In the Fall of 1816, as already mentioned, with a body much reduced by nursing our last child, she took a cold, which, after continuing some weeks, was attended with other symptoms of that disease which had within a few years been fatal to several of her family. The usual means of checking the first approaches of the disorder were resorted to, and seemed likely to be effectual. For a time our hopes revived; but a return of the same symptoms in the month of March, 1817, again awakened our serious fears. After a few weeks, a physician was again called in. Never can I forget the scene. Mary and myself were alone when he came. His questions, her answers, his looks, his prescriptions, and whole conduct were decisive. He left us; and in a moment we found ourselves clasped in each others arms, and embracing, as it were, for the last time, and endeavoring to reconcile each other to the will of God."

"A choice was now given between a journey and voyage, or a long and sickening course of medicine. We did not hesitate, but determined to adopt the former."

About the middle of April, they left their home for the South—journeying by carriage and steamboat to Norfolk, and thence by water to Charleston, S. C., before reaching which, the Bishop's "hopes were entirely gone." He "feared they would not be able to reach land and find some comfortable house in which Mrs. Meade might breathe out her last. Heaven ordered it otherwise." "After spending a week in Charleston, and finding no benefit to her from the air of that place, I purchased a carriage and horses, and a horse for myself, with which we set out for our home, at a distance of six hundred miles from it. What a journey for such a frame! Her patience, and meekness, and resignation were remarkable throughout."

"It was my office to bear her in my arms from the carriage to the houses where we stopped and back again." "As her body weakened, her hope was strengthened."

"After a long journey, during which not an accident occurred to delay us on the way, we reached our friends at home. In ten days her journey of life was over."

"During the night of the 2nd of July, I insisted upon watching over her more entirely and exclusively than on any other night, though I always spent my nights in the same room, and near her side. She slept but little, though she did not appear to suffer. At length I was overcome with sleep, and my head sank beside her's. She put her hand upon me, and asked if I could not keep myself awake. Had she not a presentiment that she was soon to be called, and did she not wish me to be awake to receive her last farewell?"

"Her words have often sounded in my ears like those of the blessed Saviour to His disciples on the night before His death: 'Could ye not watch with me one hour?'"

"Just as the day dawned she called me to her side; her

eyes, her hand, her voice, all said to me, 'I am going, William,' for by that name she always called me. 'I trust you are ready, my dear,' was all I could say. 'I trust so,' was her answer. She asked for her parents. Through mistake they were not called immediately. I believe she asked for them a second time, when her father and sister and some other friends came into the room. But she was too far gone to speak to them. Life was expiring. It was some comfort to him, that she died in her husband's arms. He heard the last breath that left her lips; he felt the last pulse which beat in her veins. It was just as the glorious sun arose, that her blessed spirit ascended to the realms of glory, leaving below a most unworthy but fondly attached husband, and three motherless boys, to mourn their loss."

"Her remains were deposited in the grave-yard at the old Chapel, where she and her husband had from their childhood been accustomed to attend, and where the latter had preached ever since his ordination, and where he continued to preach many years afterward." On a marble slab which covers that sacred deposit, the following words are inscribed:

"'But Mary has chosen that good part, which shall not be taken from her.'"

"A silent and loving woman is a gift from the Lord, and there is nothing of so much worth as a mind well instructed."

"If there be kindness, meekness, and comfort in her tongue, then is not her husband like other men."

Of his second sorrow of like nature, no other narrative is needed than that which is annexed to the second part of the "Recollections" in the form of an Obituary, prepared by his own hand. Whilst it commemorates the eminent virtues and lovely spirit of the wife for whom he mourned, it discloses the devoted affection and exquisite tenderness of the husband in a manner which must elevate him more and more in the estimation of all who appreciate intense, intelligent and delicate love.

OBITUARY OF MRS. THOMASIA MEADE, WRITTEN BY HER HUSBAND FOR THE "SOUTHERN CHURCHMAN," AT THE TIME OF HER DEATH.

"Died, July 26th, 1836, at the seat of Dr. Carter Berkeley, in the county of Hanover, in the 41st year of her age, Mrs. Thomasia Meade, wife of the Right Rev. WILLIAM MEADE.

"This event, though long and certainly expected by many, while only feared by some, will affect the hearts of all who knew the deceased, with emotions not easily described, nor soon to be allayed.

"There are some few among our poor simple race, who seem by nature to be cast in so fine a mould, and then to be so highly polished and beautifully adorned, as to attract almost irresistibly the hearts of all who come within their reach.

"It will not be considered too much to say that such was eminently the case with the deceased. Her mind, her person, her countenance, her voice and speech, her gentle manners, and affectionate disposition, her fine flow of animal spirits, and, above all, her pious feelings and habits, all concurred to make her one of the most interesting and perfect specimens of human nature which we are permitted to see. There was indeed a kind of magic charm about her, which immediately seized upon the affections, and made her a favorite wherever she went, with whomsoever she became acquainted. Even little children, attracted by her smiles, would, as though by instinct, be ready to leave their nurse's and mother's arms, to leap into her's. The servants of every household which she visited, won by her kindness, loved her at once and never forgot her. She was always cheerful, always happy, and there was so much of strong natural affection in her heart, that it seemed always ready to pour itself forth, in words and deeds of kindness, such as flowed spontaneously from her. There was such a quick discernment of all the proprieties of life, such a constant consideration for the feelings of others, that she seemed in no danger of ever giving offence. Nor did she excite an envious feeling in one human bosom, for it was evident that the last thing she sought, was to be admired. With a mind of the first order, and with a store of information possessed by few of her sex, she was never guilty of anything which even savored of vanity, or looked like display.

"But are we not describing one of those pure spirits of another world, to whom virtue and holiness are natural, rather than one of the fallen daughters of Adam? If any be disposed to advocate the doctrine of native goodness from this happy specimen, and to maintain that virtue and natural religion, without penitence and faith, are sufficient for Heaven, we hasten to inform them, that, however happy and amiable by nature, however high the order of her mind, and great the elevation of her character, by comparison with many others, yet, at an early period of life, she was taught by the Spirit and Word of God, that the very angels are charged with folly, and the Heavens are unclean in His sight, and that, among the children of men, 'there is none good, no, not one.' While in the bloom of youth, and in all the gayety and sprightliness of her heart, and loved and caressed by all her companions, she was made to feel that she was a sinner, and such a sinner, that for a long time her soul refused all comfort; her pleasant food lost all its relish; the merry song and dance in which she delighted ceased to please, and were deserted, and it was not until after much tribulation that she entered that 'Kingdom which is righteousness, peace and joy in the Holy Ghost.' Though she never for a moment turned back to the world or felt a desire for its vain amusements, yet she ever preserved her cheerful and happy spirit, and her fine natural disposition and cultivated understanding were all sanctified and rendered more useful and interesting. She became the steady Sunday School teacher, the active friend of every good work in the parish, the strict economist in dress and everything relating to herself. Her melodious voice and fine musical powers were now entirely consecrated to the service of God; and in the social circle, and in the house of God, she was always wont to lead this interesting part of the worship of Jehovah. It has now been more than fifteen years since she became the wife of the Rev. W. MEADE, now assistant Bishop of Virginia, at which time she took the charge of his three children, whom she at once began, and ever continued to love, with a mother's fondest affection, and conscientiously sought, in conjunction with their father, to train for Heaven. Concerning them, she would often say during her life, as she did, most emphatically, in death, that she could scarcely conceive how a mother could have a stronger affection for her own children than she felt for them. And they also, now in sorrow, ask whether it is possible for children to feel more love towards the mother who gives them birth than they have ever felt for her.—In the relation of wife to a minister of God, she was a pattern to all. His usefulness and her happiness were inseparably connected. To have hindered the one would have destroyed the other. A proof of this occurred within the last two years, when he was suddenly and unexpectedly called to leave a place rendered dear to them, both by the society of many beloved friends and relations, and a thousand tender recollections, in order to go to a distant part of the Diocese—Norfolk. Painful as was the thought of separating from so many beloved relatives, and bidding adieu to a home so delightful, to go amongst strangers, she hesitated not one moment, uttered not one word of remonstrance, but at once made ready to go where duty seemed to call. As usual, many and affectionate friends were soon gathered around, and in her new situation she was, as heretofore, cheerful and happy. It was not, however, the intention of Providence, that either new or old friends should long enjoy the pleasure of her society here below. God had a better place and better friends prepared for her elsewhere. During the last summer she took a severe cold, which, accompanied by high fever, so seriously affected a constitution always frail, as to threaten her life. From this, however, she so far recovered in the fall as to give good hope of a restoration to her usual health. But a worm unseen had insinuated itself into her vitals, and was there silently awaiting his time to do the work of destruction. In the month of December she was again attacked, and soon there was reason to believe that the complaint was that insidious one, which, while it is surely doing the work of death, deceives with the promise of life. At once, though still believing it not only possible, but sometimes even probable, that she would recover, she began to set her house in order and prepare for death. Her language to one with whom she often and freely conversed, was, 'I desire to feel myself in God's hands, and to have Him to do His will without being at all anxious about the event.' When medicine and pain would allow, she was the same happy, cheerful being as before; always considerate of her friends, and pouring forth the affections of her heart towards them. Her gratitude to God was in continual exercise. In the intervals of pain she would speak of His tender mercies to her, and ask how it was possible any one could be surrounded with more comfort and blessings. With this theme she never wearied. God's mercies seemed ever new to her. Could those in the full enjoyment of health experience half the happiness in their health that she did during the intervals of pain, how much would the sum of human happiness be increased! All manner of kindnesses from her numerous friends in Norfolk flowed in upon her every day and every hour, and kept her affectionate heart in constant exercise of gratitude towards them. She often exclaimed, 'Surely there were never so many kind people in any one place as in this!' But she had a beloved mother, and a kind step-father, who had been her physician from early youth, and other dear and near relatives who were not with her, and she wished to die in the midst of them.

"In the early part of May, by the kindness of God, for which she was always praising Him, she was enabled to reach Hanover county, where that mother and those relatives lived. The effort was almost too much for her exhausted and emaciated frame. Scarce alive, she reached the last stage of her earthly pilgrimage.

"But now, to the surprise of all, hope sprung up anew in the hearts of her friends, and she herself, conscious of a favorable change, began to think and speak of longer life on earth. It was a short-lived impression. In a few weeks the destroyer resumed his work, and slowly, though surely, carried it on for two long months of suffering. She was wasted to a shadow. 'All my bones,' she would say, with Job, 'stand staring and looking upon me.' To find one easy posture by day or night, was sometimes impossible. No murmur escaped her lips, but sometimes after seeking in vain for relief in every varied posture, by a silent flood of tears she would show the intensity of her sufferings. And yet, even now, there were intervals of ease, and occasionally some relish for food. And what voluptuary ever enjoyed his abundant feast as she did the little morsel which she could eat? What man of health ever rejoiced as she did in the comfort experienced in her intervals of ease? She was enabled, generally, at an early hour of the morning, to read or hear a portion of God's Word, and sometimes she would lift her enfeebled, though still melodious voice, in the sacred song. She usually awoke at the dawn of day, and was then in her best state of body and mind. Near the house were some large and beautiful forest trees in their most interesting state, where numbers of birds collected, and made a sweet concert at that early hour. Their notes were ecstacy to her ear and to her soul, and she would choose that time to mingle the sounds of her voice with theirs in hymns of praise to their Creator and her Redeemer. Not many mornings before her death, weak as she was, she sang alone two stanzas of Heber's beautiful hymn,

'From Greenland's icy mountains.'

"As death approached, her sufferings diminished, and, a few days before the event, her power to suffer seemed to be almost gone, and yet her mind was in its most perfect state.

"On the Sunday evening before her death, some of her devoted relatives from the neighborhood, thinking that her end was near, gathered round her. She understood its meaning well, and felt that there was cause for it. About one o'clock in the morning, she assembled them all around her bed, and spoke in such a manner as we would expect a Christian, a wife, a mother, and a relative would do on so solemn an occasion. She particularly spoke of her dear boys, as she called them, and said that if it pleased Providence, she would be thankful to remain until they came, that she might see them once more. After this she fell asleep. On the following day she revived a little, and enjoyed food and the society of her friends more than usual. It was not until ten o'clock on Tuesday morning, that she felt her hour to be come, that hour for which, during the preceding night, she had often prayed, saying: 'Blessed Saviour, come and take me to Thyself;' 'Heavenly Father, if it please Thee, take me to Thyself.' All her most loved relatives and friends were around her bed, when she told them that her hour was come, she was almost gone. She took leave of them separately, calling first her mother, her precious mother, as she often repeated, and giving her a small present; then her sister and brother; then the rest; giving to each some token of love, accompanied by expressions of tenderness. After this, all were requested to leave the room for a few moments, when her husband approached to receive her last farewell. As he leaned his head towards her, she put her arms around his neck, pressed his face to hers, laid her hand gently upon his cheek and forehead, as if to soothe him, and said, 'What a dear husband you have been to me,' spoke of their former happiness, and their hope of meeting again; told him to give her love to her dear boys, declaring, as she had often done before, that she did not know what to say to them—she loved them so much; then spoke of the servants; then enjoined him to give her love to all her dear friends in Frederick and Norfolk. After this, she signified her wish that her mother should come to her. Her mother, with all the others came, and the room was again full of pious and affectionate relatives. She then asked her husband to place one of his hands under her head, to support it, and in the other to hold both of her hands. This being done, she said she would endeavor to sing a hymn, and proceeded, in distinct and sweet tones, to sing:

'O Thou, from whom all goodness flows!
I give myself to Thee.'

"Here her voice failed; but she said, 'I will try again presently.' But that voice was lost in death. At that moment it was evident that the hand of death was upon her. Her eye wandered. She busied herself for a moment—not knowing what she was doing—in adjusting the clothes about her neck and arms; then her head sunk a little, and the last struggle came on; but it was a gentle struggle, and as it proceeded, a number of sweet voices joined in the following hymn for a departing soul:

'Happy soul! thy days are ended,' etc.

"A short time after this was ended, the pulse ceased to beat, the bosom to heave, and the eye was closed forever.

"On the following day, her remains were interred in the grave-yard around the Old Fork Church, St. Martin's parish, Hanover, by the side of her aged grandmother, the venerable relict of General Nelson, of Yorktown, Virginia.

"To lose such a friend, one so sweet, so pious, so interesting, is indeed hard to bear; but God's will (which must be best) be done. 'Blessed are the dead which die in the Lord.'

"How blessed the righteous when he dies!
When sinks a weary soul to rest,
How mildly beam the closing eyes,
How gently heaves the expiring breast!

"So fades a summer cloud away;
So sinks the gale, when storms are o'er;
So gently shuts the eye of day;
So dies a wave along the shore.

"A holy quiet reigns around,
A calm which life nor death destroys,
Nothing disturbs that peace profound,
Which the unfettered soul enjoys.

"Farewell, conflicting hopes and fears,
Where lights and shades alternate dwell!
How bright the unchanging moon appears —
Farewell, inconstant world, farewell!

"Life's duty done, as sinks the clay,
Light from its load the spirit flies;
While Heaven and earth combine to say
How blessed the righteous when he dies."

The two letters which follow manifest a depth of feeling both for his own and others' bereavement, not always united with the firmness and force of character for which he was so distinguished. The first is addressed to Dr. Carter Berkeley, who, by marriage, sustained the paternal relation to Mrs. Meade, and at whose house she died. It bears date four years after her decease. The second is to one of his grandsons, on the death of his beloved mother.

PETERSBURG, July 2, 1839.

My Dear Sir:

I wrote you a few days since, mentioning my unsuccessful effort to get to Hanover last week, and my expectation to be with you and all our dear friends on Monday, the 8th, on my way to Alexandria. Since then, I perceive that the day of meeting is Tuesday, instead of Wednesday, as I had supposed. This will prevent the indulgence of one of those gratifications which my heart, sometimes, even in the midst of many high and holy duties and pleasures, yearns after most earnestly. I love to look at the place where the remains of my beloved wife are laid, and to be in the house where she loved to be, and to see those who were so dear to her. I wanted to have brought some little presents for Kate's children, and their dear mother and grandmother; but my happiness must be henceforth more than ever in duty. Although I trust that God is making me more willing to live for Him, and upon Him, yet my heart is sometimes sad at the thought of the manner of my remaining life — that I shall probably be almost a stranger even to my own children and children's children. May we all be together in Heaven, is my comfort.

As I cannot come, I send something which I wish spent in a better manner than I could have done it, in some articles of clothing for those dear objects of my affection mentioned above. Love to all.

Yours, very truly,
W. MEADE.

MOUNTAIN VIEW, Feb. 29, 1839.

To my Dear Grandson. Dear Motherless Babe:

In times of old the name of Grandfather was scarce known. Father was the only word. His children's children were his own dear children, living in his heart. My heart tells me that it was nature's language, for how does it yearn over thee, my child; how it swells within me, and sends tears into mine eyes at the thought of thee! I feel as though my youth were renewed, and all the affections of my nature drawn out. But there is one painful thought that will enter — how little shall I be with thee, my child — how seldom take thee in mine arms. Thou wilt scarcely know me, dear. Thou wilt not love me, as a child his father — as thy dear father did, when a babe. Even now, after seeing thee only for a few moments, I feel thine absence, and the distance between us; and my heart is aching for thee, and I feel sadness come over me, because thou art so far away. If it be thus with me, oh, what must be thine own dear father's feelings, at parting with thee though only for a time! Oh how can he tear himself away, after having doted on thee for more than three months, in the presence and arms of thy mother! What shall sustain his heart when slowly and sorrowfully traveling back the dreary road thy mother's corpse was brought? The thought of thee and that dear mother shall rush into his soul. And when he reaches that deserted home, enters that vacant chamber, once so blessed with those so loved — when he looks upon that bed upon which she lay and nursed thee at her side — that cradle in which he so often rocked thee, and finds no mother there to answer when he speaks, no child to take in his arms, and press to his heart. Oh! what can keep that heart from breaking? God only. Thou wilt never know, dear, what a blessing thou, and thy father, and I have lost. Oh! how dear was she to my heart! An own and only daughter could scarce have been more so. I am told that her mother, in her dying hour, as it were, bequeathed her unto me, that is, she commended her to my special prayers and pastoral care, and have I not ever felt the yearnings of a father's heart towards her? Thine own father, dear child, loved her early, loved her long, loved her tenderly, and loved her only; and on the night of their espousals, as I clasped her to my bosom, and called her my own child, I felt (and told her so) as if Heaven had restored me one, whom thou canst never see on earth, my dear ———, in a daughter who resembled her. How often have I looked forward to happy days with my children and children's children, and sometimes have I thought that perhaps, in the course of duty and of Providence, I might end my days with them. But God is good and wise and gracious, and hath dealt otherwise with us all. Dear ——— has no mother below Heaven.

Dear ———, thy father has no one now to lie on his bosom, and thy grandfather has lost a loving daughter, but still we all have many dear friends. There are many who would gladly be tender mothers to thee, for thine own sake, and thy sainted mother's sake, if it would not break thy dear father's heart to part with thee, and God will make him to be both thy father and thy mother, and thou wilt have friends most kind in every one who knew and loved thy mother. Oh! that they may not be too kind, cruelly kind to thee! Let them love thee with their prayers, and nourish thee with words of Heavenly wisdom, and make thee ready for thy mother, when she shall come down to meet thee on the shores of Heaven. Even now, may their holy charity begin. When she, who was as a mother to thy mother, and who so loves to nurse thee, shall bathe thy tender limbs in the pure water from the streams of earth, may her soul be lifted up in prayer, that the purer waters of Heaven may be poured over thy soul. And when she shall bind the needful raiment about thy little body, may her prayer be, that thy soul may be wrapped in the robe of Christ. And when thou art troubled, and she hushes thee to rest, may the prayer be, so let his soul he calmed when the troubled waves of life pass over him.

I write thus, my child, because it soothes my heart when I think of thee, thy mother, and my dear ——, thy father, and because I may never see thee more. Should I be called away suddenly, as thy mother was, I leave this as a memorial of my love to thee. Thy father or some other will read it to thee, when thou canst know its meaning, and will tell thee that I am gone where thy mother is, and that we will meet thee at the shore, and carry thee to Christ. Farewell, dear child, and Heaven save thee from the evil to come.

Thy loving grandfather,
W. M.

WRITINGS.

It may be conjectured that one who was so constantly engaged in active parochial duties—in voluntary missionary labors and in personal services in connection with the general enterprises of Christian benevolence, would have no time to supply the delinquency which must have been occasioned by the irregular and desultory character of his early professional studies—certainly none to aid in promoting those important objects by means of the press. And yet, he was through life a diligent reader of works calculated to further him him in the Divine life, and to increase his capability for ministerial usefulness. He was, however, rigidly eclectic with regard to books, resolutely, and with great discernment, eschewing all which were not to edification, and happily appreciating both in religious and secular literature whatever of real value he could command. And as for his pen, he began to employ it for the benefit of others, almost as soon as he was licensed to preach—first in adapting the productions of other persons and times to the wants of his own people, and then by preparing and publishing occasionally sermons and treatises upon subjects suggested by his knowledge of what his parishioners needed or the state of the Church required.

In a letter to the Assistant Bishop, he writes:

MILLWOOD, Feb. 10, '44.

* * * * * * * * * "I have been much confined this winter, now for more than five weeks at home, so as not even to be at Church. A cold, toothache, and sore eyes have beset me. I have, however, not been idle, having written a very long criticism on Mr. Park's sermons, having thrown into more form and written out my lectures on Pastoral Theology, most of which were only in notes before, and scribbled something for the press. In the *Protestant Churchman* are two pieces signed 'Senex on the Church System.' In the next *Recorder* you will see one on Maurice's Kingdom of Christ. In the next *S. Churchman and Recorder* you will see two letters over my name addressed to Bishop Hopkins and Bishop Onderdonk of New York. Perhaps not merely those who differ from me, but those who agree with me, may think I take too much upon me. I wish I could have counsel at hand, and sincerely desire that any friend, and none more than yourself, would honestly say, if they think it. A mere hint will suffice to make me retire.

"But I have felt that in these times, when some are boasting of all the churchmanship, and seem disposed to take all the power, that any one has a right to come forward and do a little in opposition. I am now getting old and grey by comparison with most, even of the Bishops, and perhaps may not live long to do anything for the truth as I see it. Under such influences I wrote the letter, which you will probably see next week.

"I feel very weak from confinement and study or writing, and, as soon as the weather will allow, mean to ride about as much as possible, and get all the health and strength I can for the Spring work. I go to the Seminary immediately after Easter, spend three weeks there, and then proceed probably on horseback, through Albemarle to Lynchburg.

"Perhaps you will wonder what I have said to Bishop Hopkins and Bishop Onderdonk. I have thanked the former most heartily for his pamphlet, and advised the latter to let his case be referred to the House of Bishops next Fall, with a request to give him their candid opinion and fraternal counsel about it."

The following are the letters referred to:

"TO THE BISHOP OF THE PROTESTANT EPISCOPAL CHURCH OF THE DIOCESE OF VERMONT.

Right Rev. and Dear Brother:

"I have recently received, and with great pleasure read your four printed letters to the Bishops and clergy of the Episcopal Church in these United States, on certain points of doctrine and discipline now agitating our beloved Church in England and America. If it be lawful and expedient for you thus to make known your sentiments, and seek to influence others to adopt what you think most likely to conduce to the peace and welfare of our Zion, and I can see no reason to the contrary, it may also be to one, such as myself, conscious of inability to follow your example, at least to take this public method of acknowledging the receipt of your communications, and to thank you most sincerely and heartily for them. I desire, also, in this public manner, to do what I have done in private, that is, to render thanks to the Giver of all grace, that he has granted to you the talents, the learning, the opportunity, and, above all, the spirit, to perform the task you have undertaken, in so able, so learned, so judicious, temperate and courteous a manner as must ensure the respect of the candid, the wise and pious, even though some of them may not in everything agree with you. You have set an example to those who write on disputed points, of a candor which enters into the feelings and prejudices of both parties, and makes all due allowance for their influence over the judgment, while at the same time you are entirely free from the weakness of indecorous reserve or ambiguity — prevailing errors of our day.

"You have done what it seems to me the Bishops and clergy in their several degrees and stations are now imperatively called on to do, in such manner as may seem most suitable — that is — in reference to the doubts, which are but too prevalent, and the questions that are continually asked, to assert in terms not to be misunderstood, the Protestant character of our Church, in opposition to all the glosses and perversions of her doctrine by those who favor the party which, within the last few years, has sprung up at Oxford.

"You have, as I conceive, set forth the true, moderate and Scriptural views of our Reformers on the subject of the ministry, the Church and sacraments, in opposition to those extravagant ones which some very few, at different times since the Reformation, have held, and which, I am persuaded ever have been, and ever must be, injurious to the cause of true piety within our Church, and opposed to her outward extension.

"Thus estimating your letters, I rejoice in their publication, and most heartily recommend them to any with whom my opinion may have the slightest weight, especially to my brethren of the clergy and laity in Virginia.

"It may not be amiss to add, that I have not extended my remarks to the suggestions in your fourth letter as to some Court of appeal in the General Church — a subject worthy of serious consideration by the wisdom of our triennial assembly, and on which I should be unwilling to express, or even to form an opinion without full examination. In relation to what may be considered as almost a new order in the Church — an order increasing in numbers and influence — I mean the editors of our religious newspapers, I much doubt whether any plan — such as you hint at — can be devised for restraining them or their contributors from making an ill-use, at times, of the power of the press, without producing greater evil. If the solemn vows taken at their ordination to "maintain as much as lieth in them quietness, peace, and love among all Christian people"—if the fatherly remonstrance of the House of Bishops, a few years since conveyed in the pastoral letter written by the venerable White, or sainted Griswold—if their own responsibility to Heaven will not preserve them from bitterness—from violence and misrepresentation, I know not what can avail. So deeply do I feel the injury done to religion by the misconduct of some of them in this respect, that were it for me to decide whether or not, every religious paper of all denominations in our land should cease, or not, I should be strongly tempted to conclude that their evil so out-weighs their good, that we had better try some other method of circulating religious intelligence and commending religious truth, than those cheap weekly messengers, the vehicles alike of blessing and cursing, of error and of truth. Such an experiment, however, being impossible, we must try and render the established method as innocent and as useful as may be. Let those in which truth is set forth in the best spirit, be most encouraged—let the Bishops use their influence in restraining the abuses of the press within their Dioceses—let subscribers send in their private protests, and, if these be unavailing, withdraw their names; and, lastly, if the editors would only follow the example you have set them in all your publications, but especially in those for which I thus publicly thank you, we might hope that the press uniting with the pulpit, would be a powerful instrument for making our Church a praise in our land. Praying that the divine blessing may be vouchsafed to your labors of love, I remain your affectionate friend and brother in the Lord,

WILLIAM MEADE,

"Bishop of the Prot. Epis. Church in the Diocese of Virginia.

"*Millwood*, Feb. 3, 1844.

"P. S.—In what I have written above, I hope I shall not be understood as reflecting unkindly on worthy men who either for an honest support for their families, or for no pecuniary consideration adopt, this method of promoting what they conceive to be right views of religious truth, or, that I am unaware of the difficulties of conducting an agency where so many are to be satisfied; and especially, of excluding from their paper communications containing some sentiments and expressions not approved by the editors. These difficulties should make them the more resolute in the discharge of duty. They should let the contributors know that such communications, will either be rejected or corrected at the pleasure of the editors. Unfortunately, however, the spirits of too many of their readers delight most in personal, sarcastic, controversal pieces. Let truth be fearlessly maintained at this time especially, but let it be in love. None have need of more grace to avoid a wrong spirit than editors of religious papers."

LETTER FROM BISHOP MEADE OF VIRGINIA TO THE BISHOP OF NEW YORK.

MILLWOOD, Feb. 8, 1844.

Right Rev. and Dear Sir :

The last mail brought me your circular to the Bishops of the Church, in which by reason of some animadversions on your Episcopal act in the ordination of Mr. Carey, you invite a public trial according to the Canon for the trial of Bishops. Will you allow me, in a spirit of friendship for all concerned in this unhappy affair, to suggest to you and to them, what seems to me a more excellent way of its disposal? There seems to be a very general impression throughout our Church and country, extending to many who in our mother Church take a deep interest in our affairs, that at our next General Convention, something will be done evincive of the sentiment of the Church on some matters now agitating its peace. I have often been, both by letter and otherwise, inquired of, whether this may not be reasonably calculated on, and is not very necessary? My reply has ever been that too much in this way, must not be expected of the General Convention — that it has a most important, but difficult and delicate task to perform — that is, to preserve the bond of union between the different dioceses — to legislate on main points for the whole, so as not to interfere with the rights of each part, producing alienation and tempting to separation. Controversal points must be kept as much as possible away from it. With matters of discipline — that is, the execution of it, it has nothing to do, for that would greatly endanger peace and brotherly love.

Still it is impossible but that in some shape or other, disputed points will be discussed in the course of general legislation, and the prevailing sentiment of the Church be thus exhibited. More especially will this be the case with the House of Bishops, who in their Pastoral letter address a triennial charge to the Church on matters of chief importance.

My object in this communication is to suggest to you the propriety of deferring all consideration of this question until the meeting of all the Bishops, and then ask their candid brotherly opinion on the subject in dispute. You will thus have the opinion — not of a selected Court, which might be charged with prejudice or partiality, and thus be destitute of weight — but of the whole body of your brethren, which will be given, I am sure, not in the way of severe condemnation, if unfavorable, but of brotherly regret and disappointment. As to myself, I have no hesitation in expressing what, from the first, have been my views of the case. Entirely opposed to many sentiments, uttered at the time and since, by many concerned in the transaction, as contrary to the principles of our Church, I still regard it as a new case, coming unexpectedly and by surprise upon yourself and others; attended by personal and party considerations — influencing the judgment and feelings, and through them the conduct of those concerned. Time was wanting, though I think it should have been taken, at all events, for full consideration. You acted, it is stated, by the advice of two brethren in the Episcopate, and nine Presbyters, and not without some hesitation. On all these accounts, however much many of us may condemn the act, we must be disposed to appreciate the motives and circumstances of the actor. As to the trial of a Bishop for this the first act of the kind occurring in our Church, and under such circumstances, except it be for the purpose of declaring to the Church and world our condemnation of the act, I should be entirely opposed to it, especially when a far more Christian and effectual method is open to us in the manner I have suggested. Your own public call for a trial may be regarded as a voluntary invitation to the expression of such an opinion by the assembled Bishops. Meanwhile, I do not think it should be regarded as a matter of wrong, if after the full public exposure of the whole transaction, and after each Bishop has probably made up his own mind on the subject (though but few of them are made known) any of them should feel constrained, out of duty to the Church, and to meet the continual inquiries made, and charges alleged, to express themselves, so as to remove from the Church and themselves injurious impressions.

It appears to me that, in the peculiar circumstances of the Church, such an expression of opinion would meet the general expectation and demand as to the sentiment of the American Church on subjects now disturbing our peace. I mean not to interfere with the rights of clergy and laity to express their sentiments as individuals or in Diocesan and General Convention, but only to suggest this as the mode by which the fraternal sentiment and advice of all the Bishops may be had, rather than by impeachment and trial conducted by a portion of them. As your circular is published in the religious papers, I send this to one of them, for the consideration of those who may be interested on the subject.

Praying that God may guide us in all our opinions, feelings and conduct in relation to this and all other matters affecting the welfare of religion and our beloved Church, and that His blessing may rest on yourself and Diocese, I remain your faithful brother in Christ,

W. Meade,
Bishop of the Prot. Epis. Church of Virginia.

The pamphlets thus issued are by no means of transient interest. If collected, as they certainly should be, they would form several columns, and be an invaluable legacy to the Church in Virginia.

His large works are,—1st. "*Lectures on the Pastoral Office,*" delivered to the students of the Theological Seminary, at Alexandria, Virginia. The modest preface is sufficiently descriptive to supersede the necessity of any other notice, and too characteristic of its author to be overlooked.

"Had the undersigned any reputation as an author to sustain, or were he in pursuit of one, he certainly would not publish the following lectures. Of the sincerity of this declaration the reader will not doubt, when he shall perceive how large a portion of the work, not merely as to sentiments, but also language, is borrowed from others. Although there is also much which is the result of the author's own reflections and experience, yet that is of so plain and practical a character, and expressed in such unadorned language, that no one will impute to him the folly of expecting to acquire fame by it. Happily, however, for the cause of true piety, God has so ordained it, that one may be useful to others without securing for himself any reputation for talents or learning. Diligence in using the labor of others, and in exerting one's own powers, however moderate, may effect something which, with God's blessing, may be useful. Such is the only merit claimed, and hope cherished, for the following lectures. * * * * * Two considerations have led to the publication of the lectures at this time.

1. That the author might the better discharge his duties to the young candidates, by furnishing them with a text-book which they may carefully study, and thus, by relieving him from the delivery of the lectures, enable him more thoroughly to examine the class, and more freely to expatiate on the subjects under consideration.

2. That if there be anything useful in them, others might have an opportunity of profiting thereby.

To the favor of that Being, without whose blessing no success can be hoped for, the volume is now humbly commended.

WILLIAM MEADE,
Bishop of the P. E. C. of Virginia.

A learned medical professor remarked that he had read these lectures with much interest and benefit, and thought them more admirably adapted for usefulness to students of other professions than the one for which they were prepared.

2. "*Old Churches, Ministers, and Families of Virginia.*"—2 vols., 1857.—The author states that "In the fall of 1855, being solicited to furnish some personal reminiscences of the Episcopal Church in Virginia, he promised two articles to one of our Quarterly Reviews, which have, most unexpectedly, grown into two octavo volumes. He was led into this enlargement, by the further solicitation of friends, that he would extend his inquiries into former times, and, by the discovery that there were materials not yet lost to history, of which good use might be made."—In prosecuting his work he succeeded in "the recovery of many old vestry books, or fragments thereof"—found much that was interesting in the old records of the State, "now in a mutilated and mouldering condition in the Clerk's office of various counties." Other documents were furnished from old family records and papers, which would soon have perished. He had inscriptions copied from old tomb stones, and describes them and the old churches, or ruins, after having carefully inspected them—in some instances having them daguerreotyped for preservation. And, in addition to all this, he procured from the archives of Parliament, and of Lambeth, and of Fulham Palaces, many important, deeply interesting, and hitherto unpublished documents belonging "to the history of the State and Church in Virginia." No other man had the opportunities and facilities which he could command, for the successful performance of this work. The research, correspondence, and various other forms of labor which it required, were prodigious, and, if it had been his only gift to his State and Diocese, entitle him to their great admiration, and lasting gratitude.

3. "*The Bible and the Classics,*" 1861.—The history of this remarkable volume, remarkable for the great research which it evinces, and as the production of a writer who

had passed his seventieth year before the work was completed, may be briefly gathered from his own statement:

"When a youth at school, studying the Greek and Latin poets, I was, as doubtless other youths are, much struck with the accounts there given of the heathen gods and goddesses; of their visits to the earth and intercourse with mortals; of the miracles ascribed to them; and especially of their frequent assumption of the human form. I could not but observe the strong resemblance between some of their fables in the ancient poets and certain things in the Old and New Testaments. While noticing this resemblance, I well remember that unbelieving thoughts would sometimes enter my mind, in opposition to the faith in which I had been trained, and that I was tempted to say, 'perhaps all these marvellous things in the Bible are false.' To the blessing of God, on a religious education I owe it, that the impression was not an abiding one."

"When it pleased God more deeply to affect my heart with the truth and importance of our holy religion, and I saw how many classically-educated youth of our country were disposed to regard alike the most sacred truths of the Bible and the wild fables of pagan writers, and how much impurity was learned from the latter, I began to dread the effects of a classical education, and to think that more harm than good resulted therefrom. But, on continuing and enlarging my reading with a view to the ministry, and carefully examining the sacred Scriptures and the heathen poets and mythologists, my mind was relieved of this apprehension, and I became satisfied that a candid study and comparison of the same with the Bible, would produce quite a different result. All my subsequent examinations have only confirmed me in the conviction that one of the strongest arguments in favor of all that seems marvellous in the Bible may be drawn from the remarkable resemblance between the marvellous in it and the marvellous in the religious history and systems of the ancient heathen world."

"Who can question the importance of some work which shall bring within a moderate compass a comparative view of the leading principles and facts of the Bible, and of all the false religions of earth, showing that they had the same origin, but how, under the latter, men gradually turned the truth of God into a lie, and came to worship the creature more than the Creator, and at length were given up by God to all the abominations which abounded in the heathen world."

During "forty years" he was engaged in the fruitless effort to persuade some one either in this or the mother country to undertake "what he thought himself" incompetent to execute in a manner worthy of its great importance. He adverted to it through the press,—spoke and wrote to pious men, urging the subject on their attention; but in vain. When in England he made a special visit to the Rev. Mr. Faber, who has written so learnedly and voluminously on the subject, to persuade him to condense in a small volume, for the use of schools, the substance of what he had published to the world, but the years and increasing infirmities of that venerable man and most useful author forbade the attempt.

"Disappointed in all my efforts of help from others, and feeling that old age and infirmities might soon unfit me even for the attempt at something which I had so long deemed important, I hope that my presumption may not seem greater than my zeal, if I make an humble experiment myself."

In a letter to the Assistant Bishop, dated Millwood, January 26, 1859, he wrote:

"After attempting for forty years and more to get some one in England or America to do it, I have at last begun on my book, 'The Bible and the Classics,' which engrosses my time and my thoughts. I think I can, in this and the next winter, prepare a duodecimo volume of four hundred pages, tract type, which will be of some service in Christian schools, having primarily in view our High School."

"I have collected in these forty years about forty or fifty volumes, folio, quarto and octavo, bearing on the subject."

In the list of books which he consulted during the preparation of his book, he enumerates more than a hundred volumes, a goodly proportion of them folios and quartos.

Extract from another letter, dated February 15, 1859: "I am in the midst of folios, quartos, etc., and my clothes show much of their old dust; but am deeply interested in my work. About six hours a day I devote to it; I can do nothing at night." This was owing to the weakness of his eyes, to which through life he was subject. And then, his general health had now become so impaired, that he was liable to frequent attacks similar to that which he alludes in the following letter:

MILWOOD, *Sunday morn, April* 10, 1859.

"MY DEAR BROTHER:

I had hoped by to-morrow's mail, to have specified a day on which you might expect me, but Providence orders it otherwise, and I submit, not doubting but that all is for the best. My cough is such that I cannot utter even the few words of grace at table, without being certainly arrested by it; so that even if I were, in other respects, in a condition for it, I could not propose to question the class. But besides this, I have now been housed for four weeks, except little walks about the place on good days, and am very weak and without appetite, and, of course, most liable, by any undue effort or exposure, to be made worse. Duty, therefore, seems to require that I remain where I am as long as possible, and gain the largest amount of health that Providence may think best to afford me.

I begin to fear that most of my appointments between this and Convention may be unfulfilled; but I shall not despair, or withdraw them until it shall appear indispensable. I shall still cherish the hope of being with you and the class, at least the last two days of this week, for I am very anxious to see you, and be with it a few days. I am very glad to see you are about to spend several days of next week in Fredericksburg. If the weather permits, and I am able, I shall come to Mr. Lee's one day, and you will see me out the next morning.

I am somewhat encouraged to hope for improvement, from the fact that last night, by the blessing of God on warm applications internal and external, I had a more comfortable night than I have enjoyed for some time. These have been before tried, but without effect.

Love to your household.

Yours truly,

W. MEADE."

It is difficult to imagine the resolution which, at his advanced age, and with his many bodily infirmities, not only carried him through his regular services, as Bishop and Professor, but determined him to attempt the preparation of a work requiring so much labor and research, and to persevere to its successful completion. No one would suppose that it had not been composed in his prime, and as his agreeable employment in seasons of professional leisure. It was, indeed, a striking fulfilment of the promise to the righteous—"He shall bring forth fruit in old age."

DEVOTIONAL AND OTHER PAPERS.

"What man knoweth the things of a man save the spirit of man which is in him." But if the spirit of a man has manifested what is in him by briefly recorded meditations—written rules for personal government—and has expressed his aspirations in written forms of devotion for his private use, and if these drafts were evidently penned only for the individual's own eye, the experience so disclosed is a most reliable exponent of character.—There are but few documents of this description in the handwriting of Bishop MEADE. These are found in three little unbound books, of which they occupy but a small part, and are penned in a manner so unstudied as, in addition to their own nature, to indicate that they were prepared exclusively for himself. There is, however, nothing in them which it would now be improper to publish, and, as they furnish a very interesting revelation of his mind, and heart, and conscience, which may be instructive and otherwise useful to many, there would be no excuse for omitting them in this Memoir.

The first extract was evidently written immediately after the heavy affliction to which it refers.

"This little book was gotten by me in Norfolk, for my beloved Thomasia, the winter before her death, at her particular request. She designed writing something for me in it, but was too unwell to do it without pain.

"I will try and make a good use of it by writing such things as may do my soul good.

"I have found peculiar comfort in my present sorrows at her loss, and in my apprehensions for myself in the future part of my life, by that promise of our Lord, 'as thy days so shall thy strength be.' God will, in answer to faithful prayer, comfort me, and enable me to honor Him all my life, most assuredly; that is, if the Gospel be true—and it is true."

"Henceforth let me divide self from my heart, and have neither love nor resentment but for others. I would be no man's enemy, but the brother of all mankind. Nothing now binds me to life but the desire to do some good. I have nothing to do with this world, but as I am the instrument of good to others."

"Things in which I ought to be very particular and conscientious:

1. In not exaggerating, but always being moderate in language.

2. In all parts of my duty as guardian, in feeling and speaking tenderly towards the mother and children.

3. In the judicious and liberal appropriation of my property. Remember Annanias and Sapphira.

4. In obtaining a command over myself, positively refusing and turning away from things improper, though so in a slight degree, thus acquiring a habit of self-denial.

5. In expressive silence, or speaking in love and to edification.

6. In the constant prayer, "Set a guard, O Lord, before my mouth, and keep the doors of my lips."

7. In always remembering my high and holy office, and what feelings, words, looks and deeds become me in it.

8. In a constant watchfulness against inattention and wandering in prayer, public or private."

"In what state of mind I ought to be towards God and man."

I ought to be "careful for nothing, but in everything, by prayer and thanksgiving, make my requests known unto God," 'learning, in whatsoever state I am, therewith to be content;' doing all the good I can during the time being, and under present circumstances, leaving the issue to God."

"E'en be content with God."

I would let nothing interfere with kind feelings to all men, and yet not confound good and bad together.

"I would not be uneasy as to what may happen in Church or State, to myself or family, but trust in Providence. 'The Lord reigneth.' 'The right hand of the Lord hath the pre-eminence.'

"Our bodies are required by our Lord to be temples of the Holy Ghost."

We may know how pure and holy they should be kept by seeing how clean and undefiled the temple was required to be; and, although beasts were slain and blood shed and sprinkled, and the bodies roasted and boiled, it is said to have been the purest place in Jerusalem.

Let us learn hence not only to keep our bodies washed with pure water, and our persons and clothes neat and clean, but honor our bodies as God's temples, by letting no unclean thought lodge there; by indulging no forbidden lusts; by no kind of intemperance in eating, drinking or sleeping, or any other animal enjoyments, which might defile the body, injure the soul, or offend and grieve the Holy Spirit.

"Through faith in the Son of God, and in true repentance,

I desire to go forth each day as Milton's angel bid our first parents go forth from Paradise, "though sorrowing, yet in peace, by reason of the promised seed.

" 'The rule of *not too much* by temperance taught,
'In what thou eatest and drinkest; seeking from thence
'Due nourishment, not gluttonous delight,
'Nor lose thy life; but what thou livest
'Live well; how long or short, permit to Heaven.'—*Milton.*

"As to my health and ability to work in my Lord's service, I must take due care of them, and be content with just as much as God allows. More might be misspent. Resolved to speak as little as possible of my infirmities of body, or of my trials, or of my labors, or of my charities. Instead of either thinking or speaking of them, let me rather think and speak of those of others, or of the duty of laboring and suffering for Christ."

"Resolved to think and speak as little as may consist with duty, of the faults of others, but when tempted to do so, to turn to my own infirmities and sins."

"If it requires some time every day to wash and dress ourselves, and adjust our clothes and persons, so as to be seen of men, ought we to expect to adjust our souls and prepare our hearts for God, and for the trials of life in a few moments of hurried prayer?"

"It is good to think of God as a Father and Saviour, and call up all those feelings which affectionate children and grateful rescued friends have."

"I will try in the future and never more be in a hurry or impatient, but do present things well—take all things as they come in a right spirit—enjoy present things, and not put off happiness to the future. "All things are yours, whether life or death; things present or things to come."

"Let me resolve on the entrance of each day, and the setting down to each meal; the taking of each walk or ride; the commencement of any work, either of body or mind; reading or writing; the decision of any question; the thought of any trouble — that I will be calm, considerate, conscientious; trying to do them right, as to God, leaving events to Him, being happy and content myself."

The different forms of devotional exercises which follow were specially intended for use on the morning of the Lord's day. The first in order is headed—

"*Confession of Sin.*—"The sacrifice of God is a broken spirit; a broken and contrite heart, O, God, Thou wilt not despise."

"How shall I humble myself before the Lord, for my sins and my corruptions? Where shall I begin with those sins, which are more in number than the hairs of my head?"

After a particular enumeration in very strong language of the transgressions and delinquencies with which he charges and for which he judges himself, he closes thus: "It must be grace that 'saves to the uttermost,' which can avail for me."

"*Supplication.*—'Ask and ye shall receive; seek and ye shall find; knock and it shall be opened unto you.' 'In every thing by prayer and thanksgiving let your requests be made known unto God.'

O that the spirit of prayer and of supplication might come down upon us! O that I might have the spirit of Jacob when he wrestled all night with the angel, and would not let him go, except he blessed him! Let me wait still upon God, until He have mercy upon me. O God, pardon my many offences which I still commit against Thee and my fellow beings, knowing, and in opposition to the warnings of Thy word, the upbraidings of my conscience, and the voice of Thy Spirit speaking in my heart. For His sake, who is our Advocate with Thee, forgive and blot them out of Thy book. Let me have such a sense of Thy pardoning love as shall fill me with peace and joy, and make me resolve to sin no more, knowing that I am accounted Thine."

"O Thou who hatest iniquity with a perfect hatred, give me to see the evil of sin, that I also may abhor it, and be made to see and feel that it richly deserves whatever Thou shalt assign it as its due punishment. O for a heart truly penitent for sin and ashamed of it, and humbled to the dust on account of it. O that I could see it as my Lord and Saviour on the cross saw it, as the angels of Heaven see it, and as the demons of Hell feel it, that I might hate it and forsake it."

O that the love and admiration of holiness might take full possession of my soul! O that I might be holy and perfect as Thou Lord, art holy and perfect!"

Make me a clean heart, and renew a right spirit within me; purge me with hyssop that my inward parts may be clean. Wash me, that I may be all over whiter than snow.

O for a more entire devotion to my God and Saviour, an eye singly directed to heaven, doing all to the glory of God, living, not for myself, but for my fellow beings, seeking to bless them by extending the Redeemer's kingdom.

O that God, by His spirit of love would drive out of my heart the spirit of selfishness which is so deeply rooted there, which is ever springing up amidst all my thoughts, and mingling itself with all my actions, so that I scarce know whether I do anything for the love of God or man.

O for a calm and quiet state of mind which is entirely satisfied after having done its duty, to leave all in the hands of God, and never be uneasy at any disappointments.

O for more pure and ardent affection towards my fellow beings, desiring and seeking their eternal welfare.

O for more undoubting and enlightened faith, clearer

and stronger views of the great doctrines of religion — more knowledge and love of Jesus Christ, more dependence upon the spirit of grace, more lively hope, more joyful anticipation of Heaven.

"O for more self-command, and self-denial; a better government of my thoughts and feelings, all my appetites, so that all may at once obey when my conscience, instructed by Thy word, shall give its directions. 'Set a guard before my mouth, and keep the doors of my lips,' that nothing improper may ever escape me. May my tongue bless God, and speak no evil of man, but rather speak in love unto edification. May my heart ever abound in love, so that my mouth may speak kind words without dissimulation."

"O that I could ever feel what I preach, and thus speak from the deep of my heart. O for the true spirit of my high and holy office; a spirit rising above all trivial and selfish considerations; a spirit of holy zeal for God's glory, of tender affection for all the brethren, a largeness of soul towards the whole Church of God, and the whole family of man. A spirit of candor, sincerity, firmness and true courage; a spirit of martyrs and confessors, which is willing to spend and be spent, to live and die for Christ's sake."

"O that Christ himself might dwell more and more in my heart, that I were more intimately acquainted with Him; that all my actions proceeded more from gratitude to Him; that my sermons and exhortations were more deeply imbued with the Spirit of Christ, so that I might, like the Apostles, know no other among men than Jesus Christ and Him crucified."

"O that God would enlighten my mind to know what is right, that I might be able not only to do my duty, but to give an answer to them who ask counsel of me.

"O that I could live more as one who is soon to die, preparing to meet my God by dying daily to things of and living to those of eternity.

"O God, assist me by Thy grace to be more punctual and earnest and particular in praying and reading Thy holy word; to be more watchful over my thoughts, words and actions; more given to meditation on holy subjects."

"Grant unto me a more tender and charitable heart towards others; one which hopeth all things, which covereth a multitude of sins, suffereth long, and is kind."

"O God, how near am I oftentimes to sin, seeing that I have no power of myself to resist temptation. O be with me in the hour of trial, and save me from disgrace and ruin."

Intercession.—"Pray one for another." "The effectual, fervent prayer of the righteous availeth much."

O! merciful God, who hast chosen to bestow Thy good and perfect gifts, not merely through the intercession of Thy Son, Jesus Christ, but even through the prayers of poor sinful beings, one for another; enable me with strong faith and desire to come before Thee at this time, imploring Thee, for our great Redeemer's sake, to grant the blessings which I ask for those whose welfare ought to be very dear unto my soul. O! for that spirit which fell on Thy servant, Abraham, when he took it upon him to speak unto the Lord!

For my Children and Grandchildren.—O! Heavenly Father, since it has pleased Thee to grant unto Thy servant's children and children's children with immortal souls, which must live forever in bliss or woe, first and ever let me pray that Thou wouldst be a Father unto them all, blessing them on earth, and providing a place in heaven for them.

Keep them from all evil, especially from sin. Prosper them in all their earthly pursuits just as far as may be good for their never-dying souls. May they find favor in Thy sight, and in the sight of all men.

Bless, especially, that dear son who is serving Thee in

the Sanctuary. Give him grace to be diligent in all his preparations for the pulpit, and holy, zealous, faithful and prudent in all his labors, and may many souls be his wages.

And O! God of grace, hear me in behalf of that child of many prayers, whose heart is yet unchanged. Send Thy converting spirit into his soul, and save him ere he be hardened in the ways of this world. Keep him from evil communications, and lead him in the paths of righteousness. O! God, hast thou not one blessing more? One for this, my only child, who is yet living without a saving faith in Thy dear Son. O! for a speedy blessing from Heaven, lest he be suddenly taken away from me, and without hope!

For the Families of my Deceased Brethren.—And next, O! God, let me pray for those families, who, by Thy Providence, have been bereaved of their chief protectors and rulers on earth. O! Thou Husband of the widow, and Father of the fatherless, watch over and bless them all. Give wisdom and firmness to the mothers, that they may guide their children with discretion, and train them up in the nurture and admonition of the Lord. Be a Father unto them, and as they grow in age, so may they grow in grace, and in the knowledge of Christ. Oh, save them from the snares and temptations which are all around, and especially, from evil companions. Give me grace ever to feel for them and consult for them as though they were my own children.

"*For my God-Children.*—And since I have united in the solemn act of presenting unto Thee, O Lord, in the ordinance of baptism, a number of immortal beings for whom I am especially bound to care and pray, I do here most earnestly beseech Thy blessing upon them. However negligent others may be of them—do Thou send Thine invisible Spirit into their hearts, and prepare them for a contest with this world of sin. O! may they have grace to renew at an early age, their baptismal vows, and be a comfort to parents, and friends, and blessings to mankind. And may I have grace to perform all that rests on me.

"*For the Church in Virginia and its ministers.*

"O, Thou great Head of the Church which Thou hast purchased with Thine own blood, since Thou hast been pleased to honor Thine unworthy servant with a charge of a portion of Thy vineyard, grant him the needed grace to tend it, so that it may yield much fruit to Thine honor and glory. Thou hast been very gracious to this once barren wilderness—be yet more gracious, and bless it more abundantly. May the care of all the Churches be ever on my heart before Thee. May my trust ever be in the Lord, to supply them with faithful ministers, and to bless their labors. May I ever feel as a brother to each one, exhorting, counselling and encouraging them. O! God, let no reproach rest upon Thy Church because of the unworthiness of Thy minister or members. May they all walk worthy of their high vocation; fill them with zeal for Thy truth and make them to abound in good works. May brotherly love bind all our hearts together. Bless our conventions and associations, and the visits of Thy servants the chief pastors more and more. May this Diocese be, deservedly, a praise to Thee among the Churches of our land.

Bless our Seminary for training up faithful ministers. May its teachers be filled with the Holy Ghost and with wisdom. Put it into the hearts of more and more of our young men to covet the work of the ministry. Draw to Thy ministers should labor. Enlarge my heart in love to all of every name, and of every character, and teach me how to make the best use of all the talents committed to my trust. Lord, what am I, or what my father's house, that I should be able to serve Thee thus?

"*For the whole Church and all Mankind.*—Nor pray I for these alone, but for all, by whatever name they be called, throughout this land, and every land.

Bless the Bishops and other ministers of the Church, in which Thy servant labors, in this, and all other lands. May their souls be knit together in love and holy zeal. May they agree in the truth of Thy holy word and preach faithfully and live holily, and exercise the godly discipline of the Church wisely and firmly. O! God, if there be any who now do Thy work deceitfully, and preach not the truth as it is in Jesus, show them their awful guilt and danger, and let not immortal souls perish in their hands. Thyself the hearts of parents and ministers in prayer for such a blessing on the young. O! that God would endue all parents with more wisdom and firmness, that they might command their households after them.

Bless all the citizens and christians of this State, and make me an instrument of good, in every way wherein

O God, raise up faithful ministers for every part of Thy Church in these United States, and when Bishops are to be chosen to govern, may they be men of faith and zeal as the apostles were. Look in mercy on our whole land, but especially visit with Thy mighty power, the increasing millions of the West. Increase and multiply among them zealous and faithful preachers of the gospel, who may rebuke vice, and resist the torrent of iniquity which is sweeping through the land.

Bless our rulers with true wisdom from on high, and let them be men fearing God. O! let this great people whom Thou hast blessed above all lands, be a peculiar people unto Thee, zealous of good works, a mighty instrument in Thy hands for consummating all Thy glorious designs towards our fallen race.

Bless all societies for the promotion of religion and virtue, and the suppression of vice through our land. Let them be wisely and zealously conducted, nor ever cease their labors because of the scorn or ridicule of the lukewarm and impious.

Especially bless all the efforts made for sending the gospel into heathen lands, and to the fallen Churches of Christendom. O! for an increase of that zeal which first preached the gospel throughout the then known world. O! for the spirit of martyrs and confessors, to animate our souls in this glorious cause! O! for hearts of love to perishing sinners, and souls of holy zeal for the glory of the Lord! May the liberality of Christians be greatly increased toward the heathen; and the number of missionaries be multiplied a thousand-fold. Especially may the efforts made by members of our Church in this land be enlarged more and more, and the hearts of the people be opened towards them.

Bless our dear brethren and sisters who are laboring in foreign lands. May the abundance of Thy grace rest upon them, and fill them with a joy and peace which will comfort them under every trial. O! grant an increase to what they plant and water, and may their labors be very effectual in bringing about the happy period when all the world shall call upon the name of the true God and Saviour. O! Let the time to favor Zion come. May the nations which have forsaken the Lord return unto Him. From the rising of the sun unto the going down of the same, may Thy name be great among the heathen, and the knowledge of the Lord cover the whole earth, as the waters do the great deep. Thus, may Thy Kingdom come and Thy will be done on earth, even as it is done in Heaven. Grant it! O! God, for Thy Son Jesus Christ's sake."

The preceding rules of living, and forms of private prayer, affectingly disclose the noble Christian principles, and the elevated devotion of the writer. And it may be presumed, that no one competent to judge, can consider what has been exhibited, without the highest admiration of his religious experience and character, and true love for the excellent grace of heavenly charity which animated his devotions towards God, and kept his heart warm towards men.

DECLINE OF HEALTH—APPOINTMENT OF ASSISTANT BISHOP—OCCURRENCE AT LAWRENCEVILLE—CONSECRATION OF SEMINARY BUILDINGS.

Few persons have been blessed with a more vigorous constitution than Bishop MEADE. This he never spared, but rather imposed upon it, and sometimes to a degree beyond what a reasonable regard for health justified.—How he accustomed himself to endure hardness as a good soldier of Christ, is related by one of his daughters-in-law, who long formed one of his family at Mountain View.

"At the time I was married and came to this house, or rather the old house, since burnt, his habit was to walk miles between four o'clock, of a winter morning, and the rising of the sun. Then to the family prayers with cheerfulness, and a hearty appetite for his breakfast. Once an humble neighbor of ours asked me, 'Does the old Parson walk and ride in all weather as he used to do?' I replied, 'Yes, he goes to Winchester by church-time, the very coldest Sunday morning.' She then remarked, 'The earliest recollection I have of anything is of the Parson,' as we used to call him, then, 'coming in on his way to Winchester, to preach. My father lived on the road side; he would say, if the weather was cold, 'Make up a good fire, for the Parson will be here to warm soon.' And sure enough, he seemed to me, a little child, to come oftenest when the weather was violently cold or snowing. He used to bring us little ones apples in his big coat pockets.'

"I recollect stopping at a toll gate on the Blue Ridge mountains once. The keeper of the gate asked Mr. M. are you Bishop MEADE's son?" On his replying in the

20

affirmative, "Oh," said he, "then you must drink some of my spring-water, for your father has done so for forty years." The old man then said, "the Parson used to ride on horseback to Alexandria, when it was too cold for any human being to turn out." "Once he did it when the mail rider was frozen to death on this very road. We inquired of the Bishop whether this was true? He said 'Yes, and I remember stopping to warm at that toll house on my way.' 'It was to meet an appointment; the sleet was so heavy I had to protect myself by tying my silk handkerchief over my face, and I would frequently take it off and shake it.' 'I would not advise others to do as I did, but I thought it right.'"

Some years ago the last of February was made memorable by the deepest snow ever seen in our neighborhood. After breakfast, (the storm over,) to our surprise the men were brought and pieces of plank and timber were taken into the garden, where the soft snow, which was very deep, was shovelled out of the way, post holes dug, and a trellis for the grape vines was put up before night, when the rest of our neighbors were frightened and unable to think of any work, beyond feeding the animals and keeping good fires. Often would we think, after a whole day spent out of doors on the damp earth in thin shoes, that an illness would follow, but he would escape with a headache or cold, not sufficient to shut him up."

Bishop MEADE said that for a large part of his life it was only by a sense of hunger that he knew of having a stomach, and as to nerves, he knew nothing of their existence from his own experience. The various ailments which would now be considered as different forms of neuralgia, he was disposed to regard as imaginary, and when a minister was given to complaining of fatigue from his professional services, and to be economical of himself in his ministrations, he was apt to think the infirmity more moral than physical; not so much corporeal feebleness as indolence, which found no favor with him. But then his own iron frame and nerves of steel were not impassible. His hale constitution honored without remonstrance the constant and heavy drafts made upon it, and allowed the account to run on for a long time. At last, however, payment began to be exacted, and it was some five and twenty years, with varying indulgence, before the final settlement. He now learned what it is to pass painful days and restless nights; to have to spare himself in the work of the study, and in the services of the sanctuary; to be obliged to recognize and accommodate himself to infirmities of which in others he had been incredulous, and sometimes, perhaps, impatient. He never, indeed, backed an inch beyond what he was forced to surrender, and often by persisting when he should have yielded, suffered and lost more than was needful, till sad experience disciplined his brave spirit to a right understanding of the policy proper for one who is partially disabled.

With the first serious impression of disease upon his system, he adopted the opinion that his heart was organically affected, and referred all his ailments to this derangement, which he expected would, sooner or later, suddenly terminate his life.

Whereever the seat of his malady may have been, its distressing influence extended to his nervous system generally, and at times to his head, with a painfulness that drove sleep from his eyes and interfered with his ordinary duties. Yet he persevered in his long and fatiguing visitations.

In 1841, both his friends and himself perceived that some intermission of his labors was indispensable, and in his address to the Convention of that year, after a narrative of the services which he had been enabled to perform, he thus alluded to his own case:

"Perhaps it may not be improper to add that they have been performed with less comfort of body than those of any previous period, and that at some times I have been seriously admonished of infirmities which, except duly attended to, might bring my ministry to a close at a period earlier than might otherwise be. God has in times past been truly gracious in giving me a readiness of utterance which made the preaching of the Word and other services, for the most part easy and delightful. During the last twelve years, with the exception of that just ended, my health seemed to have increased with the increasing duties devolved upon me, so that with considerable comfort I have engaged in the performance of ministerial duties, more or less various, and extended during at least two-thirds of the days of each year. This, indeed, was actually required, in order to meet the reasonable wishes and wants of the brethren and their congregations in regard to Episcopal services, for such is the number and distance of the congregations to be visited in this large Diocese, that even with the frequent services mentioned, I have not been able to visit the congregations once in two years. From my present feelings, I fear that should it please Providence to continue my ministry for a number of years, I shall scarcely be able to go beyond a triennial visitation. By a more leisurely movement from place to place, and by availing myself more of the aid of my brethren in the ministry, I hope while life is continued to render some service to our beloved Church in Virginia. During the present season I have before me four or five months of duty which I am anxious to perform, and shall postpone most reluctantly; but the wishes of relatives, and friends, and brethren, coinciding with my own conviction of what is due to Providence, induce me to ask of the Convention a release from the same, or rather the postponement of it for a season. Perhaps the relaxation from effort at this time, may strengthen me the more for the performance of such duties as lie before me in years that are to come.

Commending our beloved brethren and friends to the protection of Heaven,

I remain,
Your faithful brother in Christ,
WILLIAM MEADE."

Journal, 1841.

The response of the Convention at the close of the Report of the Committee upon the state of the Church:

"In fine, as our Right Reverend Assistant Bishop, in a state of health greatly impaired by his unwearied and exhausting labors, is about to travel abroad in pursuit of more vigorous health, affection and duty concur in prompting us to invoke upon him the Divine blessing, and recommend him to the special protection of Almighty God, and to pray that with reinvigorated health and strength, He may in due time restore him to his loved duties and his Diocesan home."

Just after the adjournment of the Convention, as he was on his way North to embark for Europe, he received the following beautiful note, with the gift to which it refers:

MOUNT VERNON, May 23, 1841.

Will our honored and beloved Diocesan accept a staff cut from the tomb of the Father of our Country? and, should weariness come over him during his sojourn in a far distant land, let this be in his hand, and remind him of his country, where so many affectionate hearts put up humble petitions to God, for his safety and happiness. And in his prayers for those he leaves, will he sometimes remember

THE FAMILY AT MOUNT VERNON.

On the first of June, at 3 P. M., he left Boston in the steamer Caledonia. On the 14th reached Liverpool, having made the voyage in "just thirteen days, lacking one and a half hours, tarrying ten hours at Halifax." He was absent from the United States just four months, his return being hastened that he might attend the General Convention which met in New York the first Wednesday in October.

During his absence he visited the principal towns, the Universities, and other places of interest, both in England and Scotland, not entirely neglecting Paris. In his address to his Convention, after his return, alluding to the partial services rendered, he adds : "They have been fewer in number than in any past year through bodily indisposition, which led me to ask (what was kindly granted) a respite from labor during the last summer. I need not inform you that the period of relaxation was spent in a visit to the land and Church of our fathers. Having already, in a few brief letters, published in our Diocesan papers, stated the great kindness experienced while there, and the satisfaction enjoyed in witnessing much that came under observation, mentioning some facts which might not only interest but edify my brethren and friends, I shall forbear the repetition of the same, except simply to advert to the wonderful providence of God over our mother Church in times past, and His great grace in making her what she now is, in comparison with what she has been."

The only memoranda of his "foreign travel" are found in a small book with this heading, "This book was presented to me by my valued friend, Dr. Milnor, of New York, on leaving that city for England, on the last day of May, 1841." Only two of the leaves have been used, and on these the entries are so very brief and fragmentary, that though they might aid the writer's recollection, they communicate little of interest to a reader.

His reception by Bishops and other clergy and prominent laymen was most gratifying. Wherever he went he was cordially welcomed and hospitably entertained. He greatly enjoyed his association with the pious and intelligent ministers and members of the establishment, and whilst he saw and heard occasionally what he did not approve, there was so much to admire and love, that his visit very much increased his appreciation of the "Mother Church." One or two brief personal notices may be introduced without impinging the proprieties of social intercourse.

"I heard the Bishop of Chester preach in the Cathedral, back part of the choir, to a good congregation, on Sunday evening at 6½ o'clock. In the morning at 8 he ordained fifty-two, only using the ordination service, the morning prayer and communion being at 11 A. M. The Bishop stood up while asking the questions, and did not wait for them to kneel down and pray privately and silently at a certain place in 'the ordering of Priests,' as we do, but simply called on them to pray, and then said, 'Come Holy Ghost, Creator, come,' &c. Perhaps it was because there were none but themselves to pray."

I took breakfast with the Bishop of Chester. He had all the servants (ten) in (to prayers), each with Bible, reading it with him. He read and expounded, for twenty minutes, three chapters of St. John. No baptismal regeneration in his exposition. He spoke during and after breakfast on Oxfordism—he, very decided.

Mr. Raikes, his Vice Chancellor, a tall, fine-looking, amiable man—hope he will be a Bishop—examiner of his candidates first; then the Bishop three days, from nine in the morning until ten at night; intermission at dinner; pleased with the appearance of the young men."

"Mr. Faber, small man, like Hartwell Home. He expressed to me his views of tradition, very different from the Tractarians. His provincial letters in the Churchman considers the Tractarians as Jesuitical, and very unsound in doctrine."

Mr. Faber, and all the clergy I have seen, live well—high, I should say; the English certainly eat and drink more than the Americans can afford to do, either by reason of our purse or health."

Among the many valuable acquaintances made during his visit, none was prized more than the Rev. W. Goode. Several of his admirable works, on the points involved in the Tractarian controversy, the Bishop imported, and had reprinted in this country. Their sympathy on this exciting subject animated their Christian friendship, and led to a correspondence which terminated only with the Bishop's life.

On the voyage home a storm was encountered, so violent, that no one supposed the vessel would survive it. Some time after his return, one of his clergy asked him how he felt when they were expecting every moment to go to the bottom? Instead of the description of the danger, and of his fearlessness and composure, which was expected, his brief and quiet reply was, "You know I was never nervous."

After his return Bishop MEADE prepared for publication in the Diocesan paper, several letters, in which he gives his impression of the countries through which he had passed, and the people with whom he had been associated. His motive he states thus: I have been encouraged to this by the consideration that as my brethren of the ministry and friends of the laity of this Diocese had kindly consented to release me from the duties which would have devolved upon me during the summer, in order to the relaxation and benefit of the journey of which I am speaking, I ought to hold myself a debtor to them so far as to communicate any facts, hints, or suggestions, which might, by God's blessing, be of use to them as a substitute for the personal services relinquished."

It is to be presumed that these instructive and interesting letters will appear in a volume with other miscellaneous writings. His preliminary remark, therefore, is all that need be quoted: "Let me at once premise that I return to my own county and State, Church and Diocese, with all my attachments increased, on account of many advantages which a kind Providence has bountifully lavished upon us, but of which many of us are not duly aware, and for which none of us are sufficiently thankful. And yet, at the same time, I return with a heart more disposed than ever to love and venerate the land and Church of our forefathers, for all the good, temporal and spiritual, which God has made to abound therein, and rather to lament than severely condemn those evils from which we are happily freed, and which greatly hinder the more perfect accomplishment of all those great and glorious works which the pious and benevolent are so anxious to achieve."

He was very much impressed by the beauty of the trees which adorned the grounds of the nobility and gentry of England. The taste, so formed and cultivated, became a passion, which sought its innocent and refined gratification in transplanting, to the lots around his residence, the choicest growth of his own and of foreign lands. There was scarcely an ornamental evergreen, or deciduous tree in one woods, or in the nurseries, a fine specimen of which might not be seen in the enclosure around Mountain View, and with the history and habits of which he had not made himself perfectly familiar. It was one of his ways of entertaining his visitors, to conduct them from tree to tree, telling of its derivation, and giving a kind of running commentary on its peculiarities, with an animation which could scarcely fail to interest. Often in his visitations he carried with him a piece of oiled silk, with which, and the aid of his trunk cover, he conveyed to his home such plants as he desired to add to his collection, and so had transferred to his grounds representations from the different parts of his Diocese—from the counties on the Eastern Shore, to those on the Kanawha—forming objects not only pleasing to the eye, but possessing very agreeable associations.

In this matter, the Bishop was truly a propagandist. When Bishop Johns was preparing for the residence of his family, the place which he had purchased in the vicinity of the Seminary, Bishop Meade asked to be permitted to select the ornamental trees. On their return from a

General Convention, he accompanied Bishop Johns to nurseries near Philadelphia and Baltimore, and chose, and had labeled tree after tree, until Bishop Johns found it necessary to interfere, saying, "Bishop, not your inclination, but my purse must limit the purchase; we had better stop." And yet, the next evening, on reaching his home, he covered a page with the names of other trees, and wrote to Bishop Johns, that he must add them to those already ordered. This was the only letter, during a correspondence of twenty-three years, in which there was not the slightest allusion to the great interests to which he was devoted. *

In sending his contributions to aid in purchasing and fitting up premises to be used as parsonages, he would add to a generous subscription, a sum to be specially appropriated to the purchase of ornamental trees, sometimes giving their names.

Another illustration of this passion, combined with his interest for everything connected with the old Churches of Virginia, is related in his History—vol. I, p. 309. It relates to the old church near Smithfield—Isle of Wight—the oldest in the State, and probably the oldest now standing in the United States.

"Some years since, in the month of November, towards the close of day, I passed by the church in company with an active young man, and, as usual, turning aside to survey it, I saw among the shrubs a delicate young cedar, about a foot long, issuing out of the wall, just under the cornice of the roof. On expressing a wish that I had it, without dreaming that it could be gotten, my companion

* On one of his vernal visits to the Seminary Hill, he stepped from the carriage at the door of Bishop Johns' residence, holding in his hands two trimmed branches, and observed, "I cut these from my Napoleon willow, and wish to plant them myself at your spring," which was just below the house, in a clump of fine forest trees. He selected the spot, and planted the branches with his own hands. They are not there now. With the entire clump near which they stood, they have disappeared amidst the devastations attendant on war.

immediately began to clamber up the pillar nearest to it, and, ascending twelve feet, got in a position which enabled him to remove several of the loosened bricks, and got the young plant, with good roots, from its nest. It is now a flourishing tree, eight feet high, near my study window."

After the adjournment of the General Convention of 1841, Bishop MEADE returned to his home in Clark county. On his way, he held a Confirmation in Alexandria, and performed some duties at the Seminary and High School. The domestic enjoyments for which he had so fine a relish, and which now, after so long a separation, must have been peculiarly delightful to him, were soon interrupted by the melancholy tidings of the death of Bishop Moore, who finished his course on the 11th of November, 1841, in Lynchburg, to which place he had gone a few days before to administer confirmation in St. Paul's Church.

By the removal of this venerable and much beloved Diocesan, Bishop MEADE was deeply impressed. In an irregular kind of memorandum of official services from which he was accustomed to make up his annual Address to the Convention, but which had been discontinued for ten years—he now resumes the notices with this solemn record:

December 3, 1841.—"I now find myself alone in the Episcopate by the death of Bishop Moore, and recommence my journal on the following pages, which may be more than sufficient to record all the acts of my uncertain and unprofitable life." "Oh! God, help me to discharge my duties more faithfully, more lovingly, more effectually for the few years allotted to me."

His address to the next Convention commences with a tender and affecting reference to the bereavement that the Diocese had sustained, and an earnest request for the prayers of his brethren that he might have grace adequate for his increasing responsibilities.

"The great Head of the Church, who, for a long time

has continued to the Diocese of Virginia the counsel and superintendence of a very beloved father, has, since our last meeting been pleased very suddenly to take him away. I hope it will only make us look the more humbly, and steadily to Him, from whom all good counsels come, that the interests of true religion may not suffer in our hands. If there be any of you, my friends, who deeply feel the absence of our beloved father, (and which of you does not?) how much more must I, who, for so many years had been unitedly and harmoniously laboring at his side, as a son with a father, and who had begun seriously to think, that my auxiliary services might probably be over, before he should be called to his rest. God has otherwise determined, and permitted to devolve on one, ill able either in body or mind to sustain it, the undivided responsibility of superintending this Diocese.

It is not my intention to undertake either an eulogy, or biography, of our dear departed father—that having been already done, and often, and well done by others, both from the pulpit and the press. And indeed, there was something so peculiarly amiable in his character, and so correspondingly interesting and venerable in his form, and countenance, and manner, that it were worse than useless to attempt a delineation of one who has been so recently among us, and who can be so much better remembered than described. May God rather give us grace to imitate those traits which endeared him to the heart. For myself, who of necessity must now take his place, and enter more entirely upon all the anxieties and responsibilities of the Episcopal office, I must ask of you, my brethren, both of the clergy and laity, not only great indulgence for infirmities and unfitness, of which I am daily more and more sensible, but a very large share in your most earnest entreaties at a Throne of Grace, that the cause you have entrusted to me may not suffer. This, I ask, not in feigned humility, but, as God knows, from the very depth of a heart which feels more of its deficiencies than can be known to any human *being*."

Assistant Bishop.—The relaxation, change of scene and habits connected with the Atlantic voyage and European tour, no doubt benefitted Bishop MEADE's health. Under the influence of the relief which he experienced, he resumed his duties at once. During the early part of the winter he officiated in the churches in the vicinity of his residence. In January, he preached in Alexandria and Fredericksburg, on his way to Richmond and to Petersburg, where he spent a week "enjoying much pleasure in beholding the rich fruits of God's grace in blessing the word, frequently and faithfully preached, and the services of the Church zealously and devotedly used by the Rector and many other brethren, who, for the last three months, had been almost daily meeting with the people in the house of God, where they never seemed weary with calling on Him in prayer, and hearing His truth. One of the results of this great grace on the means of Heaven's appointment was the confirmation of ninety-three persons, who, it is hoped, not merely with the mouth, but the full consent of their heart, renewed that solemn vow, promise and profession made in their baptism, and which none can make except those who are renewed in the spirit of their minds."—*Journal* 1842, *p.* 11.

Returning by the same route, and officiating at the same places, he tarried at his own home long enough to preach and administer confirmation in the three neighboring churches, when he set off on a visitation of the western section of the Diocese, embracing the churches in Harrison and Lewis counties, and on the Ohio and Kanawha rivers. By this extensive, and in those days, tedious and fatiguing tour, he was again so seriously disabled that he no longer hesitated as to the course which the interests of the Diocese, as well as his own comfort, and perhaps life, required. His experience, and the expedient he desired, were made the subject of a special communication to the Convention which met in Staunton on the 18th of May.

BRETHREN AND FRIENDS:

Since the decease of our beloved father, Bishop Moore, my thoughts have often been led to a subject which I now wish to propose for your consideration. I mean the appointment of an Assistant Bishop, to aid me in the arduous duties of this extensive Diocese. During the last twelve years I have, with the exception of a very few places, performed the whole of the itinerant duties of the Diocese. It has required, on an average, at least eight months in each year, of successive services from day to day, to render what has still appeared to me, very inefficient supervision of the Diocese The effect of this incessant labor of mind and body has been so injurious to me already, especially to my voice, which is often insufficient for duty, and the attempt to continue the same so likely to result in entire disability, that I feel it a duty to ask, according to the provisions of the constitution of the Church, that I may have an Assistant who may divide with me the labors of a Diocese which, for its extent, and other circumstances, is much more difficult to be served than any other in our country. I do this under the advice of many friends, and also of physicians, who are competent to judge of my infirmities.

Hoping that you will accede to my request, and that God may guide you in the choice of a suitable person,

I remain,
Your faithful friend and brother in Christ,
WILLIAM MEADE.

Journal, 1842.

The select Committee appointed to consider and report upon the preceding communication, having disposed of another mode of relief which had been suggested, conclude their report in these words:

"With respect to the election of an Assistant Bishop, the only remaining subject submitted to their consideration, your committee deem it highly expedient that it should be done at once. The Bishop's health imperatively demands repose. If he attempts to discharge the duties which will devolve upon him during the present season, unaided by an Assistant, the worst consequences are to be apprehended. His physicians prescribe repose as absolutely necessary to the continuance of even his present health. They therefore respectfully recommend to the Convention the election of an Assistant Bishop."—*Journal*, 1842.

This report was adopted, and the next day appointed for the election. It resulted in the choice of the Rev. John Johns, D. D., then Rector of Christ Church, Baltimore, Maryland, who accepted the appointment, and was consecrated in the Monumental Church, Richmond, on the 13th of October, 1842.

After the Convention, Bishop MEADE embraced the first opportunity to say to the Assistant Bishop, "I will aid you in making the appointments till you have visited all the churches, and then you can arrange them to suit yourself. The Diocese is before you; whatever you find to be done, do it, except matters of discipline and letters dimissory. These I am obliged to attend to myself. In all other respects the whole Diocese is open to you, without the necessity of a reference to me, unless when you desire information or counsel—only let us be careful so to arrange our movements that each parish may be visited at least once in eighteen months, that all may be regularly and equally served. We will meet statedly at Convention, at the examination of the Seminary and High School, and as often as may be convenient, and in the intervals communicate by letter." His letters were frequent, though generally concise. He rarely acted in any matter of importance, without conferring personally, or by mail. The only instance in which he manifested dissatisfaction was connected with a series of appointments published by Bishop Johns, in reference to a part of which, Bishop MEADE proposed the substitution of some other places in a different section of the Diocese, which he thought had not received its proper proportion of Episcopal services.—Bishop Johns explained that he had visited those places with punctuality, in regular rotation, and was not yet due there again, but would certainly make the change if the Bishop so directed. The next mail brought a brief reply, requesting that Bishop Johns would never again use that odious word, "direct," in such connection. This is the only instance of interference, or whisper of dissatisfaction during the constant and intimate intercourse of twenty years. The occurrence was a small matter, but in its spirit and singleness, very significant of character.

How conscious the Bishop was of the serious impairment of his health, few were fully aware. From the Convention at Staunton he proceeded on a visitation through Goochland, where he began a letter to his sister, but desisted after writing a few lines and requested another to finish it.

BOLLING HALL, *June* 10, 1842.

"*My dear Sister:*

I cannot go any further without a line to let you and all I most love know that I am alive, and as well as I could expect. I get along by adopting short exhortations generally, instead of sermons."

The friend who filled the sheet writes:

"I felt I was truly favored to be with him, and regretted his short visit, as the moments in his presence were precious to my soul. I endeavored to gain all the instruction I could from his valuable company. I am sorry to find his health not entirely restored. He will exert himself too much, or, I am sure his health would be better."

In his letter to his sister, the Bishop alluded to the expedient which he adopted in "substituting short exhortations for sermons." He was careful to secure at the places of his appointments the presence of some clergyman, other than the resident minister, who, if the Bishop did not feel able to preach, might take his place in the pulpit. The necessity for this substitution became more frequent every year, until at last he ceased to preach on his visitations, and confined himself to addresses from the chancel, and to the performance of those services which were strictly Episcopal. These addresses being extemporaneous, depended for their animation and impressiveness on the state of the speaker's feelings, and of his bodily health, which were very different at different times—occasionally animating him to eloquence of the highest order, and again leaving him to utterances quite desultory and feeble.

One of his addresses delivered in the church at Lawrenceville, Brunswick County, in May 1856, was the occasion of a violent assault on him by an anonymous writer in the *Democrat*, published in Petersburg. The writer was not present when the address was made, and allowed himself to pen his inflammatory accusation upon hear-say. His drift evidently was to direct public indignation against the Bishop as having, in his remarks to the servants whom he confirmed, spoken in a way calculated unduly to elevate the slaves, socially and politically, and of course to render them dissatisfied and lead to insurrection. The accusation was copied in other papers, with the usual expressions of astonishment, and reluctance to credit it, and hopes that so serious a charge from one whom the editor indorsed as reliable, would receive a speedy and satisfactory response from the venerable prelate. Others, both clerical and lay, who were present when the Address was delivered responded promptly in vindication of the Bishop. His own statement, which soon appeared, disposed of the accusation so satisfactorily, that the attempt at excitement utterly failed.

"Bishop Meade's statement of his remarks at a Confirmation at Lawrenceville, being made at the request of some of his friends:

"In my address at Lawrenceville, I adverted to the fact that a number of servants were about to be confirmed—eleven out of twelve—that something suitable to them was proper from me; that God, who, of one blood had made all nations upon earth, had given us a religion suitable to all — rich and poor, bond and free; that the larger portion of the human race had always been in some form of bondage to the other, being poor and dependent; that God, in His providence, had permitted a large number to come to this country from Africa, intending to make it a blessing to them, their posterity, and Africa itself, by bringing them to the light of the gospel and sending the gospel back to that country; that there were some persons who, by denying the unity of the human race and ascribing different nations to different origins, and not to the one first pair mentioned in the Bible, made an invidious assault upon our holy religion — for in maintaining different origin, and great original differences, a way was prepared for denying that Christianity was suitable to all, unless modified and accommodated to the variation's in the human family. Whereas, one great argument for the divinity of our religion is, that it is suitable to all; was received and understood by all, rich and poor, bond and free, learned and unlearned.

"I exhorted the servants to rejoice that they had been born in this Christian land, and not in a heathen land — to seek that liberty of soul from sin, which Christ alone could give, and which was infinitely better than any other liberty — to obey all those instructions to servants which God had given in His word — to be humble, faithful, honest, obedient to their masters, not eye-servants, but doing their duty as in the sight of God. The whole Address was based on the supposition that their lot was assigned them by Providence, and that they should rejoice in the many spiritual blessings connected with it. Just in proportion as they received and obeyed my admonitions, will they be happy, contented and faithful servants to their earthly and to their heavenly masters."

The above was written on hearing that something had appeared in the Petersburg papers on the subject, but not knowing the precise character of the article. Having now seen it, I add the following remarks: I have, for forty-six years, been addressing our slaves in the presence, as well as in the absence, of their owners. Twenty-seven years I have been publicly laying my hands on them in Confirmation, and as publicly addressing special exhortations to them. During all this period of my ministry, I have never heard it intimated that a word was uttered by me, which was found fault with by any. More than twenty years ago I opened one of our largest Conventions, which met in the Monumental Church in Richmond, with a sermon on the religious instruction of servants. It was unanimously approved of, and a copy requested for general circulation. Several editions have been issued. I have never varied from the sentiments contained in that sermon; I have on several occasions of late years adverted to the fact, that there were two classes of persons who were making assaults upon the Bible in connection with this subject; the one consisting of those who, unable to resist the arguments in favor of the lawfulness of slavery, from the Bible, had gone to the extreme of denying the Divine authority of the Bible; the other, consisting of those who, not satisfied with the sanction afforded to this institution by the Bible, sought to strengthen it by affirming that different races, and especially the African, came from different origins, and that the latter was very diverse and inferior to the others. Of course the same religion would not be equally suitable to all. Against all such assaults upon our holy religion, I trust the ministers of the gospel will be ever ready to defend it.

On the occasion spoken of, I briefly alluded to these assaults upon our holy religion, and, referring to the many notices of servants in the Bible, and especially to what St. Paul had addressed to them, and his instructions to Timothy as to exhortations to them, said I never felt myself more as the minister of Christ and follower of the Apostles, than when laying my hands on the heads of this portion of our fellow-beings. I have ever rejoiced to say to those who upbraid us with being indifferent to the souls of our servants, that our ministers seem to delight in preaching to them, and our people encourage them to do so. On that occasion I said, that from the earliest period, the most pious of our forefathers, who declared that they came to America chiefly to bring the Christian religion to the natives, also regarded the Africans as sent here, not merely to fell the forests and cultivate the fields—though this was part of the design of Providence—but chiefly for the far more glorious purpose of hearing the gospel of salvation. I felt that while speaking I was defending Southern Christians against charges of neglect from distant quarters, though I by no means affirm that they do the half of their duty towards them.

"If I was not so understood, I can only ascribe it to the most sensitive and morbid state of some minds on the subject. "WILLIAM MEADE."

The position of Bishop MEADE in reference to this exciting subject may be concisely stated without any discussion.

Slavery, as a civil institution, was never to his taste. He had, however, no conscientious scruples as to its lawfulness, because he believed it to have been distinctly recognized, and formally legislated about, by divine authority in the Sacred Scriptures.

As an institution existing in the United States, he did not hold with those who professed to regard it as a blessing to the country, but with the distinguished statesmen of Virginia who considered it politically disadvantageous, and hoped it would, in process of time, be happily terminated. How such termination was to be effected, he did not as yet perceive. In early life he had manumitted and conveyed to non-slaveholding States, such of his servants as he thought capable of taking care of themselves.

The results of this, and other similar experiments, which he had watched with much interest, satisfied him that manumission was generally a failure, if the persons freed were to remain in this country, and he decidedly advised against it.

His zeal in the cause of the Colonization Society was kindled by the hope that though it was, in its principles and action, distinctly limited to the free people of color, it might ultimately lead to some arrangement for the removal of the entire colored population, without violence or wrong.

Meanwhile, with the Apostle, he taught masters and servants to conform to the relations in which they were providentially placed. Servants by "obeying their masters according to the flesh, not with eye-service as men-pleasers, but in singleness of heart, fearing God," and masters by giving unto their servants that which is just and equal, knowing that they also have a Master in heaven."

Notwithstanding the appointment of an assistant, Bishop MEADE continued as heretofore to visit all the parishes in the Diocese, except that, instead of two, he now took for its accomplishment, the three years canonically prescribed. This, and the substitution of addresses from the chancel for discourses from the pulpit, was all the indulgence he allowed himself. His malady returned upon him with increased power—yet, with that indomitable resolution for which he was so very remarkable, he persevered in his visitations, though often distressing to him, and occasioning much concern to the sympathizing people for whom he officiated. Instances of failure to officiate according to appointment became more frequent, and acted unfavorably on his health and spirits. Several times, as he said to a friend, he had come to the conclusion that he ought to surrender the whole supervision of the Diocese to the assistant: but, he worked on as he could, and his assistant, besides his own visitations, was able and glad to go to his help, and finish out any line of appointments which the Bishop found himself incapable of completing. This was just what he needed, relief of body, and relief from mental anxiety in reference to his engagements—which, in reality, often brought on the very disability it dreaded. Seeing, however, that the Diocese was regularly visited, and that occasional lack of service on his part could be promptly supplied, one cause of painful disturbance subsided, and so he found himself working with less and less inconvenience, and when at home reposing with more comfort. As was to be expected, there were still painful vicissitudes in his experience, yet his maladies ceased to advance, and when this was realized, it was encouraging, and contributed, in connection with the use of other means, to abate—slowly indeed, but to abate—the most distressing symptoms in his case, and gradually led, not to health, for that was never fully restored, but to such relief, as neither he, or his friends, ever supposed could be attained.

The Bishop continued for a number of years to refrain from formal preaching, and officiated only in his place in the chancel—the most appropriate position for the ministrations of a Bishop on any ordinary visitation.

He resorted to it at first to avoid being obliged to speak as long as custom prescribed for the delivery of a sermon, or to appear to have failed. The apprehension of this, in his state of health, really disqualified him for the effort, and produced a kind of nervous disinclination to ascend the pulpit, which grew by indulgence, and kept him from occupying it for some time after the infirmity in which the practice originated, had ceased to render it necessary.

The Bishop's duties as Professor of Pastoral Theology brought him to the Seminary every year, where, before commencing his spring visitation, he spent about a fortnight in instructing the senior class. His home at such times was at Malvern, the residence of Bishop Johns, contiguous to the Seminary grounds. During one of these visits Bishop Johns had an appointment to preach and confirm in Christ Church, Alexandria, on April 11, 1858. Knowing how agreeable it would be to his old congregation, Bishop Johns proposed to him to administer the rite of Confirmation. This he promptly declined, but added in a very animated voice, "If you please, I will preach the sermon." The proposal was cheerfully accepted, though with much surprise, and no little distrust as to performance. Bishop Johns deemed it prudent to be ready himself in case of the Bishop's resolution failing when the hour arrived. But the precaution was unnecessary. The idea of beginning again to preach, and in the very church of his early ministrations, stirred his spirit within him, and braced him for the experiment. The people were astonished when they saw him, with firm step, ascend the pulpit, and heard him deliver his sermon with a sonorous voice, which made the old church ring with tones with which, for sixteen years, they had ceased to be familiar.—Some could go back to a remoter date, when the youthful parson, in his home-spun suit, boyish collar, and black necktie, first stood in that pulpit, charming their ears by the music of his lips, and wooing their souls with the grace of the gospel. But those privileged days, and also the powerful ministrations of his manhood, had long passed away. The congregation were now accustomed to see him serve under the disabilities of disease, and infirmities of advancing life. The unexpected manifestation of the morning seemed to them like a resurrection, and the people wept for joy!

It was not the last luminous flash of an expiring flame—the mysterious rally of energies which sometimes precedes and indicates sudden and final collapse—but the elasticity of a naturally vigorous life, partially relieved from the incubus of a destroying disease, and so far springing into salutary action under the happiest influences incident to humanity. From that time onward he continued to officiate in the pulpit, preaching occasionally twice on the same day to the edification and delight of his devoted Diocese—himself as much interested and pleased at resuming this form of ministration, as when he first began as a young deacon, at the stone chapel in Clarke.

His devotion to the Theological Seminary has been noticed in its place. With the first move for its establishment at Williamsburg he had no sympathy. He believed it, what it soon proved to be, a mistake. But from the time of its transfer to Alexandria it was prominent in his thoughts and affections, and shared largely in his labors. Besides the services required by a general superintendence as President of the Board of Trustees, his duties as Professor brought him for several weeks every spring into personal intercourse with professors and students. These annual visits were exceedingly pleasant to the other preceptors and to the students, with whom his association was always that of an affectionate and wise parent with sons just maturing into manhood. Year after year he thus watched over the beloved Seminary, and he was amply remunerated for his care and toil. He had the happiness to see it advance with healthy growth from the few pupils and limited accommodations in Alexandria, till it covered with its spacious and imposing buildings, and those of the adjacent High School, the commanding hill to which it has given its name—was filled with students from all parts of our country, and had its alumni ministering in every State in the Union, and at every foreign missionary station of the Church.

Among the buildings then recently erected were "St. George's Hall," by funds furnished by a lady of St. George's Church, New York, through the friendly agency of the Rev. S. H. Tyng, D. D.—a handsome fire proof library, the contribution of Mr. John Bohlen, of Philadelphia, and a legacy of Miss Sophia Jones, of Virginia—and the noble central building, "Aspinwall Hall," the gift of the brothers of that name, at the suggestion of the Rev. G. T. Bedell, D. D., then Rector of the Church of the Ascension, New York, with which the liberal donors were connected.

It was eminently proper that these gifts should be publicly and formally recognized in connection with their solemn dedication to God for the purposes contemplated by the several benefactors of the Seminary. A most suitable occasion presented itself by the approaching General Convention which was to assemble in Richmond, and the day preceding its meeting was appointed for the interesting services. Due notice was given, special invitations sent, and every proper preparation made for the accommodation of visitors.

On Tuesday, October 5, 1859, being the day appointed for the consecration of "Aspinwall Hall," and other buildings forming the group on the Seminary Hill, a large number of clergy and laity assembled for the purpose.

The spacious hall and the three lecture rooms, with the wide entry and stairway were soon occupied. Among the welcome visitors were the Bishops of Vermont, Kentucky, and Louisiana, the last being an alumnus of the Seminary. The presence of the generous friends by whose liberality the new buildings were erected, added largely to the interest of the occasion.

As the Bishops, clergy and lay members of the Board of Trustees entered the west door of the new Hall, and proceeded to the platform provided for the speakers, they repeated the 19th Psalm alternately.

A form of consecration modeled after that prescribed for the consecration of a church had been prepared by Bishop Johns, and was now used, and, after an appropriate Psalm sung by the large congregation, Bishop MEADE delivered an interesting address, in which he gave a history of the Seminary, recited a list of its generous benefactors in and beyond the Diocese, and dwelt with expressions of gratitude and praise on the signal blessings of God which had rested on the Institution, as evidenced by the number and character and usefulness of its alumni. He then alluded briefly to what was necessary to carry out the architect's plan for completing the central structure, and having appealed for means to accomplish this, to those friends of the Church whom God had prospered, he closed with a prayer for "our kind benefactors yet on earth, that when they rest from their labors their works may follow them in the good which they are still doing upon earth, and their own happiness even in heaven, be increased by the sight of souls once lost, but now saved, and in some degree prepared for the abodes of bliss by the instrumentality of this institution."

The next speaker was the Rev. Dr. Bedell, the Assistant Bishop elect of the Diocese of Ohio—a favorite alumnus of the Seminary, always its generous friend, and recently having manifested his great interest by procuring for it a participation in the munificence of two of his liberal parishioners. In his address he gratefully recognized his individual obligations to the Seminary for its faithful theological training, and "its atmosphere of true spiritual religion," which he there enjoyed during his student life, ascribing to them, "under the grace of God," the ability "he might" possess to preach with profit, and in all other ways minister well and wisely to his cure. He bore decided testimony to the excellency of his professors, and, on the intellectual and religious character of one since deceased, (the Rev. Reuel Keith, D. D.,) he passed an eulogium as just as it was delicate and affecting. He related with much interest his reminiscences of Seminary life, especially its devotional exercises among themselves, and the lay agencies of the students at the different stations for religious service in the surrounding country, the influence of all which, he considered, as worth more to the future pastor than any amount of mere theological instruction. He delivered his judgment in favor of a few large and well endowed seminaries, rather than many with limited advantages. Specified "the missionary spirit, which had always characterized 'the Hill' as the consideration which had "engaged the hearts of his friends from the Church of the Ascension," and given direction to their Christian liberality. The address closed thus: "I thank my friends for permitting me to be an instrument in their behalf of building here a tabernacle for the children of God. Most happily has my share in its dedication been the final act of a very blessed pastorate. God's holy name be praised who put it into their hearts. His be the glory. May He hear our prayers. May He follow this gift with His richest blessing. May many a generation of faithful ministers nurtured here, praise Him, through them, for the privileges they have secured to this institution by the erection of Aspinwall Hall."

After a short address by Bishop Johns, the congregation sang a portion of the "Veni Creator," united in prayer, and were dismissed with the benediction.

In the basement rooms of the old Seminary building, which was then standing just in the rear of Aspinwall Hall, the ladies of the Hill had prepared a bountiful and beautiful collation, to which all were invited, and of which they now partook with hearts cheered by the services of the morning, and enjoying the blessed charities of Christian fellowship—a day to be entered in capitals on the Seminary calendar.

In a note annexed to his address, Bishop MEADE mentions with merited distinction the name of another friend, to whose long continued services as Treasurer and Agent we are much indebted.

"Mr. Cassius F. Lee, of Alexandria." "From an early period to the present time, he has been actively engaged, by correspondence, in raising funds for the Education Society, for the various buildings which have been put up, acting as receiver and disburser of the same, as well as making contracts, and superintending the works. Much care and trouble have devolved upon him in the performance of these duties, and to no individual in the Diocese are we indebted for so large a share of labor and anxiety in our behalf, as to himself, besides the occasional advance of moneys when our funds were low."

Mr. Lee, by his judicious counsel, efficient and varied personal agencies, and generous pecuniary aid, has certainly laid the institution under obligations which no amount of coin could cancel, nor any words adequately express. Wherever his invaluable services are understood, he is with one consent considered as eminently

"THE SEMINARY'S BENEFACTOR."

It may be proper to state that the additional buildings to which Bishop MEADE referred, as necessary to complete the architect's plan, have since been erected,—"Bohlen Hall," by the generous friend whose name it bears, and "Meade Hall," by the members of the Church in Virginia.

General Convention of 1859.—The day after the consecration of the buildings on the Seminary Hill, the General Convention met in Richmond, Virginia. It brought together the Bishops of the Church, and a large number of clerical and lay deputies from the several States of the Union. It was an assembly, which, for learning, talents, piety and influence, was very distinguished.

In the absence of Bishop Brownell, who was detained at his home, in Connecticut, by ill-health, Bishop MEADE, by seniority of consecration, became the presiding officer in the House of Bishops. He was by no means remarkable for his acquaintance with parliamentary rules. For any such deficiency, his gentlemanly instincts and Christian spirit made ample amends. For all the duties of the Chair he proved himself quite competent, directing the proceedings of the House with courteous address and dignified decision.

It would be remarkable, if, even in an assembly of Bishops, no one were found who did not fancy himself slighted in the distribution of its agencies, and think it hard that he was not selected for a more honorable position than had been assigned to him. Such complaints are oftener to be imputed to the common infirmity of "thinking more highly of one's self than one ought to think," than to neglect, or partiality, on the part of the presiding officer. And then, there is in some very excellent persons a morbid sensitiveness, quick to take offence where none was intended, and where, in fact, no cause had been given.

Two illustrations of these remarks occurred in the Convention at Richmond, as appears from a manuscript in the Bishop's handwriting, designed to vindicate himself, if the necessity should occur. For this, happily, no occasion has been given, and the occurrences were of no importance, unless it be to sustain others similarly tried, by the assurance that "no strange thing has happened to them."

His official duties were laborious, and superadded to these was a constant, just concern, that the proceedings of the Convention should be honorable to the Church, and promotive of its true prosperity. He shared with the resident clergy in the responsibility of arranging for the accommodation of that body, and for the personal comfort of its members.

But its session in Richmond was a happy episode in his Episcopal life. Except in his mountain home, and in the midst of his children and grandchildren, he rarely, perhaps, appeared to more advantage than when participating with the good people of that part of his Diocese, in welcoming to their houses their fellow-churchmen who had come to the Convention, and in studying to render their visit as pleasant and profitable as possible.

It must have been impossible for him to avoid contrasting that grand assemblage with another, which met in that same city six and forty years before, and of which he was himself a member. It has already been described. "Only seven clergymen attended. Our deliberations were conducted in one of the committee rooms of the Capitol, sitting around a table." "There was nothing to encourage us to meet again." Now, that little handful had become a host, and in one of their own spacious and beautiful buildings receiving as their guests the thirty-six Bishops, 129 clerical and 106 lay delegates, assembled to legislate for a Church extending over the entire territory of the United States. Then, as he returned alone on horseback to his ministrations in the Stone Chapel in the distant county of Frederick, never expecting to cross the mountain again to attend another Convention, he found himself continually exclaiming in reference to the Church in Virginia, "Lost! lost! lost!" Now, as he looked upon the Church of which his own flourishing Diocese was a prominent portion, and saw its extent, and order, and beauty, and was thrilled by the *Gloria in Excelsis*, which again and again burst from the lips of the assembled brethren, gladdened by the blessing of God on their procedures, how could he refrain from exclaiming, in holy admiration and joy, "What hath God wrought?" "Not unto us, O Lord, not unto us, but unto Thy name give glory, for Thy mercy, and for Thy truth's sake!"

Usually at General Conventions, his infirmities rendered it necessary for him to take a recumbent posture, either on a bench or lounge, considerately provided for his accommodation. But he kept himself familiar with the business of the House, and was on his feet the moment his action was required. "Bishop Alonzo Potter was asked by a clergyman of Virginia, 'who was the ruling spirit in the House of Bishops?' He replied: 'There is a man who lies on the sofa from ill-health, who often seems half asleep, but let any question of moment come up, and he is wide awake, and wields an influence which no other man in the House of Bishops comes near.'"

After the business of the Convention is completed, and before adjourning without day, it is customary for the two Houses to meet for the purpose of listening to the Pastoral Letter. On this occasion (1859) no Pastoral was prepared. Both Houses, however, assembled as usual, and after appropriate prayers, the Senior Bishop delivered a very impressive Address, of which nothing has been preserved.

The annexed very imperfect and scarcely legible sketch, in his own handwriting, of an Address delivered at the close of one of his own Diocesan Conventions may not be unacceptable, as a specimen of his style, and spirit on such occasions.

"*Order.*" In a few short moments our services are over, and we part, some of us to meet no more on this side eternity. God has been, we trust, in the midst of us for good. If our acts have been noted down for the eyes of others, God has kept a record of the doings of our hearts, and we shall know them one day when the secrets of all hearts shall be revealed, at the great meeting above.

These, our meetings in the Church below, are highly important, and most fearfully interesting. Men will meet together in large numbers on earth for business, pleasure, for the display of talent, for war, or trade, literature. These will be. Shall not the most important of all subjects have its great assemblages and celebrations? God, Himself hath appointed them. Beside the weekly Sabbath and other assemblies; great feasts, three times a year from all parts of the land. "O 'twas a joyful sound to hear." Our Lord, when very young, attended one with His parents. At one of them, where the Apostles and first disciples were assembled, three thousand were converted by the plainest of sermons.

What are all the nations of Christendom? What are all the States of our Union? all the churches in the same Judeas, and Canaans and Jerusalems? And what our great meetings, but so many feasts of the Lord, where numbers come together?

I trust that the Spirit which was so bountifully poured out on thousands on the day of Pentecost, being sent down by our Lord, from the right hand of the Father, in answer to the prayers offered up with one accord from waiting hearts, has not been withheld from us; that it has been helping our infirmities, interceding within some with groaning for sin; that we have felt it good to be here. If only we have felt the spirit of penitence, truly it is good to set under the gospel ever new to sing the new and everlasting song for redeeming love, making melody in our hearts to the Lord—if our love to Christ and the brethren has been increased, and the promises been precious to us, our hearts enlarged towards the poor heathen, by the statements; if our desire after greater holiness, and more usefulness has been increased, and if we go home determined to be more faithful in our families and co-operate more with God's ministers.

We are parting, and which of us will assemble thus again? How many of those who meet at the last (Convention) have passed away? How many have lost friends who were not there? (something here is unintelligible). The manuscript continues: "When our children are thus early removed, there is good hope of them. But, when they have been admonished, and good and evil set before them, where is our hope? How many, during the last year, have died, whose friends have been obliged to mourn as those who have no hope? How many may, the present year? And oh! to be thus bereaved of friends, especially children, it is indeed to be bereaved. Oh Absalom, my son Absalom! how many Christian fathers may say, would I had died for thee, and left thee behind with the sweet hope that

God would have mercy on thee. Let this stimulate us to more prayer, and effort for their salvation, while living! Such is our parting counsel this night.

But I must address a parting word to my brethren of the ministry. We have great need to exhort each other, being poor weak creatures, earthen vessels. We have a great work. Who is sufficient for it? Oh how blessed the thought that our sufficiency is of God! And how short the time in which to do it! In the midst of life, God's ministers, as well as others, are in death—often cut off in the midst of their days. Some in the beginning, in youth. Death has been in the midst of us, and our families, brethren. Two of our number are wanting. They were victims to labor and exposure—fast spending and being spent during the short time of labor, and died in the cause. Blessed are such dead who "died in the Lord! They rest from their labors, and their works do follow and bless them! Let us follow their examples, and whatever our hands find to do, do it with all our might, lest the night come, when we cannot work. Who shall say, "my time is not yet?" The arrow may be on the wing. The youngest may die. The oldest must die early. Some of us are fast approaching the end of our course. Our eyes are dimmed, our natural force fast abating; our steps are becoming unsteady. We are tottering towards the grave, which may even now be open for us. We need help from God. Even if this be not so, if we are left over, some of those dearest may be taken. We may be bereaved of our children, of those dearer than children, than life itself, as some now feel in the deep of their hearts. But though life, friends, be spared, still, my brethren, we have sorrows and trials peculiar. If every heart knows its own bitterness, the hearts of God's ministers have bitterness to which the world is a stranger. From the oldest Bishop having the care of many Churches pressing on his soul, to the youngest deacon, there are fears and troubles. God

*21

alone can sustain us under trials, disappointments, mortifications, removals, want, sometimes poverty coming on like armed men upon wife and children. But, brethren, that God who sustained so many prophets, apostles and confessors under greater trials, will uphold us. The glorious privilege of laboring for souls is ours. Even though the more we love, the less we are loved, what a thought that, as Christ died to save His enemies, we may be instrumental in good to such. Our days of sorrow will soon be over, and we have much joy mingled with it. Let none be afraid to enter.

Ours is the sweetest, safest life after all. Our families will not perish from hunger; our sons and daughters will be provided for. It is a well proved fact, more of the sons of pious ministers become pious ministers of the gospel. [Incomplete.]

Let us, then, go to our several fields of labor, thanking God that we have such fields, and resolved to make them gardens of the Lord. Not by the sweat of our brow to make bread, but by the toil of our souls to save sinners, so far as man can do it. Let us begin anew, and abound more and more in love and good works; preaching more zealously, and in season and out of season make full trial of our ministry. Then, whether we meet again on earth —our ministry be abridged or lengthened—when we meet before the Lord, it will be with joy, and not with grief.

State of the Country.—Bishop MEADE's father, who, as has been related, was aid-de-camp to General Washington, was a Federalist of the old school. The principles and patriotism of the son were part of his patrimony. They commended themselves, in due time, to his own intelligent conviction, and, as he came to maturity, grew with his growth, and strengthened with his strength. They had his conscience and affection also, and became part of his religion, or they were so happily fused, that his patriotism was religious, and his religion patriotic. Next to his church, was his devotion to his country. To whatever promoted its prosperity, he was alive. Any discordant note or movement which affected this, disturbed his national sensibilities, which partook of his general character, and were very decided in their tone. It was not without the deepest concern that he perceived the strong sectional antagonism which obtained, and which was yearly becoming more violent. Against this, no matter in which quarter of its manifestation, he testified, in language of decided condemnation and solemn warning.

Whatever may have been his views on the subject of secession as a right, he was, with the great majority of the people of Virginia, opposed to it in fact, and, as the danger became more imminent, exerted himself the more to prevent the apprehended evil. At home he spoke with no uncertain sound. To his correspondents in the North, he wrote as one deeply anxious to avoid the apprehended calamity, and, even to brethren in England, he appealed for their aid in changing the current of public sentiment, which was sweeping the country into evils most devoutly to be deprecated.

In his address at the dedication of the Seminary Buildings, alluding to the generous donation of the Messrs. Aspinwall, he said, "We were the more ready to accept the proffered donation, because well assured that it was suggested and offered, not only in approbation of the views entertained and taught in this place, but in a spirit of the truest patriotism, and most enlarged philanthropy, by persons who soared above all party and sectional distinction in our country, and desired to patronize an institution which might continue to be, what it ever has been, *a bond of union to all its parts*, and, at the same time, a source whence faithful missionaries should issue to all the lands of the earth. Such, by God's blessing, we trust *it ever will be.*"

His letters to Bishop M'Ilvaine are of great interest:

MILLWOOD, Dec. 15, 1860.

MY DEAR BROTHER:

Yours of the seventh is just received. I have this morning written to Dr. Dyer that you would publish 2000 copies of your pamphlet, and that you would tell him how to dispose of them. My plan has been to take a Church Almanac, and mark the names of such of the clergy as I wished to supply, and send it to the printer, or some one who would envelope and direct them; you might not care to send to all the clergy. I should like one hundred myself, and you could reserve as many as you want. Bedell and Wharton should have fifty copies each.

Touching the affairs of our country, nothing but a most remarkable interposition of Providence can save the Union, and prevent an incalculable amount of mischief, poverty, and perhaps bloodshed. An article in the last *Southern Episcopalian*, and the uncommon action of the late Presbyterian Synod, show that the Churches sympathize with and sustain the politicians of the South. To a certain, and, I fear, a large extent, the union of both Church and country is no more. The division of the different denominations for some years past has sadly foreboded the present unhappy state of things. If Christian ministers, a body of more intelligence than any other in the land, and who may be supposed to excel all others in piety, cannot continue together to consult about the Kingdom of the Prince of Peace, even while the civil rulers have preserved their union, can we expect the selfish politicians to do it? You see that I am almost in despair. I am told that our clergy in Charleston and New Orleans speak and preach in favor of disunion. I fear some of our Bishops consent, or why have we heard of no remonstrance? In a few days the die will be cast, and South Carolina, the last to enter into the confederacy of Churches or States, will be first to leave it. Would that I could hope she would go alone, and not be followed. I will think and pray on the subject you have proposed to me, though as yet I see no path of action opened to me. It may be that South Carolina can be induced to suspend action for a few months, and then will be the time for something. Meanwhile, I should rejoice to have something from your pen, which might serve as a help to Bishop Brownell.

Most truly, yours in the Lord,

W. MEADE.

In the *Southern Churchman*, of last week, you will see a form of prayer for the present crisis, and a circular about our Education Society, in which my sentiments as to union are set forth.

MILLWOOD, Jan. 12, 1861.

MY DEAR BROTHER:

Your last came by yesterday's mail. I sympathize with you in your feelings as to the present state of our country, though I believe that good sense, self interest, religion, and other things will prevail, through God's good Providence, to avert the calamity of disunion; still it is proper to use all proper preventives on our part. The address you propose may have some effect, and might even turn the wavering scale.

I hope our Bishops would all concur in it. I should like to have had more time for consideration, but as you ask an immediate reply, I will say thus much, that I prefer your drawing up the letters, and think God has called you to it, putting the thought and desire in your heart. Bishop Brownell is too old and feeble in mind and body to do it. He would doubtless unite in it, for I see that his name stood first on the list of persons calling for a union meeting at Hartford some time since. * * * * * If you will draw up one and send it to me, and I approve the plan after more consideration, I will send it to Bishops Brownell and Hopkins for their concurrence, or rejection. It ought to be short, not political or argumentative—an entreaty and warning.

I send you our new Governor's inaugural address, which will show his views as to the probability of disunion. It strikes me as assuming too much on that side—that it is not well to treat disunion as so probable an event; we should beware of that in our address.

Hoping soon to hear from you, I commend you and your plan to the guidance and blessing of Heaven.

Yours truly,

W. MEADE.

January 15th.—"Through mistake or neglect, the above was not sent to the post-office, as intended, for the first mail. On thinking over the subject since, it has occurred to me that perhaps some of our Bishops might not enter fully with us into our views, and might object to be put into the position of recusants, if not signing it. Were we all together for consultation, it would be easier to decide the question. Possibly, the trial might betray some difference of sentiment not now apparent, or supposed to be even probable. Any approach to meddling in politics is considered *non episcopal*. Perhaps your first plan of a pastoral address to your own people might be the best as an example to the Bishops; though I expect some, both North and South, would be unwilling to contradict the opinions and feelings of a number of their people.

I have just set down my thoughts hastily for your consideration. I still think that self-interest with the men of the world, religion with the pious, and patriotism with the few who know the feeling, *will* save us."

RICHMOND, *May* 8, 1861.

MY DEAR BROTHER:

Most cordially do I reciprocate all that you say as to the probable separation between us in national and ecclesiastical associations; but I feel an assured confidence that such separation will never affect in the slightest degree the affectionate intercourse, and entire agreement which has ever existed between us. Still, it is most distressing to think that any such change will occur, as I fear is too probable.

A meeting of delegates from the Southern Dioceses is called, for the 4th of July, at Montgomery, which will, I suppose, inaugurate a Southern General Convention.

In relation to the late secession of students from our Seminary, I have heard from several students and others, that a most friendly relation subsisted between the Northern and Southern students to the last, and that the parting scene was a touching one. It had been determined some time before, that in case of the secession of Virginia, it would be prudent on the part of the Northern students to leave, as it would be impossible to tell what would be the effect of the act in many ways. The Southern students left two weeks after, as also the High School boys. The account of it in the New York papers was a gross mistake, and was contradicted by the *Southern Churchman.*

I have run down for a day to this place, in order to ascertain more accurately the state of our affairs. All Eastern Virginia is in continual expectation of assaults from the Federal forces, at one or two of various points. We are as yet unprepared for a proper defence, and may suffer much for some time, but final success in maintaining a state of secession is undoubted. I have slowly and reluctantly come to the conclusion, that we must separate. May God overrule all for the furtherance of the gospel, and the true welfare of our country.

I have just received your letter, and answer it by candle-light (contrary to the welfare of my eyes), as I must leave early in the morning. I have moved the Convention from Alexandria to Richmond, and expect to be here again on the 15th, if war does not prevent.

Most truly, yours in Christ.

W. MEADE.

RICHMOND, *May* 17, 1861.

MY DEAR BROTHER:

The transfer of Mr. —— is just received and accepted. I enclose you my views of the present crisis. You will see where we differ.

We are in daily expectation of an invasion from the Federal forces in various points. They outnumber us greatly, and have many advantages, bnt will be met with courage and determination by those who believe that they are unjustly and wantonly assailed. Virginia may soon be drenched with the blood of the flower of her youth, and the strength of her manhood. The piety of all denominations, especially of our Church, will be well represented. In great haste, and with true love.

Yours truly,
W. Meade.

The following extracts from a few of his letters to the Assistant Bishop, which were rescued from the destruction to which his library and many valuable papers were consigned, are of the same tone, and show the mind of Bishop Meade in reference to the sad state of civil affairs, then hastening to a crisis:

Dec. 9, 1860.

My Dear Brother:

The Governor having refused to appoint a Fast-day, the clergy of Richmond have agreed on one, and have united on that day. I wish I could have had you for consultation. Time and circumstances did not even allow my sending these through you. I fear, however, that all will be of no avail, and that God will not grant our prayer." *Quem Deus vult perdere, prius dementat.*

Millwood, *Jan.* 4, 1861.

"The news from the Virginia Legislature is somewhat cheering, and I hope this evening's mail will bring something of the same kind from Congress."

(*Without date*). "I am almost in despair about the Union. The action of the Episcopal and Presbyterian Clergy in South Carolina, as seen in the *Southern Episcopalian* and other papers, settles the point." "If the clergy in other denominations, after quarrelling for so many years on the subject of slavery, were obliged or preferred to separate, can we expect anything else of half the politicians and people. The Churches are the most guilty, before God.

Yours truly,
W. Meade.

The extracts are few and brief, but nothing more is needed to show the strong Union feeling of the writer; and such, without the slightest abatement, continued to be his spirit up to the day when he received intelligence of the proclamation which declared the coercive policy of the General Government, and called for an army to carry that policy into effect. This action, which united the South in resistance of invasion, completely changed the views and feelings of the Bishop. His convictions of duty now accorded with the course to which his State had been driven, and although his sense of professional propriety prevented him from any active participation in its defence, he believed it to be right, and with deep sorrow of soul for the sad necessity, gave it his warm sympathy and decided approval.

The correctness of this representation is rendered unquestionable by his own communication to the Convention of his Diocese, which met in Richmond, May 16, 1861.

Having disposed of matters usually embraced in the Address required by the Canons, he proceeds:

"I now ask your attention to a few remarks concerning the present unhappy condition of our State and country.

"My brethren and friends will bear me witness, how carefully I have ever avoided, in all my communications, the least reference to anything partaking of a political character, and how I have earnestly warned my younger brethren against the danger of injuring the effect of their sacred ministry by engaging in discussions which are so apt to disturb the peace of society. But in the present circumstances of our country, the cause of religion is so deeply involved, that I feel not only justified, but constrained, to offer a few remarks for your consideration.

"It has pleased God to permit a great calamity to come upon us. Our whole country is preparing for war. Our own State, after failing in her earnest effort for the promotion of peace, is, perhaps, more actively engaged in all needful measures for maintaining the position which she has, after much consideration, deliberately assumed, than any portion of the land.

"A deeper and more honest conviction, that if war

should actually come upon us, it will be, on our part, one of self-defence, and, therefore, justifiable before God, seldom, if ever, animated the breasts of those who appealed to arms. From this consideration, and from my knowledge of the character of our people, I believe that the object sought for will be most perseveringly pursued, whatever sacrifice of life, and comfort, and treasure may be required. Nor do I entertain any doubt as to the final result, though I shudder at the thought of what may intervene before that result is secured. May God in great mercy, and with His mighty power, interpose, and grant us speedy peace instead of protracted war!

"But can it be, that at this period of the world, when so many prayers are offered up for the establishment of Christ's kingdom in all the earth, and such high hopes are entertained that the zealous efforts put forth will be successful, and our country be one of the most effective and honored instruments for producing the same,—that the great work shall be arrested by such fratricidal war, as that which is now so seriously threatened? Is there not room enough for us all to dwell together in peace in this widely-extended country, so large a portion of which is yet unsettled, and may not be until the world that now is shall be no more? The families or nations which sprung from two venerable patriarchs of old, could find room enough in the little pent-up land of Judea to live in peace, by going the one to one hand, and the other to the opposite. At a later period, when Israel and Judah separated, and the latter, having the city and temple in possession, and the supremacy, according to prophecy, was preparing to go up against the former and reduce the people to submission, and bring them back to union, the Lord himself came down and forbade it, saying: 'Thou shalt not go up nor fight against your brethren, the children of Israel. Return every man to his house, for this thing is of me.' And they hearkened unto the Lord, and ever after, the history of the two kingdoms is written in the same volume, in which are also recorded the evidences of God's favor to both; and though sometimes at controversy, yet how often were they found side by side defending the ancient boundaries of Judea against surrounding nations. God grant that our country may learn a lesson from this sacred narrative! Let none think that I am unmindful of law and order, and of the blessings of union. I was trained in a different school. I have clung with tenacity to the hope of preserving the Union to the last moment. If I know my own heart, could the sacrifice of the poor remnant of my life have contributed in any degree to its maintenance, such sacrifice would have been cheerfully made. But the developments of public feeling, and the course of our rulers, have brought me slowly, reluctantly, sorrowfully, yet most decidedly, to the painful conviction, that, notwithstanding attendant dangers and evils, we shall consult the welfare and happiness of the whole land by separation. And who can desire to retain a Union which has become so hateful, and by the application of armed force, which, if successful, would make it ten times more hateful, and soon lead to the repetition of the same bloody contests?

"I trust, therefore, that the present actual separation of so many and such important portions of our country may take place without further collision, which might greatly hinder the establishment of the most friendly and intimate relations which can exist with separate establishments. I trust that our friends at a distance, and now in opposition to us, will most seriously review their judgment, and inquire whether the evils resulting from a war to sustain their wishes and opinions as to a single confederacy, will not far exceed those apprehended from the establishment of a second — an event far more certain than the result of the American Revolution at the time of its occurrence.

In connection with this civil and geographical separation in our country, and almost necessarily resulting from it, the subject of some change of the ecclesiastical relations of our Diocese must come under consideration. There is a general and a strong desire, I believe, to retain as much as possible of our past and present happy intercourse with those from whom we shall be in other matters divided. A meeting is already proposed for this purpose in one of the seceded States, whose plans, so far as developed, I will submit to the consideration of this body at its present session.

"I cannot conclude without expressing the earnest desire that the ministers and members of our Church, and all the citizens of our State, who are so deeply interested in the present contest, may conduct it in the most elevated Christian spirit, rising above uncharitable and indiscriminate imputations on all who are opposed. Many there are, equally sincere, on both sides, as there ever have been in all the wars and controversies that have been waged on earth; though it does not follow that all have the same grounds of justice and truth on which to base their warfare.

"It was the maxim of an ancient sage, that we should always treat our friends as those who might one day be our enemies, and to treat our enemies as those who may one day be our friends. While abhorring, as I am sure we all do, the former part of this cold-hearted maxim, let us cherish and adopt the latter, so congenial with the spirit of our holy religion. The thought of even a partial separation from those who have been so long dear to me, is anguish to my soul. But there is a union of heart in our common faith and hope which can never be broken. The Church in Virginia has more dear friends and generous patrons amongst those who are on the opposite side of this painful controversy than any other, and feels most deeply the unhappy position in which we are placed.

"As our State has, to its high praise, endeavored to avert the evils now threatened, so may our Church, and all the others in Virginia, by prayer and the exercise of true charity, endeavor to diminish that large amount of prejudice and ill-will which so unhappily abounds in our land.

"Let me, in conclusion, commend to your special prayers all those who have devoted themselves to the defence of the State. From personal knowledge of many of them, and from the information of others, there is, already, I believe, a large portion of religious principle and genuine piety to be found among them. I rejoice to learn that in many companies, not only are the services of chaplains and other ministers earnestly sought for, but social prayer meetings held among themselves. Our own Church has a very large proportion of communicants among the officers of our army, and not a few among the soldiers. Let us pray that grace may be given them to be faithful soldiers of the Cross, as well as valiant and successful defenders of the State.

"If all of us do our part faithfully, and according to the principles of our holy religion, we may confidently leave the issue with God, who will overrule all for good."—(*Journal*, 1861.)

This admirable address, so expressive of the composure and clearness, and charity and active piety of the Bishop, at a time when the storm of political excitement was coming to its height, and sweeping with disturbing power even the Church itself, possesses a permanent and very peculiar interest, and it presents the character of its author in an elevation, easier to be admired, than attained.

The committee to whom it was referred reported the following resolutions, which were unanimously adopted:

"1. *Resolved*, That this Convention, having heard with deep interest the true and timely statements of our venerable Diocesan, in reference to the present political and ecclesiastical condition of our affairs, cordially concur in the views presented, and sympathize fully in the kind and Christian spirit in which they are so wisely declared.

"2. *Resolved*, That a committee, consisting of the two Bishops, three other clergymen, and three laymen, be appointed, as a provisional committee, to act during the recess of the Convention on all matters connected with our relations to other Dioceses, and the clerical and lay members of the Committee shall serve as delegates in any Convention which may be agreed upon by other similarly situated Dioceses. All the proceedings of this Committee to be reported for the approval of the Convention of the Diocese of Virginia.

"J. JOHNS,
"WILLIAM SPARROW,
"J. GRAMMER,
"THOS. S. GHOSLSTON,
"JAMES GALT,
"R. H. CUNNINGHAM."

In the Fall of 1861, the Bishop wrote an appeal, which will sufficiently explain itself and furnish another evidence of his humane consideration for others, and his readiness to deny himself in providing for their necessities.

"*Dear Brethren and Friends* :

The approach of winter, at all times, admonishes us to make some preparation in the way of clothing and covering for ourselves and families, lest we suffer, either by day or night, from the severity of the weather. On those who abound in such things, the duty devolves of remembering the claims of the poor and suffering. A most urgent appeal is made to us now, in view of the approaching winter, for suitable covering for our soldiers, when their only houses may be light tents. Our peculiar circumstances render it impossible to obtain a supply of blankets and coverlids in the usual way, and through former channels, and the families of Virginia have been called on to examine their household stores, and from them draw forth the needed supply. I doubt not but that this call has already been heard, and in a good degree answered, but feeling anxious that those who are in some measure committed to my spiritual care, should abound in this liberality, I have determined to address a few words to them, rather as suggestive of the mode of performing this duty, than as exhorting to the duty itself; believing that to the latter, there is little or no need of exhortation.

It has pleased Providence to bless a large portion of those whom I address with the means of a generous hospitality, by day and by night, in winter and in summer, which they delight to exercise. Their bedrooms are abundantly supplied with coverings in a cold winter night for numerous guests, more numerous oftentimes than the demands of charity require. Let us look over our stores, and see whether in the present emergency some articles might not be spared to the soldiers who are fighting for our dearest rights, even though our accustomed hospitality be, for a time, somewhat diminished. And if we have already done this, and more be needed, let us look down upon our floors and see if some of those luxuries of which our Revolutionary fathers were ignorant, might not, if necessity exists, be converted into the means of affording comfort to the soldier in his tent.

I am well aware how much our mothers, wives, sisters and daughters have done in behalf of the poor, the sick and the wounded, and how cheerfully they have done it, and how much the young and the old of our own sex have sacrificed in this cause; how much more they are prepared to sacrifice, and, therefore, I am sure that they will rightly receive these suggestions. It is only in this way that I can contribute my mite to the furtherance of that war of self-defence, which has been forced upon us, and which is waged in such a manner as to show that all our energies are required to secure to ourselves and transmit to our children those blessings which our forefathers purchased for us, by similar labors and sufferings. Commending you and our cause to the blessing of that God, without whom all our efforts and suffering will fail,

I remain,

Your friend and brother,

WILLIAM MEADE,

Bishop of the Prot. Epis. Church of Virginia."

The extreme Southern Dioceses had early entered upon the formation of a separate ecclesiastical organization within the limits of the Confederacy. Meetings had been held, committees appointed, a draft of a constitution and a body of canons prepared, and a provisional Convention called, to meet in Columbia, South Carolina, in November 1861, to which all the Southern Dioceses were requested to send delegates, and all the Bishops were invited to be present. The Diocese of Virginia had therefore taken no part in the preliminary movement. By the adoption of the 2nd Resolution reported by the special Committee on the Bishop's Address of 1851, and the election of a provisional committee to act for the Diocese after the adjournment of the Convention, and also to represent the Diocese in any Convention which might assemble the Diocese was in a position of readiness to act as circumstances might require.

When the Convention assembled in Columbia, the Bishops of Virginia, with the clerical and lay delegates, were there, and took part in the last review of the constitutions and canons, which were afterwards adopted by the conventions of the several dioceses, and because the Law of the Protestant Episcopal Church in the Southern Confederacy.

In anticipation of that Convention, Bishop Meade committed to paper his thoughts on certain matters as proper to be considered.

"Some thoughts in view of the proposed and probable connection of the Diocese of Virginia, with those of the other seceded States."

"It has pleased the great Head of the Church to give to the Diocese of Virginia a peculiar history among her sister Dioceses, both before and since our civil and ecclesiastical severance from England. In point of numbers, both as to the clergy and laity, she was far before all others, under the colonial establishment, and her influence on the Revolution was in due proportion. Her fall, from power and numbers, was also great in like proportion, so that, in a few years after, she had scarce a name to live, and was despaired of by the rest of the Church in the General Convention of 1808.

God, in His wisdom and goodness (who chooses ofttimes to use weak things, and things that are not, to effect His most gracious purposes), determined to put life into the dry bones of the Church in Virginia, or, at least, to strengthen the things that remained, and were ready to die, and to make use of her for no little good, not only among the citizens of Virginia, attached to our own and other denominations, but also to many beyond the bounds of our State, especially to those of our communion.

This He has done by raising up a number of pious and evangelical young ministers in Virginia, and elsewhere, and sending them to our vineyard, especially by placing over us a zealous Bishop, (Bishop Moore,) who presented the Gospel instead of a mere moral system, such as was too common with many ministers at that day, both in England and America.

But the great instrument for giving the Church in Virginia an influence for good in our own State, and elsewhere, was the establishment of a Theological Seminary.

While most other Dioceses wished and endeavored to establish a general Seminary, to which candidates from all parts of the Church should be sent, and where the greatest uniformity of sentiment should be promoted under the same Professors and Trustees, the Church of Virginia, fearing some evil effects of this system, and seeing many advantages in having a school of her own, determined upon the effort to establish the same, which, by the blessing of God, has been most happily successful.

For the same reason, the Bishops, clergy, and laity of Virginia, in the General Councils of the Church, and elsewhere, have opposed the consolidation of power in the General Convention, whether as to the training of ministers, the publication of books and tracts, the management of Sunday schools, the conduct of missions, foreign or domestic. Experience has confirmed us in the wisdom of such a course. We have seen that confusion, unhappiness, strife and disappointment have attended the contrary.

A civil division which has taken place in our country, leading to the proposal for a new ecclesiastical confederation, imposes upon us the duty of considering what old things are to be retained, and what new things to be introduced.

In a reconstruction of our ecclesiastical system, we have the benefit of the experience of more than three-fourths of a century, during which the trial of the best means of promoting the welfare of our Zion has been diligently made. The successes and the failures of ourselves and our fathers are before us, and it becomes us to learn wisdom from the same.

Our earliest fathers, with a wise foresight, warned against too much legislation on the part of the General Convention, as endangering the most attainable unity in sentiment and action through our widely extended Church. Such warning has not been lost upon the Church. Though experiments have been made in the way of consolidation, they have been found so productive of discord, and have so failed of effect, that they have been either relinquished, or modified in their execution, so as to prove the wisdom of our fathers, and to furnish no encouragement for their repetition.

So strong is the opposition to the consolidation of power in any central representative body, in our Southern mind, arising from the past and present history of the United States, that there can be little danger of our erring much in the way of attempting undue legislation, or of placing too much power in the hands of any agency of our Southern Ecclesiastical Convention.

Voluntary associations, or Diocesan societies, in which individuals or congregations may exercise their charities, and put forth their efforts in such manner as shall seem most likely to effect most good, will doubtless be encouraged.

The Bishops, clergy, and laity of Virginia will never surely relinquish to any other confederation, that liberty of action for which they have so long and successfully contended under our former one, and by which they have effected so much good in our own Diocese and in the Church at large. In nothing has the doctrines and con-

22

duct of Virginia been more approved and followed by others throughout the land, than in regard to the establishment of seminaries and other associations of a Diocesan character, independent of the General Convention.

Our Bishops, and other delegates to the meeting at Columbia, will doubtless see that no power of usefulness belonging to the Diocese of Virginia be surrendered into other hands, and thus be a cause of future strife.

The subject of representation, which has been the subject of recrimination and complaint for the last forty years, will doubtless be considered, and equitably settled. Some difficulties in the way of it in the old confederation will, I think, be so diminished in our new, as to present no serious hindrance to the disposition of this part of the subject."

No General Theological Seminary was proposed or desired. No General Missionary Society connected with the General Council was, or could have been, organized. The ratio of representation, which he wished to have equitably adjusted, found no favor. Yet the statement of his views is too important to be omitted here, and may yet be of service to the Church.

Bishop Meade, being by date of consecration, the senior of the Southern Bishops, was the Presiding Bishop of the Church in the Confederate States. The only service pertaining to this position which he had occasion to perform, was that which was connected with the consecration of the Rev. R. H. Wilmer, D. D., Bishop elect of Alabama. The frequent occupancy of the railroads for military purposes, interfered with the regular transmission of letters, and rendered travelling very uncertain, so that the requisite arrangements were not made without difficulty and delay. It was ascertained that the presence of three Bishops could not be relied on, unless Richmond was selected as the place for the consecration, and the Presiding Bishop be present as one of the consecrators. His advanced age, his infirmities at the time, and the inclement season, combined to render the journey from Clarke to Richmond, very hazardous. But he was so impressed with the importance of the object, that he would not allow any personal inconvenience, or apparent risk, to prevent its accomplishment. He promptly appointed Richmond as the place for the consecration, and engaged, Providence permitting, to preside in the service; which he faithfully kept, and on the 6th of March, in St. Paul's Church, Richmond, consecrated the Rev. R. H. Wilmer, D. D., as Bishop of the Protestant Episcopal Church in the Diocese of Alabama, Bishops Elliott and Johns uniting in the imposition of hands.

The sad sequel is furnished in the funeral Address delivered in the same Church, March 17, by the Right Rev. J. Johns, D. D., which is therefore annexed, with the addition of notes relative to particulars not included in the Address.

ADDRESS.

"And His disciples came and took up the body, and buried it, and went and told Jesus."—Matt. 14 : 12.

My Christian Brethren :—I have scarcely courage for the sad service which devolves upon me I could not brace myself for the effort, but for the special commission which I dare not decline. A commission not from the living, but from the now dead; from the lips of the honored and beloved father in God, whose departure has stricken our hearts with sorrow, and around whose mortal remains we are assembled, to render them the last tribute of respect and affection.

My commision is not to present for your admiration the rare and decided excellencies of his character, and recite the deeds of his remarkable life. All such eulogy, either from the pulpit or the press, he strongly deprecated. A just regard for his wishes on that subject repeatedly and explicitly expressed, measurably restrains utterances for which every feeling of my heart pleads, and which usage, on such occasions, authorizes you to expect. Happily, though it may be that formal panegyric was never more deserved, it certainly has rarely, if ever, been less needed. He, who, more than any other man was honored, as the instrument in raising the Church in Virginia, from what was pronounced hopeless extinction, who gave to this work his early manhood, his vigorous maturity, and the wisdom and efficiency of advanced life, whose extensive itinerations in this service year after year, for more than half a century, had made his name a household word and his face familiar throughout the Diocese; his patriarchal presence, the privilege of the people, and his wise instructions prized as precious precepts; surely he needs no formal panegyric. His praise is in all the churches of his cure, and his spiritual children are his living epistles of commendation, written, not with ink, but with the Spirit of the living God—not on tables of stone, but in fleshy tables of the heart.

It was unusual to find our good Bishop here at this time of the year, and nothing but a case of great importance would have justified his leaving his home in the valley, and encountering the fatigue and exposure of the tedious journey. Such he deemed the accomplishment of the consecration of Dr. Wilmer. Repeated arrangements had been proposed to effect it without the presence of our venerable Bishop, for we were unwilling that a life so invaluable, should be subjected to the least unnecessary danger. But, when all other arrangements failed, and he was informed that Richmond was selected for another experiment, which would also be unsuccessful, for the want of the requisite number of consecrators, unless he could be here, he thought his duty clear, and though laboring under a deep seated cold, he essayed, and accomplished the journey on a very inclement day, and under circumstances of great discomfort. The result was, the serious aggravation of his malady, rendering it exceedingly doubtful whether he would, after all his efforts, be able to unite in the consecration. When the day appointed came, he was in truth more fitted for the repose of his chamber and couch, than for the services of the chancel. But, with a resolution and energy which never failed him when duty seemed plain, he roused his enfeebled physical powers to action just adequate to the emergency, and came only when his presence could no longer be dispensed with, and officiated merely in the act of consecration. As he moved slowly up the aisle to his seat in the chancel, the impairment of his once powerful frame was affectingly apparent. And when the Bishops present helped him from his chair to his feet, and supported and united with him in the imposition of hands, whilst that voice, once of such sweetness and compass, now tremulous and broken, enunciated with difficulty the Apostolic Commission—whose heart was not saddened by the spectacle?

It proved to be the last official act of his long and laborious, faithful and fruitful ministry; an act to him of great and varied interest and importance. It elevated to the Episcopate the son of a valued friend and fellow-laborer in the successful enterprise of resuscitating the Church in Virginia. It provided an active and earnest and capable Bishop to supply the vacancy in the Diocese of Alabama occasioned by the death of the lamented Bishop Cobbs, and it unmistakably declared the conviction of the Church in the several Confederate States, that the disruption of the civil government rendered necessary the cessation of the general ecclesiastical system, under which, by conventional arrangement, the different Dioceses had been united, and consequently devolved on us the responsibility of perpetuating evangelical truth and order in our churches, by independent ecclesiastical action. It was its significancy in this respect that gave the consecration of Dr. Wilmer its peculiar interest to Bishop MEADE, and decided him to encounter the exposure and fatigue of the journey to Richmond, leaving the issue in the hands of God.*

---

*The residence of Bishop MEADE was in Clarke Co., near Millwood, at the western base of the Blue Ridge; a county of remarkable fertility and beauty, and endeared to him by the associations of his youth, and as the happy home where his children and his children's children had grown up around him.

The undulating ground about the house, covered with its rich turf, he had adorned with every variety of the fir and cedar, interspersed with the most beautiful shade trees which the nurseries could furnish. The adjacent garden abounded in choice grapes and other fruits of which the Bishop was very fond, and which he was gratified to gather with his own hand,

The important object has been accomplished, but to us, at a cost which no one can compute. The mental and corporeal effort required, produced and prolonged an unnatural excitement in the Bishop's system, which at the time seemed like genuine strength returning, and, as he mingled so genially during the afternoon, in social intercourse with his brethren, and friends, under the roof where he had been received and cherished with Christian hospitality and filial devotion, we were ready to interpret the whole transaction of the memorable day, as a token for good, full of promise. But our exposition of the scene, and the sequences was sadly mistaken. The apparent glow which gladdened us was not the animation of returning health, but of the nature of those unaccountable transient re-kindlings which precede and indicate approaching dissolution. The inspiriting influence of the impressive occasion declined as the interval increased, and was not renewed. An accession of disease, an increasing embarrassment of vital organs soon became apparent.*

The chronic affection of the heart, of which for years he was conscious, and from which he long expected sudden death, now developed itself in fearful action. For several days and nights his manly frame bore the assault with ex-

---

for the refreshment of his visitors, as he conducted them about the grounds.

No one could be his companion in these walks, without perceiving his strong attachment to "Mountain View." When he left this loved home he expected to be back in a few days, and carried with him but a single change of raiment. How mercifully it was hidden from him, that the cherished spot was soon to pass under the control of the invaders of our soil, and could no longer be a home for him!

God, who veiled the coming sad event from his vision, prepared better things for his faithful servant; led him by a way he had not anticipated to another "Mountain View," showed him the Celestial Hills in their attractiveness, kindled to greater ardor his heavenly longings, and then translated him to his Father's house, and its incorruptible inheritance, its blessed company of loved ones, and to Jesus, his Redeemer.

His journey from his earthly to his heavenly home was short. The single change of raiment was sufficient. The vestments of the way were needed but a few days; then the robes of light and glory, for ever and ever.

*On the following Monday, (March 17,) when I entered his room, I found him still in bed. After some conversation in reference to his state of health, he said, "Let me rise, and walk a little." I assisted him to put on a dressing-gown. Then, with his arm around my neck for support, he moved a few steps, but with so much difficulty that he begged me to take him back to his bed again. When I laid him down he remarked, "It is all over, my strength is gone," and after a moments reflection, "It is as good a time as any for me to die."

traordinary powers of endurance, and his Christian spirit, strengthened by the word of God, sustained his great bodily suffering with exemplary patience. "Read me," he said, to a friend, "a portion of the Sacred Scriptures." "What shall I read?" "The history of the Crucifixion." And when this was done, he observed, "Yes, six hours did our Lord suffer the intense agony of the Cross, and that for us, for our sins, and shall we complain of our sufferings? 'The cup which my Father hath given me, shall I not drink it?'" Throughout the severe struggle of nature his mind was clear, his faith strong, and his hope steadfast.

Few things impressed me more during the last days of his life than his perfect naturalness. Affectation in every form and degree was always disgusting to him. What are termed scenes in connection with religious character and experience, especially on the supposed nearness of death, he regarded with no favor. He was so accustomed to bear his religion about with him in all his intercourse with men and all his secular business, and so in the habit of bearing both, with him, in his hours of devotion at a throne of grace, that they were not kept separate and apart, as if incompatible, but intermingled continually in his thoughts and sympathies, and came out in close relation in his speech. It was strikingly and instructively so during his last illness. In health he habitually thought and acted as if there was but a step between him and death, judgment and eternity; and when he knew and said, that the ensuing night or following day would end his connection with earth, the welfare of his country and the interests of his friends were as near his heart, and as emphatically on his lips, as if he expected to share their portion here for many years. To one of his respected presbyters who was at his bedside taking leave of him, he thus closed his solemn counsel: "Speak boldly to your people. Tell them to persevere in sustaining their country in this struggle. The war against us is iniquitous. I am persuaded that God is with us, and will give us success."

He knew that the courageous spirit of a living General would not be hindered, but helped, by the presence and power of the constraining love of Christ, and he had uo fear that the faith and purity of a dying Bishop would be impaired by the glow of genuine patriotism. He was on his death-bed precisely what we all saw him to be in life, except his sufferings.

On Thursday morning, the day before his death, he requested others who were present to retire, that he might communicate something to me in private. When we were alone he said:

"I wish to bear my testimony on some things of importance.

"The views of evangelical truth and order which I have held and advocated for fifty years, I approve, and exhort my brethren, North and South, to promote more than ever.

"My course in civil affairs I also approve: resistance to secession at first, till circumstances made it unavoidable. I trust the South will persevere in separation.

"I believe there are thousands in the North who condemn the course of their administration towards us, and in time will express themselves openly.

"The prospect of rest from sin and suffering is attractive, though I am willing to remain and take my part in the labors and trials which may be before us.

"My hope is in Christ, 'the Rock of Ages.'

"I have no fear of death, and this, not from my courage, but from my faith.

"The present seems a proper time for my departure. I am at peace with God through Jesus Christ, my Lord, and in charity with all men, even our bitterest enemies.

"All that has ever been said in commendation of me I loathe and abhor, as utterly inconsistent with my consciousness of sin.

"I commend you and all my brethren to the tender mercies of Christ, and pray for his blessing on the Church in Virginia."

When he ceased I withdrew to the adjoining room, and in conformity with his suggestion, immediately committed the testimony to writing, and availed myself of the earliest opportunity to read it to him, and receive his affirmation of its accuracy.*

* He observed, "It is accurate, but alter one expression. Instead of 'approve our cause,' write, 'condemn the course of their administration towards us.' "

NOTE 2. On Thursday evening he asked, "What o'clock is it?" On being told, he said, "Then I shall not see Richard," who at his father's request had gone to "Mountain View" to bring away certain papers of importance, that they might be deposited in some place of less exposure. The Bishop perceived that the hour for the arrival of the cars had passed,

Such, beloved brethren, was the special commission to which I referred, and from the painful execution of which I could not shrink.

The message is duly delivered. The weighty words of the wise leader, his legacy of love, are with you.

Death has since sealed his lips in silence. He has fought a good fight — finished his course — kept the faith — received the crown of righteousness, and entered into his glorious rest. If the gift which I covet for you and myself, "a double portion of his spirit," depended on the condition named to Elisha, that blessing would be ours — for I witnessed his departure, and cried from my heart, "My father, my father, the chariot of Israel, and the horsemen thereof."

Our bereavement — the bereavement of our Church and country — how inexpressibly afflicting!

What can we do — to whom can we go in our sorrow and bewilderment, but to Jesus, who was "anointed to bind up the broken-hearted, to appoint to those who mourn, beauty for ashes, the oil of joy for mourning, and the garment of praise for the spirit of heaviness." What can we tell Him, but that we can have no compensation for our great loss, but His own self, by the special gift of the Comforter, and so pray humbly, and earnestly, and perseveringly, "Come, Lord Jesus, manifest Thyself to us with greater vividness and power; draw us into more in-

---

and as he felt, and had so expressed himself, that he "would not live through the day," he meekly relinquished all hope of seeing "Richard." The other sons were in Clarke county, and as there was no mail to that section of the State, they were ignorant of their father's illness. The only one of his own family privileged to be with him, was the Rev. Wm. H. Meade, the eldest son of that son whose return he had so earnestly desired.

NOTE 3. A Convention for the purpose of forming a General Bible Society was about so assemble in Augusta, Georgia. The Bishop adverted to this with great satisfaction, spoke of the interest with which Bishops White, Griswold and others had regarded the U. S. Bible Society, expressed his own earnest desire for the success of the proposed Society for the South, and his hope and belief that it would be zealously sustained by Southern Bishops and their Dioceses, and directed that a telegraphic communication should be sent immediately to Augusta, requesting that his name might be enrolled among the Life Members.

The communication was unnecessary. Before the Convention was organized he had passed to the participation of the glorious privileges of a Life Member of the "General Assembly of the Church of the first-born in Heaven."

timate and transforming fellowship with Thee; come, perfect Thy strength in us, and possess our hearts more and more with Thy love; enlighten our understanding with the illumination of the Holy Ghost, that all our wishes and desires may centre in the advancement of Thy glory and in the salvation of Thy people."

So, dear brethren, the prayer of our departed father in God for us all will be soon and fully answered. "The tender mercies of Christ will be upon us, and His blessing upon the Church in Virginia."

After the service in the church, the funeral procession moved to Hollywood Cemetery, where the coffin was laid in a vault, till suitable arrangements could be made for its permanent interment.

In the afternoon of the same day, there was a meeting of the clergy then in Richmond, the proceedings of which are thus reported:

"The Committee, through their chairman, having retired for a short time, returned with the following resolutions, which were unanimously adopted:

"WHEREAS, It has pleased Almighty God to remove from his labors to his rest, our beloved Bishop, the Rt. Rev. WILLIAM MEADE, D. D., and we, a portion of his clergy, providentially assembled in the city of Richmond, do desire to record our deep sense of the loss sustained by ourselves, by the Diocese over which he presided, and the Church at large; therefore, be it resolved,

1. That in the loss of Bishop MEADE, we feel, as individuals, that we have been bereaved of a father most loved and most revered; and, as members of the Church, of a leader, the loss of whose godly counsel and faithful guidance we most deeply mourn.

2. That in the midst of our sorrow we would bow meekly to the will of God in this dispensation, acknowledging His mercy to us, and to His Church, in sparing our

late Bishop to us so long, and preserving him through so many dangers; and that though prevented, by Bishop MEADE's own expressed wishes, from heaping praise and commendation upon him, we yet feel it our privilege and our duty to thank our Heavenly Father for the grace of God which was in him, and are constrained to say, that he was unsurpassed in all the qualities which can adorn the highest office in the Church on earth.

3. That as the noblest tribute we can pay to his memory, we will, by the aid of the Spirit of God, endeavor to follow in his footsteps as he followed Christ.

4. That we do hereby express our deepest sympathy with the afflicted family and relations of our beloved Diocesan in this our common bereavement; and trust that in the love and mercy of God, they may find support and abundant consolation."

In his address to the Convention which met in Richmond the ensuing May, Bishop Johns, in reporting the services which he had performed during the past year, introduced, in its proper connection, the following reference to the affliction with which the Diocese had been visited:

"March 9th.—I preached in St. John's Church, Richmond. This, dear brethren, was the week of our bereavement. On Friday, the 14th, at 7 A. M., it pleased Almighty God to remove from us our venerable and beloved Bishop, whom He had chosen to cherish our Church in Virginia during its infancy; to aid in bringing it up in the nurture and admonition of the Lord, and long honored and blessed as its chief pastor. The habit which forms by duration, and the love which excellence and usefulness inspire and invigorate, had so bound and endeared him to us all, that the thought of being without him was not seriously entertained, and we were ill prepared for the afflictive separation. Perhaps we ought to have been more discerning, and gathered premonitions from the significant service with which our last Convention was opened. When the Bishop, under a solemn sense of the appropriateness and duty, officiating as the preacher, delivered his semi-centenary discourse, spoke of the experience of his long and eventful life with the deep humility of a sage, that the benefit of his carefully acquired knowledge might accrue to us, there was impressively evident 'a ripeness and perfectness of age in Christ,' which might have advised us that his maturity for heaven was attained, and 'the time of his departure at hand.' For many years, his bodily infirmities, though they did not abate his intellectual labors or suspend the use of his pen, but only rendered them more abundant and beneficial, yet did deprive us of his impressive services in the pulpit. His capability for these, however, was recently restored, and in that memorable discourse there was an unction of piety, and a rich melody of religious thought, in which our ears should have recognized the dying notes of our aged apostle.

The last few pages of this discourse, preached "in the fifty first year of his ministry, and thirty-second of his Episcopate," are of very peculiar interest.

"And now, if I may be permitted to close with some personal reflections, I would say, that in reviewing my life, since entering the ministry, I can truly say, that not a day or waking hour has been so spent that the word evil may not justly be applied to it, because so largely partaking of sin. I know that I have never performed one single act without some sin intermingling with it, either as to the motive or manner; not doing all to the glory of God, but allowing the desire of human praise to get into the heart and dwell there. Thus has "my sin been ever before me," and when my eye has caught some near glimpse of God, I have said, "I abhor myself," feeling "that no clean thing can come out of such an unclean one." When I have read that God "charges even His angels with folly," how often and from the deep of my heart have I exclaimed with David, "O God, thou knowest my foolishness, and my sins are not hid from Thee." Thus do I declare my doctrine and experience as to human depravity. It has ever been a source of shame to me that so many of my friends and brethren were conscious and observant of my infirmities, and the more so, because they have dealt so forbearingly and kindly towards them. Had I these fifty years to live over again, I see many things to be amended, and would fain hope that I should be enabled so to do; and yet, I would not ask or wish such a repetition, lest even greater dishonor come, through me, to the sacred cause. As already declared, I have now gone beyond my three-score years and ten, and have no desire or expectation of reaching that period when "age is nothing but labor and sorrow, and the grasshopper might be a burthen." At present I have cause to be thankful for a most unexpected share of health, though but little strength is connected with it, my eyes having become dim and my natural force much abated. With such as I have, and as long as it lasts, I desire to serve my Lord and Master and my poor fellow-sinners, hoping that in some small degree "for me to live is Christ," though "to die would be gain." The same kind allowance will, I trust, still be made for my imperfections, and if, in the course of that brief remnant of life which may yet remain, my understanding (such as it is) should fail, my friends and brethren will remember the injunction to children in behalf of a declining father, "If his understanding fail, have patience with him and despise him not."*

But, while with humility and shame looking back on the sins and neglects of the past, I must not omit what I am sure the patriarch felt in his heart, special gratitude for special favors and honors from God and man. While the office of a Bishop, by reason of its many cares and responsibilities, has been a heavy burden to many, I have indeed found it both in its lower and higher grade, "a good

---

*Ecclesiasticus, 3: 13.

thing." Some painful cases I have had, some offences given which I could wish to have avoided; some old friends in a measure alienated, whom I would have retained nearest my heart; some enemies made, whose friendship I desired; some censure incurred, which I would gladly have avoided, if it could have been done with a good conscience; still, such has been the favor and kindness experienced that "my cup has run over." Such has been the honor received from my brethren, and the hospitality from the members and families of the Church, that my visits, though sometimes attended with exhaustion, have been delightful recreations, while the sacred duties of the Episcopal office have been high and delightful privileges. On the heads of hundreds have I laid my hands in ordination, on thousands in baptism and confirmation, and to more numerous thousands have I administered the memorials of the dying love of our Lord, besides, for many years, the almost daily privilege of preaching the glorious gospel to perishing sinners. In all these ways I have felt that a sacred relation was established with them to whom I ministered. I trust, also, that I have been thus drawn nearer myself to the Great Shepherd and Bishop of souls above; and oh, may He one day lay His hands on my head, confirming all my hopes, admitting me to the fellowship of the first-born above, and allowing me to partake anew with Him and them, in some ineffable manner, the Supper of the Lord, in the Church triumphant above!

Would to God that I could thus conclude. Mingled emotions have attended our brief review of the last half century; but what if the veil could be raised which now shrouds in darkness the history of our country for the next fifty years, (should the world itself continue thus long,) who might not shrink back from the awful sight? O! the divisions, the wars, the miseries which may make up that history, the mere beginning of which is now before our eyes and at our doors. God in mercy hides from us the sight of garments rolled in blood, of fields strewed with mangled bodies, of proud cities crumbled into heaps of ruins, of fertile valleys become desolations, of republics and kingdoms rising and falling, and being no more forever. Such has been the history of nations once prosperous like our own. Such may be the end of our own, unless the Prince of Peace shall speedily come down and establish that kingdom which is to be forever and ever. Come, Lord Jesus, come quickly."

He has since finished his course in peace and hope, and added to his wholesome example and salutary instructions of his self-denying and laborious life, the solemn seal of a fearless death. It was my privilege to minister to him during his sickness, receive his dying testimony, watch his waning strength, catch his expiring breath, and then close those eyes, which, in an intimate association of twenty years, had never been turned on mine and me, but in true friendship and tender love.

The particulars of his illness, and his dying testimony to his brethren and country, I have communicated in the address delivered at the funeral. That testimony will be long and religiously preserved as the precious legacy of a Christian patriot, to the Church and people, whose prosperity was so dear to his heart, both in life and in death. May our devoted love for our departed father in God, and our sympathy in sorrow under our sore bereavement, be so sanctified as to unite us in closer Christian affection and animate us to greater zeal and diligence in the cause of our Lord and Master, that we "lose not those things which have been wrought," but may behold his pleasure still prospering in our hands.

In the address of Bishop Johns to the council of 1863, the following statement occurs:

"The last Convention entrusted to a committee consisting of the Rectors and Vestries of the Churches in Richmond and its vicinity, the arrangements for the permanent interment of our late Rt. Rev. Father in God. The wish of the sons of the deceased being ascertained, a lot was selected in Holywood Cemetery.

On the 4th of March, at 2 P. M., the Rev. R. K. Meade and children, accompanied by clergy and laity of the city and its vicinity, repaired to the Cemetery, and reverently removed the venerated remains from the vault in which they had been temporarily laid, to the spot chosen for permanent interment, where, with appropriate religious services, we committed the body to the ground, looking for the general resurrection, and the life of the world to come, through Jesus Christ, our Lord.

The proposed monument and inclosure are postponed till they can be more satisfactorily accomplished than under existing circumstances.

The ground for the interment was purchased by two gentlemen of Virginia, Wm. H. Macfarland, Esq., and Mr. John Stewart, and presented to the Church in Virginia. Its position is eligible, and it is completely isolated by roads which pass along its sides. In shape, it is mound like. Nearly midway on one of its sides stands a large oak tree, an appropriate emblem of the sainted servant of God, whose remains repose under its wide spreading branches, a hallowed spot, where angels will keep their vigils, and where every son of the Church may reverently stand, with uncovered head, and thank God for WILLIAM MEADE.

APPENDIX.

A SERMON

PREACHED IN STAUNTON, VA., MAY 24, 1863, IN MEMORY OF RIGHT REV. WILLIAM MEADE, D. D., LATE BISHOP OF THE DIOCESE,

BY

REV. WILLIAM SPARROW, D. D.

"Seeing we are compassed about with so great a cloud of witnesses, let us lay aside every weight."—*Hebrews*, 12 : 1.

The Church of Christ is a mighty power in the earth, the mightiest beyond all comparison, known to man. At first it was but as a grain of mustard seed; but it has long since grown to be a great tree, which unlike every other planting of the divine hand in this world, and much more of any human hand, is not destined to decay, but to increase, striking its roots downward, and bearing fruits upward, till it overspreads the world, and blesses all mankind.

Now this power of the Church lies chiefly in its testimony to the truth which has been committed to it, and this testimony is continually increasing through the multiplication of the witnesses, who, by their example in word and deed, by holy living, and peaceful and happy dying, give to those who know or remember them, a reason for the hope that is, or was, in them; a reason which no man of any conscience and reflection can make light of. So widespread is the Church of Christ, and so numerous its members, that not a year passes by that does not add some precious name to that cloud of witnesses for Jesus. Yes, annually, and at even shorter periods still, we are called to mourn the departure from our earth of God's faithful servants who are gone to join the redeemed of the Lord in heaven. They are personally gone, but not gone altogether. Their testimony is still with us for our instruction and encouragement. They being dead, yet speak to us. Of this class is our late Diocesan.

The eventful times in which we live, and in which he died, dispose us to speak of Bishop MEADE, first, though but briefly, as a *patriot*. The importance of passing events, and the deep interest he took in them, might invite to more extended remarks; but the higher relations of the character and office of the deceased claim our chief attention. Patriotism, after all, it should be remembered, at least in this place and hour, is, in itself, and as commonly exhibited in the world, only a natural feeling, a local attachment, a social affection formed by long intercourse, and identity of secular interest in property, reputation, habits, customs and tastes. And though, when stimulated, it may perform prodigies of valor, and may consummate revolutions, which under the hand of God may be greatly beneficent to the country and the world; still, all this may be, and alas, too often is, where God is not in all the thoughts of the actors, and where it cannot be said that He is the origin, the support, or the end of the procedure; being called in, if called in at all, only in an extremity, to sanction and sustain man's foregone conclusions. But such was not the patriotism of the venerable man of whom I speak. The love of country, or section of country in which his lot was cast, was with him at once a transformed and subordinated affection; transformed, so as to be elevated, and subordinated, so as to be controlled by other, higher, broader, and purer principles. It was denied the right of supreme rule in the Christian heart. Like every other natural affection, to have real value according to the Christian standard, he held it must be entirely subject to the paramount considerations of God's spiritual law, and spiritual kingdom, and must be cherished and put forth in full recollection of that divine sovereignty, which, in the ordering of human affairs, often acts on principles which we, for the present, do not understand,—at one time granting us prosperity beyond our guilty fears; at another disappointing our most ardent wishes and confident and (as we deem them) reasonable expectations. Moderation, therefore, marked the movements and expressions of his patriotic feelings. His final testimony on his death-bed, as immediately after utterance put on record by Bishop Johns, and afterwards revised by himself, indicates, as I have said, that patriotism was not only a subordinate principle in his heart, but a transformed principle, free from bitterness, adopting only the measures and means, the language and sentiments which God approves, submitting all errors to be corrected by His infinite wisdom, and all events to be regulated by those higher considerations of State which belong to the Court of Heaven. It was, in short, just what you might expect from a man of God, who loved his country, expressing his opinions on a great national question, standing on the confines of the eternal world, and conscious of his fallibility.

Let us pass to his services to the Church in Virginia. He was the *restorer* of that Church. So far as I have been able to read the history of that Church, this title belongs to him more than to any other man. He was fitted for it by personal character, and social connections, in eminent degree; formally and understandingly, he took it in hand, in the strength of God's grace to do; and by the grace of God, he *did it.* His very idiosyncrasies conduced to this end. In early life, as is well known, he observed a plainness of style in his family arrangements, and personal appearance, which was much remarked upon. The motive was neither vain affectation, nor idle caprice. It was designed, I doubt not, to indicate that he did not wish to continue, but rather to break the continuity of that secular mode of life, into which the ministry too generally had fallen, and to inaugurate, if possible, a new state of things —a new style of practical religion, in which was mingled as little as might be, of "*the lust of the flesh, the lust of the eye*, and *the pride of life*;" *new*, I mean, as compared with that of the generation which had gone before, but *not* new, according to the principles and early history of the Church from which we sprung. His prime and immediate object in entering the ministry of course was, by preaching the gospel to *convert*, and *build up* the converted; but he also had a further object germain to this; he would do this in the Church of his fathers, as, all things considered, the best and most Scriptural organization, in his judgment, for carrying forward the reign of Christ among men. Friends endeavored to dissuade him from his whole purpose, the ministry generally, and especially the ministry in our Church. Episcopalians, so-called, thought it folly for a young man of his talents and surroundings to attach himself to a fallen Church, that never could rise again! But, he had formed his purpose considerately and prayerfully, and he adhered to it with the firmness which ever characterized him. He saw that the Church had not sunk so low from inherent weakness, either of doctrine or order. It had fallen either from that *general* cause found in the depravity of human nature, through which all churches, like individual Christians, are liable to declension in long spaces of time; or else, from particular causes which were incidental and remediable; as, for instance, the prejudicial influence of the union of Church and State—the want of powers of self-government, and the absence of the characteristic feature of our system, Episcopal oversight. And as he understood the causes of its decline, so, also, did he clearly see what would prove effectual to its restoration. The Church being now like the State, independent, self-governed, and complete in its organization at the beginning of this century, he was prepared to go forward in his task. By man it had sunk: by God must it rise. *Human policy* could not do it. Ecclesiastical pretention could not do it. A *narrow spirit* of seclusion from the people and a want of sympathy with them, could not do it. The *restoration* of confiscated glebes and parsonages could not do it. Nothing, he saw and felt, could effect this object, but evangelical principles and practice, spiritual preaching, and holy living; and to these he consecrated his life with a singleness of aim, an industry, perseverance and consistency that few have equalled.

And he had his reward. He lived to see the Church in Virginia "in great prosperity." Never was it so prosperous as at the commencement of our national troubles. The Bishop then saw around him a body of parochial clergy (I venture the expression of the opinion, because unhappily I am not of that class), surpassed by none for faithfulness and efficiency as pastors. He saw the congregations committed to their care increasing yearly in all the fruits of the Spirit. Missionary zeal was spreading on every hand, and substantial aid more and more afforded to the cause. Neither Foreign, Domestic, or Diocesan Missions were overlooked. The Education Society for the aid of young men preparing for the ministry, was deriving an adequate support from Virginia alone, though helping young men from all the States. Educational institutions for both sexes, in connection with the Church, were prospering; and the Theological Seminary was far better provided with every species of accommodation, and better filled with students, than it ever had been before. In the progress of things towards this point of prosperity, it should also be mentioned, there had been very little fluctuation, and no "back-sets." Owing to the consummate prudence of him who took a leading part in all these matters, the progress of the Diocese had been as continuous and unbroken, as the advance of the dawn to broad daylight.

Let me next speak of him as a Diocesan Bishop. The Episcopal office is one of great responsibility, and not a little difficulty. The performance of Episcopal acts, as they are called, Confirmation, Ordination, Consecration, and the giving and receiving Letters Dimissory:—these functions are the most easy, by far, of all those which devolve upon a Bishop. Next after the preaching of the gospel (which, where not providentially prevented, is the first work of every minister of Christ, of whatever grade, being first in his commission); next after this, the most weighty, and altogether the most onerous duty of a Bishop is, "the care of all the churches," including both ministers and people; seeing as far as the canons appoint and permit, that the parishes be supplied with suitable pastors; counselling with these ministers in the various perplexities which beset their path; sympathizing and comforting them in their peculiar trials; more difficult still, when serious complications arise, which affect parochial standing, or clerical efficiency, or personal character of the minister, managing such delicate matters with strict impartiality, tenderness towards all the parties concerned, a true concern for the honor of Christ, a desire to avoid scandal, where it can be done without screening iniquity, or laying the Church open to the charge of so doing; and an unfailing caution in the midst of all this, that no one be able to say that any prerogative has been exercised which is not perfectly legitimate and canonical. What constant and laborious occupation of mind and heart must such an office occasion! What judgment, and moderation, and conscientiousness, and firmness, it calls for! With reference to such an accumulation of sacred duties, how appropriate the inquiry of the Apostle, "Who is sufficient for these things?"

In the discharge of these arduous duties, I do not say our departed father in God was perfect. He would not say it himself; he would reject the thought with abhorrence. But, surely, all will admit, that with a vigorous mind, a sound judgment, an honest intention, and great and self sacrificing industry, *he aimed at* it. Those who had an opportunity of observing him when weighing matters which belonged to his Episcopal oversight, and endeavoring to find out what was due to the Church and to individuals, to justice and to mercy, to the rights of men and to the claims of truth; such persons if not very much warped by prejudice, or by personal interest in the questions handled, will also admit that the administration of the affairs of the Diocese was, in this regard, in the main, eminently successful, through his great wisdom and fairness.

But a Bishop is a debtor to those without, as well as those within, the pale of his own communion. To stand aloof and ignore them is absurd, and worse than absurd. There are relations subsisting between him and them, not of his creation, and out of these relations grow duties not to be put aside. In regard to them, the course of our late Diocesan was most honorable to himself, to the Church, and to Christianity. We know how the Church has arisen in this Diocese, not only from small beginnings, but from deep depression. It had not only to struggle in great weakness, but under a heavy load. As the daughter of the Church of England, all the political prejudices felt against the parent, descended upon the offspring. Nor descended only, through a spirit of rivalry, but none the less reprehensible, these prejudices seemed to have been studiously cherished in certain quarters, even to the asserting that true, vital religion was impossible within our pale. I speak of this as past; it lingers, I trust, in few of our Christian brethren round us,— only the very narrow-minded and very weak. But in the first decades of our history as an independent Church, it was a dead and heavy weight, as inevitable as gravitation. Against it our Bishop struggled manfully, not only never bating a jot of heart and hope, but, what was specially to his honor, because so difficult of achievement, without evincing any bitterness, or contracting a sectarian spirit. Many a liberal mind has been narrowed by coming into contact and collision, with those that are illiberal. Few indeed can resist the perverting influence of such association. Bishop MEADE was one of those few. In twenty-seven years' acquaintance with him, often conversing on religious subjects, I can testify, I never heard from him anything, in regard to Christians, and Christian Churches, which I would not be willing they should hear; on the contrary, I often heard remarks from him, which, uttered in their hearing, could not fail to soften and conciliate. And, as were his words, so was his conduct. He went on quietly and lovingly in the work which Christ had given him to do; never turning aside to forbid those who were casting out devils in Christ's name. He did not approve of some of the ways in which Christ is preached among other denominations, but still it was a pleasant reflection to him that Christ was preached. *That* was with him the point of paramount importance to the world, and therein he rejoiced, and continued to rejoice even to the end.

Let me mention another temptation to which Bishop MEADE was perfectly proof: Ministers wish to increase their congregations, Bishops their Dioceses. This is a matter of course, and very proper. The Church of Christ was not meant to be stationary. Let it be firm and stable, and let it resist decay; but let it be progressive also. That is its mission; and the clergy of all grades are appointed and commanded to further this object. But there is a weakness here to which they are liable, but which should be conscientiously and firmly resisted. In their desire for the growth of the Church, they may overlook the quality of the increase, and, in adding to its membership, may subtract from its strength. In this matter too, our late Diocesan was a wise and faithful shepherd. In things pertaining to God, he had no confidence in mere numerical strength. He manifestly believed that the Christian Church, like Gideon's army, is often greater in power for being less in numbers. All compromises that involved a denial of this principle, he was opposed to. For this reason it was, that he did not approve admission to Confirmation, unless the candidate contemplated enrolling himself also as a communicant of the Church. He would not sanction an enlargement of the Church merely by something like what the Congregationalists of New England, called their "halfway covenant." Better be out of the Church altogether than IN IT but not *of it*. Christianity that is not hearty, deep, spiritual and thorough, did not, in his judgment, answer its purpose, or correspond to its own idea. To his firm conviction of this truth, and his efforts to promote its practical adoption, the Episcopal Church in Virginia is largely indebted for the sound tone of religion which distinguishes her adult membership. Those who came forward to Confirmation, he considered bound, in consistency, to go forward to the Table of the Lord. The soundness of the principle he deemed manifest from the language of the Confirmation Service. The opposite opinion, wherever held, has proved most disastrous to our Church. It belongs, indeed, to the *parish minister* to indoctrinate the candidates for this rite upon the point; but of course the weight of Bishop Meade's teaching and influence in regard to it, could not fail to be felt. It was felt, and I hope it long will be.

4. Let us next consider his position and work, as a leading *member of our highest legislative councils.* While yet a presbyter, he made himself distinctly felt in these assemblies of the general Church. His great practical sense and high moral integrity must have given him prominence and weight. But it was in our House of Bishops his influence matured and culminated. In learning, eloquence and literary accomplishments, he was confessedly surpassed by several of his brethren on the Episcopal bench; but in wisdom without cunning, in firmness without stubbornness, in unflinching integrity unstained by harshness, he had no superior, if any equal. It was his lot to be placed twice or thrice, or even oftener, before the Church in most trying circumstances, and to act as leader in them. Of course he had to bear the censure of hot misguided partisans, of weak men who suffered themselves to be controlled by them, and sometimes, perhaps, of men void of seriousness and true principle. But there were few men of his day who could bear such a trial with more firmness and tranquility. He had great faith, as I have noticed in other matters, in the ultimate power and success of truth. He could do his duty and possess his soul in patience, relying upon it. "Wisdom will," doubtless, "be justified of her children;" integrity must, sooner or later, be acknowledged and applauded. Alas! I fear, when the present generation has passed away, and history takes up her impartial pen to give a narrative of the events now

referred to, the only passages bright and cheering, and creditable to our communion, which she will leave on record, will be those pertaining to the part which the Bishop and his coadjutors acted on these occasions.

The Protestant Episcopal Church is not given to change, as it should not be; but neither is it sworn against it. While neither fickle nor unsteady, neither is it stationary or petrified. Since its first organization it has changed, but most of the changes have been progress and improvement. The same may be said in remarkable degree of the mother Church of England. In the changes which have taken place among ourselves Bishop MEADE took an active part from the time he entered our councils, and always exercised great influence; and when *injudicious* changes were proposed, he was found just as efficient in checking the wheels of precipitation and rashness. To him in full proportion are due our improved selection of the metrical Psalms, our excellent collection of hymns, the expressions of opinions drawn from the House of Bishops by the Memorial, and other matters.

In *Diocesan* legislation and action his influence was greater still. It is no wonder we were all so ready to defer to his judgment. It was given, neither in an imperious tone, on one hand, nor with flattering lips on the other. It was dictated by a disinterested and enlightened desire for the spiritual welfare of his charge; and it was sustained by an amount of knowledge and of anxious reflection, which none of us brought to the decision of the questions before us. He ruled with diligence. His Diocese was never out of his mind. As a father thinks for his children, so did he for us; with the same continuous self-forgetting, self-sacrificing, unbiased, anxious, laborious, and experienced love. If the occasion was one of sufficient importance to draw him out, he almost always made us feel that he knew more of the facts, and had reflected more deeply on the principles, and had calculated more accurately the consequences than most of us; and sometimes, more than all of us put together. Our experience of this, may occasionally, perhaps, have led us to lean too much upon his judgment, but looking back upon all the legislation of the Episcopal Church in Virginia since he acquired such influence among us, we all must feel that, taken as a whole, it has been both safe and salutary; partly because not excessive.

5. We have next to consider Bishop MEADE as a *theologian;* the most important aspect of all. The life of religion is truth. The chief efficiency of the ministry consists in its propagation. False religions rely on other things; Christianity upon this. As a theologian he is to be admired and followed. Some of the furniture of mind which belongs to the present race of divines, he did not possess. His early lot was so cast, and his subsequent life was so full of parochial and Diocesan labors, that the attainments alluded to were impossible to him. But he had very large compensation in the gifts both of nature and of grace, of an active and well balanced mind, and a pious heart. He read extensively to the end of life, but reflected much more. If not a man of deep learning, he was a man of earnest thought. Better than that; his thinking was not mere scientific speculation, but a devout searching after truth; and all for practical and experimental purposes, for the regulation of the heart and life. Accompanying this, and naturally growing out of it, was a spiritual intuition and taste, which to the minister is above all price. The result of the whole was, that while he disliked all refinements and idle questions as a stumbling block to some, a false boast to others, and a snare to all, he was for "substance of doctrine," clear, decided, ready and firm. The properly descriptive epithet of his system of opinions was EVANGELICAL—meaning by that, nothing partisan or narrow, but just the reverse; that system, namely, which eschewing the revolting and the chilling extremes of the prevailing ISMS of the day, at the same time does not run into dry orthodoxy, legal morality, or worldly ceremonialism. The doctrine of gratuitous salvation through faith, as a principle of simple trust in Jesus Christ was, as of the Reformation, so of his individual system, the very corner-stone. To it every other opinion was assimilated, and by it was squared. If we are actual sinners, verily and indeed, we must be freely forgiven, if God's favor be attained at all; and the fitness of a Mediator, therefore, becomes apparent at once. But as the fitness of a Mediator becomes apparent, so does the necessity of exclusive trust in Him, as being the only link to connect us with the grace of pardon, and the hope of eternal

life. But we *are* guilty sinners, transgressors of known law, and need, therefore, to be thus justified freely by God's grace, through faith in the redemption which is in Christ Jesus. But this is not, alas, all. We have not only become guilty by our deeds, but also in our very nature corrupt, even born so. Born depraved, we cannot purify ourselves, escape further guilt, and restore ourselves to happiness. The stream cannot rise above its fountain; and a *Sanctifier*, therefore, becomes just as urgent a necessity, as an Atoner; *self*-salvation is as impossible in the one case, as in the other. Here we can do nothing of ourselves. If not drawn to the Father by the Spirit, we never can come to Him, any more than we can find acceptance with Him, without a Propitiator and Advocate.—These two principles, then, built as they are on the holiness, justice and mercy of God, on the one hand, and on the guilt and depravity of man on the other, were ever uppermost in the mind and foremost on the lip of our late venerated teacher. The necessity of holiness, and the obligation of gospel ordinances, he was ever careful to maintain; but *that holiness* he regarded as an unfailing fruit of true faith, and the only satisfactory evidence of a state of justification; and *these ordinances*, as most salutary in operation and bounden in duty, yet not necessarily conveying grace, nor, except ecclesiastically, necessarily taking effect by virtue of the mere outward act, *opere operato.*

The style of his churchmanship, as it is called, is known to us all, and I trust approved by most of us. No man could be more unwaveringly attached to the Church of his birth, education and intelligent convictions, than Bishop MEADE was to his. His early life and choice—choosing rather to suffer affliction with her, than, as with his talents and other advantages, he might well have done, look for wealth and distinction in some *secular* calling; or rather than attach himself to some orthodox church suffering less from unjust popular odium;—these things, together with his whole subsequent career, put this point—the point of his loving allegiance to our Church beyond dispute.

While thus decided in his Church attachment, he never advocated our peculiarities on ultraistic grounds. He deemed Episcopacy, and Confirmation, and a Liturgy, and such like things, necessary to the perfection, but not to the *being*, of the Church. This being so, to talk darkly and mysteriously about our peculiarities, and to press them as something without which salvation somehow or other is questionable, is to be inconsistent with our own admission of cardinal facts, and consequently to tempt men to conclude from the extravagance of the claim set up for our system, that it has no just claims at all. He that proves too much, often proves, so to say, less than nothing. There is a most damaging recoil in such extravagant argumentation. And to this may be added another consideration. If perchance some *few* persons having a natural proclivity to ultraism, and exclusiveness, *are* attracted by such arguments, and converted, as the expression is, to our communion, they are frequently found no real acquisition. They are apt to prove fierce champions, but not eminently Christian members.

These principles were very dear to our late Diocesan. On his death-bed he remembered the part he had borne in reference to them, and there renewed his testimony to their excellence. The nearer eternity came, the closer were they pressed to his heart. Doubtless the reason was, that he felt, to use the words of that eminent man of God, Rev. C. Simeon, that they best "humbled the sinner, exalted the Saviour, and promoted holiness." By these principles, sown in large measure also by his predecessor, he was the instrument, under God's blessing, of raising up the Church in Virginia from the dust, and giving her a position of influence in the General Church, as it existed at the commencement of the pending revolution, altogether unmatched in the South, and hardly matched anywhere else. Bishop Meade had scanned our whole Church with a most thoughtful eye, comparing its several parts with one another, and the totality of these parts with th ebodies of Christians, orthodox and heterodox around; and these latter again in their relations to one another. He saw the excellences and defects of all; freely confessing the good, and, when necessary, not denying the bad. And his matured conviction was, that for the sound conversion of sinners, and the healthful nurture of Christians, there was no instrumentality like the faithful preaching of evangelical doctrine, united with a temperate advocacy of our own ecclesiastical system, and a conscientious and diligent, but not slavish use of the means which it supplies and enjoins. In this conviction he began, he lived, he labored, and he died.

6. And now, in conclusion, I would like to speak at large, if time permitted, of Bishop MEADE as a *Christian man;* though already several hints have been dropped, which bear upon the subject. When public men are spoken of in a commendatory way in this country, the first remark you usually hear is, that they are *popular.* The traits which secure this advantage most promptly and most widely, are made most prominent; namely, those which please all classes of men alike, and demand on their part no reflection, or discrimination, or thorough testing, to find them out. For such traits Bishop MEADE was not remarkable. He never cultivated them; perhaps had too low an opinion of their value. He could not court favor. To flatter or be flattered, was his abhorrence. He never sought — as men in elevated positions, and men seeking them, are apt to do—to win others over to their views by playing upon their vanity, or ambition, or any other weakness; and to attempt to sway him in that way, was to ensure failure and excite disgust. It was only another phase of the same trait, that he so much abhorred all affectation and cant; so much so indeed, that it may be, he did not always make due allowance for the difference of training, temperaments, and manners of different persons and classes. Be that as it may, "*To be—not appear,*" was evidently his motto; and though by carrying it too far he may have forfeited some noisy, superficial popularity, it in the end enhanced his influence, and is a full explanation of the great control which he exercised in his latter years over the affairs of the Diocese. Our men of discernment knew that in him they had to do with substantial character, real worth, sterling integrity, in short, with one who was "no sham." Amid the hollowness, pretension and selfishness of the world, it is no wonder persons of intelligence and virtue should be ready to rely much on so true a man.

Another element of this influence thus acquired through long years, but never sought by questionable means, was his great practical *good sense.* Naturally sound of judgment, he was, as every mature Christian *is,* acquainted with *human nature;* and, as every mature Christian is *not,* with the *world* also; being very observant, and having had large opportunity for observation. But on this subject I need not dwell. All who know anything about his administration and character will admit, that Bishop MEADE was emphatically a wise man.

This wisdom, let me further add, was made largely available to the Church by his *great industry.* He was ever about his Master's business. No duty was overlooked through inattention, or because of its irksomeness declined. Called to a high office in the Church, he felt its obligation, and gave himself wholly to it. In his fiftieth year, when about to make a visit to the Canadas, he remarked to a friend, "This is my first pleasure trip, since I entered on public life." He was always at work, though for many years he had to struggle with great bodily infirmity. His activity of mind he retained to the last. When, after the seasons of Diocesan visitation, he retired to his quiet modest home at Mountain View, it was not to hybernate in idleness and self-indulgence. Besides keeping up an active correspondence, he generally selected some topic, and read extensively upon it, either with a view to general improvement, or to the preparation of some work which he thought might be useful to others. His last winter had been thus devoted to prophetic studies.

Bishop Meade wrote and published a good deal; but no man ever took up the pen of authorship, with less of the ambition of an author. He valued truth above all price; he believed he had grasped it in its essence; he had great confidence in its naked, unadorned and inherent power; and therefore he published. It was simply to benefit others, not enhance his own reputation. Indeed he was well aware, as we see from the Preface to his Lectures on Pastoral Theology, that to win applause as a writer, he must elaborate; a thing which neither his taste inclined him to, nor his duties permitted. In order to do good in his day he did not deem this necessary; and with simply doing good he was content.

In both natural and acquired *firmness* of character our departed friend and father was most remarkable. Timidity in no form made a part of it. Though ever prudent and cautious in the highest degree, it was never from the mere fear of trouble. Hence in these times of war, and of a high appreciation of military talent, it has been often said, by those aware of these traits of his mind, together with his great powers of combination, that he would have made, if duly trained, a general of high order. This absence of fear, it is pleasing to observe, did not lead him to indulge in irascibility of temper, or overbearing conduct. I once witnessed on his part, under gross and continual provocation, merely from a sense of official propriety, and from a determined natural *fairness*, an amount of quiet endurance and patience, which very few in his position would have exhibited. Not that I suppose such rule over his own spirit was entirely a natural gift, rather the reverse; he he had *learned* self-restraint; that is, to deny self on Christian principles. I do not say that his manner was not sometimes blunt and even *brusque,* but in twenty years, frequent intercourse with him, I can truly say, I never saw in him anything like the slightest exhibition of passion; he was always calm and self-controlled.

Bishop MEADE, from various causes, not having made it his special duty to cultivate the little amenities of life, which, with some, constitute the substantial things of character, may have been considered by such persons occasionally *destitute of feeling.* And it may be, I admit, that he was not a man of feeling, such as Mackenzie would love to portray. In other words he was not a man of extreme *sensibility;* but, my friends, he was, what is a great deal better, lying far nearer the foundations of character, and resting far more upon the rock which sustains all real moral excellence, he was a man of *genuine benevolence,* just such practical benevolence as his divine Master exhibited, He loved to do good, and make others happy. Little children seemed favorite objects of his kindly feelings. Among his grandchildren, at least, it was delightful to see how much pains he bestowed upon them, and how much thought he took that he might contribute to their enjoyment. Hospitality in him, Virginian as he was, was a matter of course, and hardly to be mentioned; but no one ever spent a few days at his residence, without being convinced that the foundation of it in his case was neither hereditary usage, nor fondness of company, nor household pride, but rather a simple spirit of overflowing benevolence. That spirit indeed spread itself everywhere, and was manifested towards all persons and causes, that might be considered as having any claims upon him. He was a liberal giver through life; as will be seen in that day when the books are opened, in which are recorded the doings of the right hand, which the left hand knoweth not. To *individuals* he gave with a considerateness and delicacy of which some remarkable instances have come to my knowledge; and on *societies*, his money and influence were freely bestowed; provided, in any fair way, and for a reasonable time they promised to advance the welfare of the community at large, or any substantive part of it. That he might be better able to give, was one great object of the simple and inexpensive style of living which ever characterized him. Indeed he seems in the true spirit of Christianity to have seen no proper use or end in those riches which men so much covet, but to promote the cause of God and man in their essential relation and connection upon earth.

About his last end I shall not speak; though it was just what was to be looked for after the course he had run. It has already been handled publicly in a most effective way, and doubtless in due time, will be put in a more permanent form, and given all the minuteness of detail to be expected in a book. I do not repeat therefore what has been said, or attempt to anticipate what may be done. It is enough to allude to the fact that Bishop MEADE declared on his death bed, that the principles which sustained him, were the principles which he had preached, and that his whole deportment on the occasion was that of a man of God, going to his reward, in the avowed character of a sinner saved by grace.

The removal of such a man from the Church ought not to be allowed to take place in silence. It is meet that as each worthy of marked eminence is added to the cloud of heavenly witnesses, we should take note of the fact, and try to gather up the lessons taught or suggested by the event: especially where, as in this case, the Church owes so much to the life and labors of the deceased. He has left us a private example and a public history that ought to be very precious to Virginia, whilst the principles out of which they grew, and which it was the great labor of his life to propagate, should be more precious still. By them Virginia arose like the Phœnix from its own ashes. By them only can it stand. *Supplant* them by others to which they are opposed, and we fall back at once into formalism, exclusiveness, secularity, and spiritual deadness. *Develop* them into knotty questions, metaphysical enigmas, and you may engender a spirit of controversy and bitterness, which may involve life enough indeed, but not the "life of God in the soul of man." It will only be the contest of Saracens und Crusaders over again, contending for an empty sepulchre. Jesus "*is risen; He is not there.*'

I have not been indulging a spirit of hero-worship — one of the great weaknesses of our age. Neither have I indulged that indiscriminate eulogy which naturally is connected with it. *That* is a falsehood, and idolatry which the servant of God, of whom I have been speaking, would be the first to condemn, even while he was upon earth; how much more now, as he stands in heaven, with the glory of the infinite God shining full upon him! This egoism and pride which so abound among men, were unknown in Paradise, and are unknown in heaven, and, when observed here below by those dwelling above, (if observed they can be), it is only to be pitied as weak, and condemned as wicked. Let the potsherd strive with the potsherd of the earth, and vaunt themselves one against the other, but in connection with religion, and in the sanctuary of God, and when in our thoughts following the departed to the other world, let all such feelings be banished. as at once profane and childish, from the heart and mind alike of him who speaks, and them who hear.

To God be all glory! Glory for His own infinite perfections; His wondrous works; His gracious dispensations! Especially be it to the praise of the riches if His love in Christ Jesus, that while His grace is exhibited towards all, it is from time to time magnified in raising up some, eminently, to fight the good fight, to finish their course consistently, to keep the faith unsullied by human refinements and earthly mixtures, and then, when the time of their departure has come, that that grace is further magnified, in transferring them to another world, and adding them to that cloud of witnesses that encircle the throne of eternal truth and purity. Just such an instance of God's grace have we in the life, career and death of our departed father in God. While we recognize the hand of God in raising him up, and making him a blessing; let us, as the best thank-offering we can present, accept his testimony to gospel truth, and in our lives follow him, as he followed Christ.

WRITINGS OF BISHOP MEADE.

From a Catalogue of the writings of Bishop MEADE, with a brief account of the occasions on which they were written, and a synopsis of the principal publications, prepared by the Rev. Cornelius Walker, D. D., Professor in the Theological Seminary of Virginia, the following list is made. It is much to be regretted that the entire notice cannot be inserted here. Its extent renders this inexpedient. But it is hoped that a review, so judicious and instructive, will be reserved as an appropriate introduction to such of the Bishop's writings as may be selected for publication.

LIST.

1. SECOND ANNUAL REPORT OF THE BIBLE SOCIETY OF FREDERICK COUNTY, VIRGINIA. Printed by order of the Society. Winchester: 1815.
2. SERMON AT THE OPENING OF THE VIRGINIA CONVENTION, at Winchester, May 20th, 1818.
3. A SERMON ON THE DEATH OF THE REV. OLIVER NORRIS. Preached in Christ Church, Alexandria, Sept. 18, 1825.
4. SERMON ON THE DEATH OF THE REV. JOHN DUNN, Rector of Shelbourne parish, Loudoun County. Published in the Theological Repertory.
5. SERMON DELIVERED IN THE ROTUNDA OF THE UNIVERSITY OF VIRGINIA, on Sunday, May 24, 1829, on the occasion of the death of nine young men, who fell victims to the diseases which visited that place during the summer of 1828, and the following winter.
6. A SERMON AT THE OPENING OF THE CONVENTION OF THE PROTESTANT EPISCOPAL CHURCH in Petersburg, May 15, 1828.
7. A SERMON ON CONFIRMATION. Preached in Winchester, Dec. 12, 1834.
8. PASTORAL LETTER on the duty of affording religious instruction to those in bondage. Alexandria: 1839.
9. SERMONS, DIALOGUES, AND NARRATIVES FOR SERVANTS. To be read to them in families, abridged, altered, and adapted to their condition chiefly. Richmond: 1834.
10. SERMON (CONNECTED WITH THE TEMPERANCE CAUSE). Preached before the Convention in Staunton, May, 1834. Published by request of the same. Richmond: 1835.
11. SERMON PREACHED AT THE OPENING OF THE GENERAL CONVENTION of the Protestant Episcopal Church in Philadelphia, Sept. 5, 1838.
12. SERMON TO THE STUDENTS OF THE THEOLOGICAL SEMINARY near Alexandria. Published by their request. Washington: 1839.
13. "THE WISDOM, MODERATION AND CHARITY OF THE ENGLISH REFORMERS, AND FATHERS OF THE PROTESTANT EPISCOPAL CHURCH IN THE UNITED STATES." A sermon preached before the Students of the Theological Seminary of the Diocese of Virginia, February 5, 1840. Washington.
14. SERMON BEFORE THE STUDENTS OF THE HIGH SCHOOL, in the Prayer Hall of the Theological Seminary, Feb. 16, 1840.
15. DITTO. Oct. 3, 1840.
16. SERMON DELIVERED AT THE CONSECRATION OF THE RIGHT REV. STEPHEN ELLIOT, D. D., for the Diocese of Georgia, in Christ Church, Savannah. With an appendix on the rule of Faith; in which the opinions of the Oxford Divines, and others agreeing with them, are considered, and some of the consequences thereof set forth. Washington: 1841.
17. LIFE OF THE REV. DEVEREUX JARRATT. By himself. Abridged by Bishop MEADE. With a sermon of Mr. Jarratt's on Justification.

18. FAMILY PRAYERS. Collected from the Sacred Scriptures, the Book of Common Prayer, and the works of Bishop Wilson. 1834.
19. RELIGIOUS EDUCATION OF CHILDREN.
20. THE LAW OF PROPORTION IN THE CHURCH OF GOD, considered in a Pastoral Address. 1843.
21. THE DOCTRINES OF THE EPISCOPAL CHURCH NOT ROMISH. An Address to the Convention of the Protestant Episcopal Church, Lynchburg, May 16, 1844.
22. A TRACT ON THE MINISTRY. For the Episcopal Tract Society of Virginia. An answer to the question, "What does the Protestant Episcopal Church believe and set forth concerning the ministry?" Extracted from the Book of Common Prayer, the writings of the Rev. William Goode, and the Rev. George Stanley Faber.
23. A TRACT FOR THE TIMES.
24. A BRIEF REVIEW OF THE EPISCOPAL CHURCH IN VIRGINIA, from its establishment to the present time; being part of an address to the Convention in Fredericksburg, May 22, 1845.
25. TRACT ON INDUSTRY. Being one of the Homilies, with a sermon on the same subject, (preached and published in 1838). Alexandria: 1845.
26. TWO LETTERS TO THE BOARD OF MANAGERS AND EXECUTIVE COMMITTEE OF THE PROTESTANT EPISCOPAL SUNDAY SCHOOL UNION. 1847.
27. PASTORAL LETTER OF THE HOUSE OF BISHOPS. 1847.
28. ADDRESS TO THE EPISCOPALIANS OF WESTERN VIRGINIA, on the proposition to divide the Diocese, &c. 1851.
29. WILBERFORCE, CRANMER, JEWETT AND THE PRAYER BOOK ON THE INCARNATION. 1850.
30. LETTERS TO A MOTHER, on the birth of a child, &c. 1849.
31. EXPLANATION OF THE CHURCH CATECHISM. Chiefly from the Catechism by the Rev. James Stittingfleet, Jr., with an Appendix. 1849.
32. REVIEW OF A WORK ENTITLED "THE DOCTRINE OF THE CHURCH OF ENGLAND AS TO THE EFFECTS OF BAPTISM IN THE CASE OF INFANTS." With an Appendix. 1849.
33. ECCLESIASTICAL LAW AND DISCIPLINE. A charge to the Clergy of Virginia. 1850.
34. REMARKS ON A PAMPHLET CONCERNING A CANON ON LAY DISCIPLINE. Passed at the Convention recently held in Alexandria. 1850.
35. COMPANION OF THE FONT AND PULPIT. 1846.
36. PASTORAL LETTER to the Congregations of the Protestant Episcopal Church of Virginia. 1847.
37. STATEMENT IN REPLY TO SOME PARTS OF "BISHOP ONDERDONK'S STATEMENT OF FACTS CONNECTED WITH HIS TRIAL." 1845.
38. REASONS FOR LOVING THE EPISCOPAL CHURCH. 1852.
39. A COUNTER-STATEMENT OF THE CASE OF BISHOP H. U. ONDERDONK, in reply to one signed "A Member of the Church." 1854.
40. PASTORAL LETTER ON SCHOOLS AND TEACHING. 1858.
41. PASTORAL TO LAITY OF THE EPISCOPAL CHURCH IN VIRGINIA. (Without date.)
42. SERMON ON THE OPENING OF THE CONVENTION OF THE PROTESTANT EPISCOPAL CHURCH IN VIRGINIA, in the fifty-first year of his ministry and the thirty-second of his Episcopate. Published by order of the Convention. 1861.
43. "LECTURE, ON THE PASTORAL OFFICE, delivered to the Students," &c. 1849.
44. "OLD CHURCHES, MINISTERS AND FAMILIES OF VIRGINIA." 1857.
45. "THE BIBLE AND THE CLASSICS." 1861.
46. "ADDRESS ON THE DAY OF FASTING, HUMILIATION AND PRAYER. June 13, 1861.

www.ingramcontent.com/pod-product-compliance
Lightning Source LLC
LaVergne TN
LVHW021259110826
845150LV00003B/436

* 9 7 8 1 4 2 5 5 6 0 7 8 2 *